MILLER, C.

954.912

-0 FEB.

D1549729

Please return this book
on or before the last
date shown or ask for

ESSEX 4/12/08
12/11

Hertfordshire
COUNTY COUNCIL
Community Information

18 DEC 2001
8ᴿ Jaway 2002

15 FEB 2003

29 AUG 2006

L32a

OTHER BOOKS BY CHARLES MILLER
PUBLISHED BY MACMILLAN

The Lunatic Express
Battle for the Bundu

KHYBER

British India's North West Frontier

The Story of an Imperial Migraine

CHARLES MILLER

MACDONALD AND JANE'S · LONDON

To John H. Hemingway, Jr.

Copyright © 1977 by Charles Miller

All rights reserved. No part of this book may be reproduced or
transmitted in any form or by any means, electronic or mechanical,
including photocopying, recording or by any information storage
and retrieval system, without permission in writing from
the Publisher.

First published in Great Britain in 1977 by
Macdonald and Jane's Publishers Limited
Paulton House
8 Shepherdess Walk
London N1 7LW.

ISBN 0-354-04167-3

The extracts from *Campaign in Tirah* by Col. H. D. Hutchinson
and *The Pathans* by Sir Olaf Caroe are reprinted by permission
of Macmillan London and Basingstoke.
The extracts from *My Early Life* by Winston Churchill, copyright
1930 Charles Scribner's Sons, reprinted by permission of
Charles Scribner's Sons.
The extracts from *Tales of Travel* by Lord Curzon are reprinted
by permission of the Estate of the late Lord Curzon.
The extracts from *Eighteen Years in the Khyber* by
Col. Sir Robert Warburton are reprinted by permission of
John Murray (Publishers) Ltd.

Printed in the United States of America

CENTRAL STOCKS UNIT
TAMWORTH ROAD
HERTFORD SG13 7DG
TEL: 586 863

HERTFORDSHIRE
COUNTY LIBRARY
954.Q203
19.1.78
6708597

Contents

[vii]

Author's Note

GRATEFUL ACKNOWLEDGMENT is expressed to the many organizations and individuals who granted permission to quote from sources or to reproduce illustrations used in this book.

I should like to add a word of personal thanks to my editors—Jody Ward and Fred Honig in the United States and Penelope Hoare in England —for their advice, cooperation, and patience. Thanks also to Mrs. Gunn Brinson of London, for important help with illustrations. And I owe a continuing debt of gratitude to my agent, Gunther Stuhlmann; as always, he kept my morale shored up whenever it began to get mired down.

While I take pleasure in acknowledging all of the above professional and personal help, I only wish I could find a whipping boy for any factual errors that may crop up in the following pages. Regrettably, however, the buck stops here.

A quick note on pronunciation. Hindi, Urdu, Pushtu, Farsi (Persian), and other regional tongues bristle with tricks that are tailor-made to stump Westerners. Probably the most common and deceptive are words containing an "a" that must be pronounced as "u." Thus Amritsar is really "Umritsar," Bannu should come out "Bunnu," Ambela "Umbela," the Kohat Pass the "Kohut" Pass, Ghazni (the city) "Ghuzni," and so forth, down an almost endless list. *But*: a Ghazi (a religious fanatic) keeps his "a," as do Jalalabad, Kandahar, Swat, the Malakand Pass, Parachinar, and a host of others including every khan that turns up. How to differentiate? Unless one has some basic working knowledge of Indian and Central Asian languages (my own grasp falls just short of being even

[ix]

x

rudimentary), probably the best and most sensible thing to do is forget about it.

Still, two place names continually used in this book might merit the slightest bit more respect. Kabul is "Cobble," while Peshawar takes its accent on the second syllable, as do many other words that sometimes seem (on paper at least) to need their stress elsewhere. Of course, I suspect that the planet will continue to spin if readers decide that "Ka-*bull*" and "*Peshawar*" come over more comforably.

Even, God forbid, if they think of a Pathan as a "*Paythan*" and not a "*P'tan*."

PROLOGUE

Mission Aborted

ON A CRISP February morning in 1809, the Lahore Gate of the city of Peshawar was thrown open to admit a train of 600 heavily laden camels. Caravans seldom entered through the easterly Lahore Gate, but rather by the Kabuli Gate on the city's western walls. That was because they usually approached Peshawar through the Khyber Pass, about ten miles to the west, after journeying down on the long trade routes from Kashgar, Tashkent, Samarkand, Bokhara and Kabul. But this caravan had come from the east, from British India, and it was not a party of merchants—its official character being attested to by the scarlet tunics and pipe-clayed white crossbelts of 400 sepoy escorts. The loads that the camels carried were supplies for these troops, and for their leader, the Honourable Mountstuart Elphinstone, the first Englishman ever to visit Peshawar.

A man of slight build, sensitive features, and urbane manner, the thirty-year-old Elphinstone did not quite seem the sort to go venturing into dimly known regions far beyond the borders of British India. But he had been chosen specifically by India's Governor General, Lord Minto, to carry out a delicate diplomatic mission in Afghanistan—or, as it was usually called at the time, the Kingdom of Kabul.

The name was not inappropriate, the city of Kabul, about 100 miles west of Peshawar, having then become more or less acknowledged as Afghanistan's capital. Elphinstone himself never got to Kabul, nor did he need to. At the time of his visit, the incumbent monarch, Shah Shuja-

[xi]

ul-Mulk, was holding court at his palace in Peshawar, where Afghan rulers usually wintered.

Peshawar was in many respects more important than Kabul. It was the terminus of the great trade arteries from Persia, Turkestan and China, the point of departure for waterborne passengers and freight sailing down the Indus River to the Arabian Sea and the oceans beyond. As Elphinstone made his way through the Street of the Storytellers, his European garb went all but unnoticed in a busy traffic jam of Asiatic humanity. He was jostled by Chinese silk merchants from Kashgar, by Bokhara rug dealers, by Chitrali almond growers from the Hindu Kush, by Turkestan horse breeders, by Uzbek pilgrims from Kokand passing through Peshawar on their *haj* to Mecca. There were white-robed Afghans whose turbans resembled well-packed bundles of laundry. Tall, hawk-eyed Pathans from the nearby hills stalked everywhere, each a walking arsenal of matchlocks and long knives: Khyber Pass Afridis, Yusufzais in roomy pajamas, Orak-zais swathed in pearl grey *chaddars*; gaunt Waziris with falcons on their wrists. The slant-eyed features of Mongol-descended Hazara tribesmen from the Bamian Valley presented a smooth-cheeked contrast to a forest of beards. Peshawari women in ankle-length veils somehow contrived to glide through the throng like wraiths.

Elphinstone soon became thirsty in the billowing cloud of thick yellow dust raised by at least 200,000 bare and sandaled feet. Near the Chowk Yad Gar, the central square beneath the great white minarets of the Mahabat Khan Mosque, he managed to find room in one of Peshawar's uncountable tea shops. It was no more than an oversize, open-fronted closet furnished with a few wooden stools, a brass samovar and some chipped chinaware cups. One could choose from several popular brews. Some customers enjoyed a strong black leaf boiled in a mixture of water and buffalo milk, others the Kashmiri tea that was flavored with salt instead of sugar. Elphinstone decided to sample the Pathan favorite, *qahwa*, a light green Chinese tea spiced with crushed cardamon seeds.

He drank several cups, glancing up from time to time at the rooftops and balconies of three- and four-story houses of sun-dried brick, where Peshawaris in white turbans and blue cotton shirts puffed contentedly on the small water pipes called *chillums*. Mainly, however, his attention remained on the square, which teemed with beggars, charm sellers, magicians and itinerant holy men. One fakir drew laughter and gasps as he rubbed a pasty substance on his arm and then held out the arm to be bitten by a cobra. This and other performances were continually inter-rupted as paths were cleared for squadrons of royal cavalry, whose troopers held aloft red and green banners and were followed by strings of dromedaries with swivel guns on their panniers.

In the manner of countless tourists who would, one day, follow him to Peshawar, Elphinstone made a point of walking through the bazaar.

In this rackety sprawl of cramped streets were the wares of the great Central Asian caravans: silks, rugs, precious stones, muskets, swords and knives, copper and brassware, racing horses and cavalry mounts, hides and skins, tea, fruits and nuts, and a galaxy of other imports. Each trade had its own street—the Street of the Goldsmiths, the Street of the Jewelers, the Coppersmiths, the Waxworkers. Elphinstone blinked in the glare of 10,000 curved steel scimitar blades in the Street of the Armorers. He watched carpet merchants hold up Samarkand and Bokhara prayer rugs so that their patterns would catch fingers of sunlight. On the Street of the Clothiers, tailors wound silk *lungis*, spun in Kashgar and Yarkand, around gold-threaded peaked caps to make turbans; cobblers stitched gold embroidery and silk pompons on the delicate slippers called *chaplis*. In the fruit stalls were great heaps of football-sized Samarkand melons; deep crimson Kandahar pomegranates; white Kabul grapes, carefully wrapped in cotton wool; walnuts from Kashmir; apricots from Swat; and mountains of almonds, pistachios and *chilgosas*, the tiny pine kernels that Peshawaris chewed like gum.

The Street of the Money Changers was a place to linger. Elphinstone examined silver and copper coins minted during Hindu dynasties that had ruled in the Peshawar Valley ten centuries earlier. The coins bore Sanskrit characters and the images of bulls, lions, elephants and lance-wielding horsemen. Other money went even farther back in time; Elphinstone fingered gold and silver pieces dating to the Kushan dynasty in the first century A.D., copper "Menandars" and "Eucratides" embossed with the helmeted busts of soldiers from the Graeco-Bactrian empire that had flourished in eastern Central Asia before the birth of Christ. Peshawar's money changers operated what was literally a museum of the currency of antiquity.

The entire city, in fact, spilled over with history. Peshawar had belonged to the Gandhara satrapy of Darius the Great. Alexander's Macedonian hoplites had marched through Peshawar's environs when the region was known as Peucelaotis. Genghis Khan and his swarm of iron locusts from Mongolia had left a bad mark here—only partially erased by Genghis' descendant Tamerlane. And Tamerlane's great-great-great-grandson Babur had cut his way through the Khyber Pass to make Peshawar a stronghold and showplace for a long succession of Mogul emperors. The neighboring hills were a vast archaeological dig of Persian, Greek, Buddhist, Hindu and Muslim civilizations spread across nearly two and a half millennia. It seemed only fitting that Shah Shuja and other rulers of Afghanistan should choose Peshawar as their second capital.

Afghanistan itself was something of a blur, certainly in terms of national boundaries. The country's northern borderline could be delineated by the ice-cloaked 700-mile wall of the Hindu Kush range, but there were those who drew the line even farther north, along the banks of the Oxus River on the equally hazy frontier of Turkestan. In the mutilated desert and mountain country to the west, it was impossible to say where Afghanistan ended and Persia began. A similar murk hung over the southern marches, where Afghan and Persian influence—if "influence" was the word—faded off into the howling wilderness of Baluchistan. Only in the east, along the Indus River, did Afghanistan possess anything like a clear-cut boundary. To be sure, even the Indus could be disputed; from a military standpoint, a southerly pointing thumb of the Hindu Kush west of Peshawar seemed a more realistic defensive frontier. But the Indus had long been a natural ethnic and linguistic dividing line between the peoples of Central Asia and the Indian subcontinent. To all intents and purposes, the Indus was Afghanistan's eastern moat.

At the time of Elphinstone's visit, the frontiers of British India had not yet advanced to the Indus. Between Afghanistan and British territory lay the independent state of the Punjab, a sort of inverted pyramidal wedge some 300 miles broad at its northern base. But the 300 miles might just as well have been 300,000. Indeed, the British in India and the Afghans could have been as far distant from each other as the inhabitants of Earth and Jupiter, considering that no communication of any kind had ever existed between the two countries.

One could reasonably have asked, in fact, why Elphinstone had been sent to Afghanistan at all. India had little, if anything, to gain from a commercial standpoint. Despite the great market of Peshawar, Afghanistan was for the most part barren and churchmouse-poor. British statesmen would have recoiled in horror from the faintest suggestion of territorial aggrandizement at Shah Shuja's expense. The Afghans for their part were known to be fanatical Muslims whose religious isolationism was expressed in an almost homicidal suspicion of infidels—especially those white unbelievers whom they called *Feringhis*. On the face of it, there seemed no valid purpose whatever in establishing even a facade of diplomatic relations between Britain's flourishing Indian possessions and the stagnant, all but inaccessible waste of scorched deserts and frozen mountain ranges at the bottom of central Asia.

In fact, however, both the British government and the king of Kabul had urgent reasons for cultivating each other's friendship.

If Afghanistan's national boundaries were uncertain, Shah Shuja's rule was even more so. Afghanistan could be seen not so much as a state than as an uneasy state of mind—a murkily defined patchwork of ever-shifting regional and clan alliances. The country seemed to reenact the *Arabian Nights*. Its princes lived in Babylonian opulence and wove tortuous Machiavellian plots against each other, while its ragged masses slit one another's throats to avenge real or imagined insults, or simply for the hell of it. Shah Shuja held precarious sway over a fickle, rapacious citizenry of unlettered, bearded sharpshooters and knifemen whose allegiance was split up capriciously among several of his own relatives, each seeking the throne himself. Indeed, at the time of Elphinstone's visit, a tatterdemalion but well-armed military force, mobilized by Shah Shuja's half-brother Mahmud, had captured Kabul and was marching toward the Khyber Pass to lay siege to Peshawar.

And if internal dissensions were not enough, Shah Shuja was also feeling pressure from the Punjab, a virile nation of breakaway Hindus known as Sikhs. Ranjit Singh, the Punjab's half-blind ruler, had staked out a claim to Peshawar and all of eastern Afghanistan as far as the Khyber and the frontier hills. Although Ranjit had not yet made his move, he almost certainly had the military muscle to enforce the claim whenever he chose to.

But Shah Shuja was resolved to meet the challenges. It was his belief that if, with Allah's will, he could secure the friendship and assistance of so mighty a world power as England, his place on the Afghan throne would be made secure. Afghanistan's great unwashed, deserting Mahmud to back a winner, would rally round his own standard as he became the country's de facto as well as de jure ruler. As for Ranjit Singh, that unbelieving dog must surely reconsider his own designs on the Afghan trans-Indus territories. All hinged on Britain.

The British, to be sure, were not sitting up nights over Shah Shuja's fate, but the British had enemies of their own. In 1807, after settling their differences in a treaty signed on a raft near Tilsit on the Niemen River in East Prussia, Napoleon and Russia's Czar Alexander I had tentatively discussed a possible joint invasion of India through Persia. For all practical purposes, this meant a French invasion—although "practical" was hardly the word. It mattered little to Lord Portland, the British prime minister, or his foreign secretary, George Canning, that such an offensive was even less realistic than Napoleon's subsequent plan to take Moscow. During England's 350-year rule of India, it seldom required much more than even the accidental blink of an alien eye in the direction of the subcontinent to spread panic through British cabinets and deprive otherwise keen-minded British statesmen of rudimentary common sense. Decisive measures were seen as imperative if the Tricolor were to be kept from flying over Fort William, the Calcutta nerve center of British rule in India.

Britain had accordingly moved to seek friendly buffer states along the path of invasion. Although Persia was something of a French satellite, envoys had nonetheless been dispatched to Teheran, where an Anglo-Persian treaty of mutual defense was concluded, for whatever it may have been worth, which was nothing. Of equal if not greater strategic importance, however, were the possible results of missions sent by Calcutta to the Punjab and to Afghanistan. For these were the two countries standing directly between Persia and India. Alliances with their rulers, it was hoped, would at least discourage the French at the diplomatic level, if not actually halt the French army.

The Punjab turned out to be a piece of cake, more or less. Although Ranjit Singh had been making a practice of sending his Sikh armies into adjoining British territory on minor harassing expeditions, he had more than enough respect for force majeure to heed the warning of Minto's envoy, Charles Metcalfe, that the patience of the Raj was wearing thin. So accommodating did Ranjit prove that he not only agreed to call off his trans-border forays but he also actually ceded a small portion of his own country to British India. Given his designs on Afghanistan's eastern frontier region, a well-disposed England was very much in Ranjit Singh's interest.

The Punjab, however, was contiguous with British India and, as such, a relatively known quantity. Under Ranjit, moreover, its government was strongly centralized and, in that respect at least, could be considered a reliable ally. But Afghanistan was not only a house divided against itself; it was uneasily managed by kings who came and went as if through a revolving door. A treaty with an Afghan monarch might remain in force for decades, but a more realistic life-span had to be measured in months, if not weeks or even days. Indeed, Elphinstone's mission to Afghanistan loomed as one of the more futile in the history of British diplomacy.

Yet if the attempt had to be made, Elphinstone seemed the right man to make it. He had held responsible positions in the Indian government for thirteen years; among his appointments had been that of political adviser to General Arthur Wellesley—later and better known as the Duke of Wellington—in the first Mahratta War. He would subsequently become Governor of Bombay, the second highest-ranking official in India, and would also decline two offers of the governor generalship itself. Besides this, Elphinstone was a scholar and orientalist of note; his fluency in Persian—the language of the Afghan court—as well as Sanskrit and other eastern tongues was expected to smooth the path of his negotiations with Shah Shuja. Above all, he was a humanist; it can be said that he personified the compassionate detachment of an eighteenth-century Age of Reason that was soon to be swept away by Victorian righteousness. There was nothing of the imperious Pukka Sahib in Elphinstone's makeup; behavior, not pigmentation, was his measure of his fellow man.

To be sure, these qualifications may not have been needed at the time, since Shah Shuja's dire straits might have made him receptive to terms offered by a Calcutta street sweeper. On Elphinstone's arrival in Peshawar, the Afghan ruler had not yet learned that Mahmud had captured Kabul, but he did know of the uprising. The military force at his disposal, although tough and acceptably well armed, more likely than not would go over to Mahmud if the usurper took Peshawar. No one felt more keenly than did Shah Shuja how uneasy lay the head beneath his own crown. At that moment, only massive outside assistance could keep his foundering throne afloat. And time was of the essence. Elphinstone held all the cards.

Shah Shuja received the British envoy and his party in Peshawar's Bala Hissar, the name given to massive Afghan citadels that usually enclosed royal palaces. Elphinstone got the full treatment, and the treatment was impressive. Attendants salaamed the visitors through high-ceilinged, tapestried passageways into a large, sunlit chamber, along whose walls, painted to represent cypress groves, stood the king's ministers and other officials, resplendent in jeweled robes. Smartly uniformed troops of the household guard came to attention as the British party walked past. Fountains played in the center of the room, and, through the open arches at its far end, Elphinstone could see the famous Shahi Bagh, the royal gardens—acre upon endless acre of immaculately landscaped flowerbeds and orchards, divided by pebbled pathways and shining with fish ponds. Near the end of the room and only partly screening this vista was a white gazebo-like structure, its roof supported by fluted pillars and Moorish arches. Here, on a gold throne, sat Shah Shuja.

Elphinstone almost gasped aloud. "We thought at first the king had on armour of jewels," he later wrote, "but, on close inspection, we found this to be a mistake, and his real dress to consist of a green tunic, with large flowers in gold, and precious stones, over which were a large breast-plate of diamonds, shaped like two fleurs-de-lis, large emerald bracelets on the arms, and many other jewels in different places. . . . The crown was about nine inches high—the whole so complicated, and so dazzling that it was difficult to understand and impossible to describe." Elphinstone was not so blinded, however, as to fail to notice that Shah Shuja also had on the Koh-i-Nur.

Now Elphinstone was formally presented. "On coming in sight of the King, we all pulled off our hats and made a low bow; we then held up our hands towards heaven, as praying for the King; and afterwards advanced to the fountain where the Chaous Bashee repeated our names, without any title or addition of respect, ending, 'They have come from Europe as ambassadors to Your Majesty. May your misfortunes be turned upon me!' The King answered in a loud and sonorous voice, 'They are welcome,' on which we prayed for him again, and repeated the ceremony once more."

Beneath the layers of jewels and ritual, Shah Shuja proved human and amiable. The black beard which cascaded to his chest did not conceal a man barely emerged from boyhood, but the twenty-year-old monarch conducted himself with mature poise. "The King of Caubul was dignified . . . and his address princely. . . . It will scarcely be believed how much he had the manners of a gentleman, while he seemed only anxious to please."

He was also anxious to get down to business, and after an exchange of fulsome compliments and lavish gifts with Elphinstone, started the ball rolling with a request for a British loan. Elphinstone said this could be arranged on condition that Shah Shuja throw in his lot with Britain against Napoleon and bar all Frenchmen from Afghanistan. Without hesitation, Shah Shuja agreed and forthwith placed his signature above Elphinstone's on a treaty of eternal friendship, which proclaimed that "the veil of separation" between Afghanistan and Britain "shall be lifted up." Elphinstone's mission was accomplished. It was almost as simple as that.

Exactly what England had gained from her new ally was not even a matter of conjecture. England had gained nothing. If Napoleon had ever presented a real threat to India (which he had not), that threat had since vanished in Spain, where French military might was reeling under Wellington's blows. And even if one accepted the hypothesis that any European power could keep an army supplied for a march of at least 2,000 miles across some of the most intimidating terrain on the planet to strike at India through Afghanistan, Elphinstone's treaty was cellophane armor. Shah Shuja could hardly have halted the French legions for half a day.

Besides which, the question became academic almost at once. Hardly had the ink dried on Shah Shuja's signature than messengers galloped into Peshawar with news of Mahmud's approach. The insurgent troops would be mounting their scaling ladders on the walls of the Bala Hissar in a matter of days. The British loan, if it ever arrived, would take months to reach Peshawar.

And Shah Shuja knew that the loan would not arrive: He was realist enough to recognize that the defenses of India were hardly going to be bolstered by a lame-duck monarch. He therefore fled from Peshawar, his only solace lying in the knowledge that Elphinstone would seek no alliance with Mahmud as the de facto ruler of Afghanistan. For by this time, news had reached the British envoy of Napoleon's reverses in Spain. Afghanistan had just been eliminated as a pawn on the Anglo-French chessboard.

Elphinstone now reported to Minto that "a very unfavourable turn has taken place in the King of Caubul's affairs." Then he, too, quit Peshawar, never to return. Calcutta and London might well have considered themselves fortunate in being disencumbered forever of entangle-ment with a country whose labyrinthine politics and uncertain fortunes could offer them nothing but tribulation.

What no one realized at the time was that Shah Shuja would return to the scene as a cog in the British imperial engine. Nor could even the most farsighted have dreamed that Elphinstone's aborted mission was only the first step in a sequence of events that would lead to British rule of Peshawar, the Khyber Pass and all eastern Afghanistan—the country that was to become known as the North West Frontier of India.

It was to prove the only part of the British Empire that the British were never able to conquer.

PART ONE

Filibuster

1

The Vales of Treachery

THE HARDEST WAY to reach India is by land, but until the end of the fifteenth century, when Portuguese navigators opened up the longer but less arduous sea route, every India-bound merchant and aspiring conqueror went there on foot. The journey was a very real test of endurance because it meant traversing the Iranian Plateau, a region nearly as vast as India itself. Bounded by the Indus and Tigris rivers on east and west, by the Hindu Kush and Arabian Sea on north and south, the Iranian Plateau might be likened to a free-form pool table that has been run through a meat grinder, a blast furnace and a deep freezer. One can find parts of the globe that are less inviting, but one cannot find many.

Crossing the plateau, however, is less difficult than reaching it or even leaving it. Just as the ancient Chinese, the Romans in Britain and the Germans in East Berlin saw fit to guard their estates with walls, so too is the Iranian Plateau fenced off on all sides by nature. Caravans and armies coming in from the north may have had the stiffest hikes. There was no way to scale the impregnable, icebound battlements of the Himalayas, so a detour through the passes of the Himalayas' western elbow, the Hindu Kush range, became necessary. And access to the Hindu Kush was blocked by the Ust-Urt Plateau and the Kara Kum and Kyzyl Kum deserts, which spread out like decomposing blankets across an area twice the size of France.

Such badlands were not to be conquered by pantywaists. According to a sixteenth-century description of the region, "the greater part of the countrey is covered over with baraine sands, and withered up for want of moisture, nourishing neither man, nor bringing forth fruite." As recently as the 1880s, when the Russian Transcaspian Railway finally crossed the Kara Kum, a British passenger called it "the sorriest waste that ever met the human eye," adding that "from time immemorial nature's curse has been on this spot." The desert's summer temperatures, he said, were "of a seven times heated furnace, [and] the winter cold is sometimes arctic. . . . many human lives are lost in the storms."

Early travelers did find a few places in this wilderness where enough water flowed or fell to generate explosions of fertility: where fat lambs grazed on rich green throw rugs, where date and fig palms offered sustenance and shade, where ponderous clusters of grapes glistened in their own beads of sweat, where melons grew like women's breasts. But such oases appeared as not much more than tiny emerald crystals in the horizonless, crumpled boneyard of rock and sand that could fry the brains and turn the blood to ice. The approaches to the Hindu Kush did not encourage life.

And the Hindu Kush itself was only barely negotiable. The name means "Hindu Killer," because, according to the great fourteenth-century Moorish traveler Ibn Batuta, "the slave boys and girls who are brought from India die there in large numbers as a result of the extreme cold and the quantity of snow." The passes of the Hindu Kush were given names like "Tooth Breaker" and "Horseshoe Breaker." For six months of every year, the entire range would be locked and bolted to caravans and armies by the *sharmal*, the winter wind that slices down the glacier-lined slopes like a giant's razor blade and halts even the flight of birds.

Yet these obstacles were surmountable, if only just. It can be said that the Hindu Kush was conquered because it had to be—because it divides India and Eurasia, which Arnold Toynbee has called "two worlds that will not submit to being insulated from each other . . . notwithstanding the rigours of the passage across the intervening barrier." In the course of time, the Hindu Kush passes became not only a military and commercial highway but a conduit of civilizations.

One did not necessarily have to scale the Hindu Kush to reach the Iranian Plateau and India. Darius and Alexander the Great, who were the earliest invaders, crossed the plateau by a more southerly route, approaching India from Persia. But theirs was no royal road. Whether one traveled to India from north or west, the final several hundred miles of any such journey followed a winding, soaring, plunging path across present-day Afghanistan, which was and still is an earthquake-convulsed moonscape. Nor was there any easy exit from this madman's funhouse. One either had to turn back or overcome a mountain barrier at least as challenging as the Hindu Kush. These heights are in fact a sort of knuckle of the Hindu Kush, jabbing southward for some 250 miles to join with the great Suleiman range, which hovers over upper Baluchistan. The entire chain forms the easternmost watershed of the Iranian Plateau. In the nineteenth century it was to acquire a magnetic notoriety as British India's North West frontier.

For earlier India-bound merchants and soldiers, however, the region was an eastern rather than a western boundary. Once an invader put it behind him, he had only to ford the Indus River and all of the subcontinent would lie more or less supine at his feet. But hauling oneself and one's army or caravan over the hump was far easier contemplated than accomplished. Although nature has favored the frontier with a few places—such as Swat and the Kuram Valley—that make the Vale of Kashmir look like a used-car lot, their beauty did not make the going any less stiff for a traveler. Anyone viewing the frontier skyline can legitimately wonder why it is usually referred to only as hill country. The Grand Canyon might seem a shallow gully compared to many of the boulder-strewn gorges that knife through a scar tissue of near-vertical ridges and spires rearing up to ten times the height of the Empire State Building as they lurch across an area that would blanket the state of Missouri.

Like the Hindu Kush, however, the frontier palisades are pierced in several spots by mountain passes, notably the Khyber; if not exactly freeways, they at least offer access of sorts. But the Hindu Kush presented itself simply as a topographical obstacle. To thread the needle of the eastern passes, early travelers had to cope with inhabitants as xenophobic and truculent as any community that ever slammed a door in a visitor's face.

Of the five main frontier passes leading eastward into India, two carried the bulk of the traffic. Near the southern foothills of the Suleimans, the eighty-mile-long Bolan Pass was the exit of an extreme southerly route to India via the ancient Afghan cities of Herat and Kandahar. During the nineteenth century, many British geopoliticians came to look on the Herat-Kandahar-Bolan line as the key to India's defense; an invading army, they held, would encounter fewer topographical bottlenecks and impediments to the movement of supplies on this route than on any other. That might have been so, but the line of march through the Bolan was a far less direct route than that offered by the northernmost pass, the Khyber. Because of its location astride the main trade routes from Persia, Turkestan and China as they converge on the road from Kabul to Peshawar, the Khyber Pass has always been the busiest funnel of movement between India and Central Asia. And this despite the fact that no other pass on the frontier has been so jealously and ferociously guarded.

Negotiating the thirty-mile-long Khyber Pass today is not much harder than crossing the International Bridge from El Paso to Cuidad Juarez. Apart from the border customs post at Tor Kham, the only obstacles on the paved, two-lane highway are other motor vehicles, as camel caravans use a separate parallel road and congestion is further reduced by the freight and passenger traffic carried on a narrow-gauge railway to Peshawar. Tourists driving through the Khyber between Afghanistan and Pakistan enjoy some breathtaking scenery and a glimpse of imperial history. The escarpments are studded with bronze plaques marking forgotten actions fought by British regiments in the days when the Khyber was Pax Britannica's remotest watchtower. Some of the old British forts continue to serve Pakistani frontier constabulary; the battlements of the brawny fortress at Landi Kotal not only guard the summit of the pass, but command spectacular views. Far above Landi Kotal to the north looms the cedar-quilted Tartarra Ridge with its mile-high peaks of Tor Sappar and Lakka Sur. Some fifteen miles to the southwest, with 10,000-foot crests glittering off into the haze of the mutilated Afghan foothills, stand the raggedly majestic Safed Koh—the "snow peaks"—the frontier's mightiest mountain range.

Here and there the pass widens so that it is really a small valley, speckled with cultivation and dotted with the white mud sentry towers of Afridi villages. Some sections of the road are like roller coasters, diving and vaulting over successions of switchback turns while the beetling escarpments crowd in until they are less than seventy-five yards apart; before dynamite blasted out the highway, the pass was so narrow in places that the opposite walls could almost be touched with outstretched hands. Thanks to the many hairpin turns in the road and a sometimes heavy volume of truck traffic, the drive through the Khyber can often take three hours or more.

Visitors of the pre-gasoline era considered themselves lucky if they made it in less than three days, and made it intact. The Afridi tribesmen inhabiting the Khyber also stood guard over the road with the vigilance of Apaches, waiting to exact tolls from anyone wishing safe passage to or from India. "If a single traveller endeavours to make his way through," wrote Mountstuart Elphinstone in 1809, "the noise of his horse's feet sounds up the long narrow valleys, and soon brings the Khyberees in troops from the hills and ravines. . . . If they expect a caravan, they assemble in hundreds . . . and sit patiently, with their matchlocks in their hands, watching its approach." Those unwilling to pay had to run a gauntlet of sniping from behind scores of *sangars*, the stone fortifications built by the Afridis on the heights, and face massed onslaughts by the tribal armies called *lashkars* from points of ambush at nearly every bend in the narrow, winding road.

Even payment of the toll did not necessarily guarantee safety from the Afridis. "Such are their habits of rapine," said Elphinstone, "that they can never be entirely restrained from plundering passengers. . . . On the whole, they are the greatest robbers among the Afghauns." Soldiers as well as merchants heeded the Afridi threat. Before the British came, few invaders of India ever tried to carry the Khyber Pass by force of arms.

The early conquerors of India did not really conquer India, nor did their writ on the subcontinent run far. At the end of the fifth century B.C., Darius the Great led his Persian armies eastward to carry the boundaries of the Achaemenian Empire beyond the northern slopes of the Hindu Kush to the Jaxartes River and into India as far as the Indus Valley. But Darius bit off more than he could chew; within fifty years, Persian satraps had been supplanted by local rulers in all the annexed regions. Much has been made of the Indian offensive launched in 329 B.C. by Alexander the Great, when he and 30,000 hoplites set out to conquer new worlds for the Macedonian Empire. In some quarters it is still believed that Alexander was the first invader to march through the Khyber Pass, but in all probability he crossed the Indus farther north— although one of his generals, Hephaestion, may have tried the Khyber route. In any case, the Macedonians did little more than raid a few villages in the neighborhood of the Peshawar Valley and then depart. One historian has accurately described Darius and Alexander as birds of passage on the northwest frontier.

To be sure, both invaders left enduring marks. On the frontier hills and in the Indus Valley, the ruins of ancient Buddhist shrines and statuary show the direct influence of Greek architects and sculptors. Even today, Greek coins still turn up in the bazaars, and more than a few blue-eyed Afghans are named Iskandar, for Alexander. The Persian language never departed from the region. Nor, in fact, did the Persians themselves: for nearly 1,000 years after the second century B.C., present-day Afghanistan was ruled by a succession of dynasties—Graeco-Bactrian, Saka, Indo-Parthian, Kushan, Sassanian, Kidarite, Saffarid—whose kings were of predominantly Iranian stock. Even the Hindu monarchs who held the frontier during much of the tenth century were Persian in origin.

But these Hindus soon began to feel uncomfortable pressures as the easterly march of militant Islam reached the Indus Valley with the impact of a bursting dam. The new invaders were a Mamluk Turkish people called Ghaznavids, whose power reached its apogee in the early eleventh century. Their most celebrated ruler, Mahmud of Ghazni, held court in the city of that name, 100 miles southwest of Kabul, and made his capital a center of Islamic culture that rivaled Bokhara and Samarkand. Ghazni glittered with splendid palaces and mosques; among its many artists and writers in residence was the poet Firdausi, often called the "Persian

Homer." But Mahmud of Ghazni was even more famous as a destroyer of infidels and their works. He carried out at least a dozen invasions of western and northern India, demolishing Hindu temples and other places of worship with such energy and thoroughness that he became known as the "Idol Smasher." The Prophet had arrived with a vengeance.

Although Mahmud of Ghazni and the rulers of succeeding Muslim dynasties penetrated India—some even advancing as far as Delhi and holding that city for short periods—the subcontinent had yet to be truly subjugated. The climate halted Genghis Khan in the early thirteenth century. Tamerlane carved out a Central Asian empire the size of Australia and also sacked Delhi in 1398, but he no more mastered India than did Darius and Alexander. That achievement was left to the mightiest and most enduring of all the invader dynasties before the British. Under its founder, Babur, and such successors as Akbar, Jahangir, Shah Jahan and Aurangzeb, the Turko-Iranian Moguls became the first outsiders who genuinely made India their own.

The earliest Mogul invasion took place in 1528, when Babur swooped down from northern Turkestan and captured Delhi, and more than three centuries would pass before Mogul influence faded entirely from the scene. During that interval, one of history's most magnificent imperial achievements reached full flower. Not a few Mogul administrative systems were adopted by the British and even survive in today's India. The 1,500-mile Grand Trunk Road, the main highway of the British Raj between Calcutta and Peshawar, was built by Mogul engineers. Mogul painters, poets, architects and jewelers fashioned works that matched and even surpassed the creative brilliance of ancient Athens and Rome; the Taj Mahal, the Peacock Throne, the Koh-i-Nur, the Shalimar Gardens and the Pearl Mosque are only a few items in a dazzling showcase of priceless Mogul-made wonders. The Mogul Empire was the Roman Empire of the East.

India proper was not the only part of the Mogul dominions. Conquering as he went on his southeastward march across the Hindu Kush to Delhi in 1525, Babur also annexed a large portion of present-day Afghanistan. And it was under the Moguls that the Afghan people first began coming into something like focus as a nationality, although they were still light years distant from statehood as the word is usually understood.

Actually, they had been on the scene for centuries, a bubbling ethnic stew of Persian, Greek, Scythian, Turk and Mongol, to mention only a few of the invading and migrating peoples who contributed their racial ingredients to the Afghan stock. But most Afghans were also men without a country. Prone to perpetual vendettas among themselves, they were incapable of uniting under their own leaders. To the extent that anyone could control them, they were ruled by whatever transient emperor happened to be in charge of the eastern Iranian Plateau. At best, they were the indifferent subjects of an alien prince; more often, they were locked in battle with that monarch. Afghan loyalty, such as it was, tended to be directed inward.

Nowhere did this insularity manifest itself more forcibly than among the Pushtu-speaking eastern Afghans known as Pathans, especially those tribes occupying the mountains and passes of the trans-Indus frontier region. Sometimes called "true Afghans," the Pathans have always considered themselves a race apart—indeed, as a chosen people, claiming direct descent from the Lost Tribes of Israel. It troubles the Pathans not at all that the veracity of this ancestry has been exploded many times over by modern historians. Besides which, few who know the frontier tribes will deny the Old Testament flavor of the Pathan life-style. Jehovah in his least forbearing frame of mind could hardly have shaped a more vindictive outlook on the world.

Many foreign flags have flown over Pathan country. Laws have been enacted to keep the tribes on a short leash, numberless military expeditions mounted to enforce the laws. The effect of such measures has always been uniformly negligible. In the five or six centuries of their often fragmentary recorded history, the Pathans have never acknowledged alien rule, seldom even Afghan rule. What is more, despite the various nationalities conferred on them by numerous conquerors, the tribes have never been conquered in any meaningful sense. Their xenophobia, blood lust and passion for a free-wheeling independence are perhaps described most eloquently in the writings of the seventeenth-century Pathan poet Khushhal Khan, whose verse, as often as not, was an enraged battle cry against the Moguls:

Cup-bearer, fill the flagon, fill it high;
Khushhal shall sing of war in revelry!
Now blood has stained the hands of Pakhtun youth,
The talons of the hawk that knows no ruth.

. . .

For full five years the tribal sword has flashed
Keen-edged and bright, since first the battle clashed
Upon Tartarra's peak, where at one blow
Twice twenty thousand of the Mogul foe
Perished, wives, sisters, all that they held dear
Fell captive to the all-conquering Afghan spear.
Next in Doaba smote we Husain Bek,
And crushed his unclean head, that venomous snake.

. . .

In all, our gain was glory, our glory gain;
Minstrels shall sing of us—"Yea! these were men!"

The Moguls indeed had had much to put up with from their less than obedient subjects in the trans-Indus highlands. The emperor Babur was virtually unique among foreign invaders in carrying the Khyber Pass and gaining an ascendancy of sorts over the Pathans—although it took him twenty years, five major expeditions and a marriage of convenience to a girl of the Pathan Yusufzai tribe to bring this off. But Babur cannot be said to have left any real mark on the Pathan homeland. His armies had about the same effect on the frontier mountain men as did the American military juggernaut against the ragtag guerrillas of Vietnam.

Later Mogul rulers accomplished even less. Toward the end of the sixteenth century, Babur's grandson Akbar actually had a road built through the Khyber Pass. It did him little service when his most able general barely managed to extricate a huge army from the pass after it was trapped in its own camp and badly cut up by an Afridi lashkar. At about the same time, Akbar was losing 8,000 crack Mogul troops and an uncountable number of elephants and horses during a vain attempt to subjugate the Yusufzais in their tangled mountain strongholds north of Peshawar. Akbar's son Jahangir fared no better some years later when he sent out an expeditionary force to crush rebellious Orakzai Pathans in the crumpled hills of Tirah below the Khyber. Jahangir himself described how the Orakzais, "like ants and locusts, completely surrounded the attacking force . . . plied them with stones and arrows . . . and slew the greater number of the troops most mercilessly." By way of rounding off the victory, the Orakzais hamstrung the horse of the Mogul commanding general.

While they never bent the knee to the Moguls, some Pathan tribes were willing enough to fight under the Mogul standard as mercenaries. But they also performed the same service for other Central Asian rulers, who, by the mid-eighteenth century, were beginning to challenge the Mogul supremacy. It was in this free-lance capacity that one Pathan combat team almost accidentally created the nation of Afghanistan.

Nadir Shah was the most imperially ambitious ruler of Persia since Darius the Great. He also succeeded where Darius had failed twenty-two centuries earlier, by carrying out a successful invasion of India. The cutting edge of his army was a wild mercenary force of 16,000 mounted Pathans led by a tribal chief named Ahmad Khan. In 1739, Ahmad Khan's Pathan cavalry spearheaded the Persian thrust into the heart of the Mogul Empire at Delhi. The city was sacked and thousands of its inhabitants put to the sword before Nadir Shah ordered a withdrawal. He did not depart, however, without exacting a price from the Moguls. Included in the payment were the Peacock Throne and the Koh-i-Nur, and all Mogul territory west of the Indus.

In 1747, Nadir Shah was murdered by a rival for the Persian throne, who did not, however, get control of the newly acquired regions. He was challenged at once by Ahmad Khan, who stepped into the breach and contrived to win proclamation, by his reluctant fellow-Pathan chiefs, as their sovereign. The area he claimed to rule embraced most of present-day Afghanistan, along with the southern lands of Baluchistan and Sind. Just as much to the point, Ahmad Khan had the military muscle to back up his takeover from the Persian usurper. By way of formalizing his accession, he also expropriated the Koh-i-Nur and assumed the Persian title of Shah, adding the name *Durr-i-Durran*, meaning "pearl of pearls." The Durrani family was to give the Afghan people all their rulers into the mid-twentieth century.

Ahmad Shah Durrani lost no time in following Nadir Shah's path to India, where he further pared down a Mogul Empire already shorn of its trans-Indus provinces and by then facing other challenges to its preeminence. A few decades earlier, the Mogul writ had extended across the length and breadth of the subcontinent, but by the second half of the eighteenth century the imperial borders were beginning to shrink. The Mahratta Confederacy threatened from the south. In the eastern Punjab, an embryonic Sikh nation was stirring. The frontier of British India was creeping ever closer in its steady westward march up the Ganges. And now there was Ahmad Shah. In 1752, Afghan armies wrested from the Moguls all of their western Punjab territories, and almost simultaneously annexed Kashmir. Afghan rule, in exactly five years, had come to extend over a region nearly one-fifth the size of the continental United States, while Ahmad Shah had made himself master of northwestern India and eastern Central Asia.

But the Afghan empire was doomed to a short life-span, if for no other reason than that the concept of national unity remained alien to the Afghan people. Ahmad Shah's death in 1773 left the country without a real leader for more than a half century. During that time, Afghan supremacy withered as a succession of rivals went at each other's throats in a perfect orgy of intrigue, treachery, torture and assassination. Administrative systems, to the extent that they had ever existed, vanished entirely. Corruption was an open, running sore on a putrefying body politic. Bandits infested every road in the land. Daylight robbery and murder were endemic. By the second decade of the nineteenth century, Afghanistan could no longer even be called a nation. It was a crazy, mixed-up feudal anarchy of three separate, embattled city-states, with "capitals" at Kabul, Kandahar and Herat. Each city was ruled by a faction hostile to the other two, each faction split into subfactions that made and broke alliances in an ever-shifting kaleidoscope of betrayal.

Probably the prototype of these machinations was the partnership of one ostensible ruler, Shah Mahmud, and a member of a rival family named Futeh Khan. A brilliant commander of troops and master conniver, Futeh Khan may have been the outstanding Afghan leader of his generation. In 1800, when another candidate for the throne sent an army after Mahmud, Futeh Khan won the troops over to Mahmud by kidnapping the brother of the commanding general and demanding the whole force as ransom. After Mahmud was ousted in 1803, Futeh Khan remained at his side, and in 1809 was able to blueprint the revolution against Shah Shuja that returned Mahmud to power. For these services, Futeh Khan was rewarded with the office of *wazir*, or prime minister. As Mahmud's Talleyrand, he held the real reins of power, but his own gifts eventually proved his undoing—as well as Mahmud's.

In 1818, Futeh Khan led an army against Persian forces that had placed Herat under siege, and drove off the invaders. But this act won little gratitude from the Governor of Herat, Mahmud's brother Kamran, who sensibly feared Futeh Khan's efforts to strengthen his own family's influence in that city. When Futeh Khan approached Kamran for funds to pay the Afghan troops, Kamran refused outright and Futeh Khan, therefore, sent his own younger brother, a lusty youth named Dost Muhammad, into Herat with instructions to appropriate what was needed from the city treasury. Dost Muhammad not only obeyed his orders but exceeded them, entering the harem and pursuing a princess—who happened to be Mahmud's sister—into a bath, where he relieved her of her clothes on the pretext of commandeering a jewel-studded waistband. The outrage could not go unpunished. Kamran and Mahmud plotted retribution.

But the labyrinthine complexities of Afghan politics dictated that Dost Muhammad be spared and that Futeh Khan, who had won and held the throne for Mahmud, become the victim. On returning to Kabul, the Wazir found himself thrown into a dungeon. There, Mahmud looked on as Futeh Khan was first blinded, then scalped, then had the skin pared from his body as if from an apple, and then had his limbs amputated, after which he was allowed to expire. One British historian has called this a deed of "cruelty so abominable that men still writhe at the telling of it." Actually, by Afghan standards it could have been a great deal worse, but that was small consolation to the members of Futeh Khan's increasingly powerful family. As one man, they rose in arms against Mahmud, who fled to Herat. He was eventually to be succeeded by Dost Muhammad, but not until eight years had passed.

During that interval, Afghanistan remained a rudderless ship, a nation in name only, dismembered no less thoroughly than Futeh Khan. In 1826, when Dost Muhammad finally came to power, his writ barely ran beyond the city limits of Kabul, and even his hold on this micro-kingdom was precarious, having been gained in the face of vigorous intrigue by his older brothers, the chiefs of Kandahar. So tenuous, in fact, was Dost Muhammad's position that he did not even assume the Afghan regal title of shah, but simply called himself "Amir," hoping that the show of humility might somehow dissipate fraternal jealousies.

In due course, under Dost Muhammad, the word "amir" would come to signify the de facto and de jure ruler of all Afghanistan.

It can probably be said that Dost Muhammad was born to rule. Certainly he was well suited for the part in personal appearance and demeanor. A British army officer was to describe him thus: "He was tall, of fine physical development, and he truly looked a king. An artist would have rejoiced to secure his prominent Jewish features as a typical model for an Abraham, Isaac, or Jacob. His manner was courteous, whilst his keen eyes and vigorous conversation conveyed the idea of great determination, combined with asteuteness and appreciation of humour."

But that assessment was made many years after Dost Muhammad came to the throne. Statesmanship in the Afghanistan of the nineteenth century was synonymous with making war and practicing duplicity. Dost Muhammad had become proficient in both arts before reaching his teens; during his young manhood he also enjoyed what amounted to nationwide repute as a philanderer—his invasion of the Herat seraglio being only one of many such romps. But it was not until the age of thirty-one, when he took his seat on the shaky throne of Kabul, that Dost Muhammad found it necessary to learn to read and write.

In the process of teaching himself, he underwent a transformation that has been likened to the conversion of Henry V from wastrel to national leader. Somehow, Dost Muhammad acquired a genuine concern for the welfare of his people and the unity of his country. He undertook to rebuild the machinery, albeit primitive, of government that had been smashed up in the anarchy of the previous half-century. Laws were not only enacted but enforced. Many corrupt and incompetent officials were removed from office. To encourage trade, banditry was ruthlessly stamped out; in due course, citizens and foreigners alike could travel the length and breadth of Afghanistan—except for the frontier hills—in perfect safety. The task was not accomplished overnight. It required three decades, but it elevated Dost Muhammad to an undisputed sovereignty over a united Afghanistan, and his rule was to become equated with fair play for all. To this day, when an Afghan feels that he has been wronged in some fashion, he is likely to fall back on the colloquialism: "Is Dost Muhammad dead that there is no longer justice in the land?"

But all that was in the future. The early years of Dost Muhammad's reign were a walk across a high wire, and not only because he had to outscheme a host of domestic foes. He also faced a deadly enemy outside his gates.

Since the closing years of the eighteenth century, the Sikhs of the Punjab had been having it all their way. A warrior race like the Afghans, they took more readily to discipline and showed less inclination to quarrel among themselves. Their religion preached that the profession of arms was the highest calling to which a man could aspire. In later years, Sikhs would form the backbone of the British army in India and provide very tough paramilitary police forces in many other parts of the Empire. Every Sikh's name ended with the word "Singh," meaning lion. It was not braggadocio.

Even more to the point, the Sikhs enjoyed incomparable leadership in their half-blind ruler, Ranjit Singh, one of the more commanding presences in the history of Indian royalty. Ranjit managed his country with an iron hand that could sometimes be tempered by a compassion unusual for the time and place, since he tended to frown on torture. Ranjit was also a practicing voluptuary, but he never allowed his fondness for wine, women and horseflesh to interfere with his extraordinary gifts as military strategist and bunco artist. Absolutely without fear or ethics, he softened up the victims of his swindles with a mixture of rapid-fire double-talk and irresistible personal charm. Sometimes his blazing single eye almost seemed to hypnotize. Among Ranjit's many marks was the exiled Afghan ruler Shah Shuja, who was bilked of the Koh-i-Nur as payment for military assistance that would restore him to his throne, and which was never forthcoming.

Ranjit Singh's rise to preeminence in northwestern India was accelerated by his enemies' continuing disunity. In 1819, Sikh armies pried the dis- organized Afghans from Kashmir, and in the same year denuded them of their remaining Punjab territories. In 1823, after a blood-drenched engagement near the old Mogul fort at Attock on the Indus, the river was forded and Sikh columns cut their way to Peshawar. There, they went on a spree of mass murder and vandalism, trampling the city's famous gardens into weed patches, battering into rubble the Bala Hissar and many magnificent works of Mogul architecture. Neighboring areas also caved in under Ranjit's onslaught, and it was not long before the entire trans-Indus region, extending into the frontier highlands, had become a Sikh dominion.

The conquered provinces were held by the naked force of well- equipped and smartly disciplined Sikh armies. Apart from generally keep- ing the lid on the frontier, the main task of the occupying troops was the collection of revenues, which the subject peoples were disinclined to pay unless their homes were threatened with artillery fire and their persons with cold steel. When necessary, the threats were carried out. Just as often they were carried out when it was not necessary. The word "Sikhashahi"—Sikh rule—came into local usage to describe anything burdensome or oppressive. Afghan mothers silenced rowdy children with the warning "Raghe Hari Singh"—Hari Singh is here—referring to Ranjit's ruthless commander-in-chief.

To facilitate the enforcement of martial law west of the Indus, Ranjit also fielded a team of white mercenary generals, a number of whom had commanded troops under Napoleon. The most celebrated was a formidably mustachioed Neapolitan artillery officer named Avitabile, who wore baggy, scarlet Turkish pantaloons with a laced uniform tunic and was looked on as a devil incarnate. As Military Governor of Peshawar, "Abu Tabela" ran a taut ship. When not feeding his chickens or winding his collection of musical snuffboxes, he was feathering his nest with fines from lawbreakers, whose ears, noses and hands were sliced off if they pleaded innocent. Avitabile also kept busy hanging delinquent taxpayers, sometimes at the rate of sixty per day, from a minaret of the Mahabat Khan Mosque.

But even Avitabile's draconian fund-raising methods did not suffice to wring from Peshawar anything approaching its annual revenue quota of ten *lakhs* of rupees, or £100,000. For in annexing the trans-Indus frontier, Ranjit Singh had seized a tiger by the tail. Even on the plains, where Sikh authority could be asserted most forcibly, substantial expenditures were necessary for garrisons and flying columns to hold insurrection at bay. The Pathan hill country to the west was a minefield from which the tribesmen thumbed their noses at the conquerors and defied their tax collectors to collect. More than one punitive expedition was bloodied up by Pathan *jezails* (long-barrelled matchlock muskets) and *tulwars* (the curved swords they wielded like meat cleavers). The broken terrain of the highlands also crippled the mobility of Sikh field guns and confounded generals reared on the tactical laws of Clausewitz.

Peshawar was the most vulnerable spot. The occupation of Afghanistan's second capital by a Hindu people whose name stank in the nostrils of every Muslim was a humiliation that the Afghans could not be expected to tolerate indefinitely, and the city's proximity to the Khyber Pass made it a tempting target for Pathan attack. Only tribal disunity and insufficient resources kept the hill country guerrillas from reoccupying the city. But they did carry out nuisance forays and were considered enough of a threat for Ranjit Singh to order the building of a huge fort at Jamrud near the Khyber's eastern entrance. Not everyone held out high hopes for the fort. The Indian Government's Alexander Burnes, who was passing through the region in the summer of 1837, wrote that "even with these defences the position will be a troublesome one, as both the Afreedees and the Khyberees consider it meritorious to injure the Sikhs."

Burnes' judgement was pinpoint accurate. In fact, when he wrote those words, Jamrud had already come under massive attack. By the end of April 1837, Dost Muhammad had consolidated his own power in Kabul sufficiently to permit a concerted military effort against Peshawar. Under the command of his son Akbar Khan, a large Afghan army marched through the Khyber Pass, and Hari Singh's troops sallied forth from Jamrud to hurl back the invaders. Although Sikh morale was beefed up by the presence of Ranjit Singh himself, Akbar received more useful assistance from Afridi and Mullagori tribesmen whose jezails mutilated the Sikh flanks and enabled the main Afghan column to shiver the defenders' center in a barrelling frontal assault. The end of the day saw Ranjit weeping over Hari Singh's corpse and Akbar's men exulting over two captured field pieces while the Sikh army fell back on Jamrud in total disarray. Once inside the fort, however, the Sikhs dug in their heels and held fast; even Akbar's two new guns could not dislodge them. Presently, Afghan ammunition began to run short, and Akbar was left with no option but to order a retirement. Peshawar and the trans-Indus lands remained a Punjab colony for the time being.

In a few short years, to be sure, the Sikhs were to lose the frontier. But it would never revert to the Afghans.

The redcoats were coming.

2

Ambassador in Handcuffs

WHEN THE LIKES of ITT and United Fruit began carving out stock-holder empires in Latin America and other places, they were covertly and perhaps unconsciously emulating the private corporation that once owned India for nearly three centuries. The Honourable British East India Company was founded in 1599, when a handful of London merchants received a Royal Charter from Queen Elizabeth I, grandiosely permitting a monopoly of trade in the part of the world then known variously and not too accurately as the Spice Islands, the Moluccas, the East Indies and East India. Two hundred years later, "John Company" was reaping annual profits that often exceeded the revenues of Great Britain itself. It was an institution less solvent only than the Bank of England.

In the process of transforming India into a jackpot, the Company itself had undergone a great change. Two centuries of almost uninter-rupted wars had not only eliminated Dutch, Portuguese and French competition, but had atomized the power of numerous inhospitable Indian princes; so that by the early 1800s, what had started out as a sort of waterborne variety store had become a full-scale exercise in imperialism. The Company's Court of Directors controlled three-quarters of the Indian land mass and paid at least 75,000 British and Indian em-ployees to manage the estate. After the Napoleonic Wars, the Company's army was larger than any military force in Europe; only the Royal Navy floated more ships than the Company fleet of armed merchantmen.

[17]

Officials prepared for Indian careers at two Company-owned colleges in England: Haileybury turned out the civil bureaucracy, while future army officers trained at the military academy at Addiscombe. The Governor General of India laid down the law to more subjects than any other world ruler except the czar of Russia and the emperor of China.

But by the early nineteenth century, this colossal griffon was having its wings clipped and its claws pulled. High-handed initiatives by such dynamic Indian proconsuls as Robert Clive and Warren Hastings had laid the Company open to charges of mismanagement and corruption, and there was also a growing sense of moral uneasiness over the propriety of a corporation ruling upwards of 100 million human beings. As a result, the British Government had gradually come to absorb certain key Company powers and responsibilities. In 1813, the trade monopoly was abolished; twenty years later, Parliament removed all trading rights from Company hands. Although the Directors retained vast and awesome influence, their decisions were subject to approval or veto by a Government Board of Control. In effect, the Company had become the Crown's managing agent for India.

One of the more significant reforms involved selection of the Governor General. Nominally picked by the Directors, he was really a government appointee, a fact that had the effect of introducing British party politics into Indian affairs. In 1835, when George Eden, third Baron Auckland, was chosen for the post, it was mainly because Lord Melbourne's Whig administration considered him a safe man who could be relied upon not to rock any boats. The Whigs might have been wiser if they had appointed King Kong.

A model of British upper-class noblesse oblige whose facial expression sometimes suggested that he had caught a whiff of gamy pork, Auckland was an altogether decent mediocrity and seemed just the man to guide India's destiny at that relatively tranquil hour of her history. It was not a time of crisis that cried out for the take-charge qualities of a Clive or a Wellesley. At a farewell banquet in England, Auckland spoke of looking forward eagerly to "the opportunity of doing good . . . of promoting education and knowledge—of improving the administration of justice . . . of extending the blessings of good government and happiness to millions in India." These generalities were not only exactly what the Board of Control wanted to hear; Auckland himself intended quite earnestly to give them substance. It was not long, however, before he had led his administration into uncharted waters, on a diplomatic-military adventure that was to change the face of the British Empire.

Auckland is usually thought of as the key figure in the quixotic undertaking, and, indeed, the role he played was considerable. But the real responsibility—a better word might be culpability—at least for setting the thing in motion, belonged to the man who put Auckland in his job: Britain's Foreign Secretary, Lord Palmerston.

Besides enjoying a reputation as a tireless bedroom athlete—he scandalized Queen Victoria when caught in flagrante delicto with a lady-in-waiting at Windsor Castle and was named corespondent in an adultery suit at the age of seventy-nine—Palmerston was even more celebrated as a performer on the world political stage. His enemies called him a "bully to the weak and coward to the strong," but this was an unintended tribute. Like any realistic diplomat, Palmerston was prepared to hector or cringe, depending on which posture would strengthen his country's position on the international chessboard. And if he did not always make the right moves, the fact remains that in his fifty-eight years of public life—holding various positions including that of Foreign Secretary and Prime Minister—Palmerston was the chief architect of Britain's nineteenth-century foreign policy. It can even be said that no other statesman of the era played so influential a role in the affairs of the globe itself.

Although Palmerston may have felt most at home adjusting weights and springs in the European balance of power, India always loomed large in his thinking. Indeed, the entire fabric of the British Eastern Policy that he wove was designed for the specific purpose of safeguarding the Raj against outside aggression. And India's security suddenly took on a new urgency shortly after Auckland's appointment as Governor General.

Although Waterloo had eliminated any ostensible threat to India by Napoleon, Britons of the 1830s watched with growing uneasiness as the Russian Bear began to cast its shadow across Central Asia. Since the turn of the century, the Czar's armies had been carrying out expansionist expeditions in northwestern Persia. The Caucasus had become Russian soil, and Persia itself was to all practical purposes a satellite of St. Petersburg. To mollify the Shah and reimburse him for the loss of his Caucasian provinces, Russian diplomats in Teheran were encouraging the Persians to carry out some annexations of their own in the east. In London, this could only be seen as the first step toward a further eastward extension of Russian influence—the preliminary, in fact, to an actual Russian advance on India.

The specific target was the city of Herat, part of the Khorasan border region long claimed by Persia, but tenuously held by Afghanistan. In the distant past, Herat had been a Central Asian pearl, a major center of Islamic art, literature and science. By the 1830s, however, the city had taken on the worst aspects of a ghetto and a police state. The nominal sovereign, Shah Kamran, had helped plan the torture-execution of Futeh Khan in 1818 and had since become a senescent boor who continued to perpetrate atrocities between bouts of raving and vomiting from the effects of *bhang* and opium. Mohan Lal, a Kashmiri in the Company service, visited Herat at about this time and described Kamran as "the most unmerciful man in Afghanistan." The real power, however, was held by Kamran's Wazir, Yar Muhammad, who referred to his master as "that old drunkard," while another contemporary, the British historian Sir John Kaye, remarked in turn of Yar Muhammad that "if there was an abler or worse man in Central Asia, I have not yet heard his name."

In any case, neither Kamran nor Yar Muhammad was a model of civic virtue. Herat's budget was balanced by extortion, with delinquent contributors being tied to camels and dragged through the streets after first being disemboweled. Yar Muhammad grew rich by selling towns-people—including members of Kamran's family—into slavery. Residence in Herat was not the best of insurance risks.

Herat's unstable condition seemed to offer easy pickings for Persia. The citizenry had little reason to oppose a change in administration. Herat's own ties to Afghanistan were slender. Kamran, who had never forgiven Dost Muhammad for violating his harem, claimed independence from Kabul. Yar Muhammad might prove a tougher nut for Persia to crack, but he had once considered throwing in his lot with the Shah and was more than capable of contemplating another sellout. And even if he chose to resist, Herat's ragged, poorly armed military forces would crumble swiftly under the blows of a Russian-equipped Persian army.

More to the point, the occupation of Herat would be a strategic coup. The city lay astride the main road to Kandahar, from which an invading force could either march on Kabul and then drive eastward through the Khyber Pass, or strike at India's relatively soft underbelly by the south-erly Bolan Pass route. Russia had already gained what amounted to free passage through Persia. With Herat in Persian hands, the Russians would have an important base of supplies and reinforcements for a military juggernaut that could roll virtually unopposed through Afghanistan, and then go smashing on to Delhi.

This, at any rate, was the characteristically paranoid British view of the Russian menace. Palmerston's colleague, Lord John Russell, summed it up with the solemn warning that "if we do not stop Russia on the Danube, we shall have to stop her on the Indus."

No one was more alive to the threat than Palmerston. In 1835, he had stepped into his role as bully to the weak, with instructions to the British Ambassador in Teheran: "You will especially warn the Persian Gov-ernment against being made the Tool of Russian policy, by allowing themselves to be pushed on to make war against the Afghans. Russia has objects of Her own to gain by exciting the Persian Government to quarrel with its Eastern Neighbours." That tentative exercise in muscle-flexing set the tone of the policy that Auckland was to pursue.

Auckland had more clear-cut instructions. They took the form of a memorandum drawn up by a secret committee of the Company's Court of Directors, bidding him "watch more closely than has hitherto been attempted the progress of events in Afghanistan" with a view toward neutralizing any Russian overtures to Dost Muhammad. But Auckland's brief did not stop here. He was further empowered to "interfere decidedly in the affairs of Afghanistan" if and when he felt that the Russian threat warranted such action, and to "take any other measures that may appear to you desirable in order to counteract Russian advances in that quarter."

In effect, Auckland had been given a free hand to manipulate Afghanistan in any way he chose. His instructions reflected Palmerstonian gunboat diplomacy at its most brazen.

Initially, Auckland did not leap to implement the directive; he genuinely shrank from becoming embroiled in the unpredictable twists and turns of Afghan politics. Shortly after his appointment he had received a letter of congratulation from Dost Muhammad, who expressed the hope that "your Lordship will consider me and my country as your own." Auckland may have gulped. Dost Muhammad went on to ask: "Communicate to me whatever may suggest itself to your wisdom for the settlement of the affairs of this country." The Amir was referring specifically to Peshawar and the Afghan eastern frontier, and the request for advice was in fact a thinly veiled bid for British aid in ousting the "reckless and misguided" Sikhs. Auckland's response was a courteous whopper: "My friend, you are aware that it is not the practice of the British Government to interfere with the affairs of other independent states."

And as for that sort of interference, Auckland already had more than enough on his plate with the importunities of the land-greedy Ranjit Singh, who was then seeking British assistance in his plan to annex Sind on the Punjab's southwest border. Since the Punjab was contiguous with British India, and thus a vital buffer against invasion from the west, Ranjit had been able to exploit that accident of geography and make himself seem indispensable as a partner of the British. Yet, whereas Auckland normally recoiled from aggravating this ostensible friend, he was also resolved not to become party to the Sikh ruler's expansionist schemes. "I have entreated Runjeet Singh to be quiet," he wrote a colleague at this time, "and in regard to his last two requests I have refused to give him 50,000 musquets, and am ready to send him a doctor and a dentist."

Events soon tumbled Auckland from his neutral perch. In November 1837, in defiance of Palmerston's earlier warning, the Shah of Persia ordered his army and its siege guns to the walls of Herat for the long-feared assault on that city. It had suddenly become urgent that Palmerston's policy be implemented by a formal alliance with Afghanistan.

Indeed, Auckland had already acted. His special envoy to the court of Dost Muhammad was even then conferring with the Amir in Kabul.

The robes and turban that Alexander Burnes often wore in Afghanistan did not conceal a youthful, merry face and an expression that suggested a boy who had just stolen a box of sweetmeats. In 1837, Burnes was perhaps the most glamorous figure on the Indian scene. A relative of the poet Robert Burns, he had been born in Scotland in 1805 and joined the Company at the age of sixteen as an ensign in the Indian Army. But Burnes swiftly established himself as a wunderkind in less warlike specialties. A gifted linguist and cartographer, he also showed skills in high-level wheeling and dealing more often found in older men of vast diplomatic experience. Though hardly touched with genius, as some writers have implied, Burnes may have been born with an intuitive affability; it carried him far in his career and was exceeded only by his patriotism, ambition, ego and bedsmanship—listed in no special order.

Burnes' future with the Company seemed limitless. In 1832, he had wangled permission from the Indian Government to lead an expedition into Central Asia. His route took him across Afghanistan, over the hump of the Hindu Kush and north of the Oxus River to the little-known and all but forbidden city of Bokhara. In the 1830s, a European visiting Bokhara faced more dangers than he would have on a trek through Central Africa. Although Burnes and his party were treated civilly during their two-month stay in the city, they were literally marked men, being required to wear black caps and ropes around their waists, the mandatory garb of aliens. From one moment to the next they could never be certain that they would not fall prey to a caprice of Bokhara's crazy Amir Nasrullah. Had this happened, they probably would have been thrown into the city's infamous "bug pit," a deep well, crawling with insects and reptiles that fed on decomposing corpses while living captives waited their turn. Providentially, the expedition was able to depart intact—a fact on which, Burnes later wrote, "I have never ceased to congratulate myself." When he returned to England and described his adventures in an overnight best-seller, he was lionized in London society as "Bokhara Burnes."

One of the high points of the journey had been Burnes' stay in Kabul, where he accepted an invitation to dine with Dost Muhammad at the Bala Hissar. Burnes wrote of being "quite charmed" by the Amir's "accomplished address and manners," and impressed with his lively interest in European affairs. On the strength of that abbreviated meeting, Burnes seemed to commend himself, in the eyes of British Indian officialdom, as just the man to head up a mission that would lay the foundations of Anglo-Afghan friendship.

There was something in it for both parties. What Dost Muhammad wanted from India was help in recovering Peshawar from the Sikhs. What Auckland wanted from Dost Muhammad was the assurance that he would resist Persian and Russian moves on Afghanistan. While the Governor General could certainly bring effective pressure to bear on Ranjit Singh, the Amir was not in the best position to guarantee a cordon sanitaire against Russia or even Persia. Many parts of Afghanistan still lay outside his real authority. Kandahar to the south was governed by a posse of his brothers; almost certifiably insane in their jealousy of him, they were known to be considering an accommodation with the Shah of Persia. Herat could cave in under the Persian siege guns at any time, and even if it did not, Kamran could never be expected to subordinate himself to his sworn enemy in Kabul. For all this, however, Dost Muhammad came closer than anyone else to being the legitimate ruler of Afghanistan. It must be with him alone that Burnes could make a treaty.

In fact, Burnes was empowered to do no such thing.

This might have seemed odd. Thirty years earlier, Mountstuart Elphinstone had been directed to conclude an alliance with Shah Shuja because of a threat to India that was much less tangible—even less visible—than the Russian-Persian designs on Herat in 1837. And yet, even as Persia prepared to pound on the Afghan gates, Burnes went to Kabul with express orders to keep clear of political engagements in Afghanistan. The purpose of his mission was to explore the possibility of opening the Indus River to navigation—although merchants had been plying the Indus for generations—and to discuss with Dost Muhammad in general terms the prospects of commerce between Afghanistan and India. In short, Auckland was continuing to shrink from political entanglements in the never-never land west of the Indus.

Or so it might have seemed at first. "As yet I have no authority beyond that of conducting a *commercial* mission," wrote Burnes in a letter during his journey up the Indus in the spring of 1837, "but various hints and letters, together with the chain of events now in progress, convince me that a stirring time of *political* action has now arrived, and I shall have to show what my government is made of, as well as myself. . . . Why, zounds! . . . we must be on the alert." Sir John Kaye, whose monumental history of Anglo-Afghan relations at this time is still considered the definitive work, put it another way when he remarked that "it would be hard to say what our Oriental diplomatists would do if they were forbidden the use of the word 'commerce.'" In any case, Burnes' original harmless objective was soon forgotten.

Burnes left India for Kabul at the end of November 1836, and enjoyed a leisurely seven-month boat ride up the Indus to a point not far from Peshawar. The journey was for the most part uneventful, although there were some tense moments in July 1837, when the party crossed the

Khyber Pass without an escort. No one was molested, however, and on September 20 Burnes reached the outskirts of Kabul. There, the mission was greeted by Dost Muhammad's son Akbar Khan, leading a squadron of Afghan cavalry and several royal elephants, one of which had been brought out so that Burnes could ride into Kabul in the fashion of a conquering hero.

The following day, Burnes presented his credentials to Dost Muhammad and told the Amir that he had brought as gifts "some of the rarities of Europe," to which Dost Muhammad "promptly replied that we ourselves were the rarities, the sight of which best pleased him." It was not many days after this exchange of compliments that Burnes' mission began coming apart at the seams.

One version of the fiasco lays the blame squarely on Burnes' shoulders. At the time of the talks, the East India Company had in Kabul a sort of quasi-official political observer named Charles Masson. A Kentuckian, of all things, Masson had spent much time in Afghanistan and was very well informed on the country's affairs. It is also possible that he had a personal axe to grind with Burnes; certainly his portrait of the Envoy is less than flattering, but neither can it be dismissed entirely as the product of a grudge.

Among other things, Masson accused Burnes of getting off on the wrong foot immediately by his lack of "decorum" with the women of Kabul—another way of saying that the Envoy's randiness outraged his Afghan hosts, who had their own ideas about sex. Burnes might not have given Masson much of an argument here. He himself wrote that "I must not . . . lightly pass over so important a part of the population of Cabool as the ladies. Their ghost-like figures when they walk abroad make one melancholy, but if all be true of them that is reported, they make ample amends when indoors for all such sombre exhibitions in public." The suggestion of only second-hand knowledge was a sop to Victorian readers. Burnes had long enjoyed a reputation as a womanizer, and his orgies in Kabul were quite uninhibited. At one point, Masson himself was approached by a high-ranking Afghan official with the sarcastic proposal "that I should imitate the example of my illustrious superior, and fill my house with black-eyed damsels." Burnes was later to pay the price for his philandering.

Masson also deplored Burnes' personal conduct as a diplomat—in which he underwent a transformation from Hugh Hefner to Uriah Heep. In audiences at the Bala Hissar, said Masson, Burnes gave Dost Muhammad "every reason to exult in the humility of his new guest, who never addressed him but with his hands closed, in the attitude of supplication." In Masson's view, this was no way to deal with a ruler who was "anything but an angel," and who "had, indeed, shown the cloven foot." And, in fact, Burnes' submissive behavior, if depicted accurately, could hardly have enabled him to lead from strength or improve the British bargaining position.

Nor did Burnes seem to enhance his image as an unruffled emissary of the Crown when, on December 19, 1837, a handsome young Cossack officer named Ivan Viktorovich Vitkevich arrived in Kabul with letters to Dost Muhammad from the Czar and the Shah of Persia. Burnes wrote that he invited Vitkevich to dinner and enjoyed his guest's company; the Russian "had been three times to Bokhara, and we had therefore a common subject to converse upon." Burnes also voiced regret that policy dictated against cultivating a friendship with this "gentlemanly and agreeable man." But, according to Masson, that was not the way it happened; instead of welcoming Vitkevich, Burnes "abandoned himself to despair. He bound his head with wet towels and handkerchiefs, and took to the smelling-bottle. It was humiliating to witness such an exhibition, and the ridicule to which it gave rise."

These, of course, were relatively minor points. Quite correctly, Masson saw the success of Burnes' mission turning on the question of restoring Peshawar to Afghanistan. Auckland had offered a compromise whereby the Indian Government would arrange to have Ranjit Singh hand over the city to one of Dost Muhammad's brothers, one Sultan Muhammad Khan. The Amir's fraternal relations being what they were, Dost Muhammad likened the proposal to "placing a snake in my bosom," but, according to Masson, Burnes could and should have prevailed on the Amir to accept the compromise without delay: "The settlement was in our power at the time . . . it is extraordinary that Captain Burnes should not have seen the matter in the light every one but himself did." Instead, said Masson, Burnes encouraged Dost Muhammad to hold out for a series of unrealistic counterproposals that only had the effect of alienating the Indian Government. This doomed the mission to failure.

Certainly no one could question its collapse. By April 1838, with the British and Afghans unable to reach agreement, Dost Muhammad finally turned to Vitkevich, and Burnes had to stand and watch as the Russian emissary was escorted to the Bala Hissar with the same elephantine pomp in which he himself had reveled seven months earlier. There was nothing left for Burnes but to quit Kabul.

Although Masson had a ringside seat at the diplomatic miscarriage, Kaye's account is the most commonly accepted. Here, Burnes is portrayed as anything but a bumbling playboy. With access to originally unpublished correspondence, official and personal, Kaye shows it highly likely that Burnes was not merely hobbled by insufficient authority, but actually betrayed by a barely comprehensible policy volte-face on the part of two high-ranking British officials far removed from the scene.

The villains of Kaye's piece are Auckland and the Indian Government's

Chief Secretary, Sir William Macnaghten. According to Kaye, both men were party to the underhanded doctoring and suppression of Burnes' reports, because both had somehow decided that Dost Muhammad constituted a threat to the security of India and had to be exposed as such to the British public.

There were two ostensible reasons for the mistake of viewing Dost Muhammad as a menace. One was the Amir's continuing effort to regain Peshawar from Ranjit Singh. While the Sikh ruler could be a terrible nuisance to the British, the common border shared by the Punjab and British India tended to dictate a kid-gloves policy toward Ranjit. This in turn allowed Ranjit to insinuate himself shrewdly into a position of inflated importance as an ally: anyone who opposed him had to be anti-British by definition. Thus, Akbar Khan's near-successful attack on Jamrud in the spring of 1837 was a very bad mark against Dost Muhammad. Furthermore, with the restoration of Peshawar in mind, Dost Muhammad had also considered, and at one point even sought, aid from Persia and Russia. To Auckland and Macnaghten, that act could only brand the Amir as a potential, if not open, enemy.

That was Dost Muhammad as Auckland and Macnaghten saw him from afar. Yet in his talks with Burnes in the informal atmosphere of his throne room—where he usually ignored the throne itself for a more comfortable seat on a carpet—the Amir showed himself to be anything but unyielding on the crucial Peshawar issue. Auckland could easily have won from Ranjit Singh an agreement to relinquish Peshawar to Dost Muhammad without loss of face, particularly since it was known that the city had become a liability to the Sikhs. Yet Auckland and Macnaghten would only go so far as to restore Peshawar to the Amir's brother. Although Dost Muhammad found that proposal unacceptable, he did not slam the door entirely on compromise, and Burnes looked to Calcutta for new instructions that might enable him to submit more flexible terms.

It also became clear that Dost Muhammad was ready to turn his back on Russia and Persia if he could win British friendship. When Burnes told him that he must not expect material aid from an alliance, Dost Muhammad responded by severing all connections with the Czar and the Shah. Burnes was able to report to Auckland: "Russia has come forward with offers that are certainly substantial. Persia has been lavish in her promises. . . . Yet, in all that has passed or is daily transpiring, the chief of Caubul declares that he prefers the sympathy and friendly offices of the British to all these offers, however alluring they may seem." That passage, writes Kaye, "was not published in the official correspondence. It was thought better to suppress it."

While waiting for his instructions on Peshawar, Burnes found his hands full in another quarter. Dost Muhammad's brothers, the chiefs of

Kandahar, had been welcoming Russian and Persian overtures. They received a Persian emissary and were preparing to send gifts to the Russian Ambassador in Teheran when Burnes stepped in. He swiftly quashed the budding alliances, first with a threat to the chiefs ("I have sent them such a Junius," he wrote a friend, "as, I believe, will astonish them."), then with a promise of military aid. He was without authority to take this step and knew it, but as he said in another private letter: "Am I to stand by and see us ruined at Candahar? . . . Herat has been besieged fifty days, and if the Persians move on Candahar, I am off there with the Ameer and his forces, and mean to pay the piper myself."

Burnes never had to go to Kandahar; his gesture was enough to send the Persian envoy packing. But his reward for ridding Kandahar of Russian and Persian influence was a severe rebuke from Macnaghten for "having exceeded your instructions and held out hopes which . . . cannot be realised." This left Burnes with no choice but to renege on his promise of aid, whereupon the Kandahar chiefs promptly concluded a formal treaty with Persia.

Perhaps the most revealing aspect of this episode concerned the text of the official reprimand to Burnes. It ran to twenty-four paragraphs, of which only three ever saw print, causing Kaye to charge "a studious suppression of the entire history of the offers made to the Candahar chiefs." Kaye also notes that Auckland, "subsequently, with praiseworthy candour, admitted that the authorities at home were of opinion that [Burnes' proposal] was the very best that could have been adopted." By then it was too late.

At about the same time that Burnes was being admonished for trying to keep Kandahar out of the enemy camp, he received Calcutta's final word on Peshawar. "Under any circumstances," Macnaghten wrote him, "our first feeling must be that of regard for the honour and just wishes of our old and firm ally Runjit Singh"; and Burnes was also instructed to "discourage all extravagant pretensions on the part of Dost Muhammad." In effect, Macnaghten was making it clear that the Amir could forget about recovering Peshawar. By way of driving this home, a further directive underscored the need for "bringing Dost Muhammad to his senses." Another historian has said of this rigid stand that "never can an envoy have received more . . . unpalatable instructions on which to base a bid for the friendship of a foreign potentate."

On learning of Auckland's refusal to budge on Peshawar, Dost Muhammad might have been expected to break off the talks with Burnes. As it proved, his eagerness to win British friendship transcended even his wish to get back his country's winter capital. No clearer evidence of this could have been manifested than on Vitkevich's arrival in Kabul. Burnes wrote to a friend that after the Russian envoy had presented his letters to Dost Muhammad, "the Ameer came over to me sharp, and offered to do as I liked, kick him out, or anything . . . and since he was so friendly to us, said I, give me the letters the agent has brought; all of which he surrendered sharp; and I sent an express at once to my Lord A. . . . How all this will go down I know not, but I know my duty too well to be silent."

Dost Muhammad did more than just hand over Vitkevich's letters. Apart from receiving the Russian formally, he thenceforth locked and bolted the Bala Hissar to him. Although this did not quite make Vitkevich persona non grata in Kabul, he could only cool his heels and write ruefully that the Amir's pro-British position "has occasioned [him] to conduct himself very coldly towards me."

This and other acts of good faith gained Dost Muhammad no credit with the government whose friendship he vainly sought. As late as the end of January 1838, he told Burnes that he was ready to remove Peshawar from the agenda entirely, and Burnes reported to Calcutta that the Amir "has declared that his interests are all bound up in an alliance with the British Government, which he will never desert as long as there is a hope of securing one." Kaye points to this as one more of innumerable passages that were deleted from Burnes' official correspondence, with the intention not only of misrepresenting Dost Muhammad's motives and character, but of creating the impression that Burnes himself had sought a break with the Amir.

It should be noted that the physical tampering with Burnes' dispatches was not the work of Auckland or Macnaghten, but of Palmerston. The Foreign Secretary, however, was acting on the Governor General's recommendation that Britain sever relations with Dost Muhammad. Despite the urgings of his man on the spot that India had everything to gain from an alliance with the Amir, Auckland would not be swayed from his decision that Ranjit Singh was the man to back and Dost Muhammad a plague to be shunned. Burnes might just as well have stayed in Bokhara.

As it was, by April 1838, Dost Muhammad had reluctantly arrived at the realization that he could expect nothing from the government that shrank from discomfiting his enemy Ranjit Singh in the smallest way. Like Third World rulers before and after him, he by then felt bound to protect his country's interests by making a strong friend wherever he might find one. Vitkevich thus became the man of the hour, and Russia seemed to have gained her foothold in Afghanistan—the very step that Auckland had sought to thwart when he sent Burnes to Kabul and that he had facilitated by rejecting Burnes' advice.

Vitkevich was well rewarded by his own government. In the spring of 1839, he returned to St. Petersburg to report to Count Nesselrode, the Russian Foreign Minister, and to his astonishment was informed that

Nesselrode "knew no Captain Vitkevich, except an adventurer of that name, who it was reported, had been lately engaged in some unauthorized intrigues at Kabul and Kandahar." Fearing—not without reason—that he had been made a dupe in high-level diplomatic maneuvering, Vitkevich promptly blew his brains out. Although other reasons have been given for his suicide,* the fact remains that Russia, by early 1839, had come to entertain second thoughts about the wisdom of a direct thrust into Afghanistan. The change of heart stemmed partly from strong representations by Palmerston and partly from a serious setback to Russian fortunes in Persia. A by-product of this modified policy was Dost Muhammad's fall from favor with Russia. But that development in no way softened Auckland's own attitude toward the Amir. In fact, Auckland had, by this time, made Dost Muhammad the target of a political-military campaign that was only less ambitious than it was mad. Auckland's objective was nothing less than the forcible removal of Dost Muhammad as amir—after the invasion and conquest of Afghanistan.

---

* It is known that he was depressed at this time over the conviction that in serving Russia he had betrayed the cause of Polish nationalism for which he had fought as a youth, and for which he had been exiled to Central Asia, where the Russians allowed him to redeem himself in their eyes by carrying out various military and diplomatic missions.

3

Juggernaut on Crutches

In 1836, when the secret committee of the Company's Court of Directors furnished Auckland with the guidelines that empowered him to "interfere decidedly in the affairs of Afghanistan," its members knew they were allowing him an almost breathtaking degree of latitude. But in leaving not only the timing but the manner of the intrusion to the Governor General's discretion, the committee had presumably never dreamed that he would come up with so crazy a scheme as a full-scale military invasion.

In fact, the idea was probably not Auckland's alone. At the very least, it appears to have sprung partly from the mind of the Indian Government's Chief Secretary, Sir William Macnaghten, whose judgement the Governor General may have respected more than that of any other subordinate. In some respects, one can almost think of Macnaghten as Auckland's Svengali.

This man, whose mustache, eyebrows and spectacles gave him the look of a pensive Groucho Marx, had been a faithful and dedicated servant of the Company for three decades. His gifts as scholar and linguist took a back seat only to his reputation as a chillingly efficient and almost hypercautious bureaucrat. But in a few instances, Macnaghten was known to have taken bold positions; one contemporary in India even called him "our Lord Palmerston." And, paradoxically, Macnaghten's prudence was also capable of being cancelled out by a kind of supercharged optimism that could mangle reality beyond recognition. These qualities may well have combined, in 1838, to make Macnaghten party to—if not the actual instigator of—a perfect model of reckless unwisdom.

To be sure, there was a rationale of sorts for the thing. In Auckland's and Macnaghten's eyes, Dost Muhammad had proved himself a clear and present danger to India, both by refusing to accept the Peshawar compromise—which was, in effect, to threaten India's "old and firm ally," Ranjit Singh—and by having welcomed Russian influence in his country. In the spring of 1838, moreover, the defenses of Herat seemed about to buckle and collapse under the hammering of the Persian siege guns, and if Herat fell, opening the path of invasion for Russia, it would become imperative that a pro-British amir hold the reins in Kabul. The only flaw in this reasoning was the evaluation of Dost Muhammad as an enemy. Auckland and Macnaghten seemed unable or unwilling to realize that they alone had driven the Amir into the Russian embrace. And now, carrying their error to its illogical conclusion, they proposed to defend Afghanistan from Russia by overthrowing the man who had been prepared to forsake Peshawar unconditionally if that sacrifice would prove his friendship for the British.

But Dost Muhammad was not to be ejected by British troops. Auckland and Macnaghten saw no need to burden the British taxpayer with the expense of a military expedition when Ranjit Singh's army was on hand to perform the chore—with the help, perhaps, of a few troops from India as window dressing. It was also planned to replace Dost Muhammad with Shah Shuja, the ruler who had been ousted thirty years earlier and who had subsequently gone for aid to Afghanistan's archenemy Ranjit. If they had been trying, Auckland and Macnaghten could not have devised a more foolproof way of bringing together the faction-ridden Afghans in a united front against a common foe.

In May 1838, Macnaghten went to Lahore, the Punjab's capital, to visit Ranjit Singh in his trillionaire's palace and win him over to the scheme. As expected, the Sikh ruler was elated at the prospect of marching on Kabul alongside his British friends, but no one had anticipated that he might have terms of his own, or how shrewd a bargainer he might prove. While being plied with a fiery local vintage wine, Macnaghten was subjected to a barrage of strategic and political queries. When it became clear to Ranjit that the British intended to play only a token role in the invasion, his questions began to take on a demanding tone. Almost before he realized what was happening, Macnaghten found himself asking whether Ranjit might feel more secure with a small addition of British military assistance. "That," replied Ranjit, "would be adding sugar to milk," and the snowball started rolling. When the talks ended and Macnaghten returned to India, Auckland informed the Secret Committee that it had now been decided to "give the direct and powerful assistance of the British Government to the enterprise." The reason, he explained, was that "the measure could not be trusted mainly to the support of the Sikh ruler and army without imminent hazard of failure."

Thus, British troops would carry the burden of the invasion and the Sikhs would provide the token force, Ranjit becoming merely a signatory to a tripartite treaty with the Indian Government and Shah Shuja. By the terms of the treaty, Ranjit engaged to give Shah Shuja fifty-five loads of rice in return for fifty-five horses of "approved color and pleasant paces," along with a shipment of Kabul musk melons. More significantly, Shah Shuja also confirmed Ranjit's title of ownership to the earlier Sikh conquests of Afghanistan's trans-Indus border regions. Shah Shuja, living the humiliating but opulent life of a royal emigré in British India, had hardly been consulted on the upcoming invasion, but he seemed agreeable enough to anything that would take him out of cold storage and give him the chance to sit again on the Kabul throne. In any event, the commitment and expenses that the British had sought to avoid had now been deftly thrust back on them by their old and firm ally.

All this became official on October 1, 1838, when Auckland issued a proclamation that came to be known as the "Simla Manifesto," because it was published in British India's summer capital of Simla—described by Kaye as "that pleasant hill Sanitarium . . . which has been the cradle of more political insanity than any place within the limits of Hindostan." Among other things, the Simla Manifesto declared that Dost Muhammad had made an unprovoked attack on Ranjit Singh and that, in concert with Persia, had "avowed schemes of aggrandizement and ambition injurious to the security and peace of the frontier of India." Particular stress was laid on the siege of Herat, not only as a further menace to India, but as urgent reason for the presence of a pro-British ruler in Kabul. Given so grave a crisis, said Auckland, the Government of India saw no alternative but to remove the threat by removing the treacherous Dost Muhammad and reinstalling Shah Shuja under the protection of British bayonets. It was further noted that this move would enable the British to plug the leak in the dam at Herat. Auckland concluded with what might be called famous last words of British imperialism: "When once [Shah Shuja] shall be secure in power, and the independence and integrity of Afghanistan established, the British army will be withdrawn."

Apart from the fact that the charges against Dost Muhammad were unfounded, if not downright fabrications, the real raison d'être of the British invasion no longer existed at the time of the Simla Manifesto. The siege of Herat had been lifted.

That the city had been able to hold out was due largely to the almost single-handed efforts of a youthful British army lieutenant named Eldred Pottinger. Some months earlier, Pottinger had entered Herat in the disguise of a fakir, taken command of the defenses and rallied the apathetic Herati troops, who dug in and began fighting back with spirit. During one particularly furious Persian assault on the walls, Pottinger had literally dragged a despairing Yar Muhammad to his feet and insulted him into leading a berserk counterattack that sent the enemy sprawling. By such aggressive improvisations had the Persian army been held at arm's length.

Pottinger's gallantry and resourcefulness were presently rewarded. In mid-August, Muhammad Mirza, the Shah of Persia, who had personally assumed command of the assaulting troops, received notice from Palmerston that if the siege continued Britain would "take such steps as [she] may think best calculated" to safeguard India's frontier. Muhammad Mirza realized at once that unlike Palmerston's earlier warning, this was no idle baring of fangs: the Royal Navy had already dispatched a squadron to the Persian Gulf. Even in the face of Russian threats, the Shah was not prepared to try Britannia's wrath. Mounting his horse, he rode off to Teheran, followed by the Persian army. Herat had been delivered. The need for a British invasion of Afghanistan had vanished.

Auckland and Macnaghten thought otherwise. On November 8, a second proclamation brought the Simla Manifesto up to date. The invasion was to proceed as scheduled, it said, "with a view to the substitution of a friendly for a hostile power in the eastern provinces of Afghanistan and to the establishment of a permanent barrier against schemes of aggression upon our north-west frontier." This geopolitical reasoning might possibly be likened to the strategy, thirteen decades later, of defending Los Angeles and San Francisco from Mao Tse-tung by sending an American army to Vietnam.

If the Court of Directors was stunned by the impending filibuster, its hands were tied by the Palmerston-dominated Board of Control, and the members could only voice impotent dismay. Indeed, few Britons who understood Indian and Central Asian politics rejoiced. "The very last men in the world I should have expected of such folly!" exclaimed a former governor general, speaking of Auckland and Macnaghten. "The Afghans were neutral," wrote Mountstuart Elphinstone to a friend, "and would have received [British] aid against invaders with gratitude—they will now be disaffected and glad to join any invader to drive [us] out." Another high-ranking Indian official predicted: "Depend on it, the surest way to bring Russia down on us is to cross the Indus and meddle with the countries beyond it."

The Russians were soon to fulfill that last prophecy. Barely a year later, they launched a military expedition against the Central Asian khanate of Khiva, which hovered over Afghanistan's vaguely defined northwest frontier. Auckland and Macnaghten could consider themselves fortunate that the Czar's army, marching at the worst possible time of year, was wiped out almost to a man by ice storms on the Ust Urt Plateau.

Fazed not in the least by the voices of gloom and doom in England, Auckland set out for the Punjab in the autumn of 1838 to greet his brother-in-arms Ranjit and bid godspeed to the invading force, now known as the Army of the Indus. The Governor General's entourage combined the features of a military parade and a traveling circus. Besides Auckland and his sister, the Honourable Emily Eden, there was an over-size staff of army officers and political advisers in costume ball uniforms; their gaily bedecked wives; some 15,000 troops and followers; and at least that many horses, camels and elephants. At the end of November, when Ranjit greeted the procession a few miles south of Lahore, the meeting was literally a collision as Sikh and British state elephants thundered head-on into each other, flinging Ranjit unceremoniously from his howdah to the ground. But this was the only embarrassing moment in the pageant of ostentation that took place over the next few days.

Ranjit shone as a host. He took Auckland on personally conducted tours of the palace grounds, the royal treasury (never before seen by an outsider) and the temple where he had discussed the proposed British alliance with an oracle. Emily Eden gasped at this last place: "The temple is of pure gold," she wrote in a letter to her sister, "really and truly covered completely with gold, most beautifully carved, till within eight feet from the ground, and then there are panels of marble inlaid with flowers and birds—very *Solomonish* altogether." The Sikh ruler also staged an endless round of entertainments. He brought out nautch dancers (Miss Eden thought them "a very ugly lot"), fireworks, illuminated fish in crystal tanks, attendants garbed in gold cloth and, at one evening party, 42,000 lamps to replace the flowers. One of Ranjit's many orches-tras caught Miss Eden's ear when it "began playing 'God Save the Queen' with every other bar left out, which makes a rather pretty air." At all these affairs, "the old mouse," as Miss Eden called Ranjit, proved to have not only one eye but a hollow leg. He favored "a sort of liquid fire . . . which he pours down like water. . . . He insisted on my just touch-ing it . . . and one drop actually burnt the outside of my lips."

Fittingly, a martial atmosphere prevailed in a continual spectacle of parading and maneuvering. Auckland's forces put on a fine show, their battalion bands thumping out bold cadences for rank on rank of British and Indian foot soldiery, ablaze with gold-faced scarlet tunics, pipe-clayed crossbelts, gaily plumed shakos, and jaunty turbans beneath a glory of Union Jacks and regimental colors. Cavalry squadrons wheeled and pirou-etted, their harnesses a jingling counterpoint to the yelp of bugles, the troopers' lances and sabers flashing like jewelry in the autumn sun. Small earthquakes were set in motion by endless tiers of horses, camels and elephants hauling the carriages of ponderous, muzzle-loading field guns. Some of these cannons had probably been fired at the American colonists six decades earlier, as had the force's colossal, ungainly .75 caliber "Brown Bess" muskets, still the standard issue infantry weapon. The climax of the extravaganza was a stirring sham battle, in which the Army of the Indus defeated itself with such realism that one of its own generals remarked: "Oh, how I wished . . . to have done in half an hour what they all bungled at from six to ten o'clock."

The invasion of Afghanistan was not to be carried out by punching directly from Lahore to Kabul on the 350-mile road that ran through the Khyber Pass—although the Afridis could have been contained by sheer weight of numbers or simply bought off. Instead, the Army of the Indus would march nearly five times that distance, following a 1,100-mile southwesterly route to Kandahar via the Bolan Pass, then driving another 300 miles northeastward to Kabul. There were two reasons for bypassing the Khyber, one being Ranjit Singh's objection to his allies marching through his country. But a southerly approach to Afghanistan would also take the army into Sind. Since both Kabul and Lahore claimed allegiance of sorts from the fractious amirs of this scrofulous principality, and the British had cast an imperial eye in that direction, there would be no harm in showing the flag and a little muscle to the amirs of Sind.

Certainly the Army of the Indus had what it took to intimidate. All told, the expedition numbered slightly under 10,000 British and Indian soldiers, divided into eighteen infantry battalions, six cavalry regiments and two artillery brigades. In addition, there was a 6,000-man Afghan-Indian force, ostensibly Shah Shuja's army, but led by British officers. Under the overall command of Lieutenant General Sir John Keane, the army consisted of two striking columns: a Bombay force led by Keane himself and a Bengal contingent under Major General Sir Willoughby Cotton. Keane was to sail with his troops from Bombay to Karachi and link up with Cotton in Sind. With nearly 17,000 fighting men to deploy, Keane had little cause for concern over Afghan resistance.

The British troops for the most part were faceless robots. Little attention was ever paid to a private soldier except when he responded to a fraudulent recruiting poster and was given a uniform that made him look like a field marshal, although for the twenty-one years of his enlistment he was treated like a felon, which he very often was. Armies in those days tended to be dumping grounds for the criminal, the alcoholic, the incompetent and the illiterate elements of society. In England, soldiers of the Queen were usually put in the same class as India's Untouchables. Their annual pay would not have supported a present-day men's room attendant for a week. They had no such thing as a NAAFI or USO, although the army did give them two meals daily and a beer or rum ration. Their only on-post diversions took place when they were formed up to witness punishment; some commanders ordered floggings so regularly that the troops gave their regiments such nicknames as the "Steelbacks" or the "Bendovers." In this rabble of derelicts, ability stood out like a sore thumb and could be rewarded with the stripes and awesome authority of a corporal or sergeant, or even the demigod status of a regimental sergeant-major. Otherwise, the rank and file of the British army was good for nothing but fighting. In this calling, the men had covered themselves with glory since Crécy and Agincourt. But, as the Duke of Wellington himself had pointed out, they were really the scum of the earth.

That designation did not apply to the sepoys of the Company's infantry or to the sowars of its cavalry, who came mainly from warrior castes and took an almost savage pride in their martial traditions. All the same, they tended to complain loudly and even shirk when called on to fight at any distance from their homes. In general, the Indians were a conspicuously brave but sullen lot, known to skirmish occasionally with British regiments. Perhaps because the Company had abolished flogging, they took somewhat less readily to discipline than did their British enlisted counterparts, but just how much less readily would not be realized fully until 1857, when they staged the protest demonstration that has come to be known as the Indian Mutiny.

The force's top-level leadership, if not overburdened with military genius, was at least experienced and tough. Keane was a sewer-mouthed veteran of Wellington's Peninsular campaigns. Cotton had three decades of army service under his ever-widening sword belt; he had also demonstrated a brawler's instincts at an early age, when he was expelled from Rugby after blasting open the headmaster's door with gunpowder during a school mutiny. Major General Sir William Nott, commanding one of Keane's divisions, was an old India hand who had been campaigning for the Company since the end of the eighteenth century. Brigadier Robert Sale of Cotton's force was known for being free with the lash, often ordering as many as three or four hundred of the best for barely discernible signs of insubordination. He also enjoyed challenging mutinous troops to shoot him, and although the offer was never accepted, "Fighting Bob's" own frame was a patchwork of scars gained in more battle actions than he could remember.

The worst that could be said about Keane as supreme commander was that he served in the British, rather than the Company's army. Rivalry between the two forces was a continual source of friction in any combined operation. Queen's officers, who bought their commissions, looked down on their Company counterparts as loutish riffraff, while the latter thought of the former as a rookery of fops, ill suited, if suited at all, for the harsh demands of Indian service. "A Queen's officer should never command in India," wrote the Company's General Nott; "whatever his talents may be, he is for a thousand reasons unfit. . . . Sir John Keane's appointment was from the first a dirty job and has paralyzed and nearly given a death blow to [our] enterprize." A self-educated man and a born fighter who thought one sepoy worth ten British soldiers and a thousand Afghans, Nott also suffered from a persecution complex and continually squabbled with Keane, whom he accused of placing him in a subordinate position because of his Company status. But Nott's complaints were not atypical in a climate of juvenile disharmony, and his feud with Keane was to have a crucial effect on the outcome of the campaign.

Much was expected of the junior officers, a bright-eyed and bushy-tailed lot. Not a few would go on to long and distinguished military careers in India. Pottinger, by then a major, had already gained a slice of glory at Herat. The puritanical Major Henry Havelock was known for his fire-and-brimstone lectures against the Demon Rum; he would become even more celebrated as a hero of the Indian Mutiny, as would the sixteen-year-old Ensign John Nicholson. Captain Colin Mackenzie had one of the highest pain thresholds in the medical records of the Company army; he was to sustain upwards of two dozen bullet and knife wounds on his road to becoming a lieutenant general. Macnaghten's aide, Captain George Lawrence, was the oldest of three brothers who made their family name the most honored in British India. The bespectacled Captain George Broadfoot loked like a divinity student, but was to become known by his sepoys as a savage disciplinarian and even more barbaric in combat. Lieutenant Vincent Eyre would put his career on the line with continual criticism of his superiors and, in due course, would become a general himself. There was hardly a single junior officer in the force who did not possess enough leadership, initiative and physical courage to fill a dozen Henty novels.*

At the political level, the two most important figures were Macnaghten and Burnes. The latter—by then Lieutenant Colonel Sir Alexander Burnes—had initially balked at accompanying the force, feeling that his presence would be a betrayal of Dost Muhammad, whose cause he had so fervently pleaded. Under Company orders, however, Burnes was obliged to smile on Shah Shuja and also made a virtue of necessity by recommending himself for appointment as Shuja's principal political adviser. But he did not think it necessary to install the puppet with an army; two regiments "as an honorary escort," he said, would be more than enough "to ensure

* The only bad apple, Lieutenant Harry Flashman of the General Staff, cheerily admits to being a model of poltroonery in his uproarious memoirs of the campaign.

his being fixed forever on the throne." This was not one of Burnes' wisest judgements, and the proposal would have gone down the drain under any circumstances.

So too did Burnes' hopes for the political plum—even though he saw himself as the only man qualified for the post. "I can tell them plainly," he wrote at this time, "that it is *aut Caesar aut nullus*." Auckland, however, passed up Caesar for Macnaghten, on grounds of broader experience, and the Chief Secretary, who had never crossed the Indus, became the British "Envoy and Minister to the Court of Shah Soojah-ool-Moolk," while Burnes had to content himself with Auckland's promise to give him Macnaghten's job once the new amir was safely ensconced. Until then he would serve as British Resident in Kabul, functioning as a sort of executive officer-cum-filing-clerk for Macnaghten. During the actual invasion, he would also be an advance ambassador without portfolio, smoothing the army's path with a supply of flattery, bribes or intimidation for various petty chiefs on the line of march.

Logistically, the army seemed more than able to look after itself should supply lines be cut. Its pack animals, including 30,000 camels, had a carrying capacity of at least 3,000 tons. Commissariat officers were to ride out ahead of the columns to gather emergency stores of food and fodder. No necessity or comfort had been overlooked. Upwards of 40,000 Indian followers would tote supplies, act as personal servants and perform a galaxy of other menial tasks. A large number of the baggage animals staggered under loads of glassware, cutlery, table linen, tinned meats and jams, cases of cheroots and vintage wines, together with other specialties for the officers. One brigadier had sixty camels rounded up to carry his personal belongings. The 16th Lancers remembered to take along their pack of foxhounds. Subalterns were allowed forty servants apiece. A correspondent with the force commented that "many young officers would as soon have thought of leaving behind their swords and double-barrelled pistols as march without their dressing-cases, their perfumes, Windsor soap and eau-de-cologne."

On December 10, 1838, the juggernaut lurched into motion, officers and men in high spirits as the columns began the march south, along the east bank of the Indus, in bracing, wine-clear winter air. Cotton and his staff looked forward eagerly to enforcing their will on Sind, and when the Bengal army reached the sand-swept northern frontiers of that country it met virtually no resistance. Only a token complaint was registered by the amirs when Cotton demanded and received a back tax (which had already been paid) of £250,000, to be shared by Shah Shuja and Ranjit Singh. His appetite whetted, Cotton ordered an advance farther south, to Sind's capital of Hyderabad, where the amirs' treasuries were said to contain nearly £10 million. But Macnaghten stepped in and reminded the General that the army's objective was Kabul. Although Macnaghten was a civilian, he was also the senior official with the force. Cotton let off a windstorm of Anglo-Saxon, but it was all wind, and the army executed a ponderous column-right toward the Indus.

By March 1839, the force had put the Indus behind it and the troops were staring up at the eighty-mile-long Bolan Pass. Now the going began to get tough and the tough could barely get going. The road climbing to the Bolan's summit, a mile above sea level, was not much more than a narrow, stony, goat path. It wound upward through the downward course of a roaring mountain torrent, which men, animals and guns had to ford at least six times a day. The supply camels had become a liability; unable to stand heights, they were also dying off in thousands from grazing on a local plant that rotted the walls of their stomachs. Many loads had to be abandoned. Burnes' diplomacy had not persuaded the region's Brahui tribesmen to abandon their age-old habit of banditry. They harried the expedition's flanks, gunning down or slicing up stragglers, making off with windfalls from the dwindling supplies and generally throwing the unwieldy British columns into a state of escalating confusion as the troops and their balky animals labored up the Bolan's slippery trail.

Two weeks of this before the Bolan was crossed. Then the army approached the brink of annihilation by hunger and thirst. The windslashed, sun-drilled mountain-desert wastes of Khelat in northern Baluchistan yielded barely enough millet for the survival of the inhabitants. Officers continued to live high off the hog, but the troops went on half rations while the followers lined their bellies with the skins of sheep fried in blood. Macnaghten had to report to Auckland that the force was verging on "a state of mutiny for food." There was nothing for it but to liberate subsistence from the locals. Helped mainly by the Khan of Khelat, whom Burnes won over with a combination of money and threats, the army replenished its larder just enough to keep the advance on Kandahar from floundering.

And Kandahar fell on April 25, without a single jezail fired in its defense. By this time, the Bombay and Bengal forces had linked up. All that stood in the way of a swift march on Kabul were the heat, well above 100 degrees in the unusually nonexistent shade, and disease, mainly in the form of dysentery, which poleaxed a great part of the force. For two months, several thousand British and Indian soldiers lay like newborn infants in their own liquid excrement and vomit, their tents a feeble shield against the hammering sun and great black thunderheads of flies. The army's only actions during this interval were some shouting contests between Keane and Nott, which resulted in the latter's being given command of the Kandahar garrison—a post that should have been held by a colonel or even a major.

At that point, Dost Muhammad never had a better chance to sweep down from Kabul and expel the intruder with a decisive blow. Although Kandahar had offered no resistance, it was becoming obvious that the Afghan people looked on Shah Shuja and the British as something less than liberators. A grand parade and review, choreographed by Keane to welcome Shah Shuja to the city, laid an egg when fewer than 300 Kandaharis turned up; and even they, wrote one British officer, "viewed the whole affair with the most mortifying indifference." Nor could the British expect supine apathy alone; "I really believe," said Nott, "that the people of Afghanistan will not give up their country without fighting for it." Still reeling from the tribal forays in the Bolan Pass, the army was not inclined to disagree.

Dost Muhammad did move, but not against the British. For some reason, he believed that their advance on Kandahar could only mean that they planned to march even farther west, to Herat, and defer an attempt on Kabul for a year. He accordingly sent his son Akbar Khan toward the Khyber Pass with the main Afghan army, as Ranjit Singh's forces appeared to be stirring in that neighborhood again. By that action, the Amir probably lost his only opportunity to save his throne.

Keane resumed the advance on Kabul at the end of June, marching northeast beneath the mountainous walls of the ancient "Arachosian Corridor," where Darius' Persian armies had once hacked a bloody military highway. The only remaining obstacle in Keane's path was an Afghan garrison, several thousand strong, firmly lodged in the fortress of Ghazni, about 200 miles from Kandahar. It was from this place that the great Ghaznavid Emperor Mahmud had launched his furious jihads against India seven centuries earlier, and it was at Ghazni also, on July 21, 1839, that the Army of the Indus had its first real taste of Afghan resistance.

Fittingly, the cutting edge of Dost Muhammad's only counteroffensive was a contingent of mounted irregulars known as Ghazis. The name had nothing to do with the city. Ghazis belonged to a fanatical Muslim sect whose members' single goal in life was to receive a one-way ticket to Paradise by dying in battle. They traveled first class if they managed to slay one or more infidels in the process. Ghazis were kamikaze pilots without planes.

When the Ghazis struck, their target was not Keane's force, but Shah Shuja's; the pretender had betrayed his faith by making common cause with the British camel manure, thus becoming a far more loathsome creature than any run-of-the-mill Feringhi. With curved tulwar blades flashing beneath green flags of Islam, the Ghazis spurred their horses to full gallop and came on in a screaming charge. The ground quivered under the pounding of 2,000 hooves and the sledgehammer blows of twenty-pound cannonballs from the fort's covering artillery fire. Within seconds, only a few yards separated the Ghazis from the tents of Shah Shuja's camp, where the horsemen would vivisect the enemy troops with the knife artistry for which they were dreaded. But the onslaught began to lose momentum as the Ghazis were struck on the flank by a battering countercharge of Shah Shuja's British-led Afghan cavalry. Exploiting the confusion, the Shah's infantry let go with a series of withering fusillades, and Ghazis began making the trip to Paradise in bunches.

When the smoke of the muskets cleared, however, some fifty of the attackers found themselves still among the living—prisoners bound hand and foot, to their everlasting disgrace. But they did not remain captive long. Shah Shuja ordered them beheaded forthwith, and his troops performed the task with an excess of zeal, opening stomachs and shearing off limbs before getting around to the actual decapitations. One British officer-bystander was shocked to observe that the soldiers were "laughing and joking, and seemed to look upon the work as good fun." It was no more, however, than a typical Afghan victory celebration.

It was also premature. The Ghazni citadel had yet to be taken, and the British did not seem up to it. When he marched out of Kandahar, Keane had left his heavy siege guns behind, having received intelligence that Ghazni would be a piece of cake. He paid no heed to Havelock's reminder that both Wellington and Napoleon had "each found cause to rue the hour" in which they had neglected their own siege trains. Now, as he stared at the Ghazni stronghold which reared up from the crest of a hill, Keane had his own hour to rue. The fort looked much like a child's sand castle except that it was considerably larger and not built of sand. Even if he had brought up his siege guns to fire at battlements of granite-hard dried mud that were ten feet thick and ten stories high, Keane still would have faced an iron vault with the combination to its lock thrown away.

An outside chance existed, to be sure, that a storming party might breach one of the gates if the gate itself could be blown open with gunpowder. But this likelihood seemed remote even when a disenchanted nephew of Dost Muhammad approached Keane and told him that one gate had been weakly built. Nonetheless, an officer volunteered to lay the charges; without siege guns, there was not much else that could be done.

A violent sandstorm drowned all sound and concealed the British sapper party as it crept toward the fort on the night of July 22. The men carried twelve seventy-five-pound bags of gunpowder—nearly half a ton—which were hastily but firmly planted at the foot of the gate. As the sappers made off, Lieutenant Henry Durand lit the fuse that would ignite the charge. The fuse was a long cotton tube filled with powder. It hissed and sputtered out. Durand tried again, but the wind kept him from raising even a spark. After several more attempts, the fuse at last began to burn and Durand ran for his life. He reached the awaiting assault force just as the first explosion slammed him to the ground.

The rasp of the bugle could barely be heard above the continuing detonations and the howling storm, but the assault team, its bayonets fixed, rushed the gate and collided head-on with a strong body of Afghan troops. The Afghans defended their gate with insane fury, but they were stunned by the blasts and could not hold. After only a few minutes, the British spearhead shot and stabbed and kicked a path through a rubble of masonry and bloody trunks to open the way for the main attacking force. Led by Robert Sale, that column now hurled itself toward the breach.

Then it suddenly halted in a great clattering confusion. Sale had thought he heard an officer say the gate had been blocked again. "Fighting Bob's" personal courage was that of a wounded grizzly bear, but he could be prone to panic when it came to committing troops in an uncertain situation. He now ordered a withdrawal, and cursing soldiers stumbled and dropped their muskets, some men accidentally bayoneting each other in the swirling, sandy blackness as they tried to re-form their ranks and fall back. The confusion became even worse when another officer raced up to tell Sale that the gate had been clear all along.

Eventually the column managed to untangle itself and pour into the fort, and, although the Afghans were still good for several hours of the most determined resistance, British firepower, discipline and numbers had to prevail. By noon on July 23, the Union Jack snapped from the Ghazni ramparts, above more than 1,200 corpses, 17 of them British and Indian. All that remained was to storm Kabul itself.

But Kabul, like Kandahar, proved to be another open city. With the capture of the supposedly siege-proof Ghazni, Dost Muhammad's supporters concluded that further resistance, for the immediate present, would be unrealistic, if not futile. But Dost Muhammad himself, still in a smoldering fury over the hijacking of his country, was ready to go down fighting for it. As Keane's columns approached, he made a last-ditch attempt to rally his own force. "Grant me one favor," he implored. "Allow me to die with honor. Stand by the brother of Futeh Khan while he carries out one last charge against the cavalry of the Feringhi pigs. In that assault he will fall. Then go and make your own peace with Shah Shuja."

He spoke those words even as the bulk of the Afghan army was filtering out of Kabul to melt into the hills and wait to fight another day. With an advance British cavalry detachment barely twenty-four hours from the capital, Dost Muhammad was left with no other choice but to emulate his troops. Mounting his horse, he cantered off northward, toward the fastnesses of the Hindu Kush.

On August 6, 1839, the conquerors rode into Kabul.

4

Fear and Loathing in Kabul

THE OFFICERS AND MEN of the Army of the Indus could have been forgiven if they thought that the Afghan summer sun was smiling down on them with just a little extra brightness. With minimal bloodshed they had brought off what was believed to be the victorious conclusion of the first military campaign of Queen Victoria's reign, and the achievement was celebrated in an orgy of self-congratulation. Laurels were handed out like pamphlets. Among upwards of five dozen titles and promotions were an earldom for Auckland and a baronetcy for Macnaghten. Keane's failure to bring siege guns to Ghazni was forgotten as he became Baron Keane of Ghazni, while Sale, who had almost botched the assault on the gate, was made a Knight Commander of the Bath. All but staggering under the weight of their kudos, the British settled down to a benign occupation of Afghanistan. The task was seen as neither demanding nor hazardous. The high command did not even consider it necessary for the entire army to remain. Keane handed over to Cotton and departed for India with the Bombay contingent, leaving two infantry brigades and a cavalry regiment to back up Shah Shuja's force.

Keane by this time had come to entertain second thoughts on the wisdom of installing a ruler in Afghanistan with guns and bayonets. "Mark my words," he grumbled as he took his leave, "it will not be long before there is here some signal catastrophe." Other spoilsports in England, including the Duke of Wellington, echoed those sentiments, but the British in Afghanistan could not see it that way. Had not Dost Muhammad's army deserted him? Had not the Dost himself fled in disgrace? Now that the benevolent Shah Shuja sat on the throne, receptive (without much choice) to Macnaghten's "advice," the necessary laws would be enacted and the necessary taxes levied for the well-being of what had become, in effect, a British protectorate. Macnaghten had more than enough firepower at his disposal to discourage dissident elements of the populace, but with the tyrant Dost Muhammad a fugitive, there could be no reason to, anticipate unrest. Few men on the spot questioned the firmness of the English bulldog's grip on the Afghan scruff.

Kabul provided a congenial seat of alien control, to a point. As great Asiatic capitals went, it was less than magnificent or even imposing. A ghetto-like sprawl of flat-roofed houses made of sun-dried brick, its drab skyline was relieved only by a few small minarets. The inner city was carved up into a warren of a thousand dark alleys, giving off a stench that could almost be shoveled up with the human waste choking the open drains. Many of the houses tended to lean over after heavy rains and could come crashing down in clusters during earthquakes. But the walls of the houses enclosed courtyards with gardens to delight the eye, and the air, when one left the fetid streets, was of the tingling clarity to be expected at a mile above sea level. Commanding the whole city from the brow of a hill were the frowning battlements of the Bala Hissar, the amir's citadel-palace, whose bulky outlines somewhat resembled an over-size football stadium. Most of the occupying forces enjoyed the comfort of quarters in the bowels of this architectural whale.

When off duty, officers and men could visit points of interest, although apart from Babur's tomb and a few mosques, Kabul was not really a sightseer's paradise. The handful of high-ranking officials who were invited to Afghan weddings or private entertainments could watch dancing girls perform—not very arousingly—to the mandolin-like music of *rebabs*. The city's famous public baths enjoyed a fair amount of British patronage; here, for a rupee or two, one could be pummelled to the brink of witless-ness for several hours of what was called a massage. Brothels did a land-office business and, to the extent that pay allowed, the British soldier's thirst for exotic souvenirs could be slaked in the bazaars. In late spring, an annual *juba*, or fair, was held on the outskirts of the city. Its highlights were acrobatics, wrestling matches and horse races—the last being impromptu affairs in which one rider simply challenged another for a sum of money. The "race course" was fixed on the spur of the moment; competing "jockeys" often scattered the spectators.

A different and far superior kind of horsemanship may have provided the most popular entertainment for the visitors. It was seen in the occasional game of *buzkashi*—a rough mix of polo and rugger in which the "ball" was a freshly slaughtered sheep or goat. At a signal, this bloody lump would be thrown on the ground and two teams of several dozen mounted Afghans would charge it, the swiftest rider leaning far down from his saddle to scoop up the "ball" and spur his horse off toward a goal line with everyone else in hot pursuit. The scrimmage could last several hours. It was a dusty maelstrom of thundering hooves and flying fists, punctuated by wild yells as the opposing teams fought for possession of the carcass at full gallop. The most reckless kind of trick riding was a routine part of buskashi. Whenever the carcass fell to the ground, every horseman became almost separated from his mount—one hand grasping the reins, a single foot in a stirrup, the rest of his body only inches from the flying earth, much like a Cheyenne or Comanche warrior—as he reached for the prize. During any buskashi match the sidelines were almost invariably packed with goggle-eyed British cavalry officers and troopers.

For the most part, however, leisure time was given over to the creation of an artificial English island in an alien Central Asian sea. There were band concerts, amateur theatricals, costume balls, horse racing Ascot style, tent-pegging, bird shooting and interminable cricket matches. Sale, whose sword hand had a green thumb, cultivated a kitchen garden and was emulated by other officers, who found the Afghan soil congenial to the imported seeds of such European vegetables as potatoes, peas, cauliflower, artichokes and turnips. When winter set in, army blacksmiths fashioned skates, for Kabul offered frozen lakes aplenty. The Afghans looked on and scratched their heads.

Paradoxically, the conquerors were also eager to win acceptance by the Afghans, and, indeed, the army's reluctant hosts showed more aloofness than did their uninvited guests. Despite this, a large number of individual friendships were formed, particularly with upper-class Kabulis, whose courtly manners the officers much admired and sometimes tried to copy. At the same time, however, most Afghans frowned on the British practice of acquiring common-law wives. In Kabul and elsewhere, mistresses were easy to come by. A Pathan couplet runs:

There's a boy across the river with an arse like a peach,
But alas, I cannot swim. . . .

And many of the hill tribesmen's more cultivated kinsmen in Kabul shared that gay predilection, which made his wife or wives all the more receptive to British advances. The women, moreover, were worth the courting:

Among them are beauties of every type;
Large eyes they have, long lashes, and arched brows,
Sugar lips, flowered cheeks, and foreheads like the moon,
Tiny are their mouths as pouting rosebuds,
Their teeth are even and white,
Their skin so soft and glossy, and hairless as an eggshell,

Their feet delicate, rounded the leg line and their hips magnificent,
Slender of belly, their breasts are full and firm, and small-waisted
are they. . . .

Khushhal Khan was writing of Afridi women, but they might just as
well have been the ladies of Kabul. A few officers and men had honorable
intentions; one such was Captain Robert Warburton, the commander of
Shah Shuja's artillery, who married a niece of Dost Muhammad. Generally
speaking, however, it could be said that Kabul under British occupation
was a swinging city, with Burnes (ironically one of the witnesses at
Warburton's wedding ceremony) setting the tone and pace of an almost
perpetual orgy. This came to arouse the bitterest of feelings among nearly
all Afghans, who, despite their homosexual tendencies, considered adultery
grounds for dismemberment, if not murder. But, for the time being, they
were impotent.

One might have expected Afghan resentment to subside when a directive permitted officers and men to bring their own wives into the country.
If anything, this only widened the breach. Although the British memsahib had yet to establish herself as the most noxious figure in the annals
of British imperialism, the mere presence of white women in Afghanistan
suggested that Pax Britannica had come to stay.

Actually, the army wives in Kabul numbered barely a dozen, although
they were a hardy lot, some even bearing children during their sojourn.
Lady Macnaughten headed the pecking order, and took pains to let
everyone know it, but the real voice of Kabul's British sewing circle was
that of Lady Florentia Sale, a chesty old trout whose husband had been
made second-in-command of the army. Never one to hang back from
offering an opinion on any topic, whether solicited or not, Lady Sale
was the Martha Mitchell of the occupying force. Her journal was a
voluminous catalogue of fault-finding directed, more often than not, at
the top-echelon leaders of Afghanistan's British Establishment.

Probably the most far-reaching result of importing British wives to
Kabul was Shah Shuja's decision that it was safe enough to bring in his
own not inconsiderable harem. This had the effect of crowding nearly
all of the British force out of the Bala Hissar and into new quarters on
the eastern outskirts of the city. Of this site, known as the Cantonment,
Vincent Eyre commented that "it must ever be spoken of as a disgrace
to our military skill and judgement."

Eyre did not exaggerate. A rectangular space of about 1,000 by 600
yards, the Cantonment sprawled out on a low-lying patch of swampy
ground. Towering hills flanked its northern and southern perimeters, well
within artillery range, but the British troubled to occupy only the south-

ern heights of Sia Sung, which were separated from the Cantonment itself by a canal and the Kabul River. The much loftier Bemaru hills to the north were left undisturbed, although one could almost drop rocks—not to mention bullets and cannonballs—on the British position from their crests. On all sides of the enclosure were gardens and orchards; in the event of an attack, their shrubs and trees would provide excellent cover for Afghan storming parties and would seriously shrink British fields of fire in nearly every direction.

About a dozen small stone forts also girded the Cantonment. They would have made an ideal outer defense line, but it was deemed necessary to occupy only one, which was used as the main commissary depot. Eyre called this "the most unaccountable oversight of all"; but the placing of the army's stores nearly a quarter of a mile beyond reach of its own walls was a measure of the high command's confidence that there was nothing to fear from the Afghan rabble. This was further underscored by the Cantonment's actual defense works. At each corner stood a small stone bastion, while around the enclosure ran a moat, really a shallow ditch, backed by a low earth rampart—cardboard armor against any determined assault. Eyre later wrote: "The credit of . . . having selected [this] site . . . is not a distinction now likely to be *claimed* . . . by *any one*."

The same casual attitude toward self-protection prevailed elsewhere in Afghanistan. At such key points as Kandahar, Ghazni and Jalalabad— near the entrance to the Khyber Pass—the British garrisons were pitifully small and travelers on the roads between these places and Kabul were continual prey to tribal hit-and-run attacks. To keep communications open, the British paid extortionate "fees" to the hillmen, particularly to the Pathan Ghilzais who stood astride the western approaches to the Khyber, which remained the most direct line of supply, and if necessary of reinforcement, between India and Afghanistan.

Some officers quickly came to recognize that the British positions might well prove indefensible in the event of serious trouble. They were outspoken in reminding Macnaghten, Burnes and Cotton that the Army of the Indus was not administering a settled Indian hill station. But such criticism fell on deaf or indignant ears. Macnaghten complained of having received "a most disrespectful letter" on the subject from Brigadier Abraham Roberts, the commander of Shah Shuja's force; shortly afterwards, Roberts was relieved of that command.

That the British should thus leave themselves wide open seemed all the more mystifying as the months went by and the conquered peoples became increasingly less docile. Early in 1840, the Baluchis of Khelat, which had been forcibly annexed to Afghanistan, threw off the yoke and wiped out the local British force, consisting of a boyish subaltern.

It took a sizable punitive expedition to recover the lost ground. Not long afterward there was an uprising near Kandahar. Although it was stamped out by a detachment of Nott's garrison, the regional political officer, Major Henry Rawlinson, told Macnaghten that "we may thrash [the tribes] over and over again, but this rather aggravates . . . the difficulty of overcoming the national feeling against us." Macnaghten replied: "We have enough of croakers without adding to the number needlessly."

But at that time, pressures were mounting from other quarters that caused even Macnaghten a temporary loss of cool. To the east, the Punjab could no longer be relied on. In 1839, Ranjit Singh had died, following a stroke and the effects of the powdered emerald-and-pearl compound prescribed by his astrologers. Ranjit had never been the most trustworthy of partners but he had been a partner nonetheless; the same could not be said for the rest of the Sikh leadership, which was now taking an openly anti-British position, which, in turn, threatened to slam shut the eastern entrance to the Khyber. To the west, Herat's de facto ruler, Yar Muhammad, had broken a treaty with the British and was courting the Shah of Persia. Macnaghten was all for delivering blows against Peshawar and Herat, but Auckland thought that too risky a proposition and Macnaghten could only bemoan his chief's timidity. "Oh! for a Wellesley or a Hastings at this juncture," he wrote.

The most serious trouble, however, was brewing in the north. By the summer of 1840, the Russians, frustrated in their attempt to take Khiva by force, had initiated treaty overtures to the khan of that country. And at the same time, reports were coming in that Dost Muhammad had taken refuge in Bokhara, where he was said to be mobilizing an Uzbek army for the recovery of Afghanistan. Singly or in combination, these two threats were seen by Macnaghten as urgent reason for an immediate move to the north.

Macnaghten also had a nonstrategic motive for wishing to advance on Bokhara; given the attitudes of the era, this was almost as important as forestalling Dost Muhammad. Two years earlier, Colonel Charles Stoddart of the British army had been sent to Bokhara to negotiate a treaty with the city's insane Amir Nasrullah and, if possible, to gain the release of some Russian captives, who, after all, were fellow whites. For his troubles, Stoddart was thrown into Bokhara's "bug pit" for several months, then brought up into the sunlight, where Nasrullah offered him a choice between conversion to Islam and live burial. Sensibly, Stoddart opted for the former, only to find himself back in the bug pit. Reports of his enforced presence in Bokhara sent shock waves through the occupying community in Afghanistan; even five decades before British racial arrogance was to reach its zenith, the imprisonment of an Englishman by "natives" could be a casus belli.

Thanks, however, to vacillation on Auckland's part, Macnaghten never got the chance to free Stoddart* or capture Dost Muhammad—although Dost Muhammad himself came close to sharing the bug pit with Stoddart. On a whim, the unpredictable Nasrullah decided that the former Afghan ruler should no longer be his guest but his prisoner; it was only by good luck and dyeing his beard that Dost Muhammad managed to escape. But escape he did, and as the summer of 1840 drew to a close, reports began reaching Macnaghten that the outlaw Amir had moved south and rallied most of the Afghan tribes between the Oxus River and Kabul. With dissension now growing in the ranks of Shah Shuja's army, there was every reason to go on the alert.

Things began coming to a head in September, when Dost Muhammad led a large column into the Bamian Valley, about 100 miles west of Kabul on the northern flank of the Hindu Kush. Here he was joined by a regiment of Shah Shuja's army that had deserted the puppet Amir to a man. Hot on its heels came an Indian infantry regiment commanded by a British lieutenant. The pursuit culminated in a pitched battle with the Dost's augmented forces. Almost in the shadow of two colossi of Buddha that had been carved from the solid rock of a 500-foot cliff more than a millennium earlier, British and Afghan columns collided head-on. Although ridiculously outnumbered in manpower, the sepoys had artillery and made good use of it—the well-directed case shot of twelve-pound guns ploughing big furrows in the Afghan formations and forcing Dost Muhammad to order a tactical withdrawal eastward. When his army popped up again, it was less than fifty miles north of Kabul in the region of Kohistan, a mad upheaval of hills nicely suited to evasive maneuver and surprise attack. Kohistan was also rich recruiting ground for the insurgents, who fattened their ranks with a horde of disaffected tribesmen. By the end of October, Dost Muhammad was ready to pounce on Kabul.

To head him off, Sale was sent north on a forced march with a strong column of infantry and cavalry, backstopped by several batteries of horse-drawn guns, which just barely managed to keep pace with the troops in the trackless, broken highlands. On November 2, the two armies sighted each other in a narrow valley and Dost Muhammad ordered an attack. Sale's Indian cavalry countered with a charge that fizzled out when the sowars hung back, leaving their British officers to plunge headlong into the Afghan lines and set a future example for the Light Brigade. One or two of the officers managed to slash their way free with their sabers, but Dost Muhammad's own cavalry was now in high gear. Brandishing

<hr>

* Stoddart managed to stay alive until 1842, when he was joined in the bug pit by another frustrated rescuer, Captain Arthur Conolly. Both men were presently brought before Nasrullah again, and the Amir ordered Stoddart beheaded on the spot. He then turned to Conolly and offered to spare his life if he embraced Islam. A fat lot of good that did Stoddart, replied Conolly, as he placed his head on the block. This act made the name of "Khan Ali" something of a legend in Central Asia for many years.

his tulwar and invoking the blessing of Allah, the Dost himself rode at the head of the horsemen. He tore off his turban and waved it over his head to urge the riders on as they dug in their spurs and thundered up the valley like pounding surf. Only when Sale's field guns opened up did the Afghan charge begin to falter. The guns were not just shooting off their big iron spitballs but were letting loose a cyclone of grapeshot and shrapnel whose spreading bursts quickly threatened to atomize at least a quarter of the Afghan force. Dost Muhammad could not afford that high a casualty rate. He broke off the action and his soldiers melted away into the dark maze of the hills. Once again, artillery had snatched victory from the Afghan grasp. But Dost Muhammad remained at large and his army remained intact. And they were barely three days' march from Kabul.

On the evening of November 4, Macnaghten was taking his pre-dinner ride through the outskirts of Kabul when an Afghan materialized from the dusk and seized the Envoy's bridle, shouting: "The Amir! The Amir!" Before Macnaghten could gather his wits, another robed figure sprang forward. He grasped Macnaghten's hand and kissed it. This was the Afghan gesture of submission and the man was Dost Muhammad. Despite his near-victory in Kohistan, he had reached the conclusion that his kingdom would never be regained so long as the British had so many big guns and he had so few.

With the threat of the Dost's army apparently removed, Macnaghten found room for magnanimity toward his royal prisoner. Shah Shuja urged the Envoy to have Dost Muhammad hanged, but Macnaghten coldly vetoed the suggestion. The former Amir's dignity in captivity even moved the guiding spirit of the Simla Manifesto to an astonishing declaration. In a letter to the Indian Government, he wrote that Shah Shuja "had no claim on us. We had no hand in depriving him of his kingdom, whereas we ejected the Dost, who never offended us." Macnaghten also arranged for Dost Muhammad's honorable exile to India, and Dost Muhammad in turn urged all his sons to follow him. Except for Akbar Khan, all did.

Dost Muhammad's exile quickly restored tranquility to Afghanistan—or so it seemed to the high command—and policy once more took on a business-as-usual aspect. Even an attempt to shore up the feeble defenses of the Cantonment got short shrift from the authorities. In the spring of 1841, Cotton retired and was replaced by Major General William Elphinstone, who immediately offered to buy from the Indian Government large tracts of land surrounding the Cantonment with a view to removing the orchards and other obstacles to possible British fields of fire. Elphinstone proposed to pay for the land out of his own pocket. The Government brushed his bid aside.

This was Elphinstone's first and last constructive act in command of the British army in Afghanistan. From the War Office's entire list of generals on active service, Auckland could not have chosen an officer less fitted to lead the force. As a younger man, Elphinstone had fought with conspicuous gallantry at Waterloo. He was a knowledgeable professional soldier and, like his distant relative Mountstuart Elphinstone, a gentleman in the best eighteenth-century sense of that word. Junior officers on his staff always spoke of his kindness and regarded him with a personal affection bordering on filial love. But as a leader of men, "Elphy Bey" commanded no one's respect. For some time he had been racked by gout and rheumatism; soon those infirmities became so complicated and so intensified by fever that Elphinstone was not only unable to mount his horse without being lifted into the saddle, but was almost totally incapable of reaching a clear-cut decision even on questions of posting guards and conducting inspections.

Kaye put it plainly enough. Elphinstone, he wrote, was "fit only for the invalid establishment on the day of his arrival. . . It was a mockery to talk of his commanding . . . in the quietest district of Hindostan."

By seniority and merit, the command belonged to Nott, but Nott's earlier vendetta with Keane and his outspoken views on Queen's officers had effectively sabotaged his chances of advancement in Afghanistan. It was considered safer to leave him in charge of the Kandahar garrison, and the British troops in Kabul thus came to be saddled with a basket case.

To his credit, Elphinstone never sought the appointment, knowing himself unable to meet its demands. It was "a command I should have liked," he wrote a relative, "had I been possessed of health to perform its duties, but it is one requiring great activity, mental and bodily. My stay would be useless to the public and distressing to myself." By October 1841, Elphinstone was complaining to George Broadfoot—perhaps unjustly—of cavalier treatment by Macnaghten, who, he said, had reduced him "from a General to the Lord Lieutenant's head constable." At this time he also asked to be relieved on medical grounds. "I am unfit for it," he wheezed to Broadfoot, "done up body and mind, and I have told Lord Auckland so." The application was accepted. By then it was too late.

Meanwhile, on handing over, Cotton had reassured Elphinstone: "You will have nothing to do here; all is peace."

It was hardly that. To the Afghan people, the occupation grew more oppressive as each day passed. Shah Shuja had failed completely to win over his subjects. At the personal level he remained a decent and likable man. He had displayed a cool, almost scornful bravery during the Ghazi attack on his army at Ghazni. Despite his marionette status he conducted himself with consistently regal dignity. But he seemed not to care much one way or the other for the well-being of his people. This indifference was especially reflected in his choice of ministers; almost to a man, they were incompetent, corrupt or tyrannical. "I doubt," wrote Burnes, "if ever a king had a worse set."

Under Dost Muhammad, reforms had only begun, but the Dost had at least encouraged commerce. Shah Shuja at times appeared deliberately bent on stifling free enterprise with the imposition of increasingly burdensome taxes, collected by Afghan revenue officers with the backing of armed, British-led escorts. Some food merchants, to be sure, grew rich from the extortionate prices at which they sold their provisions to British commissariat officers, but the price was also applied to ordinary Afghans, and the resulting runaway inflation reduced many to beggardom.

The conquering army, however, felt the brunt of Afghan resentment, which became steadily less covert. In Kabul, insults were shouted at British soldiers, who seldom walked the streets is groups of fever than a dozen. Rocks occasionally flew. Hands went to dagger hilts as officers rode by on the way to Burnes' almost nightly wild parties. The fuse to the powder keg burned slowly, but it burned.

And yet the mounting disaffection was invisible to anyone wearing rose-colored spectacles. Macnaghten had on a pair. "All things considered," he wrote at this time, "the perfect tranquillity of the country is to my mind perfectly miraculous." Everything, he said, was "quiet from Dan to Beersheba."

Indeed, the only clouds on Macnaghten's horizon seemed to hover over England. As the summer of 1841 drew to a close, it was beginning to look as if the Whig Government faced defeat at the polls by the Tories, and the Tories were known to favor withdrawal from Afghanistan. Macnaghten would not have it. He was firmly resolved that nothing should undermine what he considered to be an outstanding achievement in restoring unity, order and peace to the country. He had just been rewarded, in fact, with appointment as Governor of Bombay, an office second only in importance to the governor generalship itself. All this would be jeopardized by anxiety over imaginary turmoil, and Macnaghten needed to show England that he was presiding over a state of serenity.

For some time, he had been under pressure to pare the administrative costs of the occupation. In the fall of 1841, he took steps toward that end, with two moves that guaranteed an Afghan uprising.

First, in September, he reduced by half the £8,000 annual subsidy that the British had been paying to the Ghilzai tribes of the east for keeping open the road to India via Jalalabad and the Khyber Pass. The Ghilzais were Pathans first and Afghans second; their loyalty went to those who reimbursed them. For centuries they had earned their livelihood by collecting tolls from caravan leaders in return for marginally reliable safe conduct through their country en route to the Khyber (where the Afridis would collect another fee). When he cut their payment, Macnaghten automatically converted the Ghilzais from bandits to Afghan patriots.

Macnaghten's second economy measure was to order one of the two British brigades in Kabul back to India. It did not trouble him that only a few months earlier he had requested five more regiments to strengthen the Kabul garrison. Nor did it seem to matter that the brigade, under Sale's command, almost immediately ran head-on into heavy Ghilzai concentrations. For some time, the tribesmen had it all their way. The brigade was groping along a narrow caravan road that followed a madly twisting course beneath tremendous, boulder-strewn heights. In this dark maze, the troops seldom saw anything to fire at, but their scarlet tunics offered perfect targets to thousands of Ghilzai marksmen exploiting natural cover and the concealment of their aerie-like sangars on the crests of the towering slopes. Officers were methodically picked off, while occasional ragged volleys did visible damage to the tightly packed British columns. After two weeks of this, Sale made a shaky truce with the Ghilzais, who allowed him to proceed eastward in precarious safety. But in the interval, his brigade had covered barely thirty miles, or two miles per day.

Macnaghten was impressed by the Ghilzai performance, but he could or would not take it as a sign that the Afghan lid was about to blow off. As servants packed his trunks for the return to Bombay, he pooh-poohed the attacks on Sale's brigade and promised that "the rascals will be well trounced for their pains." Lady Sale, whose husband had taken a ball in the leg from the rascals, dissented. In her view, a national insurrection had begun, and Macnaghten, "without sufficient moral courage to stem the current singly," was "trying to deceive himself into an assurance that the country is in a quiescent state." But to the unruffled Envoy, comments like this were no more than the mouthings of "croakers" —his favorite expression for anyone who differed with him. The word was to gain wide currency as an epithet among all members of the force, whatever their feelings on the state of British security in Afghanistan.

Among those who did not croak at this time was Burnes. The most knowledgeable of all Britons in Kabul on the city's moods and the Afghan temperament in general, he airily dismissed the Ghilzai defiance as a "tempest in a teapot"—although this reassurance may well have stemmed in great part from Burnes' impatience to step into Macnaghten's shoes.

In any case, Burnes by then had become Number One on the Afghans' most-wanted list.

For some weeks, two of Kabul's top-ranking chiefs had been conspiring to fan the flames of insurrection in the city. They had circulated rumors that the British were about to seize all influential Afghans and send them in chains to India. They had forged Shah Shuja's signature over a petition calling on the populace to rise in revolt. By the end of October, with Sale's brigade gone and the occupation forces reduced by half, it seemed that the time had come to strike. But the two ring-leaders feared that Burnes might just upset their applecart. It was not enough that this afterbirth of a flatulent pig should openly debauch their women; he further enraged, and alarmed, the conspirators by his intimacy with the Afghan machinery of intrigue. Secrets had a way of reaching Burnes before any other Feringhi. If he were to be kept from learning of the uprising, he had to be disposed of with extreme prejudice.

Burnes was then occupying Kabul's handsome British Residency in almost solitary splendor, Macnaghten's mission compound being located next to the Cantonment, two miles away. He shared his quarters with a personal aide, Lieutenant William Broadfoot, George Broadfoot's brother, and at this time was also playing host to his own younger brother Charles, a lieutenant in the Bombay Infantry. A small guard of sepoys protected the Residency grounds; they were more than enough, it was thought, to hold down the lid on any disturbance, should that unlikelihood ever come to pass. Only two other British officers had houses within shouting distance of the Residency.

Throughout the summer, Burnes had received numerous reports of mounting Afghan unrest, but they seemed to cause him little outward concern as he wined and dined and fornicated away the days and nights while awaiting Macnaghten's departure. He referred to himself at this time as "a highly paid idler." Invitations to dinner at the Residency were much sought after, and not only because of female companionship. Burnes probably had the best-stocked cellar in Kabul, overflowing with champagne, sherry, port, claret, sauterne and a wide selection of brandies. "If rotundity and heartiness are proofs of health," wrote Burnes to another brother, "I have them." He also gave occasional thought to his impending promotion, sometimes with sardonic realism. In his journal on November 1, he remarked that "I grow very tired of praise, and I suppose I shall get tired of censure in time."

He was not given the time. That very night his Hindu secretary came to him with news of a plot on his life, and was rewarded with a string of obscenities. Some hours later, shortly before dawn on November 2, there was an urgent pounding on the Residency door. A servant admitted Shah Shuja's wazir, who had come direct from the Bala Hissar. A mob was approaching, the wazir told Burnes, begging him to leave at once for the Cantonment. I'm sure there's no need for that, replied Burnes as he stepped into his trousers; a word in their ear and they'll be off. It was a rare moment, the chance dreamed of by every gentleman-servant of the Queen on hazardous duty: to subdue, singlehandedly, by the sheer impact of his eloquence and white skin, a throng of murder-bent savages.

Burnes thereupon mounted a balcony overlooking the Residency courtyard, where he saw some three dozen armed Afghans pressing at the gates. He laughed and waved at them and told them to go to their homes before they caught a chill. He was answered by jeers, which quickly became enraged screams. The sepoys raised their muskets. Burnes shouted at them to hold their fire and continued lecturing the Afghans, now in a louder voice. There was a bang and a thud as the ball of a jezail smacked into the wall behind the balcony. The three dozen Afghans by this time had swelled to more than three hundred. They could not interrupt the flow of Burnes' harangue, but Burnes was no longer joking with them. More shots spattered about the balcony. Several Afghans began scaling the Residency wall. Burnes beckoned to a sowar and ordered him to ride to the Cantonment with a hastily scribbled note for Macnaghten: Residency under attack; request troops.

Burnes was now joined on the balcony by his brother and Broadfoot. The three men took up weapons, and Burnes ordered the sepoys to open fire. Broadfoot drilled six Afghans with his double-barrelled pistol before a jezail slug tore his chest apart. Then the mob was over the wall, throwing torches into the Residency stables and surging forward, over the bodies of dead and dying sepoys, toward the main building. The Burnes brothers no longer had any choice but to make a dash for it. As they hastily threw on Afghan robes, they were approached by a Kashmiri who had somehow entered the Residency and who offered to lead them to safety. Even in the midst of the howling mob, the guide and the disguises served.

Then the Kashmiri suddenly stopped. "Friends!" he shouted at the Afghans, "here is Sekundar Burnes!" Within sixty seconds, the brothers lay on the ground in several dozen cuts of steak.

Having tasted blood, the insurgents ran amok. They burned the two other British houses and slaughtered the occupants (but not the two officers, who happened to be in the Cantonment). Then they set to work on Kabul. Shops and houses were put to the torch, stalls in the bazaar overturned and looted, fellow-Afghans gunned down by the hundreds. Shah Shuja ordered one of his regiments to march from the Bala Hissar and pulverize the mob with artillery. The troops could not find room in the claustrophobic streets to serve the cumbersome field pieces, much less slew them into firing positions. The guns were quickly abandoned, and the soldiers began taking what cover they could find.

Now there was a crashing of drums and a barking of bugles as a British infantry detachment, three sepoy companies and another of Shah Shuja's regiments came up at double-time. The troops were able to cover the withdrawal of the beleaguered regiment and recapture the guns. But they were too late to quell the uprising. Macnaghten and Elphinstone had received Burnes' SOS at about seven o'clock in the morning. It was well after midday before a blizzard of conflicting rumors, messages and orders could be cleared sufficiently to move the relief column. By then, the situation had gotten out of hand. Most of Kabul had gone over to the insurrectionists, and Shah Shuja had been made a virtual prisoner in the Bala Hissar. Presently the British units withdrew to the Cantonment.

And by nightfall, it had become clear that the Cantonment itself was under siege.

5

Day of the Croker

If Victorian Britons salivated at tidings of their armies' victories in the field, they approached religious ecstasy whenever they learned that a beleaguered British garrison had been relieved. Such news did not seem likely to be forthcoming from Kabul in early November 1841, as the 6,000 troops of Elphinstone's force went on the defensive against 25,000 Afghan infantry and cavalry. No one had dreamed that the insurgents could mobilize so huge an army in so short a time.

Reinforcements were eagerly awaited, urgent messages having been dispatched by runners to Sale and Nott. Sale's brigade was now bivouacked near the village of Gandamak, barely five days' march from the Cantonment. Nott might reach Kabul from Kandahar inside of five weeks, perhaps four, if he drove his troops. But a relief column from either quarter was soon to prove wishful thinking. The Ghilzais stood like an electrified barbed-wire fence on Sale's route of march back to Kabul. Despite his own personal fearlessness—not to mention his anxiety for his wife—the cautious brigadier let other officers persuade him that the most prudent tactic would be to move even farther east toward Jalalabad.

Hope for a lifeline from Kandahar was also unrealistic. Even if Nott could get past Ghazni, where a tiny British garrison was also under siege, Afghanistan's fast-approaching subarctic winter would decimate the sepoys no less methodically than any tribal lashkars. Nott, in fact, was to order a relief force to Kabul; he also told its commander that "in my private opinion I am sending you all to destruction." The column was not destroyed, but found its way blocked by snowdrifts and was forced

[57]

to limp back to Kandahar. The British in Kabul presently had to swallow the realization that they were sealed off from the civilized world.

In even less time, they had begun paying the price for their choice of the Cantonment site. On November 4, a strong body of Afghans stormed and captured a small defense work called Muhammad Sharif's Fort, standing between the Cantonment's eastern wall and the unwisely selected Commissary Fort, which the enemy troops now moved to seize. Elphinstone countered by ordering out two companies of infantry—not to beef up the 100 sepoys of the Commissary Fort's garrison, but to bring them off. He had forgotten that the fort was the army's only source of provisions.

But the infantrymen were swiftly hurled back to the Cantonment by sheets of jezail fire from Muhammad Sharif's Fort and an adjoining garden. By nightfall, after a second rescue attempt had been repulsed, Elphinstone was at last made to realize that the Commissary Fort must not be abandoned. Orders were sent to Ensign Warren, the garrison commander: Hold at all costs; reinforcements to arrive no later than 2:00 A.M. But then a staff conference was called, during which Elphinstone became so rattled in a cross-fire of proposals and counterproposals that it was not until daylight that the reinforcements were ready to march out.

By then it no longer mattered. The Afghans having mined a tower of the Commissary Fort and set fire to its gate, Warren had led his sepoys through an opening in the wall and withdrawn to the Cantonment, where there was enough food to last three days if belts were tightened. Commissariat officers managed to buy grain and fodder from neighboring villages and keep the supply coming in, but the flow was irregular and placed the Cantonment barely above subsistence level. In less than forty-eight hours, the conquering army had been all but brought to its knees.

Now commenced six weeks of inconclusive skirmishing—with the British usually on the defensive. Afghan garrisons were driven from a few of the forts around the Cantonment, but at great cost and without inhibiting continued assaults on the British position from other strongpoints. If the Afghans themselves had not been poorly organized, they might have taken the Cantonment in a concerted attack. But as long as their numerical superiority enabled them to hold the Bala Hissar and most of the surrounding hills, the upper hand would remain theirs.

Nor was it just a matter of outnumbering the British. "I often hear the Afghans designated as cowards," wrote Lady Sale, "but they show no cowardice in standing as they do against guns without using any themselves." And they were particularly to be reckoned with in a fire fight. Afghan foot soldiers seldom marched wearying distances before going into action; instead, they were mounted pillion with cavalry troopers and rode fresh to their positions. "They fire from rests," said Lady Sale, "and then take excellent aim, and are capital riflemen, hiding behind any stone sufficiently large to cover their head, and quietly watching their opportunities to snipe off our people." Lady Sale also noticed that most Afghan horsemen usually carried at least two jezails. Not only did these weapons have a far greater range and accuracy than the British "Brown Bess" muskets, but the riders were "very expert in firing at the gallop." The only weapons the Afghans seemed to fear were bayonets, but they seldom let the British get close enough to use them with effect. In no way was this an enemy to be despised.

And yet, British armies had often prevailed over far greater odds. Those armies had had leadership. The troops in Kabul had Elphinstone, who amply confirmed his own earlier predictions that he was not the man for the job. Elphinstone's method of planning an action was to convene what were known as "councils of war." Here, sometimes from his sickbed, he eagerly solicited the advice of senior and junior officers alike, paying close heed to all views except his own. "Unfortunately," said Lady Sale, "it is not always in the multitude of counsellors that there is wisdom. . . . Gen. Elphinstone vacillates on every point. His own judgment appears to be good, but he is swayed by the last speaker," thus causing him to "alter his opinions and plans every moment." Lady Sale wrote not only with the authority of a soldier's wife. Her son-in-law, Captain John Sturt of the Royal Engineers, attended all the meetings, which he reported to her in detail and exasperation.

The result was a condition of too little and too late along the entire chain of command. The Afghans might launch a successful sortie while Elphinstone was trying to decide how to repel it. British troops might march from the Cantonment to recapture some outer defense work, only to find that the prolonged planning of the attack had given the Afghans time to reinforce their numbers. And when a position was retaken— such as Muhammad Sharif's Fort—as often as not the place would have lost its value. Of a typical bumbled British opportunity, Lady Sale observed that "as usual, delay was the order of the day."

At least once, Elphinstone simply failed to act at all. An Afghan strong point of much strategic worth was Mahmud Khan's Fort, which lay between the Cantonment and the Bala Hissar. At a "council of war," officers were virtually unanimous in urging Elphinstone to move on this position, with Macnaghten adding the weight of his own authority. According to Eyre, the Envoy "declared his opinion that the moral effect derived from [the fort's] possession would be more likely to create a diversion in our favour than any other blow we could strike, as the Affghans had always attached great importance to its occupation."

Elphinstone agreed, ordered a storming party readied at once. Then a junior officer raised a minor objection, whereupon the plan was dropped like a hot potato and never reintroduced.

Macnaghten and others had hoped that Elphinstone's spine would be stiffened by the new second-in-command, Brigadier John Shelton, another old hard case from the Napoleonic Wars. "The people in cantonments expect wonders from his prowess and military judgment," wrote Lady Sale. "I am of a different opinion, knowing that he is not a favourite of either his officers or men, and is most anxious to get back to Hindostan." Some others seconded this view. Mackenzie described Shelton as "personally brave" but "an incompetent officer." Eyre deplored Shelton's advocacy of retirement, which caused many a stormy session in council and "deprived the General, in his hour of need, of the strength which unanimity imparts." Aside from pressing for retreat to India and generally finding fault, Shelton's main contribution to strategy meetings was to place his bedroll on the headquarters floor and feign sleep.

Elphinstone believed that Shelton's behavior was "actuated by an ill-feeling towards me," but in fact Shelton for some reason reserved most of his bile for Macnaghten, mocking and even openly insulting the Envoy at every opportunity. Mackenzie once suggested to him that this attitude might be counterproductive. Shelton snorted: "Damn it, Mackenzie, I *will* sneer at him! I *like* to sneer at him!"

Given the case of weak knees at the high command level, it was hardly surprising that morale should have plummeted and that defeatism spread through the ranks like a virus. "It is more than shocking, it is shameful," wrote Lady Sale, "to hear the way that our officers go on croaking before the men." Said Eyre: "The cry of 'Cavalry!' was a cry which too often, during our operations, paralyzed the arms of those, whose muskets and bayonets we have been accustomed to consider as more than a match for a desultory charge of irregular horsemen." Not merely disgusted by "the number of *croakers* in garrison," Eyre was even more incensed because all this showed that the white man was failing to carry his burden: "It is a lamentable fact that some of the European soldiers, who were naturally expected to exhibit to their native brethren in arms an example of endurance and fortitude, were among the first to lose confidence."

Eyre was referring specifically to the 44th Regiment of Foot, the only British infantry unit left in Kabul. When the Afghans recaptured Muhammad Sharíf's Fort for the second time, the garrison, consisting of the 44th and the Indian 37th Infantry, put on a race back into the Cantonment. It was generally agreed that the 44th won, although the sepoys came close, having been "contaminated," as Eyre put it, "by the example set them by their European brethren." Sturt once summed it up almost insolently when Elphinstone asked him whether a recently recaptured fort was practicable for use and also tenable. "Practicable if the men will fight, tenable if they don't run away," Sturt replied curtly, and then recommended that the fort be blown up.

Still, the British position was far from hopeless; even a modest display of initiative could well have turned the tide. A number of younger officers, led by Eyre and Sturt, continually urged that the army evacuate the Cantonment, take the Bala Hissar by storm, and then dig in there. In all likelihood this was not just the best but the only move Elphinstone could have made to save the force. "Our troops, once collected in the Bala Hissar," wrote Eyre, "could have been spared for offensive operations . . . while the commanding nature of the position would have caused the enemy to despair of driving us out, and a large party would probably have been ere long formed in our favour."

But the motion was decisively overridden by higher-ranking strategists. Macnaghten joined Elphinstone in throwing up a cloud of obstacles. It would be impossible, they protested, to move the sick and wounded; there was a shortage of water and firewood in the Bala Hissar, and of fodder for the horses; the Afghans would win a moral victory if the Cantonment were abandoned. And what if the British failed to capture the Bala Hissar?

"An appalling list of objections, it must be confessed," Eyre remarked drily, "but insufficient to shake my belief that a removal of the force into the Bala Hissar was not only practicable but necessary for our safety and honour."

Not all Afghans in Kabul and its environs had declared war on the British. Some even remained friendly, among them the villagers of Bemaru at the foot of the steep hills overlooking the Cantonment from the north-west. It was from Bemaru, in fact, that commissariat officers bought most of the army's food supplies. But in mid-November, communication with Bemaru was suddenly cut off when an Afghan force marched out of Kabul, captured the village and crowned the heights. A pair of guns was even mounted on the crest of one of the hills. If the Army of the Indus was to continue eating, the Afghans had to be pried off their high ground.

After protesting energetically, Shelton finally obeyed an order to launch a counterattack. His force numbered nearly 3,000, including 12 companies of infantry and at least 500 cavalrymen, backed up by a pair of field guns. As the troops and their guns labored up the slope in ragged formation, a wave of Afghan irregular cavalry came thundering down on them. Hold your fire! Shelton roared at the riflemen of the 44th Foot; wait till they're in range! The horsemen were only 30 feet off when the 44th let go with a shattering volley. It failed to bring down a single Afghan and the 44th bolted, only to be checked by its own infuriated officers, who cursed the men as cowardly scum and clubbed them back into formation with the flats of their swords. Another attack was ordered, and the artillery gouged out a path for the 44th with a barrage that shredded the Afghan defenses and enabled the infantrymen to scale the heights. After one enemy gun had been captured and the other spiked, the force marched back down the hill to the Cantonment, singing. It was the first real British victory since the siege had begun.

Ten days later, the Afghans were once more in possession of Bemaru and the hills. There was nothing for it but to drive them off again.

The action began several hours before dawn on November 23. It stretched into an all-day donnybrook during which Shelton proved himself a tower of courage, stopping five jezail bullets but never being stopped from bringing off several wondrous tactical blunders. One was to take only a single field piece with the force, in violation of a general order that expressly required at least two in any operation in case one should malfunction. Under cover of darkness, the gun was hauled to a position overlooking the village, where the main Afghan body was bivouacked. Pouring a steady rain of grapeshot into the camp, the gun played havoc with the Afghans for nearly half an hour. Then its vent became so hot that it warped, and the gunners found themselves saddled with a ton of useless iron, of which they were finally relieved when the gun was captured later in the day.

Shelton also failed to exploit the initial confusion that the gun created; had he ordered an advance at that juncture, the Afghans would have been swept from the village. Instead, they were allowed to rally while thousands of irregulars also began pouring out of Kabul to stiffen the Bemaru defenses and launch a counterattack. By ten o'clock in the morning, Shelton's position was hemmed in on three of four sides by a force numbering at least 10,000.

The British lines now began to waver in an ever-thickening swarm of jezail bullets. To buck up the men, Shelton offered 100 rupees to anyone who captured an Afghan battle flag. Five officers, led by Mackenzie, tried to set an example by rushing directly at the enemy's forward lines. Two of the officers were instantly made into colanders by the hail of lead; the other three could not get close enough to use their swords or even their pistols, but hurled stones at the Afghans until the jezail fire drove them back. Their bravery, however, did not infect the men, and Shelton next formed his infantry into two hollow squares. This was the classic and impregnable British defense against a cavalry charge and the worst possible way to repel the long-range musket fire the British then faced. As if that were not enough, Shelton deployed his own cavalry between the two formations, so that when the forward square finally buckled and broke under a determined Afghan assault, cavalry and infantry became so entangled that organized resistance was impossible.

By that time, thanks to Shelton, the Afghans had decisively gained the upper hand, and Mackenzie urged a phased withdrawal while it remained possible. No, by God! thundered Shelton, we'll not retreat yet. The result was not a retreat but a rout, with several thousand troops streaming down the slope in a panic-crazed mob. Score upon score were picked off by Afghan sharpshooters or cut down by the Ghazi horsemen who rode freely among them, crying out that Allah was merciful and swinging their tulwars like tennis rackets. The rest of the force was probably saved from annihilation only because one chief, out of nothing less than simple compassion, ordered his own column to make a temporary halt. Even so, wrote Eyre, "it seemed as if we were under the ban of Heaven."

As the men scrambled and stumbled into the Cantonment, Elphinstone limped out to meet them, hoping that his uniformed presence might raise spirits. Later he complained to Macnaghten: "Why, Lord, sir, when I said to them, 'Eyes right!' they all looked the other way."

If Elphinstone's spine had been creaking up to now, it was shattered by the Bemaru disaster. And Macnaghten, too, was ready to throw in the sponge—although of course he did not put it that way. Hardly had the mutilated remains of Shelton's columns taken flimsy shelter in the Cantonment than the Envoy received a tentative offer of peace terms from the Afghans. However, even to discuss a cease-fire without the concurrence of the military commander would be to defy Auckland's policy and jeopardize Macnaghten's own career. Accordingly, Macnaghten went on record with a letter to Elphinstone seeking the General's views of the strategic and tactical situation.

Elphinstone eagerly, and pathetically, seized the bait: "After having held our position here for upwards of three weeks in a state of siege, from the want of provisions and forage, the reduced state of our troops, the large number of wounded and sick, the difficulty of defending the extensive and ill situated cantonment we occupy, the near approach of winter, our communications cut off, no prospect of relief, and the whole country in arms against us, I am of opinion that it is not possible any longer to maintain our position in this country, and that you ought to avail yourself of the offer to negotiate."

It was all Macnaghten needed. On November 25, he received a deputation of Afghan chiefs inside the Cantonment. Their terms were simple: the British must hand over all arms and ammunition and consider themselves prisoners of war. Macnaghten almost gasped aloud. He may have been desperate, but he was no poltroon. He rejected the ultimatum out of hand. "Very well," said the leader of the delegates, "we shall meet on the field of battle." To which Macnaghten replied: "At all events we shall meet at the day of judgement."

But this could only be the beginning. Macnaghten was in a poor bargaining position, and the Afghans had just been dealt an ace in the hole.

At about the time of the Bemaru fiasco, Dost Muhammad's son Akbar Khan had arrived in Kabul from Turkestan. Apart from augmenting Afghan armed strength by 6,000 more troops, Akbar brought to the revolutionaries the leadership for which they had been starved almost as badly as the British. After taking over Kabul and unseating Shah Shuja (who was otherwise unmolested), the Afghans had installed as amir another relative of Dost Muhammad, one Shah Muhammad Zeman. But this man proved a gentle mediocrity, totally incapable of keeping the chiefs from splitting into factions whose leaders intrigued against each other not much less enthusiastically than they went at the Feringhis. With Akbar on the scene, however, there was no longer any question of who called the signals in Kabul. Like his father, Akbar had been born to take charge.

But the British also welcomed the news of Akbar's arrival. With Dost Muhammad and his family held hostage, so to speak, in India, it was believed that the ex-Amir's son would exercise a moderating influence. Lady Sale put it plainly enough: "If once in his power we might be safe, but these Ghazees are fanatics and would cut us into mincemeat."

Certainly Akbar seemed the one to bring off a reasonable settlement. A darkly handsome, almost gorgeous man with soulful eyes and a cupid's-bow mouth, he nevertheless carried himself with towering, regal assurance and gave off an air of iron authority that few ever dared to question. But Akbar also knew how to temporize and persuade. His manners were impeccable, his affability electric and his sense of humor such that he could even laugh uproariously at himself. The British conveniently overlooked his tendency to sudden and unexpected eruptions of unmanageable fury. They did not appreciate fully the depth of the humiliation to which he had been subjected by the burglarizing of his country, or the firmness of his resolution to avenge his father. Akbar in fact was not just mad as a hatter. He was even more a patriot.

And he had not the slightest intention of wasting his time in an effort to reach accommodation with the British. His plan, quite simply, was to starve them into surrender. This would not be very hard, as famine was already overtaking the force by leaps and bounds. With Bemaru cut off, grain supplies barely trickled into the Cantonment. Once, Sturt managed to buy a bag of wheat for his sepoys, and a riot was narrowly averted as the men assaulted the sack and tore it to shreds while scrambling for the grains. Officers had begun eating the hearts of camels. Early in December, an order went out to destroy all useless horses for their flesh. The serviceable animals lived mainly on the bark of trees and their own dung, but many did not live long. "Camels and tattoos [ponies] are dying fast," wrote Lady Sale, "and the air is most unpleasantly scented at times."

Hunger was also intensified by the sudden onset of the Afghanistan winter. Temperatures plunged to near and below zero. The ground, first transformed into iron by the frozen rains, was soon quilted by several inches of snow. Campfires were not permitted at night because of a wood shortage. To most of the Indians, who came from a world of almost stupefying heat, the glacial winds that slashed down from the Hindu Kush may have been more terrible than the starvation. But the Europeans shivered only a little less. Hunger and climate had become Akbar's strongest ally.

So strong, in fact, that on December 11, Macnaghten, by now a ruined man, was ready to throw himself on Akbar's mercy. With only two days' provisions remaining in the Cantonment, the Envoy met Akbar and a group of chiefs on the bank of the Kabul River. There, Macnaghten submitted a draft of a treaty whereby the British offered to evacuate Afghanistan forthwith. When Akbar added a rider that four British officers be handed over as hostages, Macnaghten consented without demur. His only stipulations were that the Afghans not interfere with the army's retreat to India and that they furnish food supplies to the famished troops at once. Although Macnaghten was hardly in a position to impose conditions of any sort, Akbar told him that the requests were reasonable and the terms of the treaty acceptable. The siege had ended at last.

Declaring that the army would be ready to leave in three days, Macnaghten returned to the Cantonment and awaited the supplies. They did not arrive. The Afghans had not believed a word of Macnaghten's promise. The resourceful commissariat department was able to continue wringing just enough grain from the outside to hold famine at bay, but only just. "Had Sturt's wish been complied with," wrote Lady Sale, "long ago we should have been safe in the Bala Hissar, with plenty of provisions." But now, the Afghans "know that we are starving, [and] will be very magnanimous if they let us escape, now that they have fairly got us in their net."

On December 22, Captain James Skinner rode into the Cantonment from Kabul. A member of a famous half-caste family, "Gentleman Jim" had been captured in earlier fighting. He had also been captivated by Akbar's charm and had agreed to bring Macnaghten a proposal from the Afghan leader. The Envoy could scarcely believe his ears. Akbar was asking the British to stay on in Afghanistan.

The proposition was simple enough. Akbar, it appeared had concluded that his own interests would best be served by a show of magnanimity that would let the beleaguered invaders off the hook. He proposed that Shah Shuja be restored to the throne and that the British army continue to go through the motions of occupation for another six months or so, then depart as if at its commanders' own wishes. All that Akbar sought in return was appointment—and British recognition—as Shah Shuja's wazir, plus thirty lakhs of rupees (£300,000) and an annual life pension of four lakhs. Skinner hardly needed to point out to Macnaghten that the plan was top secret.

Skinner added, however, that Akbar had won over the Ghilzai chiefs and that, if Macnaghten was agreeable to the plan, he was to meet them the following morning at a designated spot outside the Cantonment. Akbar had further suggested that a contingent of British troops stand ready for a given signal, on which they would capture an outlying fort and seize Amanullah Khan, one of the two instigators of the murder plot against Burnes. The handing over of this man was to be a gesture of Akbar's good faith. To signify concurrence with the proposal, Macnaghten needed only to sign a paper to that effect.

It was a deus ex machina. By Akbar's whim, British prestige in Afghanistan would be upheld and Macnaghten's career salvaged. The Envoy took up a pen and signed at once—despite Mackenzie's warning that the whole thing smacked of a plot. Macnaghten would not have it. "A plot!" he exclaimed. "Let me alone for that! Trust me for that!"

Of course it was a plot. Clumsy, perhaps, by present-day CIA standards, but it served. Akbar no more wanted even a helpless British presence in Afghanistan than he wanted hemorrhoids. He had made his overture simply to test Macnaghten. And under ordinary circumstances, Macnaghten himself would never have accepted the Asiatic Trojan Horse. No mean intriguer in his own right, he had for some weeks been toiling in secret to win over one or another of the Afghan factions to the British camp. "If any portion of the Afghans wish our troops to remain in the country," he had written at one point, "I shall think myself at liberty to break the engagement which I have made to go away." His efforts, however, had borne little fruit (what was more, Akbar knew of them), and with his private empire toppling around him he saw only a last straw and clutched at it desperately.

Indeed, Macnaghten could hardly have been unaware that trouble was brewing. On the morning of December 23, as he prepared to leave for the meeting with Akbar, he was asked by Elphinstone if he suspected foul play. Macnaghten shook his head emphatically, but a few minutes later, when George Lawrence put the same question to him, he said: "Treachery? Of course there is, but what can I do. . . . The life I have led for the past six weeks you, Lawrence, know well, and rather than be disgraced and live it over again I would risk a hundred deaths. Success will save our honor, and more than make up for all risks."

Macnaghten saddled up and rode out, accompanied by Lawrence, Mackenzie, Captain Robert Trevor and a small Indian cavalry escort. The rendezvous was only a quarter of a mile off, in plain sight of the Cantonment. Akbar and the Ghilzai leaders had already arrived; behind them glowered several hundred Ghazis, armed to the teeth, their presence seeming to cause uneasiness even among the Afghan chiefs. But all was courtesy and good humor as the British dismounted, although Mackenzie later recalled: "Men talk of presentiment; I suppose it was something of the kind which came over me, for I could scarcely prevail on myself to quit my horse."

Persian carpets had been laid out to cover the snow. Macnaghten and Akbar exchanged pleasantries and gifts; the Afghan leader salaamed graciously when the Envoy presented him with a handsome Arab charger. Then the business at hand commenced. Akbar asked whether "Macloten Sahib" was still prepared to carry out his part of the bargain. "Why not?" said Macnaghten.

That put the seal on Macnaghten's signature. "*Bezeer!*"—Seize him!—screamed Akbar, whereupon Akbar himself and a chief grasped the Envoy by the arms and hurled him to the ground. Lawrence, Mackenzie and Trevor went for their swords, only to find themselves caught in bear hugs by several chiefs. The Indian escort was galloping in full flight for the Cantonment; only its Sikh officer, Jemadar Ram Singh, rushed to Macnaghten's aid. A dozen tulwars instantly reduced him to raw meat. Each of the three British officers was mounted pillion on a horse, and the animals were spurred into a fast canter. Mackenzie had a quick glimpse of Macnaghten, struggling vainly and crying out: "*Az barae Khooda!"*—For God's sake!

The officers were being forcibly removed from the scene not only to prevent them from assisting Macnaghten but to save them from the Ghazis, who surged forward, shrieking Allah's praise and surrounding each horseman in scores. In the wild knife contest that ensued, Trevor was quickly carved to death, but Mackenzie and Lawrence, with the help of the chiefs, managed to ride through the press to safety, although Mackenzie nearly had his skull crushed by the butt of a jezail. The man who rescued him was none other than Akbar, who then turned to Mackenzie and shouted: "*You'll seize my country, will you!"*

For their own protection as much as anything else, Lawrence and Mackenzie were thrown into a prison cell in Kabul, to be released a day or so later. That afternoon they saw a hand appear in the cell window. It had belonged to Macnaghten and was now secured to the end of a stick. The Envoy's head at that moment was being carried through the streets on a pole. His dismembered trunk, along with Trevor's, had already been impaled on a meat hook for display in the bazaar.

Meanwhile, the Ghazis had been deploying in thousands outside the main gates of Kabul, to defend the city against the attack they knew the

British would launch, at long last, to avenge the outrage. Macnaghten had been struck down in plain view of the Cantonment, and his murder had been reported directly to Elphinstone by several eyewitnesses, including a sowar of the mounted escort that had fled the scene. Elphinstone, however, was content to accept someone else's announcement that Macnaghten had simply accompanied Akbar into Kabul for further talks. The General's personal courage had not failed him, but his will to act was paralyzed. The entire Cantonment, in fact, presented its usual aspect of befuddled apathy. "Not a soldier was stirred from his post," wrote Eyre; "no sortie was even thought of; treachery was allowed to triumph in open day." During all this inactivity, large bands of armed Afghans rode near the Cantonment several times, as if preparing to attack. "Not a gun was opened on them," said Eyre.

It was not Elphinstone's finest hour.

With the British Envoy out of the way and the British army commander reduced to a jellyfish, there was little to keep Akbar from storming the Cantonment and massacring every man, woman and child within its walls. That he stayed his hand was probably due in part to fear of massive retaliation from India, but Akbar also wanted to play cat to the British mouse. So the charade of peace talks was resumed. To replace Macnaghten as chief negotiator, Elphinstone chose Pottinger. It was a distasteful task for the man who had saved Herat and who even now was urging Elphinstone to order a massed assault on Kabul. The army, he said, had come out of its stupor; every man had gone into a fighting fury over Macnaghten's betrayal and assassination. But Elphinstone would not hear of it, and Pottinger went to the bargaining table with the man who had murdered his chief.

The talks nearly broke down immediately. On December 24, Akbar demanded that all British prisoners be replaced by married officers and their families. Eyre alone indicated willingness to comply if this would somehow alleviate the British plight; the others refused to a man. "Captain Anderson said he would rather put a pistol to his wife's head and shoot her," wrote Lady Sale; "and Sturt, that his wife and mother should only be taken at the point of the bayonet." Akbar must have realized that he had overreached himself, for he did not press the point. But on December 25 ("a more cheerless Christmas day perhaps never dawned upon British soldiers in a strange land," said Eyre), he laid down a set of nonnegotiable terms—the Feringhis must accept them or face the regrettable consequences.

First, the army was to move out at once, leaving behind all cash in its treasury. The garrisons at Jalalabad, Ghazni and Kandahar must quit those places also. Dost Muhammad and his family were to be freed without delay, their return to Afghanistan being insured by the British officer-hostages. Although Akbar was sensible enough not to tamper with Englishwomen again, he did insist that all Muslim wives give themselves up.*

These demands, however, were only mildly shameful. Then Akbar told Pottinger that when the army departed it could take only six of its remaining field pieces; the others must be handed over. In British military tradition, even the loss of regimental colors in battle did not approach the disgrace of abandoning guns to the enemy. But the surrender of the guns was not the crowning humiliation. That came with Akbar's promise to provide the British with a safe conduct out of the country. The army, its tail between its legs, was to be protected from harm by the foe that had beaten it to its knees.

The terms having been laid down and accepted in principle, Pottinger went to Elphinstone and begged him to repudiate them. Akbar, he said, could not be trusted for a moment to protect the army, and even if he meant to keep his word, the Ghazis he claimed to command would never restrain themselves, and Akbar would be powerless to hold them in check. According to Lady Sale, "the chiefs say they have no control over the Ghazeeas." Lady Sale also mentioned having heard a variety of warnings from friendly Afghans; one such prediction was that "it is [the Ghazis'] intention to get all our women into their possession, and to kill every man except one, who is to have his arms and legs cut off, and is to be placed with a letter *in terrorem* at the entrance of the Khyber passes, to deter all Feringhees from entering the country again."

Elphinstone turned a deaf ear to these and other cautions. On December 27, the "council of war" ratified the treaty.

The year 1841 drew to a close with the force on continual twenty-four-hour notice to evacuate Kabul. It was a condition of hurry up and wait. "The chiefs . . . now dictate to us," wrote Lady Sale, "delaying our departure, which is to be postponed according to their pleasure." Meanwhile, there was unrelenting harassment from gangs of armed Afghan hoodlums who prowled the Cantonment perimeter every day. "They committed frequent assaults on our sepoys," wrote Eyre, "[but] orders to fire on them were repeatedly solicited in vain." The troops did receive permission to frighten off the intruders by raising their muskets to their shoulders, "which," said Lady Sale, "has occasioned some ridiculous and harmless flourishes of port-fires." As a result, concluded Eyre, "our soldiers were daily constrained to endure the most insulting and contemptuous taunts from fellows whom a single charge of bayonets would have scattered like chaff."

New Year's Day came and went. Shah Shuja made a last appeal to

* He was apparently thinking chiefly of his cousin, whose marriage to the infidel Captain Warburton had driven him into a homicidal fury. Mrs. Warburton somehow managed to disobey the order.

British honor: Was the army simply going to abandon him to Akbar? Of course it was, although Lady Sale pointed out that "the Affghans do not wish to put him to death, but only to deprive him of his sight." (He would be murdered a few weeks later.) Lady Sale also noted that the high command had again raised the possibility of storming the Bala Hissar, "now that the time for action is long past." Another day of waiting went by, then another and another still, and Akbar continued to withhold the British walking papers. The chiefs had not yet been able to organize the escort, he explained, or gather enough supplies to feed the force on its retreat, he said. Officers began chopping up their furniture for firewood.

On the afternoon of January 5, 1842, Elphinstone was ordered to march the army out of Kabul at seven o'clock the following morning.

6

Death March

Seldom in Central Asia had a larger or more ragged caravan ever been seen than on the grinding cold morning of January 6, 1842, when the Army of the Indus began its withdrawal from Kabul. All told, the retreating British numbered slightly less than 17,000—five times the size of the force that had surrendered at Saratoga in 1777. But only one-fourth of this horde were fighting men: 3,800 Indian and 700 British troops. The remaining 12,000 were followers and their families, except for about three dozen British wives and children who rode on camels and ponies in the ranks of a cavalry regiment for protection. The army was formed up into an advance column, main body and rear guard. Most of the followers and some 2,000 pack animals—carrying mountainous loads of baggage and practically no food—plodded alongside the main body, although not always keeping clear of the marching troops. Many of the sepoys and British soldiers wore the heavy Afghan sheepskin coats called *poshteens*, which offered some shield against the marrow-cracking cold, but nearly as many had only their standard issue greatcoats, which might just as well have been tropical worsteds.

Whatever order existed in the formations began to disintegrate almost at once in a losing battle with arctic winds, man-high snowdrifts, hunger, exhaustion and Afghan harassment. The evacuation of the Cantonment was to have been completed by noon and, indeed, by that time the advance column and main body had managed to slog forward through the snow and to cover about two miles. But the rear guard was less punctual. As its troops formed up to march out, they were set upon by a swarm of heavily armed Afghans who had scaled the low ramparts to loot officers' quarters and barracks. In the fire fight that ensued, it was only after abandoning all its baggage and leaving behind the corpses of fifty cavalrymen that the heavily outnumbered rear guard could shoot its way free of the enclosure.

By that time, the two forward columns were having troubles of their own. The fording of the Kabul River had created a frozen logjam of men, camels, horses and gun carriages that took nearly two hours to unsnarl. When the march was resumed, large numbers of Afghans were found lining the snowbanks on both sides of the road to jeer at the half-numb troops. Presently they began hurling rocks, and it was not long before jezails were opening up and blood began staining the snow as soldiers spun and dropped in their tracks. Laughing, knife-wielding Afghan children raced about the flanks of the columns and performed amputations and disembowelments on the wounded stragglers—"one of whom, the day before," wrote Mackenzie, "could have put a dozen of those children's fathers to flight with his bayonet." The unwounded troops fired back resolutely, but frozen fingers did not make for accuracy. And British resistance was, in due course, emasculated entirely when the followers panicked and surged forward in a tidal wave that engulfed the ranks and transformed the army into a mob.

At one point, Elphinstone decided to turn back the force, ordering Mackenzie to ride ahead and so inform Shelton. In an act of open mutiny, Mackenzie replied that he would tell Shelton the march must continue. He galloped off, and Elphinstone called out plaintively: "Mackenzie, don't! Don't do it!"

Somehow, the half-paralyzed, formless mass continued its groping forward movement until four o'clock in the afternoon, when Elphinstone called a halt for the day. Six miles had been covered. Despite Akbar's so-called safe conduct, most of the officers believed that the army would not be out of immediate danger until it reached Jalalabad, where, it was hoped, its strength would be augmented by Sale's brigade. The hope also existed that the march would last no longer than a week, or ten days at most. But, even though Jalalabad lay some seventy miles due east, the actual route, over icebound heights and through snow-strangled passes, wound and twisted for a distance of more than one hundred miles. Some of the more realistic of the British may have feared, even before quitting Kabul, that the army's evacuation of Afghanistan might well make Napoleon's retreat from Moscow look like a victory parade.

Soon the anemic sun fell behind the hills to the west and the wind went to work on the British encampment like a dentist's drill. Only a few of the men had sufficient strength and know-how to keep their blood circulating more or less normally. Mackenzie and twenty Afghans under his command threw several of their poshteens on a space of ground that had been cleared of snow, then lay down in a tight circle, with feet facing the center like spokes in a wheel, and covered themselves with the remaining poshteens. Some of the women and children had small tents, but there was a shortage of pegs, and only a few of those available could be driven into the cast-iron ground. The wind sliced freely beneath the sides of the tents while mothers held their babies in vise-like embraces to generate what little body warmth they could. No one slept for more than minutes at a time. Lady Sale involuntarily kept repeating to herself some lines she had read in a volume of *Campbell's Poems* a day or so earlier:

Few, few shall part where many meet,
The snow shall be their winding sheet;
And every turf beneath their feet
Shall be a soldier's sepulchre.

"I am far from being a believer in presentiments," she wrote, with fingers as stiff as the pen she tried to hold, "but this verse is never absent from my thoughts."

Miraculously, however, only a few dozen perished from exposure on that first night.

Sunrise on January 7 brought no perceptible relief as the retreat from Kabul began in earnest. "The very air we breathed froze in its passages out of the mouth and nostrils," wrote Eyre; cavalrymen used hammers and chisels to pry lumps of ice from the insides of their horses' hoofs. At about half past seven, the advance column formed up and moved off without orders. It was soon subjected to a repeat performance of the day before when it was overtaken by a surge of followers which broke up all semblance of formation. The followers had now been joined by many sepoys. Too numb even to lift their muskets, they had left the weapons in the snow to take their chances as civilians, no longer caring whether they would be shot for desertion or simply shot—if the cold did not bring them down first.

After an hour or so, large bodies of Afghan cavalry and infantry were seen to loom up on the British flanks. Akbar's promised escort had arrived at last. Many of the sepoys and British troops, their feet already beginning to blacken with frostbite, looked dully at the layers of heavy woollen cloth in which the Afghans' legs were swathed. The men remembered Pottinger's vain recommendation, some days earlier, that surplus army blankets be torn up into winter puttees for the force.

These thoughts were interrupted when one of the mounted Afghan columns suddenly wheeled, broke into a trot and then a full gallop, hooves throwing up great divots of snow as the horsemen charged full tilt at the rear column. The British troops were not only rigid with cold but caught off guard, and the Afghans quickly scattered them, making off with three mountain guns. Brigadier Thomas Anquetil, the rear guard commander, was able to rally some of the men and personally lead a counterattack that recovered the guns. Minutes later, the guns were lost again as the riflemen of the 44th Foot hung back—or, as Lady Sale put it, "very precipitately *made themselves scarce*" from standing up to a second Afghan charge.

The 44th was not a regiment of faint hearts and pantywaists. English slums, workhouses and prisons had taught its men to endure cold and hunger in silence. British army discipline had hardened them to mindless barbarity; they thought of bullet and knife wounds as little more than surface cuts compared to the floggings that had turned many a private's back into shoe leather. But the 44th had never bargained for anything like the retreat from Kabul.

Now Akbar appeared on the crest of a hill with 600 mounted troops. Skinner rode up to him, furiously demanding to know, on Elphinstone's behalf, why the attack on the rear guard had been permitted. Akbar seemed visibly distressed. The attackers were not his men, he protested, adding that the entire incident had been the result of "Elfistan Sahib's" unfortunate mistake in breaking camp before the escort could arrive. But Akbar assured Skinner that the British would be molested no longer. He also suggested that the General Sahib might possibly wish to halt for the day. Elphinstone obeyed.

It was noon. The force had arrived at a place called Bootkhak, having now eaten up twelve miles in forty-eight hours. At that rate, Jalalabad would not be reached in less than three weeks. And two-fifths of the army's inadequate rations already had been consumed, lost or plundered.

The camp at Bootkhak offered neither rest nor warmth. Eyre's Victorian description suffices: "Night again closed over us, with its attendant train of horrors—starvation, cold, exhaustion, death; and of all the deaths I can imagine none more agonizing than that, where a nipping frost tortures every sensitive limb until the tenacious spirit itself sinks under the exquisite extreme of human suffering." When the pallid sun crept up on the morning of January 8, the bivouac site was littered with the refrigerated cadavers of sepoys and followers who had burned their greatcoats, tunics and robes, even their caps and turbans, for momentary relief from the cold. As the still living troops prepared to march, infantrymen's hands froze to the metal fittings of their muskets and cavalry troopers had to be lifted to their mounts.

The army now stumbled off in its usual confusion, with the followers rushing forward to transform the advance columns from disarray to chaos. Parties of mounted Ghilzais rode up and began nipping at the British flanks, leaning down from their saddles to lop limbs and sometimes heads from wounded stragglers, making off with supplies, loosing occasional ragged volleys into the mass of the troops. At one point, some horse artillerymen begged their commanding officer to lead them in a charge. Having found a few bottles of brandy and worked up a head of Dutch courage, they burned to restore the army's lost guns and honor. The officer cursed them as drunken swine.

Shortly before noon, Akbar rode up and demanded three more hostages: Pottinger, Lawrence and Mackenzie. It was almost as if he had deliberately chosen this moment to deprive the force of three of its best leaders. For just ahead lay the Khurd Kabul Pass, a five-mile-long funnel beneath towering cliffs that were honeycombed with recesses for sharpshooters. The Khurd Kabul was the first real danger spot on the line of march.

A spark of the old fighting spirit glowed briefly when the men of the 44th cleared the entrance of the pass in a bayonet charge, but after that the army became a school of fish in a frozen barrel as the Ghilzai jezails hurled down a Biblical deluge of lead. Above the deafening roar in the claustrophobic echo chamber, Akbar could be heard screaming at the tribesmen to cease firing. It was later learned that he added: "Slay them!" in Pushtu—a language then understood by fewer than a half dozen Britons with the force.

After only a few minutes, most of the army simply broke and ran. Weapons, ammunition and baggage were thrown aside in the mad rush to get out of the trap. Even the women and children had to fend for themselves. Lady Sale described the plight of one mother: "Mrs. Mainwaring . . . took her own baby in her arms. . . . Meeting with a pony laden with treasure, [she] endeavoured to mount and sit on the boxes, but they upset . . . and the unfortunate lady pursued her way on foot. . . . She not only had to walk a considerable distance with her child in her arms through the deep snow, but also had to pick her way over the bodies of the dead, dying, and wounded, both men and cattle, and constantly to cross the streams of water, wet up to the knees, pushed and shoved about by men and animals, the enemy keeping up a sharp fire, and several persons being killed close to her. She, however, got safe to camp with her child."

A few of the women and children failed to survive the slaughter. Lady Sale breathed a sigh of relief at her own close shave: "I had, fortunately, only *one* ball in my arm; three others passed through my poshteen . . . without doing me any injury."

The rest of the army fared less well. When it finally emerged into the thin sunlight, it had left 3,000 dead bodies in the Khurd Kabul Pass.

Late that night, Lady Sale was awakened by noise outside the shredded tent where she and other wives and children were huddled. Sepoys and followers, out of their minds with cold, were trying "to force their way, not only into the tent, but actually into our beds, if such resting places can be so called." Even if the ladies had been willing to make room, there was none to make. Some thirty women and children were jammed together in a mass so solid that no one could even turn. During the night, said Lady Sale, "many poor wretches died round the tent."

On the morning of January 9, Sturt, gut-shot in the massacre of the day before, became the first and only man in the force to be given a Christian burial. There was time for the ceremony since Elphinstone had decided to halt for the day, Akbar having told him that the promised supplies were being brought up at last. No one was astonished when the supplies did not arrive. But Akbar offered to take all the British wives and children under his personal protection, and the officers reluctantly agreed to this, having finally perceived that their families stood no other chance for survival.

Certainly the British camp was no longer fit for man or beast. Half the force suffered from wounds, frostbite or snow blindness; many were laid low by all three. Everyone had reached an advanced state of starvation. Few of the women had eaten even a crust of bread since leaving Kabul; several mothers, suckling newborn infants, could barely produce milk. Eyre wrote that one or two wives "were so far advanced in pregnancy that, under ordinary circumstances, a walk across a drawing-room would have been an exertion."

So the women and children—accompanied by several badly wounded officers, including Eyre—rode off to the enemy lines, where it was hoped that conditions might prove at least endurable. And that Akbar would honor his pledge of protection.

At dawn on January 10, there was the usual stampede of followers to the head of the column as the crippled, frozen python resumed its crawl through the snow. After two miles, the troops entered the Tunghi Tariki Gorge. This passage was only fifty yards long, but it was also barely twelve feet wide, and the men had to walk in single file, much like mechanical ducks in a shooting gallery. After the gorge had been drenched for a few minutes with sheets of jezail fire, the Afghans swarmed down and went to work methodically with their knives. The British advance guard managed to hack out a bloody exit at the far end of the defile, then deployed to cover the Indian troops of the main body when they too emerged. Presently it was realized that the main body no longer existed. The army's sepoys had been wiped out almost to a man.

Effective British fighting strength was now down to 250 officers and men of the 44th, 150 cavalry officers and troopers and 50 horse artillery-men—450 soldiers remaining of the 4,500 who had left Kabul four days earlier. The 12,000 followers had been reduced to 3,000. The Europeans might have thought that number 3,000 too many.

With the menace of Akbar's escort hovering over its rear and flanks, the derelict army stumbled into the village of Tezeen at four o'clock in the afternoon. There could be no question of any further advance that day—until Elphinstone realized that if he were to save the remnant of the force he had somehow to move it beyond a natural ambush site situated about twenty miles to the east. Here lay the two-mile-long Jagdalak Pass, whose vaulting escarpments were tailor-made for several regiments of Afghan snipers. Only a forced night march, carried out in secrecy, might allow the men to reach Jagdalak and negotiate the pass before the Ghilzais blocked them.

In a rare display of initiative, Elphinstone sent a message to Akbar, informing him that he planned to move on to a place called Seh Baba, only seven miles east of Tezeen. Then he ordered the army to its feet. With the second wind of fear, the men obeyed and stepped off at a good pace, even managing to maintain silence throughout the ranks. But, as might have been expected, something panicked the followers during the night and they swarmed to the head of the column like a rush-hour subway crowd, giving away the show. Sunrise on January 11 saw the British still ten miles from Jagdalak and the Ghilzais, fully alerted, awaiting them on the walls of the pass.

The rest of the march to Jagdalak was a running fight in two feet of snow, with the rear guard, now under Shelton, somehow beating back the assaults of Afghans, who outnumbered the column by at least seven to one. By afternoon, the force was able to take precarious cover behind a crumbling stone wall near the entrance to the pass. An icy stream flowed nearby, but anyone who approached it to drink was picked off by Ghilzai snipers. The men tried eating snow, which only intensified their thirst. But at least, and at last, they had some solid food. Three bullocks that had been brought along were slaughtered and eaten raw—small pickings for 450 starving men, but a banquet after grains of barley. There was even a letup in the Afghan sniping at about five in the afternoon, when Akbar summoned Elphinstone and Shelton to a truce talk in his camp. And night, when it came, was no worse for the British than previous nights, although neither was it any better.

In the Afghan encampment that evening, Akbar told Elphinstone and Shelton that the tribal leaders had at last agreed to call off all further attacks and that the long-awaited food supplies were even then being readied for the British troops. But when the actual cease-fire talks began on the morning of January 12, the Ghilzai chiefs immediately commenced pressing for further hostilities, shouting angrily that the Feringhi excrement had not yet received punishment enough. Akbar seemed unable to control them. Although a few of the Ghilzais were prevailed upon to accept a truce on payment of £20,000, others were less tractable. Bickering and threats ran through the morning and well into the afternoon; sporadic firing also could be heard from the direction of the British camp. At sunset, Elphinstone became uneasy and asked permission to return to his own force. Akbar said that Elfistan Sahib was an honored guest, not a prisoner, that he was quite free, of course, to depart when he chose; but would the General not consent to wait just a short while longer? Surely, matters would soon be settled to the satisfaction of all.

At that moment, a shattering, sustained crash of musketry began rolling up in waves from the entrance to Jagdalak. Beside himself with anxiety, Elphinstone now insisted that he must go at once; his honor as a Queen's officer demanded that he be with his men, die with them if need be, in their hour of peril. Salaaming, Akbar replied that it would not be possible to leave just yet. Elphinstone could only wonder what new calamity had overtaken his army.

He would presently find out, but he was never to see the army again.

The day had been a trying one for the British in their camp. While the "peace" talks were in progress barely two miles away, the army—reduced to 140 officers and men under Anquetil's temporary command —was pinned down behind its stone wall by a steady rain of potshots from the heights of Jagdalak. Several Afghan attempts to storm the fragile position were hurled back by the bayonets of the 44th, which could still rise to an occasion. By nightfall, however, it had become clear to Anquetil that unless the Jagdalak bottleneck were broken, his force would succumb to the attrition of the enemy jezails. He therefore decided to move the troops out on his own initiative and run the gauntlet of the pass.

For a while it seemed as if the darkness would protect the tiny column as the men labored up the defile. But near the summit, they found that the Afghans had blocked the narrow goat path with the cheveaux-de-frise branches of holly oak trees. The struggle to make a hole in this iron tangle allowed the Ghilzais time to mass above the position at their leisure, then let go with a series of fusillades that were punctuated at intervals by head-on knife assaults. Blind panic seized the British. Infantrymen fired at cavalry troopers, who in turn rode the foot soldiers down in the every-man-for-himself rush to break free. When the Army of the Indus finally emerged from the pass, it numbered sixty-five of all ranks, groping their way eastward as the wind went at them like a cosmic horsewhip and jezail balls continued to smash into them from the frozen blackness.

By dawn on January 13, the force had been pared down to fewer than forty, huddled together on an ice-caked rise of ground near the village of Gandamak. The officers had their swords and pistols, and perhaps a dozen or so men of the 44th still carried their muskets, with no more than three or four rounds in each ammunition pouch. Afghans in the thousands were converging on the hill from all sides. The British could only stand and wait.

They did not wait long. A small party of Afghans approached the crest of the hill, all smiles and salaams. A truce, they announced, had been agreed on at last; the British need only hand over their weapons. Not bloody likely, bellowed a sergeant as the men of the 44th fixed bayonets. Eyre was later given an eyewitness account of what happened next.

"The die was now cast . . . for the enemy, taking up their post on an opposite hill, marked off man after man, officer after officer, with unerring aim. Parties of Afghans rushed up at intervals to complete the work of extermination, but were as often driven back by the still dauntless handful of invincibles. At length, nearly all being wounded more or less, a final onset of the enemy, sword in hand, terminated the unequal struggle, and completed the dismal tragedy."

Astonishingly, not all the British were slain. About six prisoners were taken; one, Captain Thomas Souter of the 44th, inadvertently saved himself when he tried to save the regimental colors by wrapping them round his waist, thus giving the Afghans the impression that he carried high rank. Several others broke free, but were later cut down or captured. Within a day's march of Jalalabad, the Army of the Indus had at last met its end.

Not quite. That afternoon, as Havelock, Broadfoot and other officers of Sale's brigade stood on the battlements of the Jalalabad fort and searched the hills for some sign of Elphinstone's force, a lone horseman suddenly materialized in the distance. "As he got nearer," wrote Havelock, "it was distinctly seen that he wore European clothes . . . a signal was made to him by someone on the walls, which he answered by waving a private soldier's forage cap over his head." The gates of the fort were then thrown open and the man rode in. Havelock and the others recognized Dr. William Brydon, the Medical Officer of Shah Shuja's force, "covered with . . . cuts and contusions, and dreadfully exhausted." His scabbard held the six-inch stub of the cavalry saber with which he had managed to chop his way across the last twenty-five miles from the site of the massacre at Gandamak.

"Thus is verified," wrote Lady Sale when she learned of Dr. Brydon's ride, "what we were told before leaving Cabul; 'that Mahomed Akbar would annihilate the whole army except one man, who should reach Jalalabad to tell the tale.'"

Exactly one hundred years and one month later, Singapore fell to the Japanese. Until then, no British army in Asia would submit to so resounding a humiliation as that suffered by the force that had tried to retrieve the shreds of its honor in the last stand on the ice-swept hill at Gandamak.

At the end of November 1841, when the news of Burnes' murder reached Calcutta, Auckland had not acted at once. He had also received letters from Macnaghten assuring him that the situation in Kabul was well in hand, and he had no wish to create the impression among the Indian people that their masters were prone to pushing the panic button. But by January 1842, the disaster could no longer be swept under the rug. For the first time in their experience, Asiatics were being treated to the spectacle of a British army in headlong flight from a rabble of lesser breeds. Not only to rescue the survivors but to salvage the tatters of British prestige, a relief force of two brigades under Major General George Pollock was ordered to Afghanistan. But it came to a grinding halt at Peshawar. The Army of Retribution, as it was called, had to wait until spring cleared the Khyber Pass of its snows.

Meanwhile, some five dozen Englishmen, Englishwomen and English children were experiencing alternate hostility and hospitality as Akbar's prisoner-guests. At first, they were simply herded about along the British line of retreat, by then a landscape that could have been painted by Hieronymus Bosch. "It would be impossible for me to describe the feelings with which we pursued our way through the dreadful scenes that awaited us," wrote Lady Sale. "The road covered with awfully mangled bodies, all naked. . . . Numbers of camp followers, still alive, frost bitten and starving; some perfectly out of their senses and idiotic. . . . The sight was dreadful; the smell of blood sickening; and the corpses lay so thick it was impossible to look from them, as it required care to guide my horse so as not to tread upon the bodies." Lady Sale subsequently learned that many of the living followers, "driven to the extreme of hunger . . . had sustained life by feeding on their dead comrades." It might have seemed to the hostages that Akbar was deliberately rubbing their noses in their army's disgrace.

Actually, during this early marching, Akbar was not certain of what to do with his charges. On the one hand, their captivity invited the kind of retaliation he had good reason to fear, and he had originally promised to escort the hostages to Jalalabad. Eventually, however, he came to see them as bargaining chips, not only for the return of Dost Muhammad, but for ransom. Cupidity overcame prudence and, on January 17, the British party was moved into permanent minimum-security quarters in the fort at Budeabad, a village in the Laghman Valley about thirty miles north of Jalalabad.

They stayed here three months, their existence comparing favorably with that of concentration camp inmates. No one was tortured or even beaten, although the Afghan warders made free with threats and verbal abuse. Some of these keepers also stole personal belongings (including Lady Macnaghten's cat) as a matter of course, but usually returned the articles on payment of "rewards." A supply of clothes was sent to the hostages by the Jalalabad garrison. They were also allowed to write and receive letters, subject only to the most primitive censorship. Even developments that were being withheld from them (or from Jalalabad) could be conveyed, messages sometimes being exchanged in French or

Greek. Another system was to mark letters of the alphabet in old newspapers—"an easy mode of carrying on secret correspondence," wrote Eyre, "and not likely to be detected by an Asiatic."

Living conditions ranged from squalor to minimal comfort. Five small rooms in the fort were assigned to the prisoners, each room occupied by ten or twelve men, women and children crammed together without sanitary facilities. The niceties were observed by separating wives from unmarried males with strips of cloth hung from the ceilings. Afghan cuisine did not sit well in fastidious English stomachs. It consisted chiefly of boiled rice, rock-hard slices of unleavened dough, and what Eyre called "mutton boiled to rags"; but the taste improved slightly when Akbar allowed the meals to be prepared by the hostages' Hindu servants. Other discomforts and inconveniences were little more than just that. Although vermin proliferated on clothing and bodies, Eyre noticed that "even the ladies mustered up resolution to look . . . these intruders in the face without a scream." The ladies in fact went so far as to distinguish between what they designated infantry (lice) and light cavalry (fleas).

The worst hardships were inflicted by nature; from January through March, the cold never stopped knifing into poshteens and even penetrating the walls of the fort. There was also a very real danger. On February 19, Lady Sale was hanging out some wash to dry on the roof of the fort when the roof suddenly collapsed beneath her. Almost miraculously, she escaped injury, but the earthquake that had struck Budeabad was only the first of forty violent tremors that all but leveled the fort in the next twenty-four hours. Until the end of April, earthquakes rolled across eastern Afghanistan almost daily.

A few failed to come through. Three-year-old Seymour Stoker died from continual beatings by a slut called Mrs. Wade, a sergeant's wife who had converted to Islam and become an informer against her fellow-captives. Elphinstone also succumbed, overtaken at last by his multitude of afflictions and a broken heart; his only wish had been to die with his troops. For the most part, however, the prisoners survived, even adding to their numbers. Akbar's cousin, Mrs. Warburton, gave birth to a son, and several other wives also became mothers; Mrs. Sturt made Lady Sale a grandmother. Four-year-old Mary Anderson was returned to her parents, who had given her up for dead when she vanished in the confusion of the Khurd Kabul massacre. Cared for with great tenderness by an Afghan family, she had lost her command of English but spoke Persian fluently and announced: "My mother and father are infidels, but I am a Muslim."

The prisoners seldom complained of their lot; to do so would have been un-British. Besides, the Afghans were obviously sharing many of the same hardships, particularly the earthquakes, and few inconveniences were caused by deliberate malice. There were many invitations to dine with upper-class Afghan families in Budeabad. The wives of one chief helped Lady Sale celebrate her thirty-fourth wedding anniversary by asking her and several other captive women to a feast of pilaf and curds. "Those who had not taken a spoon with them," wrote Lady Sale, "ate with their fingers, Afghan fashion,—an accomplishment in which I am by no means *au fait*." And as for the cause of all the British tribulations, Akbar at this time was described by Eyre as a "perfect gentleman [who] never indulges in comparisons to the disadvantage of the English, of whom he invariably speaks with candour and respect."

Akbar also took every opportunity to protest his innocence of Macnaghten's murder, once even breaking down and weeping for two hours. The hostages, of course, gave no credit to the disclaimers, but neither were they totally unmoved by Akbar's general behavior. Once, on learning that Eyre was an amateur sketcher, Akbar asked him to do a drawing of a favorite horse. Eyre seemed to take this as a compliment, writing that "though my performance was very indifferent, [Akbar] expressed himself pleased." Even Lady Sale could unbend toward her chief jailer: "A woman's vengeance is said to be fearful . . . nothing can satisfy mine against Akbar. . . . Still I say that Akbar, having for his own political purposes done as he said he would do—that is, destroyed our army . . . has ever since we have been in his hands, treated us well:— that is, honour has been respected."

Lady Sale found less room for patience with the policy that had brought the British to Afghanistan, or with the vacillation that had caused the army's extermination and made her a hostage: "Let the Afghans have the Ameer Dost Mahomed Khan back, if they like. He and his family are only an expense to us in India; we can restore them, and make friends with him. . . . But do not let us dishonour the British name by sneaking out of the country like whipped pariah dogs."

Although it was a little late to worry about the style of the British departure from Afghanistan, the hostages by April were taking new heart from rumors and even written reports that help was on the way. Previously, Sale had been unable to come to their rescue; even though Jalalabad lay barely two marches off, Sale's brigade was too seriously reduced in numbers by death, wounds and disease for a concerted effort against the Afghans. Yet the troops at Jalalabad had not stagnated. With George Broadfoot acting as a sort of foreman, they had shored up the town's crumbling fortifications; when their work was swept away by an earthquake they rolled up their sleeves and rebuilt the fort. Lively skirmishes with detachments of Akbar's army, as well as occasional sorties to round up livestock, also helped keep the brigade in trim. After some weeks, the sick and wounded began to make a rapid recovery.* Then, early in April, news reached Jalalabad that Pollock's Army of Retribution had finally marched out of Peshawar for the Khyber Pass and that Akbar had sent his cousin, Sultan Jan, with 3,000 troops to check the British advance. Sale at last felt strong enough to have a try of his own at Akbar.

The try proved a ringing success. Although Sale's British and Indian troops were outnumbered by more than three to one, they had been aching almost physically for four months to get a little of their own back. They completely routed the Afghans, recapturing four guns and coming within an ace of making Akbar himself a prisoner. Akbar took his licking, said Eyre, "with the liberality which always marks the really brave . . . and loudly extols the bravery exhibited by our troops led on by the gallant Sale." But Akbar also lost no time in moving his force and the hostages westward toward Kabul. The beginning of the end of the captivity seemed at hand.

Once more on the march, however, the hostages received a bad shock. On April 10, wrote Eyre, "our progress was arrested by a few horsemen, who galloped up waving their hands joyfully, and crying out 'Shabash!' 'Bravo!' 'All is over! The Feringhee army has been cut up in the Khyber Pass, and all their guns taken by Sultan Jan!'" The news was impossible to believe, until Akbar ordered the prisoners to about-face and return to Budeabad.

As they retraced their steps, more details of the Afghan victory came in and presently it was realized that Pollock had not been routed at all. In fact, he had just become the first foreigner since the Mogul Emperor Babur to carry the Khyber by force of arms. He had done so by the simple tactic of sending out strong patrols to cover the heights above the pass and winkle out enemy troops, thus securing his flanks against Afghan and Afridi attack and permitting almost undisputed passage. On April 16, the Army of Retribution marched into Jalalabad as a makeshift regimental band greeted it at the gate with an old Scottish air: "Oh, But Ye've Been Long O' Comin'."

Akbar now made a desperate bid to stave off the inevitable. Twice he sent Mackenzie to Jalalabad on parole, with terms for the freeing of the hostages. But Pollock's orders did not allow him to treat with Akbar. This left the Afghan leader with no choice but to spin around once more and resume his westerly retreat, just as an astonishing order reached Jalalabad from India.

* The teetotaling Havelock attributed this to the loss of the brigade's rum ration. Had spirits been available, he said, the men would have been "inmates of the hospital and guard houses . . . coming to their work with fevered brain and trembling hand, or sulky and disaffected after their protracted debauch." Instead, he beamed, "all is health, cheerfulness, industry and resolution."

By this time, Auckland had been recalled in disgrace and the new Governor General, Lord Ellenborough, had somehow received the false report of the Afghan victory in the Khyber. Fearing another Kabul fiasco, Ellenborough issued instructions for the immediate withdrawal of the Army of Retribution. Pollock was not to punish Akbar or even rescue the hostages. The effect of this order was to create such a furor that Ellenborough finally backed down, informing Pollock in Jalalabad and Nott in Kandahar that, if they wished, they would be allowed to withdraw their forces to India via Kabul. The decision saved Ellen-borough some embarrassment, but the delay also gave Akbar a head start in his own retirement.

By summer, however, Pollock was in full cry and Akbar found himself caught up in a fighting retreat. The Afghans took a bad bruising at Jagdalak, and Akbar himself led a wild cavalry charge at Tezeen, only to see his whole army break and scatter when the British infantry fixed bayonets and drove full force into the Afghan main body. Even the dreaded tulwars seemed no match for British cold steel.

At this time also, Akbar's political fortunes were beginning to wane as a power struggle broke out in Kabul. A strong pro-British faction had surfaced among the Afghan chiefs, and for several weeks Kabul was the scene of pitched battles between rival parties seeking to gain physical possession of the Bala Hissar. At one point, Akbar even made a desperate but vain attempt to enlist Eyre as an officer with his own force. Akbar's side finally prevailed, but his mastery of Afghanistan was no longer un-disputed.

These developments tended to make him less accommodating toward his guests. "Our prospects are blacker than ever," wrote Eyre on July 29. "Mahomed Akbar declared today . . . with an expression of savage determination in his countenance, that so surely as Pollock advances, he will take us all into Toorkistan, and make presents of us to the different chiefs. And depend on it he will carry his threats into execution, for he is not a man to be trifled with." Not that the hostages had to be told this, but it still came as a jolt to them when, several days later, Akbar ordered them off on a one-hundred-mile march over the Hindu Kush to Bamian.

But by now, as Pollock and Nott converged relentlessly on Kabul, Akbar's influence was rapidly shrinking, and the prisoners began to win over many of their captors, who saw which way the wind was blowing. On September 3, when the party reached Bamian, the Afghans made no attempt to prevent Pottinger from running up the 'Union Jack over the fort. Nor did the local chiefs resist Pottinger's demand that they come in and submit to British authority. Even the merchants of passing caravans dutifully paid taxes to the hostages, who were now in a position to back up their collections, having been armed by the commander of their Afghan guard.

So liberation, when it finally came, was almost an anticlimax, although it was not without its moments. On September 16, Pollock marched into Kabul with Nott on his heels and sent a 600-man flying column to rescue the hostages, who had already started their own march east from Bamian. They were "freed" on September 17, without a shot being fired. A few days later, Sale celebrated his sixtieth birthday by riding up to collect his wife, daughter and granddaughter. "Happiness so long delayed . . . was actually painful," wrote Lady Sale, "and . . . could not obtain the relief of tears." Sale himself nearly broke down. When Mackenzie went up to congratulate him, "the gallant old gentleman turned towards me and tried to answer, but his feelings were too strong; he made a hideous series of grimaces, dug his spurs into his horse and galloped off as hard as he could." The only sour note of the whole rescue operation was sounded by Shelton, who took petulant offense because Sir Richmond Shakespeare, commanding the relief column, failed to greet him first, as was his due by rank.

All that remained was for the Army of Retribution to live up to its name. It did so by blowing up the Kabul bazaar. No other punishment was exacted—even from Akbar, who was never caught. At this point, the British wished only to put Afghanistan behind them. As swiftly as terrain and dignity permitted, the forces marched back to India, where Ellenborough had already made it known that Britain hankered after no further imperial adventures on the west bank of the Indus and would "leave it to the Afghans themselves to create a government amidst the anarchy which is the consequence of their crimes."

In effect, Ellenborough was throwing up a concrete wall between India and Afghanistan. By January 1843, Dost Muhammad, having been freed from his exile without fanfare, once more sat on the throne in Kabul as if his rule had never been interrupted. Thenceforth, as far as the British and Indian governments were concerned, Afghanistan would simply cease to exist as a political neighbor.

The new isolationist policy won loud applause from the British public, press and political establishment. The disaster of Kabul had thoroughly shamed a nation that might well have cheered itself hoarse had Auckland, Macnaghten, Burnes and Elphinstone been able to impose their will on the Afghan people. There were a few attempts to bandage self-respect. Pollock was welcomed back to India as a conquering hero. Much was made of Sale and his four-month stand at Jalalabad; the brigade became known as "the illustrious garrison," and Sale's own regiment, the 13th Foot, thenceforth carried "Jalalabad" on its colors. In England, the Afghan captivity was dramatized in a sell-out London music hall performance whose high spot showed Lady Sale—played by an Amazonesque actress—dispatching six burly Ghazis with an enormous curved sword. But there could be no escape from the reality of Britain's humiliation in the eyes of Asiatics, who would never again think of British armed might as invincible. "I could almost eat my fists from vexation," said the Duke of Wellington.

Even more to the point was the widespread conviction that no purpose whatever had been served by seeking to subjugate Afghanistan in the first place. This view may have been summed up best in the terse comment by the London *Standard* that the whole misadventure had stemmed from an "utter absurdity"—namely, "fears of an invasion of India through Afghanistan, whether from Russia, Persia or indeed at all."

Only one man stood against the tide. But Palmerston's role in the affair was to get him in hot water. In 1851, Kaye's account of the filibuster blew the whistle on the official suppression of Burnes' correspondence and the papers were finally published in full in 1858. This touched off a small Watergate, which threatened for a while to unseat Palmerston from the prime ministership. He survived the attacks, but his Central Asian interventionist policy had long fallen from favor. Britain had washed her hands of Afghanistan forever.

In fact, Britain by then had become stuck fast in the passes of the Afghan frontier.

PART TWO

Masterful Inaction

7

"Annex It! Annex It! Annex It!"

BESIDES BEING A member in good standing of the British aristocracy, Ellenborough could make two unusual claims to distinction: he was a distant relative of George Washington and his wife left him for a Bedouin sheik. He was probably not the easiest of men to get along with. Subordinates greatly resented his egotistical arrogance; one writer has called him "bombastic, masterful, vain and extremely ambitious." But at least he had something to be vain about; few contemporary Britons on the Indian scene possessed anything approaching his encyclopedic knowledge of the subcontinent and its peoples. As Governor General, Ellenborough also held decided views on Indian policy, including a widely and loudly proclaimed opinion that the Company that paid his salary should be dismantled to make way for direct rule by the Crown. Hardly less foursquare was his stand for peace at almost any price, which he had lost no time in demonstrating with the withdrawal of British troops from Afghanistan.

And at the very moment that Pollock ordered the Army of Retribution to march from Kabul, Ellenborough further underscored his noninterventionist philosophy by contradicting it in a move to annex Sind.

When the British had passed through Sind en route to Kabul in 1838, they had found little reason to linger in what had yet to become the not-so-soft underbelly of India's southwestern frontier. This perfectly frightful country was and is a desert about four times the size of Belgium, flayed regularly by sandstorms and littered with rocks that become im-

[89]

mense live coals in the summer months. In the 1830s, Sind's principal industry was banditry, but the practice made few inhabitants rich. The country's only men of means were its licentious and barbarity wealthy amirs, whose misrule set standards of corruption and barbarity probably unsurpassed by any other Central Asian monarchs, which was going some. But if one could not love Sind, the British at least had reason to covet the place. Certainly its location could hardly have escaped the notice of Indian expansionists. Lying between the Arabian Sea and southern Baluchistan, Sind also happened to sprawl out for many miles from both banks of the lower Indus. As early as the 1820s, the Company had recognized that control of navigation on the Indus would be extremely useful, if not vital, to British commercial interests. In 1831, Alexander Burnes had made a journey up the river and was told prophetically by a local chief: "The evil is done; you have seen our country."

The Company, in fact, had already made some trade treaties with Sind, and in 1840 the Indian Army's Major James Outram had been sent to the capital, Hyderabad, as British Resident. A resident was exactly the wedge Ellenborough needed, and he began casting about for an excuse to apply it. He seemed untroubled by the knowledge that interference in Sind— which meant annexation—would almost certainly lead to further penetration into Baluchistan on the southeastern Afghan frontier, and that this in turn would jeopardize, if not undermine, his own policy of isolationism toward Afghanistan. In September 1842, when the amirs of Sind protested the harsh terms of a new treaty, Ellenborough ordered General Charles Napier to pick a quarrel with the amirs and occupy their brigand-infested land.

Given the amirs' hedonistic malfeasance vis-à-vis the lofty righteousness of Victorian England, a justification for war presented no problem, although Outram, a compassionate and fair-minded man, thought it did. He called the proposed incursion "most tyrannical," and wrote Napier that "every life that may hereafter be lost in consequence will be a MURDER." Napier himself had few illusions about his country's motives. "We have no right to seize Sind," he wrote, "yet we shall do so, and a very advantageous, humane and useful piece of rascality it will be." Napier was also the right man to bring it off, if for no other reason than his burning ambition for military glory, which had eluded him despite more than three decades of active service and a respectable collection of wounds gathered in the Peninsular campaign. He also commanded the unquestioning obedience and unbounded affection of his troops, who called him "Old Fagin" for his long hair, wild eyes and colossal beak of a nose. Above all, he was impatient to move, and when the amirs hedged at signing the treaty, he thundered: "My mind is made up. If they fire a single shot, Sind will be annexed to India."

More than a single shot was fired, and Napier had to hold back until February 1843, when the amirs launched an attack on the British Residency in Hyderabad. But then, in less than three weeks, Napier's 2,600-man force scattered the amirs' 20,000 Baluchi mercenaries and marched into Hyderabad, where Napier may or may not have sent off the immortal punning signal: "Peccavi"—I have Sind. He was then appointed Governor of the country, which in effect meant dictator, and he ruled with a scrupulous honesty that was exceeded only by his draconian firmness. Once, on ordering the execution of a chief who had murdered a member of his harem, Napier was approached by a tribal deputation pleading for clemency on grounds that the man had simply been angry. "Well," replied Napier, "I am angry with him and I mean to hang him."

Napier made his presence felt in other ways. Although banditry could not be wiped out entirely, it was stamped on hard by flying columns of British-led Indian cavalry, usually the crack Sind Horse under Captain John Jacob, who looked and sometimes behaved like Ulysses S. Grant. Jacob succeeded Napier as Governor in 1848. Eight years later he was urging that the Company occupy the town of Quetta in Baluchistan; the position, he said, would be vital in protecting India's southwestern flank against invasion from Russian Central Asia. Although the proposal was shot down, it was handwriting on the wall that promised not only the eventual annexation of Baluchistan but a sea of troubles for the British rulers of India.

The troubles of course were Afghanistan. Although Baluchistan was in reality a no-man's-land, large portions of it were at least nominally Afghan territory. But in occupying Sind, the Company became Baluchistan's next-door neighbor and, in so doing, guaranteed tragic embroilment with the country that Britain was almost frantically seeking to quarantine from her Indian empire.

But even if Sind had never been marked off as Company territory, it was a foregone conclusion that the British in India would be sucked in toward Afghanistan's outer marches—and a century of endless explosions—by the vacuum of the Punjab to the north.

Sometimes known as the "Land of the Five Rivers"—each a tributary of the Indus—the Punjab, during most of the nineteenth century, embraced an alternately fertile and barren tract slightly larger than Japan, extending from Delhi in the east to the hills of Afghan territory in the west. In the early 1840s, the Punjab had not yet become British soil, but it cried out for some sort of management. Since Ranjit Singh's death, Sikh rule had fallen into a state of near-anarchy under a succession of successors and would-be successors. A return to order seemed momentarily at hand in 1845, with the accession of Ranjit's eight-year-old son Dulip Singh, who wielded no power whatever, de facto authority being shared by his mother, the Maharani Jindan, and her lover, one Lal Singh, who doubled as the country's prime minister. Although the Maharani took a no-nonsense attitude toward affairs of state, she was something less than a symbol of integrity; George Lawrence's younger brother, Major Henry Lawrence, the Company Agent in the Punjab capital of Lahore, described her as "a strange blend of the prostitute, the tigress and Machiavelli's Prince." But that assessment of political clout did not take into account the influence of the Sikh army, whose aggressive commanders were often at near-mutinous odds with the country's ostensible rulers. It was hard to find the Punjab's real seat of power.

To the extent that national unity did exist, it expressed itself in an energetic Anglophobia that was not long in finding active outlet. Resentment had been simmering for some time over the proximity of Company garrisons, totaling about 14,000 troops, along the banks of the Sutlej River, which marked the western boundary of British India. In December 1845, a Sikh army, 40,000 strong, crossed the Sutlej to challenge the might of the Raj.

Thus began what was called the First Sikh War. It lasted eight weeks and might have ended in eight days but for the British commander, General Sir Hugh Gough, an antique warhorse who thought of artillery as unsporting, effete, tactically useless and otherwise a liability. Gough nonetheless managed to hurl the Sikhs back in a blood-drenched engagement near Ferozepore, losing several thousand of his own men (including Sale and Broadfoot) in the process, and causing the new Governor General, Ellenborough's brother-in-law Lord Hardinge, to exclaim: "Another such victory and we are undone." Another such victory came a few weeks later, at a place called Sobraon, but the British were undone only in the sense that they found themselves saddled with the Punjab.

Technically, the country remained independent under the Maharani Jindan, but in fact it had all but become a British protectorate. The mighty Sikh army was disbanded and replaced by a relatively small Company force, while Henry Lawrence was made British Resident to lay down the law in Lahore. One of the monumental figures of British rule in India, Lawrence had a striking facial resemblance to Abraham Lincoln, and his outlook toward the Sikhs was not much less Lincolnesque in its empathy and compassion. It may have been the impact of his stewardship alone that kept the Sikhs from turning on their new masters for more than two years.

But with the Maharani Jindan on the scene, it was only a matter of time before trouble began. In the spring of 1848, Lawrence learned that the prostitute-tigress-Machiavelli had been working to foment mutiny among the Company sepoys in Lahore. She was swiftly arrested and exiled, but it was too late. Even as a troop of hard-case sowars forcibly removed the Maharani from her palace—while ducking her talons and marveling at the wealth of her expletives—her intrigues were bearing fruit elsewhere. About 125 miles southwest of Lahore, unrest had been simmering in the fortified city of Multan, where a minor satrap named Mulraj was openly challenging British authority. To set things straight without bloodshed, a British army officer and a civilian administrator were sent to Multan, but as they rode through the gates they were set upon by a mob and murdered. The act touched off a rising of some 4,000 demobilized Sikh veterans who rallied round Mulraj and dared the British to do their worst. Unless the insurrection were stamped out swiftly, the entire Punjab would follow Multan's example and revert to Sikh rule.

At this time, there was only one British armed force in the neighborhood. It consisted of a handful of sepoys led by a subaltern named Herbert Edwardes, who happened to be collecting taxes for the Company near the Afghan border about 100 miles north of Multan. Aware that his corporal's guard would be no match for the Multan insurgents, Edwardes played on the religious bigotry of the area's predominantly Muslim population to raise a ragged commando of 3,000 mounted Pathan irregulars—"bold villains," he called them, "ready to risk their own throats and cut those of any one else." Not even the Indus River—three miles wide in full spring flood—slowed the pace of Edwardes' forced march on Multan; his tribal guerrillas had long waited for this chance to have a real crack at the thrice-accursed Sikhs. Nor were they disappointed when they reached their objective. It took only two swift but jolting clashes outside Multan to knock the fight out of Mulraj and his rebels, who lost no time fleeing headlong into the city and sealing themselves up behind the walls, well out of harm's way.

Again it was too late. By then, other Sikh forces had begun to mobilize and were going on the offensive. Far to the north, a great army was gathering under an astute military strategist and dynamic leader named Chatar Singh. By August his columns were on the march; early in November they seized Peshawar, then wheeled around for a southeastward advance on Lahore to drive the British from the Punjab forever. And all this while urgent messages to India for reinforcements had gone unheeded. Henry Lawrence was on home leave in England and unable to bring his massive influence to bear. The new Governor General, Lord Dalhousie, had not been in India long enough—or perhaps even alive long enough, being only thirty-five—to appreciate the gravity of the crisis. Gough—by then Lord Gough, in reward for his mismanagement of the First Sikh War—had been taking his rest in the summer capital of Simla and had no intention of mounting a campaign in the hot months. When he finally deigned to stir in the autumn, the whole of the Punjab had been caught up in a holocaust that could and should have been extinguished half a year earlier.

The Second Sikh War was a much more serious conflict than the first, not only because British complacency had allowed the revolt to spread, but because it brought Afghanistan into the field against the Company. With the capture of Peshawar, Dost Muhammad finally had his long dreamed-of opportunity to regain that city. Both he and the Sikhs were prepared to submerge their differences in an alliance against the British, especially since the Sikhs had made the Amir the one offer he could not refuse: the gift of Peshawar if he joined their cause. Having lost no time funnelling Afghan troops through the Khyber Pass to reoccupy his country's historic winter capital, the Dost also found himself in effective control of the Punjab's entire trans-Indus holdings. Still, he abided by the terms of the alliance, ordering a large Afghan force to march east and link up with the main Sikh army as it prepared to do battle with the tardy Gough. On January 13, 1849, near the town of Chilianwala, the first collision took place.

It was a typical Gough operation, in which the doughty old general spurned his own ninety field pieces—nearly half the number Wellington had at Waterloo—and sent 16,000 foot soldiers and cavalrymen against twice as many Sikh and Afghan troops and three score Sikh guns. Superior British discipline just managed to carry the day, but not before 2,500 British and Indian fighting men were smashed into red paste by the Sikh artillery. "I treat it as a great victory," Dalhousie wrote Wellington in England, "but writing confidentially to you, I do not hesitate to say that I consider my position grave."

After the battle, Gough learned that he was to be replaced by Sir Charles Napier, who had been knighted since the conquest of Sind. The news at last galvanized the mossbacked commander not only into action but into a sweeping reassessment of his lifelong tactical theories. Before Napier could reach the scene and take charge, the onetime champion of musketry and cold steel was putting his despised artillery to good use near the town of Gujerat. The Company army had been beefed up to 30,000, but the Sikh-Afghan force now numbered 60,000 and occupied most of the high ground. That advantage was soon cancelled out, however, by a sustained, mind-numbing bombardment that ploughed up a broad avenue for wave after assault wave of cheering Company infantrymen. Even so, the fighting was fierce. Screaming their war cry, "Wah Guru!", the Sikhs held fast. One British soldier later wrote of how they "stood and defended their guns to the last. They threw their arms around them, kissed them, and died. Others would spit at us, when the bayonet was through their bodies. Some of the guns and carriages were streaming with blood."

But this heroism was an empty gesture. Gough had redeemed himself with an authentic victory. He not only routed the Sikhs but drove the Afghans out of the country. Dost Muhammad's mounted columns scattered in full flight as British and Indian cavalry units chased them for nearly 200 miles, splashing saddle-deep across the Jhelum and Indus rivers, not giving off the pursuit until the Afghans had become a dust cloud moving westward through the Khyber. No Afghan army would ever invade the Punjab again.

Meanwhile, there remained the question of what to do with the Punjab. Dalhousie annexed it.

But only after an impassioned plea for its continued independence by Henry Lawrence, now back from England with a knighthood. As British Resident in Lahore, Lawrence had come to be looked on by the Sikhs as one of their own; provincial status for the Punjab was not part of his hope that the country would remain a sovereign nation—if not the peer of British India then at least its ally and partner. But he had two strikes against him. One was his brother John, a former high-ranking revenue official in Delhi. Henry and John Lawrence seldom saw eye to eye on anything; they enjoyed a lifelong love-hate relationship in which the latter emotion seemed to predominate. When Dalhousie asked John Lawrence's opinion on the Punjab, he is said to have replied: "Annex it! Annex it! Annex it!"

Strike two was Dalhousie himself. An executive of unimpeachable integrity and a demon for work, this man also had a gift for rubbing some people the wrong way. Henry Lawrence, who could have been prejudiced, complained that the Governor General "vents his impertinences on us in a way that would be unbecoming if we were servants," while Napier called him "vain as a pretty woman or an ugly man." But the main thing about Dalhousie was that he was the quintessential Victorian who saw progress, with a capital *P*, as the key to India's future. He had no patience with Henry Lawrence's respect for the less urgent Indian way of life. He was also jealous of the undisputed prestige, indeed the love, that the Resident had won among the Sikhs. Henry Lawrence's arguments went down the drain, and the Punjab was welded to the Empire.

But Henry Lawrence by now had become the Company's most important and respected servant in India, and Dalhousie could ill afford to dismiss him from Lahore. Lawrence was, therefore, appointed to head up the new Punjab Government, as President of a three-man Board of Administration, which included John Lawrence—who, as Dalhousie well knew, could be counted on to clash with his older brother at every opportunity. This happened (Robert Montgomery, the third member, described himself as "a tame elephant between two wild oxen"), and Henry resigned after four years. The troika was then dismantled, and John became the Punjab's master, with the title of Chief Commissioner. But in the meanwhile the board somehow managed to function, and its achievements became a model for the rest of India.

For despite their differences, each of the two brothers was touched with his own peculiar genius, and their contrasting attitudes could even be said to have complemented one another. Henry was warm, idealistic, emotional, sometimes short-tempered, always people-oriented. He once said that "until we treat [the Indians] . . . as having much the same feelings, the same ambitions, the same perception of ability, and imbecility, as ourselves, we shall never be safe." He had no use for the bureaucratic mentality, and the loyalty and affection he gave to his subordinates was reciprocated a thousandfold. John was an icy and forbidding personality who made few friends. His human side seemed to surface only in displays of absentmindedness. (Once he almost lost the Koh-i-Nur, which had been placed in his charge after the war, simply by dropping it into a waistcoat pocket and forgetting it while changing clothes.) He was a financial wizard and had an unquenchable thirst for hard work. He frowned on leisure and forbade leave-taking by his staff except in emergencies; "there is so much to do," he once wrote Dalhousie. "Every day is of value." His decisions were always cautious, rational and cool, if not downright cold. The biographer Hesketh Pearson may have summed the two men up when he wrote that "while Henry was a great public servant, John was a great civil servant."

The brothers also shared certain outlooks. Both had spent all their adult lives in India, serving not just the Company but the Indian people. They were as fluent in Hindi, Urdu and other local tongues as they were in English. Both were rigidly incorruptible, and their unswerving belief in justice without favor was reflected everywhere in the management of the Punjab. The cadre of administrators that they created and developed became known as the "Lawrence School." It was the aristocracy of the Indian Civil Service.

And the part of the Punjab where this elite breed left its most enduring mark was also the area in which it had the least success: the dark and bloody frontier region west of the Indus River. It might be worthwhile at this point to have a closer look at a few of the Punjab's frontier administrators.

But not before meeting the wild men they tried to tame.

8

The Three Commandments

"I BELIEVE THAT our North-Western Frontier presents at this moment a spectacle unique in the world," wrote a viceroy of India in 1877; "at least I know of no other spot where, after twenty-five years of peaceful occupation, a great civilised Power has obtained so little influence over its semi-savage neighbours . . . that the country within a day's ride of its most important garrison (Peshawar) is an absolute *terra incognita* and that there is absolutely no security for British life a mile or two beyond our border."

If nothing else, this comment says something about what Britain's first administrators were up against in dealing with the not-so-lesser breeds who occupied the hills west of the Indus.

If the word "Pathan" is used in its broadest ethnic sense, the country inhabited by this tribal nation for at least five centuries can be said to embrace the eastern half of Afghanistan and a respectable slice of present-day northwest Pakistan. Mainly, however, it is the narrow belt of rugged high country straddling the Afghanistan-Pakistan border that has given the entire Pathan people its image as a sort of Asiatic Cosa Nostra.

Just as the American "families" have divided the United States into private spheres of influence, so too do some half-dozen Pathan tribal groups hold sway over fairly well defined areas of the Frontier. Reading from north to south, they are the Mohmands and Yusufzais in the swooping mountains of Bajaur, Dir, Swat and Buner, the Afridis of the Khyber Pass, the Orakzais living in the vales of Tirah (shared in uneasy coexistence with Afridis) and the Wazirs and Mahsuds who occupy Waziristan and spill over into Bannu to the east. Waziristan marks the southernmost end of the tribal region. Topographically, its majestic desolation cannot be distinguished from the vastness of Baluchistan, which in fact is sometimes considered part of the Frontier. But Baluchistan has a much different political background and its predominantly non-Pathan population places it almost literally in another world.

Besides the abovementioned major tribes, at least two dozen smaller Pathan duchies and baronies are scattered across the Frontier like small change—among them the Turis of the Arcadian Kurram Valley above Waziristan, the Mullagoris and Shinwaris of the Khyber, the Khattaks of Kohat (also occupied by Afridis) and the Bhitannis on Waziristan's eastern border. With the partial exception of the Turis, no Frontier people has ever sought or accepted alien rule, not even the rule of fellow-Muslims in Afghanistan and Pakistan. What is more, no outsider has truly conquered them. Ever.

Even to hard-case British veterans of punitive campaigns across the face of the Empire, there was not much in any Pathan's appearance or bearing that suggested submissiveness. Between a dust-layered blue turban and a shaggy, scrofulous black beard (usually dyed when it began to whiten) were fixed the eyes of a hawk, the beak of a vulture and the mouth of a shark. The owner of these features, as a rule, stood slightly taller than a jump center and moved with the silent grace of a tiger on a stalk. Beneath his long, unwashed white robe he was likely to have on a pair of tattered, ankle-length pajama pants and a loose, dirt-caked tunic festooned with charms and amulets. The cotton cummerbund holding trousers and tunic in place was also a repository for an oversize flintlock pistol, two or three knives and a long curved tulwar that could mince a floating feather. In addition to the sidearms, there was a long-barrelled jezail, held casually over the shoulder or cradled in the crook of the arm —always loaded and ready to fire. Roses, worn behind the ears, often rounded off the getup. They did nothing to dispel the notion that here was a creature whose sole purpose and pleasure in life was the inflicting of a death as uncomfortable and prolonged as it might be possible to arrange.

In their ten decades of association with this man, the British could never quite make up their minds about him. "Ruthless, cowardly robbery, cold-blooded, treacherous murder are to him the salt of life," wrote one Frontier hand; "Brought up from his earliest childhood amid scenes of appalling treachery, nothing can ever change him . . . a shameless, cruel savage." Another Briton saw the tribesman differently: "To set against his vices the Pathan is brave, sober, religious according to his lights and, on the whole, clean living; he has a ready sense of humour . . . is a lover of sport. . . . And, to those who can speak and understand his queer guttural language, he is amazingly good company." These are only two of literally thousands of conflicting British assessments of the tribal character. A Frontier official visiting a Pathan village was not always certain whether he would be dismembered and castrated or invited to enjoy grilled chicken, rice, *chapatis* and tea while watching a sword dance of balletlike elegance and fluidity. It may be that an Indian Army officer came closest to seeing the tribal persona when he wrote that Pathan "habits are not really much worse than were those of the various English tribes" some two millennia earlier.

Certainly British administrators on the Frontier were quick to recognize many Pathan traditions and customs as anything but prehistoric. The tribesman abided scrupulously by his own social contract, *Pakhtunwali*, a body of unwritten laws at once more rigid than the dictates of Emily Post and more permissive than the Marquess of Queensberry Rules. No Pathan worth his salt would dream of flouting the Three Commandments of Pakhtunwali. *Melmastia* demanded open-handed hospitality to all who crossed the doorstep of his whitewashed, mud-walled house; the deadliest enemy must dine on the mutton-rice-boiled-date stew and unleavened bread served to the most honored guest. The tribesman was no less faithful to the code of *nanawatai*, granting asylum whenever it was sought by a fugitive from the justice of an alien ruler, or even from the wrath of a fellow Pathan. But it was the Third Commandment of Pakhtunwali —*badal*, or revenge—that formed the keystone of the tribal arch and perhaps the key to a sullen vanity far touchier than the Latin machismo. Unless a Pathan wished to lose his self-esteem and court ostracism, he was bound to exact payment for the most insignificant slight to his bloated ego. And affronts were erased, almost invariably, in the blood of the offender.

The most common sparks that touched off the short Pathan fuse were (and still are) *zar, zan* and *zamin*—gold, women and land—although not necessarily in that order of importance and by no means the only provocations that could set jezails banging and tulwars flashing until the dust cleared over someone's butchered cadaver. Once a personal score was settled, however, the matter was promptly forgotten—unless the victim's kinfolk decided that badal obliged them to wipe out the stain on their own good name. This could be accomplished by the payment of blood money, sometimes in the form of land or livestock, but more often a Sicilian-style vendetta was likely to be set in motion. It could easily draw in other families—even clans and whole tribes—and last several generations before *izzat*, or honor, was satisfied, or before several clans were annihilated. Dr. Theodore Pennell, the most celebrated of Frontier missionaries, once asked a tribesman to explain all the bloodshed. He was answered with a shrug: "God has decreed that there shall always be discord among the Pathans, so what can we do?"

Apparently not a great deal. As a nineteenth-century Frontier army officer put it, "every man ploughed with his sword by his side and matchlock handy, with a piece of dried cow-dung burning near, ready to light the match, while the cattle . . . were escorted out to graze by an armed party." Only a few years ago, a Pathan lawyer practicing in London returned to the Frontier because Pakhtunwali demanded that he enter a feud as the last living member of his line. Pathan mothers still croon their infants to sleep by reciting rhythmically the names of enemies slain by their fathers and grandfathers—even if those foes are close relations, which is often the case. It is no accident that *tarbur*, the Pushtu word for "enemy," also means "cousin."

Permeating every nook and cranny of Pathan life, this Hatfield-McCoy mentality has always made itself particularly felt in tribal politics. Among the Frontier institutions that first caught British notice was the aboriginal legislature called the *jirga*, a sort of outdoor town meeting with no fixed sessions that could assemble in various shapes and sizes. Jirgas were supposed to adjudicate land, property and bride-price disputes, punish crimes, ratify treaties with other Pathan communities and generally lay down the law. In reality they were often without the power to do any of these things. Nearly every able-bodied male Pathan had a voice in the jirga but no vote, decisions being arrived at by consensus rather than ballot. What this meant was that the tribesmen with the strongest lungs could always reach for their knives. Sir Olaf Caroe, the last British Governor of the Frontier and author of the definitive history of the Pathans, has written of Waziristan's 5,000-man Mahsud jirga that it tended to "repeat the excesses of the Athenian agora, without the erudition of Athens, and with more than one Cleon to act as demagogue."

A facade of authority did exist. Jirgas were usually presided over by the elders and headmen called *maliks*, but their voices, as often as not, were the faintest of all except when the majority happened to share their views. As it was, the majority was inclined to abide by the wishes of the true powers behind any jirga: the holy men known variously as mullahs and fakirs. Practically without exception, these religious leaders were the real opinion shapers of the Pathan community. Their counsel could be sagacious and highly constructive. Just as often it was self-serving. Almost invariably it was accepted without question.

The extraordinary influence of Muslim priests in Frontier society arose largely from the Pathan's imperfect knowledge of his own religion, which ignorance could be ascribed to isolation from the rest of the world and an astronomical illiteracy rate. To be sure, certain basic forms of worship were observed. Five times daily, the faithful turned toward Mecca and prostrated themselves in prayer. Frontier mosques—usually hovels built of rough, undressed stones glued together with dried mud—were always full. But for the most part, the Pathan's creed was and still is based less on intimacy with the Koran than on a vast body of superstition. Pennell called some tribesmen so ignorant of Islam that "more civilized Muhammadans are hardly willing to admit their right to a place in the congregation of the faithful."

Among the most treasured religious artifacts of the Frontier were charms and amulets that healed the sick and warded off every imaginable evil; mullahs became rich by blessing scraps of rag and paper for this purpose and selling them. The trunks of certain magic trees were studded with nails hammered in by tribesmen who thus registered their wishes. Pathans made regular pilgrimages to the shrines called *ziarats*, usually situated atop cliffs or mountains; after a stiff climb, the votary left a scrap of colored rag in the branches of a nearby shrub or mulberry tree as evidence of his petition to Allah. The graves of holy men possessed special powers, particularly if they grew in size; one grave in Peshawar lengthened at the rate of an inch per month and eventually came to be known as the "nine-yard shrine." During the late 1930s, the British wanted to build an airstrip in the Kurram Valley, but they had chosen the site of a saint's tomb and were helpless until they arranged for one of their own Pathan political officers to disguise himself as a mullah and explain to the inhabitants that the holy man's spirit was unhappy in that particular place.

The grave of a saint, indeed, may have been more important to a Pathan than his mosque, for it was only on this tomb that tribesmen could swear their most binding oaths. It is known that the members of one Afridi clan, without such a shrine, once invited a celebrated *sayyid* (a claimant of descent from the Prophet) to visit them as an honored holy man. No sooner had he arrived than he was decapitated and buried, and the clan was thenceforth able to boast its own hallowed ground.

The tribal clergy did nothing to relieve this theological poverty. In fact they exploited it. To be a good mullah or fakir, one did not need formal instruction (although many priests were learned) so much as a gift of gab and a talent for expressing a fanaticism that not only lent muscle to whatever passages of the Koran one chose to garble to one's own ends but that appealed to the tribesman's lust for violence. As recently as the late 1930s, the Pathans in a mullah's congregation could almost always be converted into gun-toting crusaders. No other individual in tribal society commanded the respect, obedience, adoration and fear that were lavishly bestowed on the mullahs and fakirs.

Thus there is room to wonder why the fragmented Pathan nation could not have been brought together as a single state by some particularly charismatic priest. In fact, this nearly happened several times in Pathan history, but whatever unity was achieved could only be short-lived, since the holy man's writ seldom ran beyond his own community. Generally speaking, the hill tribes can be thought of as a microcosm of the present-day Arab states, almost congenitally incapable of acting in concert despite their shared objective of obliterating a common foe, whether imagined or real. When Pathans attacked or resisted an enemy, they usually did so not as Pathans but as Yusufzais or Mohmands or Afridis or Orakzais or Mahsuds or Wazirs. Yet even at the clan level, it was the holy man who was most likely to fan the flames of war. He was the tribal trigger finger.

During their century of precarious control over the Frontier, the British never ceased to marvel at the Pathan's mastery of guerrilla warfare. Typical of uncountable tributes (not all of them intentional) was a pep talk delivered by an Indian Army general during a punitive expedition in the 1890s. To encourage several crack British regiments that had just taken a bad mauling from a small Afridi lashkar, he reminded the men that they were facing, "perhaps the best skirmishers and the best natural shots, in the world, and that the country they inhabit is the most difficult on the face of the globe." The general was echoed by a war correspondent with the force, who told his British readers that the Pathans were "mountaineers of the best type. Born and bred amongst steep and rugged hills . . . inured to extremes of heat and cold, and accustomed from childhood to carry arms and to be on guard against . . . treacherous kinsmen . . . it is small wonder that they are hardy, alert, self-reliant, and active, full of resource, keen as hawks, and cruel as leopards."

Certainly they had every opportunity to enhance that image. When not defending their homeland against Moguls, Sikhs, Britons or other Pathans, they were pursuing their national and natural calling as bandits. Frontier authorities have often likened the Pathans to the early highland clans of Scotland because both peoples, occupying generally barren hills that offered marginal incentive to farming and other peaceful pursuits, had to study a more violent profession. From the earliest days of their settlement in the region, the tribes had turned their attention to the warm, fertile plains of the Indus Valley. Here has always dwelt a gentler, more industrious and comparatively wealthier populace, including even some Pathan clans whose habitat has tended to dull the edge of their belligerence. Vegetable farms, fruit orchards and livestock herds—not to mention the cash profits earned therefrom—were the targets of never-ending tribal commando raids from the high country to the west. Peshawar and other large towns yielded up juicier plums in the form of Hindu merchants and moneylenders who were kidnapped with almost clockwork regularity. Ransom was swiftly forthcoming after the man's relatives were sent one or two of his fingers or ears; should payments be slow, they were likely to receive his head.

But probably the most regular source of Pathan income was extortion, which masqueraded as the collection of tolls for safe conduct through the Frontier passes. Although the Afridis of the Khyber were the most celebrated and dreaded for this practice, the same system applied for centuries in every defile that could be negotiated by an itinerant peddler, a caravan or an army. Tolls were collected with such consistent thoroughness, and the penalties made so clear in terms of slaughter and inventive disfigurement, as to give the Pathans the image of a barracuda in Shylock's clothing.

All of which may be libel. Caroe repudiates the banditry indictment out of hand, pointing to considerable fertility in the hill country and attributing tribal belligerence to love of freedom alone. There is much to be said for that argument. Corps and livestock have never been entirely alien to the Frontier. Even before the British introduced modern farming and ranching methods, market days in some of the larger hill towns witnessed spirited buying, selling and trading of figs, dates, grapes, corn, wheat, rice, sugar cane, millet and the fodder clover called *shaftala*. The *mazarai*, or dwarf palm, produced such salable articles as sandals, ropes and baskets. Bleating herds of scrawny sheep and goats were driven many miles to a market's livestock pens. The members of one Pathan tribe, the Ghilzai Powindas, were the teamsters of Central Asia. Every autumn, their caravans, numbering tens of thousands of camels, ponies and mules, came down from Afghanistan to the bazaars of the Indus Valley, where the tribesmen traded carpets, lambskins, dried fruits and fresh grapes for salt, tea, iron cooking pots and other staples and utensils. Caroe makes a good point when he writes that "the myth of the hungry Pathan dies hard."

But the picture of the cornucopia can also mislead. Except for the Kurram Valley, Tirah, parts of Bannu, and one or two other garden spots, the country of the Pathans cannot be called a dreamland of agriculture and commerce. As recently as 1932, another Frontier veteran, C. Collin Davies, wrote that "so long as hungry tribesmen inhabit barren and almost waterless hills which command open and fertile plains, so long will they resort to plundering incursions to obtain the necessaries of life." And even conceding Caroe's erudition and intimacy with the Frontier, even accepting patriotism as the sole incentive to Pathan depredations, the fact remains that the tribes were and are and probably always will be wild men.

Besides which, the Britons who first came to administer the hills seldom had the leisure to speculate on the reasons for the delinquency of their charges.

9

Gallows and Humming Tops

D<small>URING</small> B<small>RITAIN'S</small> <small>IMPERIAL</small> salad days, if there was one thing the British held in higher esteem than the Empire's commercial and financial returns, it was the order they imposed (or tried to impose) on previously backward and savage peoples. How else, after all, could aboriginal anarchy become a sound investment if not by being systematized and pigeonholed and quadruplicated? And so it was that when ownership of the Frontier estate reverted from the Sikhs to the Indian Government, one of the first official British acts was to divide the whole region into five administrative areas.

From north to south, these were the districts of Hazara, Peshawar, Kohat, Bannu and Dera Ismail Khan. With the exception of Hazara, the only cis-Indus district, the new parishes sprawled out from the Indus' west bank to embrace a tract of Pathan territory that was about twice the size of Wales and which contained a population a little smaller than that of present-day metropolitan New York. The Peshawar district, which included the Frontier's capital, had its own commissioner. The others were presided over by officials usually known as deputy or assistant commissioners. Each was expected to serve as prime minister, cabinet, director of internal revenue, commander-in-chief of the armed forces, chief justice and foreman of the jury. He may have had one or two British aides. His armies seldom numbered more than a few hundred riflemen or mounted police. In effect, he had to act on his own in carrying out four principal duties: collecting taxes, introducing the

[104]

rudiments of Western justice, encouraging trade and keeping the peace. Each of these tasks soon proved to be an Augean stable.

Taxation came as no jolt to the Pathans. The Sikhs had been milking them of revenues for three decades, although assessments had been excessive and collections, as a rule, could be made only at gunpoint. The Indian Government lost no time in repealing the harsh Sikh revenue laws and imposing a more equitable tax system. In the machinery of juris-prudence, jirgas, with all their attendant anarchy, were not outlawed but complemented by the establishment of Frontier courts and legal pro-cedures based on the Indian Penal Code. Tribesmen were encouraged to take their disputes over zar, zan and zamin to British judges or assistant commissioners; criminals had no choice. To prime the pump of a bone-dry economy, trade fairs were held in some districts. Border clinics were opened to treat a veritable river of running sores and open wounds.

But keeping the peace held top priority. While the British did not deceive themselves that they could transform the Frontier battleground into a model of domestic tranquility, they knew at least that they could count on Pathan mercenaries in police, militia and even regular army forces. Perhaps the highest hopes, though, were held for the practice of paying annual cash allowances or subsidies to tribal communities as reward for good behavior. Payments were usually contingent not only on a clan's abstention from mischief, but on specific services to Govern-ment, such as allowing roads to be built through tribal land, guarding communications and refusing sanctuary to outlaws. Critics thought of these payments as blackmail pure and simple; Government defended the system as realpolitik.

The Pathans themselves seemed delighted with the innovation: between 1850 and 1875, Punjab authorities made formal treaties of cooperation with every major tribe in the trans-Indus region. "The agreement," writes Caroe, "would be reached in open jirga, and to it the maliks and elders of the tribe would affix their seals or, often enough, their thumb impressions. Jokes would pass, the first payment would be made, and the general atmosphere of good will would seem to promise a perpetual peace."

Caroe adds: "It was hardly ever so."

For the tribes found no reason to welcome their new masters. Relief from Sikh taxation did not mean the abolition of taxes, and the British proved more skilled and more bothersome as collectors. The new judicial codes laid an egg: what need had a Pathan for lawyers, bewigged judges, the rules of evidence and a bewildering, winding road of appeal to the High Court in Lahore? Such frills might have suited the Feringhi well enough, but feuds had always sufficed to keep the peace in the hills. Trade was a fine thing indeed, but had not the tribes themselves always allowed caravans to pass for a reasonable fee? And why should a true believer consult an infidel *hakim* when he could have the jezail bullet in his throat or the tulwar slash across his belly treated by a fakir who applied wads of flaming oil-soaked cloth to the wound?

In short, the Pathans looked on the new rulers of the Punjab as not much less an enemy than the Sikhs. By definition, a foe had to be anyone who sought to bring order out of the chaos that was the breath of life to a tribesman. Even the rupees that the Sahib handed out so generously came only with the Catch-22 of civility. So the Pathans responded to the British reforms by disregarding them, to the British lawmakers by trying to pot them or carve them up. It was not without reason that the Frontier had come to be known as Yaghistan, the land of the rebels.

The only reason why Government made so great an impact on the tribes during the 1850s—indeed, why it made any impact at all—was that the hill country at this time was managed by a remarkable pro-consulry of titans.

Although members of the Indian Civil Service, most of the men who upheld Pax Britannica on the Frontier in the 1850s were also soldiers. Colonel Frederick Mackeson, the first Commissioner of Peshawar, had been known for his intimacy with the Khyber region ever since he drew up the tactical plan that allowed Pollock to lead the Army of Retribution through the pass in 1842. Mackeson's deputy, Captain George Lawrence, has already been mentioned for his role in the defense of Kabul. The diminutive Colonel James Abbott, lord and master of Hazara, was described by Henry Lawrence as "gentle as a girl in thought," but acted differently; in the Second Sikh War, he had led a small band of mounted Yusufzai irregulars that forced the surrender of an entire Sikh army. Likewise, Captain Herbert Edwardes, by the sheer force of his personality, had raised the tribal commando that sent the Sikh insurgents sprawling at Multan. Another Afghan War veteran, Captain John Nicholson, had also personally led a regiment of Pathan horsemen that helped chase Dost Muhammad's legions out of the Punjab after the battle of Gujerat.

This accumulation of military know-how served the officers well in their capacities as lawmakers. It could not have been otherwise. One trouble with the Pathans, as all Frontier officials quickly learned, was that, like the British, they did not think they were superior to everyone else on earth but knew they were. Yet if order were to be brought to the Frontier, the Indian Government had to make it unmistakably clear that only one element was in charge. No one could put that idea across to a fighting Pathan better than a fighting Briton. The Lawrences were blessed in being able to field the flower of an English ruling class in an age when to rule meant exactly that.

Nicholson was the giant of them all, in physique as well as impact of character. A model for the expression "tall, dark and handsome," he was also a brooding thunderbolt of a man, a Cromwellian whose notions of summary justice could be barbaric. During the Indian Mutiny he was to protest that blowing sepoys from the mouths of cannon was too forbearing; "Let us propose a bill," he wrote Edwardes, "for . . . flaying alive, impalement or burning." Although Nicholson never skinned or fried a Pathan, he skewered more than one with his saber, while the force of his Old Testament fury always left its mark and is remembered even to this day.

In 1852, Nicholson was assigned to the Bannu district southwest of Peshawar. One of his predecessors in this stronghold of Wazir bandits had been Edwardes, who had managed to subdue the tribes with an army and had also called them "the most ignorant, depraved and bloodthirsty" of all Frontier Pathans. Since Edwardes' departure three years earlier, the Wazirs had lived up to that name, making a farce of British authority in an unbridled orgy of raiding, slaying and disfiguring. But within six months of Nicholson's arrival they had been tamed. Edwardes later wrote that "I only knocked down the walls of the Bannu forts. John Nicholson has since reduced the *people*." It can almost be said that Nicholson simply stared the Wazirs down.

Almost but not quite. There still stands an ancient tree in Bannu; its single remaining limb is deeply scored by the rope marks of the uncountable hangings that Nicholson ordered in his kangaroo courts. He had thousands of lesser offenders flogged senseless. When tribesmen took petitions to Bannu district headquarters, their eyes were invariably drawn to a human head mounted on Nicholson's desk. Nicholson had personally removed it from the neck of a notorious Wazir highwayman. Hesketh Pearson has written of him that he "was the first man to cow the north west frontier of India into good behaviour, and he was also the last."

Nothing could conquer him. The sun had seldom risen when he began his work day by riding ten, twenty or thirty miles before breakfast to stamp on a feud or settle a land dispute or ice a bandit. He would sit in court for ten or twelve consecutive hours, in temperatures of over 100 degrees, hearing case after endless case. His verdicts were swift, final, enraged; few tribesmen ever dared appeal. He had no use for bureaucracy. "This is the way I treat these things," he once told a colleague as he kicked a stack of Government regulations across his headquarters office. A not atypical report to John Lawrence (whom he loathed, and who returned the compliment) read:

Sir:

I have the honour to inform you that I have just shot a man who came to kill me.

Your Obedient Servant,

JOHN NICHOLSON

Such high-handed doings once drew a complaint from Dalhousie: "I know that Nicholson is a first-rate guerrilla leader, but we don't want a guerrilla policy."

Nicholson was even less patient with those who failed to show him proper respect. He once had a barber shave the beard of a mullah for neglecting to salaam him. At another time, a deputation of angry maliks met with him to air some grievance, and one elder expressed his rage by spitting on the floor. Nicholson ordered him to lick up the spit and was instantly obeyed, whereupon Nicholson threw him bodily from the room. He was probably the only Frontier administrator whom the Pathans openly feared. A malik once told another British official that "there is not a man in the hills who does not shiver in his pajamas when he hears Nikal Seyn's name mentioned."

In contrast to Nicholson's excesses was the behavior of his closest friend and temperamental opposite, Edwardes. Big in stature and heart, joyous and extroverted in nature, Edwardes preferred to win Pathan obedience with acts of fellowship, empathy and trust. He introduced the first Christian missions to the Frontier and pioneered in tribal education as the founder of Peshawar's Edwardes College, which eventually became a sort of Pathan Oxford and later produced many prominent Frontier political leaders. Yet for a proper Victorian, Edwardes could be broad-minded. "Ursulla Khan begged to be allowed to sit on the carpet and contemplate me," he informed his journal, "as he had fallen in love with me. The only way to take these things is philosophically. No offence is intended."

Edwardes also knew when to be less tolerant. During a tax collecting tour of Bannu, he had once issued a proclamation to the delinquent Wazirs of the district, "I told you last spring," he wrote, "that if you did not accept the easy terms which I offered you, and pay up your arrears, I should come to collect the balance in the winter. . . . I am now on my way to keep my word; and two forces are marching upon Bunnoo. . . . You see, therefore, that you had much better have agreed with me in the spring." The arrears were promptly forthcoming. Yet even with the "ignorant, depraved and bloodthirsty" Wazirs, Edwardes had with-held the stick until the carrot had been dangled. Nicholson, doubtless, would have reversed the procedure.

But whether it was Nicholson's bare knuckles or Edwardes' gloved fist, it remained a fist, and as such it had to command the obedience—even the reluctant admiration—of a people for whom the exercise of naked force was a mark of virtue. The Lawrences' proconsuls occupied a unique position on the Frontier because, as Caroe puts it, they were "more than half Pathans themselves." The pious Edwardes enjoyed almost as much trust among the Wazirs as any of their mullahs. Mackeson, knifed to death in 1853 by a tribal fanatic, was universally known as *Kishin* ("uncle")

"Is Dost Muhammad dead that there is no longer justice in the land?" The Amir with one of his uncountable progeny. (*National Army Museum*)

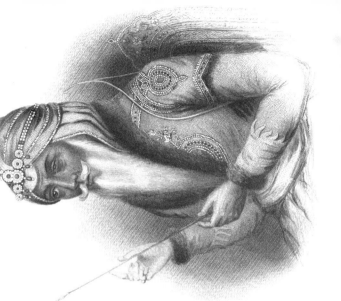

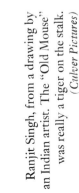

Ranjit Singh, from a drawing by an Indian artist. The "Old Mouse" was really a tiger on the stalk. (*Culver Pictures*)

Cold steel and eau de cologne: Army of the Indus enters Bolan Pass during invasion of Afghanistan, 1839. (*National Army Museum*)

The fortress at Ghazni. General Keane had his own hour to rue. (*National Army Museum*)

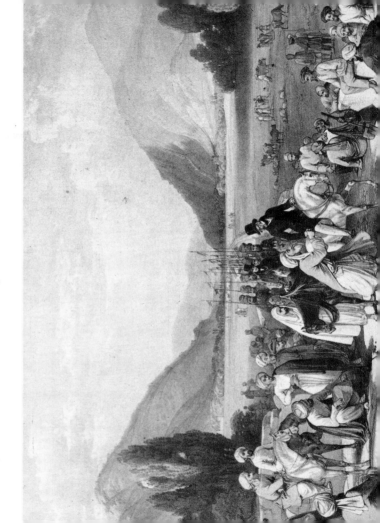

"The Amir! The Amir!" Dost Muhammad gives himself up to Macnaghten, Kabul, 1840. (*National Army Museum*)

Burnes' last few moments on earth, November 2, 1841, as depicted by an imaginative Victorian artist. (*Historical Pictures Service, Chicago*)

"Bezeer!" In a fateful double cross, Akbar orders
seizure of Macnaghten, December 23, 1841.
(*Historical Pictures Service, Chicago*)

"Fighting Bob" Sale and his pugnacious lady.
(*Culver Pictures*)

One hundred years and a month before Singapore: Dr. Brydon reaches Jalalabad after wipeout of Army of the Indus, January 1842. Painting by Lady Elizabeth Butler. (*The Tate Gallery, London*)

Pathans: keen as hawks, cruel as leopards, shameless, sober, religious, clean-living and practically never so well dressed. From *Illustrated London News*. (*Culver Pictures*)

"Nikal Seyn" made the tribesmen shiver in their pajamas.
(*National Army Museum*)

Even the enemy wanted to join them: Guides sowars scout route of march for infantry column in Frontier punitive expedition. From *Illustrated London News*. (*Culver Pictures*)

The Place of Slaughter on a quiet day. Gurkha officer's photograph of Crag Picquet shows terrain almost completely defoliated by artillery in Ambela action, late 1863. (*National Army Museum*)

Lytton, the man who would be Mogul. (*National Army Museum*)

Sher Ali, aides and younger children. He painted himself into an indefensible corner. (*National Army Museum*)

Showdown in the Khyber. At left, Cavagnari and party are about to be turned back from Ali Masjid by Sher Ali's commander. Drawing based on a sketch by Cavagnari and Maj. C. W. Wilson. *(Historical Pictures Service, Chicago)*

Not quite the real thing: Indian Army artillery covers frontal feint at Peiwar Kotal while Roberts and main body (far out of sight to right) deal victorious flanking blow against Afghan defenses, December 1878. From *Illustrated London News*. (*Culver Pictures*)

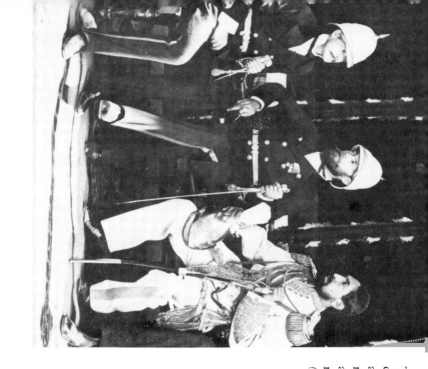

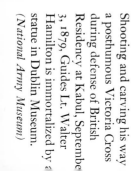

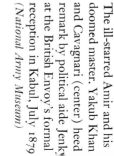

Shooting and carving his way
a posthumous Victoria Cross
during defense of British
Residency at Kabul, Septembe
3, 1879, Guides Lt. Walter
Hamilton is immoralized by
statue in Dublin Museum.
(National Army Museum)

The ill-starred Amir and his
doomed master, Yakub Khan
and Cavagnari (center) heed
remark by political aide Jenk
at the British Envoy's formal
reception in Kabul, July 1879
(National Army Museum)

The favorite rite of Empire. Roberts (invisible beneath archway) delivers his proclamation of conquest in shadow of Kabul's Bala Hissar, October 1879. From *Illustrated London News.* (*Culver Pictures*)

A section of the Sherpur defenses, Kabul, winter 1879–80. No croakers weakened the lines. Photograph by J. Burke. (*National Army Museum*)

Charge in the wrong direction. Contemporary painting shows British horse artillery and cavalry during rout by Ayub Khan's army at Maiwand, June 1880. (*Culver Pictures*)

by the wild Afridis he ruled. Another *kishin* was Abbott; Hazara Pathans used to tell British officers that he had a heart "like a fakir's." Nicholson, the most hated man in the hills, was literally worshipped. Many tribesmen belonged to a sect known as "Nikal Seyn," and when they groveled before the living god he had them flogged for their pagan obeisance. After his death, more than a few Nikal Seyns converted to Christianity.

Not a little of this uneasy good feeling was reciprocated. Edwardes remarked in his journal on "how much faith I have had occasion to place in the rudest and wildest of these people, how nobly it was deserved, and how useless I should have been without it." Next to Nicholson, Edwardes' closest confidante in the hills may have been a Wazir chieftain named Sowan Khan, "an enormous man, with a head like a lion and a hand like a polar bear . . . a more splendid specimen of human nature in the rough I never saw." The fire-eating Nicholson himself raised a Pathan foster-son whose father had been killed in action against the Sikhs. He once wrote Edwardes that "a wretched little Waziri child" had just tried to poison him, and in the next sentence asked whether "there are any humming-tops, Jews-harps, or other toys, at Peshawar, which would take with Waziri children." Nicholson even unbent on learning that the Wazirs, "well tamed as they have been, speak kindly and gratefully of me. I can't help a feeling of pride, that a savage people whom I was obliged to deal with so sternly, should appreciate and give me credit for good intentions."

Again Caroe hits the mark: "Englishmen and Pathans looked each other between the eyes, and there they found—a man. Sometimes the pledge they made was broken . . on the one side the assassin struck, on the other the avenger. But the pledge still held, the respect, the affection, survived."

Frontier administration offered fringe benefits. The officials lived in the informally opulent style of British India, with their retinues of turbaned *munshis* and *syces* and *chowkidars* and *punkah* boys and every other imaginable domestic and clerical underling to attend to needs and creature comforts. In leisure hours they took tiffin on the verandas of bungalows that were furnished in the most exquisite Victorian bad taste. The houses themselves were large and airy, ringed by immaculately tailored lawns, illuminated by gardens, shaded by colossal banyan trees. For recreation they could ride to hounds (the foxes were jackals) or hunt in Pathan fashion, using teams of hawks and greyhounds in pursuit of antelope and ravine deer. Bigger game, including markhor, bear and an occasional tiger, could be found in the foothills of the Hindu Kush. The bleak, rugged majesty of the Frontier highlands inspired Edwardes to reams of lyrical Victorian doggerel, other officials to sketch books crammed with water colors and pen-and-ink drawings. For those administrators schooled in the classics—and nearly all were—the whole trans-Indus region offered a feast of antiquity: Graeco-Bactrian sculpture, Mogul architecture, Buddhist stupas, Persian, Greek and Hindu coinage. Relaxation in the hills was nothing if not a tonic.

But even more stimulating was the sheer adventure of the job itself, the love-hate relationship with a savage but virile race, the ongoing negotiations with a people who were capable at any given moment of calling a recess with their knives and jezails. Even on quiet days it was not a life for a mollycoddle. "Dreadful toothache," reads an extract from Edwardes' journal. "Cortlandt and native doctor had three pulls. Broke two pieces off. Tooth where it was. Ditto the pain. Petitions all day." Yet one could sense that things were somehow getting done despite obstacles large and small. "To be flung into a country where anarchy prevails," wrote Edwardes to a friend in 1852, "and introduce the rights of man to man . . . is doubtless high employ. But to succeed this rough pioneering . . . to civilize those who have been subdued; to perpetuate peace by registering all rights . . . to lay the broad founda- tions of national prosperity . . . to effect, in short, a social change which the missionary alone can crown, must be allowed to be a lot of exceeding great utility. . . . And these are our labours now."

Lofty generalizations were all well and good, but Edwardes could also come to the bottom line of Frontier crusading. In 1855, describing Nicholson's work among the volatile Bannu Wazirs, he observed that the tribes had been brought "to such a state of good order and respect for the laws, that in the last year of his charge not only was there no murder, burglary or highway robbery, but not an *attempt* at any of these crimes."

This was no small thing, and Edwardes can be forgiven for inad- vertently creating the impression that he and his colleagues had brought permanent tranquility to the lands across the Indus—although it should be said that they came closer to that goal than did any of their successors over the ensuing century of the British sojourn in India. But Pax Britannica on the Frontier was always the Empire's frailest edifice. It needed more than merely administrators who happened also to be soldiers. The hills in fact cried out for a massive military presence.

10

The Piffers of Yaghistan

"I'LL TELL YOU what it is, young man. You may go without your breeches, but damn it, sir, you *shall* carry your sword!"

These words were delivered by General Sir Colin Campbell, commandant of the Peshawar garrison in the early 1850s, to a subaltern who had violated the standing order that all officers in Peshawar never go unarmed, on or off duty. The precaution was necessary. Situated outside the walls of the city itself, Peshawar's original garrison site may have been the most vulnerable defense work ever laid down by the British since they fortified the Kabul Cantonment in 1839. Although Peshawar was the largest military station in British India, there were times when it might have seemed safer against tribal forays had it been placed in the middle of the Khyber Pass. Campbell had laid out the site in 1849, with a view to cramming all troops, British and Indian, into the smallest possible space and thus reducing the size of the target offered to Pathan raiding bands. The most visible effect of this overcrowding was to give Peshawar a well-deserved reputation as the least sanitary post on the subcontinent. As a deterrent to tribal mischief it was practically useless.

One can almost think of this garrison, huddled inside its frail perimeter, as a stranded whale with the sharks closing in. When he wrote his autobiography in 1897, Field Marshal Lord Frederick Roberts, the Frontier's greatest British hero, recalled his early service as a junior officer in Peshawar: "In addition to the cordon of sentries round the cantonment, strong picquets were posted on all the principal roads leading towards the hills; and every house had to be guarded by a *chokidar*, or watchman,

[111]

belonging to one of the robber tribes. The maintaining [of] this watchman was a sort of blackmail, without consenting to which no one's horses or other property were safe. . . . No one was allowed to venture beyond the line of sentries when the sun had set, and even in broad daylight it was not safe to go any distance from the station."

And nothing, it seemed, could inhibit trespass of breathtaking audacity against Peshawar. "During the long dark nights in winter," wrote General Sir Sydney Cotton, who succeeded Campbell when the latter went to command the "thin red line" at Balaclava, "the demi-savages of the Khyber Pass, uncultivated ruffians, almost as naked as the day they were born, quite unmolested visited the cantonment. . . . They robbed and they plundered, and they got back (ninety-nine times out of one hundred) in safety to their mountain fastnesses. . . . The whole [British] force might, at any time, in their beds, have had their throats cut by the predatory tribes of Central Asia, in thousands or tens of thousands."

A legitimate question arises. What kind of army was it that would submit so tamely to this sort of thing?

Actually, when released from its Peshawar straitjacket, the Indian Army gave a good account of itself in the field. In fact, during the three decades between 1849 and 1879, no fewer than forty major punitive expeditions were mounted to deal with miscreant Pathan tribes along the 200-mile front between Swat and Waziristan. While the British always emerged victorious, they often did so with the greatest difficulty. But at least they never lost. Against tribal irregulars that was no small accomplishment.

A punitive force on the march—sometimes a full brigade strong—could be an intimidating sight as it wound its way, like a great iron worm, beneath mile-high rock escarpments in tribal country. Rifle barrels glinted in the sun like the teeth of a giant's comb as British, Sikh and Gurkha regiments stepped off to the reverberating squeal of bagpipes and the measured thump of tenor drums. Nine-pound cannons lurched and groaned in their carriages on the backs of angrily trumpeting elephants. Camel and mule trains, heavily laden with ammunition crates, tents, food and medical supplies, formed a dinosaur tail that twisted almost invisibly in a fogbank of dust. Saber blades and lances winked up and down the long line. Union Jacks, regimental colors and snapping cavalry guidons gave the whole column the aspect of a belligerent picnic.

The force was also a perfect target for methodical annihilation by every hidden Pathan marksman within jezail range.

Or would have been had it been allowed to enter tribal territory unchaperoned and without special tutoring. Despite overwhelming superiority in numbers and metal, the Company army in its original form was a lumbering, unwieldy engine, the worst possible instrument of guerrilla strategy on the Pathans' own ground. To lend spring to its muscle it needed the help of a mobile, self-contained auxiliary corps with a soldiery that could give the tribes a bit of their own back and a bit more. This lesson had been driven home as early as the rout of Elphinstone's army in 1842, and after the First Sikh War the specialist combat team known as the Punjab Frontier Force began to take shape.

Nicknamed the "Piffers," the Punjab Frontier Force came to number 11,000 picked officers and men of various British and Indian regiments. Its mainstay was the predominantly Pathan Queen's Own Corps of Guides.

The Guides were the Green Berets of the Frontier. They had been created in 1846 by Henry Lawrence, while he was Resident at Lahore, when he recognized the need for a small force of fighting men that would also do what its name implied: guide regular units in the field and provide intelligence for their commanders. The task of raising the Guides was given to a twenty-five-year-old assistant political agent in Peshawar named Harry Lumsden, who also held a lieutenant's commission and had served with Pollock's Army of Retribution in Afghanistan. Lumsden saw a rosy future in his new command. "It will be the finest appointment in the country," he wrote his father, "being the right hand of the army and the left hand of the political. I consider it as good as a majority and C.B.-ship." Lumsden also asked his father to send him "the very best telescope you can set your hands on. I do not mind . . . paying the price for it, so long as it is good enough for the officer commanding 'the Guides.'"

Although the Guides at first consisted of only one cavalry squadron and three companies of infantry—barely 300 men all told—Lumsden lost no time drawing attention to the force. Considering it tactically unwise for his troops to advertise their presence in the hills by wearing scarlet tunics, he scandalized the British military establishment by outfitting the Guides in a rough local fabric called khaki. Although the men took formal drill instruction from the 60th Royal Rifles, Lumsden also sought to make training as realistic as possible. The Guides' initial field exercise was a surprise night attack on a village of tax-dodging Afridis a few miles from Peshawar, and the tribal recruits passed the examination with high marks. "Away went the defenders," Lumsden later wrote a friend, "with my men in pursuit, so close on their heels that [one sowar] got blown up in cutting down a man who happened to be carrying a bag of powder in one hand, and a lighted matchlock in the other. This was the Guides' first taste of powder, and a most trying ordeal for raw troops, as they had to scramble up the hill in the dark, over stones and rocks, but not a man lagged behind or lost his way." The grinning recruits also returned to Peshawar with several dozen Afridi jezails, 200 or 300 sheep and goats, and the village headman.

This baptism of fire bore richer fruit in numerous hard-fought actions during the Second Sikh War, and by the early 1850s the Guides had expanded to a strength of nearly 1,000. They had also won recognition as the Frontier's *corps d'élite*. Hardly a single campaign in the hills over the next half-century did not see the Guides in the thick of it.

Lumsden himself was something of an original. Disdaining the order that officers wear swords at all times, he carried a bulky shillelagh, which his troops nicknamed "Cease Firing," because he used it on the rifle range to thump the backs of sepoys who failed to heed the bugle's cease-fire call. The rifle range was also Lumsden's recruiting office. So many aspirants were available to him that whenever a vacancy occurred he could choose from a long waiting list, and he would then take the candidates to the range for entrance examinations. The best marksman filled the opening.

Enrollment in the Guides was not restricted to Pathans. Sikhs, Gurkhas, Punjabi Muslims and even some Hindus served under Lumsden, although of the last, only members of the highest castes were accepted, since by tradition they were also the best fighting men of their faith.* The Pathans, however, made up the backbone of the force. Mainly, though not exclusively, they were Yusufzais and Khattaks, and they were characteristically delighted to tangle with other Pathans. Besides their perpetual relish for a good fight and one of the highest pay scales in the Indian Army, they coveted the prestige that went with belonging to a corps no less proud than any Guards regiment. The Guides' colors and emblem —crossed tulwars and the slogan "Rough and Ready"—were a badge of honor known across all India. Not a few aspiring sepoys and sowars attached themselves to the Guides without pay, even providing their own horses and weapons so that they could be on the spot when a soldier fell in action and created an opening in the ranks.

The Guides even attracted the enemy. The most wanted bandit on the Frontier in the 1850s was a Pathan Robin Hood named Dilawur Khan, whose head carried a dead-or-alive reward of 2,000 rupees and whose band of guerrilla merry men had led even the Guides on a hopeless chase for nearly half a decade. Lumsden eventually arranged to meet Dilawur Khan under a flag of truce, and to make a proposition. Sooner or later, he told the brigand, we'll catch you, and I'll personally supervise your hanging, but if you join my regiment we'll forget your record. Dilawur Khan spat on the ground and strode off, but several days later he rode up to the Guides' encampment again and told Lumsden he had decided to accept the offer. Many years afterward, when he had become a much-decorated *subadar* (first lieutenant), he confessed to Lumsden—by then a major general—that he had originally planned to desert after

---

* One exception was an Untouchable *bhisti*, or water carrier, who may have inspired Kipling's Gunga Din. After winning the Star for Valor—India's equivalent of the Victoria Cross—in the Mutiny, he was elevated to soldier status by unanimous vote of the troops.

learning enough about British tactics to use them against the Guides, but that regimental esprit had given him a change of heart. He grinned sheepishly as he noted that his beard had grown white in the service of a pig-eating Queen.

For a corps consisting largely of tribesmen who regarded treachery as a mark of high moral character, the Guides were conspicuous for a near-zero desertion rate. Although the Pathan troops had eaten the Company's salt, what really counted was that they had eaten Lumsden's salt. This bear of a man could tongue-lash a sepoy with more Pushtu obscenities than any of his own *havildar*-majors. He always made certain that every foot and mounted unit was amply stocked with opium and bhang. In action he rode at the head of his troops, his great black beard a battle flag. He was less the Guides' commander than their mullah.

Some idea of his stature could have been had one day when John Lawrence made a formal inspection of the Guides in the field. Lawrence happened to be in a particularly testy mood and vented his spleen on Lumsden within earshot of the troops. After dismissing the formation, Lumsden was approached by an outraged orderly who told him: "It is not right and proper that we should allow our Colonel Sahib to be harshly spoken to by anyone. There is, therefore, this alternative: the Lord Sahib [Lawrence] has arranged to leave by the straight road tomorrow morning for Peshawar, but with your honor's permission and by the grace of God, there is no reason whatever why he should ever reach it." Only Lumsden's influence with his men kept the ambush from being carried out.

Punitive action on the Frontier was not confined to military strikes alone. As a rule, troops marched only after a series of comparatively non-belligerent attempts at persuasion failed. Initial pressure frequently took the form of fines—in money, grain or livestock—against tribes known to be in violation of the peace. If payment did not bring the desired result, or if the fines were not paid, Government might then withhold the tribe's subsidies and allowances. This often sufficed to bring the tribesmen back into line. Just as often it did no such thing, which meant that a real flexing of muscle was in order.

But not yet in an overt military campaign. If the Pathan could hold Hindu moneylenders for ransom, the British could borrow a page from the tribal book. By the practice known as *barampta*, all able-bodied males —and sometimes animals—of a lawbreaking clan were rounded up and held hostage until fines were paid or the clan agreed to behave. Since barampta was something like belling the cat, however, it could not often be relied on, but there still remained one step short of open war: *bandish*, a blockade of the tribal area. Bandish promised economic disaster. Cordoned off by strong troop concentrations (and cooperative tribes whenever possible), culprit communities could no longer sell their live-stock and grain, and were likewise prevented from receiving so much as a cupful of the salt imports so essential to Pathan life. A tribe under bandish was totally isolated from the rest of the Frontier world.

One such blockade was carried out in 1853, against the Bori section of the Jowaki Afridis, a large tribal group living in the Kohat district south of Peshawar. For three years, the Boris had not only been sending regular assault-murder teams into Peshawar but had been launching continual massed amphibious attacks on the cargo vessels that plied the Indus River. However, the British blockade against the Boris made itself felt immediately. In Roberts' words, it "produced no effect."

Still trying to avoid a head-on clash, the British continued to stay their hand. John Lawrence himself came down from Lahore and offered a compromise to the entire clan jirga. Amnesty would be granted for all past violations of the peace, he said, if the Boris accepted two condi-tions. First, they had to agree to obey the law in the future; second, they were to hand over certain criminals they had been harboring in their villages. The first condition won immediate, enthusiastic and unan-imous approval, but the second was repudiated out of hand. This could hardly have come as a surprise; the maliks "stated, with truth," wrote Roberts, "that from time immemorial it was their custom to afford an asylum to anyone demanding it, and that to surrender a man who had sought and found shelter with them would be a disgrace which they could not endure." So at long last, the gloves came off.

The force that took the field against the Boris numbered more than 1,500 troops, including the Guides, three other British and Indian regi-ments, a squadron of irregular cavalry and a team of elephants carrying two batteries of nine-pounders. The Guides led the advance, which proved hard going, as the Bori villages were surrounded on all sides by an almost unbreachable wall of mountains. During the stiff climb and plunging descent, the irregular cavalrymen and the Guides troopers had to dismount and lead their horses; the elephants and guns were eventu-ally left behind. But no resistance was encountered. Even when the force approached the villages in extended skirmish lines, the Boris simply scrambled up the side of the mountain to their own rear with the still dismounted Guides hot on their heels. It began to look as if there would be no fight at all.

Meanwhile, the rest of the force proceeded methodically to pull down houses, burn fodder and crops, and round up all livestock. For this, in fact, was the real purpose of any punitive expedition: not to run up a body count but to create maximum inconvenience and total bankruptcy. Concealed from the pursuing Guides behind boulders on the upper slopes, far too distant for any jezail balls to reach the British and

Indian troops in the villages, the Boris could only sit and watch the leveling of their homes and the obliteration of their livelihood.

In fact, however, the action had yet to begin. "Afridis may be driven all day like mountain sheep," the Indian Army's Colonel G. J. Young-husband once wrote, "but when the night begins to fall, and their tired pursuers commence of necessity to draw back to lower levels for food and rest, then this redoubtable foe rises in all his strength, and with sword and gun and huge boulder hurls himself like a demon on his retiring enemy." Which was exactly what happened now, less than sixty seconds after the sun had set. At the point of the Guides' advance up the slope was a thirty-man troop of dismounted sowars led by a lieutenant named Turner. They had driven at least three times that number of Boris to cover behind a big shelf of rock near the very crest of the mountain, and they were preparing to flush the tribesmen out on the points of their sabers when the sun dropped behind the peak. Darkness made it a new ball game.

Even to the Pathans of the Guides, the broken slope had now become terra incognita, but the Boris could run across it backwards with blindfolds on. Covered by jezail fire, their knifemen began to crawl down toward Turner's platoon. In the intervals between the ragged volleys, the tribesmen opened up with their own artillery: they hurled stones and pushed larger boulders down the slopes, and thus generally held the Guides' carbine fire to a few isolated and ineffectual bursts. Turner was in no position to counterattack. But neither could he with-draw. He ordered his bugler to sound the call for reinforcements.

As it happened, Harry Lumsden was on leave in England during this particular fight, and command of the Guides had devolved temporarily on Lieutenant William Hodson, who was to make a name for himself during the Indian Mutiny for his leadership of the hell-for-leather cavalry regiment known as Hodson's Horse. No less a thruster than Lumsden, Hodson was at this moment even more hard pressed in his position on Turner's flank by a perfect typhoon of stones and jezail balls. Most of the Guides' main force were in his column but he could not spare a single man to extricate Turner. He sent over at least two companies. The troops groped their way blindly along the corrugated slope, continually stumbling over unseen rocks and roots. Some did not get up; it almost seemed as if the Bori marksmen had night sights on the barrels of their jezails. Nearly an hour went by before the reinforcements reached Turner.

They might just as well have stayed with Hodson. By then, except for a single company of Gurkha riflemen near the foot of the slope, the entire force of the Guides was pinned down like a butterfly collection. The exultant Boris were rising to their feet by the hundreds, screaming Allah's praise, reviling the Guides Pathans as pig-violating slaves of the infidel. At any moment the final onslaught would begin.

The last thing the Boris expected was a counterattack. Although the commander of the Guides' Gurkha company farther down had been killed, the Guides' surgeon, Dr. Lyell, now took over and was joined by an additional Gurkha company from another regiment. Lyell personally led the charge up the slope. It threw the Boris off balance just long enough to let Hodson and Turner carry out phased withdrawals downward to less exposed positions. They remained in trouble, however, for the shrieking Boris followed hard on their heels while the tribal jezail fire approached a crescendo.

But once again the tables turned. By then on level ground, Hodson swiftly formed the Guides infantry into a hollow square while the sowars raced for their tethered horses nearby. "Mount!" shouted Hodson, as the first wave of Boris surged forward in a whooping kamikaze assault, only momentarily jolted by a crashing volley from the square. "Carry swords! Walk, march!" The Boris were now less than 500 yards away. "Trot!" bellowed Hodson. "Fear not, Sahib, we are with you!" a sowar yelled back. Hodson dug in his spurs. "Gallop! . . . Charge!" Ten minutes later—and eighteen hours after the attack on the villages had begun— it was all over. Hundreds of Boris were in full flight back up the face of the mountain. Hundreds more had thrown down their jezails. Scores of Bori corpses marked the path of the cavalry charge. Before the sun rose, the punitive column was well on its way back to Peshawar.

Although the Bori tussle was typical of Frontier police actions, not all campaigns invariably witnessed fighting. Sometimes the simple approach of a punitive force and the prospect of losing all one's worldly goods might suffice to bring maliks into the British camp to talk peace. But a miscreant Pathan community could seldom bargain from strength, nor were British terms often lenient, with the result that the tribes usually chose to fight back. They might give the British a bad mauling before succumbing to sheer weight of numbers, but succumb they always did. They always paid, too, and paid heavily, less in human casualties than in money, crops and livestock. Scorched earth was the name of the punitive game.

The British force would then march off, its mission accomplished. The defiant clan or tribe had learned a lesson it would remember for as long as three or four months.

That was a long time on the Frontier.

11

"Their Name Is Faithlessness"

Nᴏᴛ ᴀʟʟ Bʀɪᴛᴏɴs on the Frontier applauded punitive expeditions. "Burn and Scuttle," "Butcher and Bolt," were among the pejoratives applied to the hard-line policy. Sir Charles Napier, himself no slouch at taming savages, deplored police actions against the tribes as "a proceeding at variance with humanity and contrary to the usages of civilised warfare." British troops, said Napier, should make war on men, "not upon defenceless *women and children*, by destroying their habitations and leaving them to perish without shelter." But criticism of Frontier policy was not confined to distaste for strong-arm methods. A very influential segment of the Indian Civil Service and Indian Army also questioned the value of any British presence whatever in the regions west of the Indus.

The question was by no means out of order. Why had Britain deliberately chosen to saddle herself with a barren, howling wilderness that was peopled by a race of felons?

The main answer was that the Indian Government and Whitehall thought they had no choice. If the Pathan fell short of expected standards as a British subject, the Frontier itself loomed large in imperial geopolitics because, for at least seven decades during the nineteenth century, it was seen as a vestibule for a Russian invasion of India via Afghanistan. For this reason alone, the Khyber and other trans-Indus passes shared equal strategic importance with Gibraltar and the Suez Canal. Thus, to leave the Pathans' destiny in other hands was unthinkable.

Until the early twentieth century, perhaps the highest-priority concern of the men who ruled India was the establishment of a clear-cut western border—a mountain chain or a major river where they could draw a line and say to all outsiders: thus far and no farther. There were two obvious natural boundaries. One was the Indus, the other the knuckle of the Hindu Kush that poked southward through Pathan country to join with the Suleiman range in Baluchistan. Both had serious drawbacks. From a military standpoint, the Indus was usually thought of as a weak line, and military considerations had to be an overriding factor as long as the thought of Cossacks pouring through the Khyber Pass disturbed the sleep of British statesmen. No less a strategist than the Duke of Wellington had turned thumbs down on the Indus. "The art of crossing rivers is now so well understood," he wrote, ". . . that we cannot hope to defend the Indus. . . . I have no great reliance on that river as the barrier to India."

The mountains, on the other hand, were a perfect natural fortress; if the Indian borderline were to be drawn along the western slopes, British troops could then plug up the Khyber, the Bolan and the three or four other passes that offered the only access to invaders. But the mountains also had to be ruled out. For occupation of the passes meant, in effect, occupying a large slice of eastern Afghanistan. It was a source of enough concern that Britain's trans-Indus holdings in the Punjab already violated Afghan territorial integrity, or at least challenged Afghan territorial claims. Any further annexations to the west threatened another showdown with Kabul, and British policymakers of the 1850s and 1860s shrank even from the thought of risking a reenactment of the 1842 disaster. Another such incursion, moreover, would all but guarantee the very Russian counterthrust that Britain feared.

Moreover, Anglo-Afghan relations during the early 1850s—to the extent that they existed—had reached the lowest point in the two countries' history. Ever since Dost Muhammad had thrown in his lot with the Sikhs in 1849, the British would not trust him for the time of day, while the Dost for his part was still smarting, not only from his defeat, but from the humiliation of watching Britain seize his trans-Indus lands right up to the foothills of the high country. Dost Muhammad would even make occasional tenuous but loudly voiced claims to sovereignty over the Pathans, although he could no more manage them than could the British. "The Amir of Kabul is carrying on a diplomatic war with me," wrote Edwardes to a friend at this time, "about the hill tribes here, whom he claims as his subjects, and wants me to make no arrangements with them except through him. Fancy the Khyberees as his subjects!" Still, it was enough that the Dost had asserted the right at all.

Indeed, it was largely for this reason that the British sanctioned the emergence on the Frontier of a not-so-imaginary line that came to be known as the "administrative border."

It was neither fish nor fowl. Twisting southward from Hazara to

Baluchistan like a snake in convulsions, its path wound mainly to the east of the higher Frontier mountains. Theoretically, it marked the westernmost limits of official British control over the tribes and the beginning of Afghan authority. But since Afghanistan exercised no real jurisdiction whatever in the hill country, the administrative border in fact created a no-man's-land of near-total Pathan independence. Except for some Yusufzais in the Peshawar and Hazara districts, a few Afridi clans in Peshawar and Kohat and some Wazirs in Bannu, virtually every member of the six most warlike tribes on the Frontier was the citizen of a sovereign state of anarchy.

Of course it did not work out quite that way. In certain respects, nineteenth-century imperialism can be seen as the filling of tribal vacuums. Since punitive expeditions were continually marching across the administrative border in reprisal for Pathan raids into the so-called "settled districts" of the Frontier, the British writ did in fact run a good deal farther than it was supposed to. But any meaningful exercise of authority was severely curtailed by the presence of the boundary line. It seemed almost designed to encourage tribal defiance of the Raj.

Just as significantly, this half-hearted buffer zone of neutrality weakened British defenses against possible Russian invasion, simply because the administrative border allowed the Indian Army to guard only the eastern embouchures of the passes. But that, too, was an element of a hands-off-Afghanistan credo that dominated imperial thinking during the 1850s and 1860s and was reflected on the Frontier in what came to be known as the "close-border" policy—or, as it was mockingly called by its critics, "masterful inaction."

John Lawrence was the most outspoken, eloquent and influential champion of the close-border policy. Indeed, he was its architect. Parting company with Wellington, Lawrence took the position that the Indus was the best place to make a stand against the Russians. Any invading force, he maintained, would take staggering losses from the tribes while negotiating the Frontier passes; if Russian troops ever managed to reach the Indus, the Indian Army would make short work of them. Conversely, Lawrence believed, it would be a strategic blunder for the British to extend permanent lines of communication into country infested by hostiles. And worse, it would be a sunburst of political folly because it would antagonize Dost Muhammad. To Lawrence, this was unthinkable: as he saw it, the best way to keep the Dost happy was to keep away from him.

Some Frontier officials thought of this isolationism as both self-defeating and risky. A vigorous proponent of détente was the future Lord Roberts' father, General Sir Abraham Roberts, who had been relieved of his command of Shah Shuja's force during the 1839–41 occupation but headed up an Indian Army division at Peshawar in 1852. Abraham Roberts carried on a cordial correspondence with Dost Muhammad and members of the Afghan court, which led him to the conviction, voiced repeatedly to the Indian Government, that the Frontier would become a more manageable tract if both sides buried the hatchet. This view was shared by Edwardes, then Commissioner at Peshawar; he expressed concern that the "sullenness in our present relations . . . keeps up excitement and unrest, and prevents our influence and institutions from striking root."

Indeed, Edwardes became so convinced that Dost Muhammad was ready, willing and able to consider rapprochement that in 1854 he formally proposed to Dalhousie that "a new account [be] opened on the basis of an open treaty of friendship and alliance."

Edwardes did not try to delude Dalhousie, or himself, about the nature of the friendship that could be expected with the Amir: "Neither to him nor his people can we be personally otherwise than obnoxious. . . . We succeeded in thrashing them, but not in subduing them. . . . As a mass, the people hate us, but they also fear us. [The annexation of the Punjab] has brought the conquerors of India to their door, and they cannot be insensible to their danger." Yet this was all the more reason, Edwardes concluded, for the British to "let bygones be bygones."

As expected, the proposal came under immediate fire from the close-border advocates, with Lawrence leading the pack. "I have two good reasons against it," he wrote Edwardes: "(1) that you will never be able to *get* the Afghans to sign a treaty; and (2) if they make it, they will not keep it. . . . Nothing that we could do would make [Dost Muhammad] a real ally and friend." Even Edwardes' close friend Nicholson took up the cudgel for Lawrence, because of his own deep and abiding hatred of Afghans. During the 1839–42 campaign, when his garrison at Ghazni had been captured by betrayal, he had been forced to watch Afghans torture his commanding officer. And in the Khyber Pass, he had almost tripped over the naked, castrated cadaver of his younger brother. "I hope you will never forget," he warned Edwardes, "that their *name is faithlessness*, even among themselves"; it was far too easy to be "deceived by that winning and imposing frankness of manner which it has pleased Providence to give the Afghans, as it did to the first serpent for its own purposes."

What counted, however, was the Governor General's nod. Edwardes won it. Dalhousie thought Lawrence's argument "a fallacy," arising from "the assumption that the Afghans are fools, whereas I think they are, in general, quite as clever fellows as we are." But what may really have brought Dalhousie into Edwardes' camp at this time was the impending Crimean War, which was seen in many quarters as a knife at the windpipe of India. "In England they are fidgety regarding this border beyond reason," Dalhousie wrote Edwardes, "and most anxious for that . . . renewal of friendly relations which you advocate." Dalhousie himself was a bit fidgety, hoping that a treaty might "make Afghanistan an effectual barrier against Russian aggression." He also held out little hope for fruitful results, but told Edwardes: "I give you *carte blanche.*"

And, in fact, nothing might have been accomplished had not Dost Muhammad found himself in hot water on another front. At this time, the long-simmering dispute with Persia over possession of Herat had once more come to a boil, and Dost Muhammad deemed it wise to cast about for a strong friend. Persia then being all but a Russian fief, the Dost closed his mind to past betrayal and looked to the British. In March 1855, he instructed his son and heir apparent, Ghulam Haidar Khan, to represent him at Peshawar, where, he hoped, a meeting with Edwardes—and a reluctant Lawrence—would secure the desired goodwill.

What emerged was a treaty of "perpetual peace and friendship." It expressly stated that the Company had no designs on Afghan territorial integrity, while Ghulam Haidar Khan promised that Dost Muhammad and his successors would not only "respect" Company holdings but be "the friend of its friends and the enemy of its enemies." Most Britons and Afghans present at the signing felt convinced that the value of the treaty was almost as great as the paper on which it was written. But for Dost Muhammad's ongoing tribulations, the cynics would probably have been proved correct.

In 1856, a Persian army entered and occupied Herat without firing a shot. Aware that it was very much in Britain's interest to forestall any easterly moves by a Russian-influenced Shah, Dost Muhammad hastened to exercise his prerogative as enemy of the Company's enemies with an appeal for help. He was heartened not only by an immediate British declaration of war on Persia, but also by the Indian Government's pledge to pay him a subsidy if he himself took up arms against the Shah. Persia capitulated too quickly for the Afghans to join the fray, but the agreement was nonetheless formalized in January 1857, when Dost Muhammad personally arrived in Peshawar to put his seal on a second Anglo-Afghan treaty.

In addition to reaffirming the earlier vows of perpetual fraternity and noninterference, the 1857 treaty also provided that British officers be allowed into Afghanistan to supervise payment of the subsidy for Dost Muhammad's nonparticipation in the war. This was the first time that any such permission had been granted by the Dost since Burnes' mission in 1837, and although the officers were sidetracked from Kabul, where they might have exercised some influence, to Kandahar, where they sat around for a few months, the simple fact of their presence in erstwhile enemy country marked a significant step forward.

But even more vital in breaking the ice was Dost Muhammad's willingness—indeed, his eagerness—to go to Peshawar in person. Sir Kerr Fraser-Tytler, whose history of Afghanistan may be the definitive work on Anglo-Afghan relations, has written that "the value of personal contact in oriental diplomacy is of first importance, and among Orientals it is nowhere more important than in dealing with Afghans." Dost Muhammad could have been only favorably impressed on meeting such giants of Frontier policy as Lawrence and Edwardes.* Nor could his human vanity have failed to respond warmly to the 7,000 Indian Army troops, in full-dress uniform, who lined a mile of the road outside Peshawar and stood to attention as he and his retinue rode into the city. Edwardes later wrote that the sight "inspired the Amir . . . with a very salutary feeling of awe and admiration."

Dost Muhammad also left a sweet taste in the mouths of his hosts, even—or perhaps especially—when he spoke bluntly. "He called a spade a spade," wrote Harry Lumsden's brother Peter, "and never hesitated to confess that, although personally he had the happiest remembrances of his association with the British, yet as a Muhammadan ruler . . . he would, if he had the power, sweep unbelievers from the face of the earth. 'But, Sahib,' he would say, 'as this cannot be, I must cling to the British to save me from the cursed Kujjur (Persian), and having made an alliance with the British Government, I will keep it faithfully to death.'"

In less than six months, the British would have reason to remember that pledge.

*Nicholson was not present, having deliberately stayed away out of fear that he might be "tempted," as he put it, to gun down a few Afghans.

12

The Fat of Cows and Pigs

THE SUN had not quite slipped behind the Khyber hills on the evening of May 11, 1857, when Edwardes and Nicholson, in the Company's Peshawar headquarters, read the telegraph message that came less as a surprise than as a terrible jolt. There had just been an uprising of several Indian regiments at Meerut, seventy-five miles north of Delhi. After butchering a large number of British officers and their families, the sepoys had then put a great part of the town to the torch. At that moment they were marching on Delhi itself, where other Indian units had also gone into revolt. The mutineers were supremely confident. Had not their holy men so often told them that the Raj would fall on June 27 of this year, the hundredth anniversary of Clive's victory at Plassey? The holocaust that the British had pooh-poohed and dreaded for decades was about to sweep across the northern half of India.

These pages are not the place to examine the numerous and complex causes of the Indian Mutiny, or even to describe the Mutiny itself, except in relation to the considerable role played by the Frontier and its soldier-administrators. But a word of background is necessary. For some years, British social and administrative reforms on the subcontinent had been generating as much suspicion and fear as appreciation among their Indian beneficiaries. The abolition of *suttee* (live widow burning) and female infanticide, the execution of Brahmins for capital crimes and, above all, a large missionary incursion all had contributed to a growing belief that there was a Company plot afoot to force Christianity on Hindus and Muslims alike.

Further discontent had arisen from revised property taxes, which seemed to discriminate against wealthy landowners. Enforcement of the so-called doctrine of lapse—whereby the Company annexed native states whose rulers died without heirs—was particularly resented. The British had already decided to deprive the tottering Mogul dynasty of the title of "king," as soon as Bahadur Shah, the eighty-two-year-old ruler of Delhi, died. Hindus also saw this as a threat; particularly concerned was one Nana Sahib, the scheming, warlike chief of the once-powerful Mahratta Confederacy. One way or another, all these things affected every man, woman and child in India.

Yet the changes might have been brought about peaceably had not the virus of fear and unrest also infected the army. Already bristling under a new compulsory overseas service regulation, the sepoys were given a further prod—the crucial prod, as it proved—early in 1857, when a new rifle was introduced to replace the old "Brown Bess." It was learned that the paper cartridge for this weapon had been lubricated with the fat of cows and pigs. In those days, cartridges had to be bitten open before loading, but a Hindu would be deprived of his caste if he so much as touched his lips to the flesh of the sacred cow, while eating pigs, to a Muslim, was an act of defilement. What clearer evidence was needed of a scheme to undermine the two great faiths of the subcontinent? Sir Charles Napier had once warned: "The moment those brave and able natives know how to combine, they will rush on us simultaneously and the game is up." That moment seemed at hand.

As Edwardes and Nicholson read the telegram from Delhi, they immediately perceived that Britain's survival in India probably hinged on the Frontier. A domino situation was in the making: It centered on Peshawar, which could easily fall. The city was then garrisoned by 2,000 British troops and 5,000 sepoys. The former were considered more than a match for the latter but without a hope against the Peshawar area's 50,000 Pathans, who might well exploit any outbreak and make themselves masters of the situation. With Peshawar in Pathan hands, nothing could stop a general tribal rising along the entire Frontier, and this in turn would be followed inevitably by a vast swarm of Afghans pouring like syrup through the Khyber to reoccupy their old trans-Indus dominions. Nor would insurrection stop at the banks of the Indus; the collapse of the already tenuous British control of the Frontier had to mean the loss of the entire Punjab. And when the Punjab went, it would be all up for the Raj everywhere else.

Only a few weeks earlier, in Calcutta, Edwardes had remarked to the new Governor General, Lord Canning: "You may rely on this, my Lord, that if ever there is a desperate deed to be done in India, John Nicholson is the man to do it." Now, within minutes of reading the telegram, Nicholson came up with a plan to hold the Frontier and save the Punjab. He spelled it out to Edwardes and Peshawar's military commanders in an emergency meeting. The strategy was three-pronged. First, potentially mutinous regiments in the Peshawar District would be separated from each other by immediate transfer to relatively isolated stations. At the same time, what Nicholson called a "Movable Column" of British and loyal Indian troops would be formed to carry out forced marches across the Punjab and stamp out sepoy brushfires wherever they occurred. Finally, Pathan levies would be raised, on the largest possible scale, not only to beef up the Movable Column, but to reinforce any garrisons reduced by defection.

The Pathans were the key to the plan. Nicholson hoped and believed that most if not all of the Muslim tribal leaders would be prepared to submerge—at least temporarily—their animosity toward the Company for a chance to strike a blow at a more despised enemy. He and Edwardes had not forgotten how Pathans had responded to the British SOS in the Second Sikh War; among other things, it had been a force of tribal guerrillas that had rallied round Edwardes to send the Sikh rebels sprawling at Multan. And now there was an even greater opportunity to raise the cry of jihad through the hills, to slay the thousands upon thousands of the Hindus who made up so large a part of the mutineer legions.

Nicholson's proposal won swift and unanimous approval. Implementing it was something else. Although the separation of most Indian regiments went off smoothly enough, the crucial Pathan reinforcements proved to be only a trickle. Instead of remembering Multan in 1848, the tribesmen thought of Kabul in 1842. They had no intention of joining another lost cause, especially if a sepoy outbreak anywhere near Peshawar gave them a wedge with which they could oust Indians and British alike.

That chance, moreover, seemed excellent. On May 21, news reached Peshawar that a large detachment of the 55th Native Infantry in Nowshera, some forty miles to the east, had defied its officers and seized the post magazine. Clearly, Peshawar was next.

Unless its remaining Indian forces had their teeth drawn at once, a move easier planned than carried out. During the early days of the Mutiny, nearly all British officers in India were congenitally incapable of believing that the sepoys they personally led would ever turn on their Queen. Roberts, then a lieutenant, tells of conveying a disarming order to one regimental commander who "exclaimed: 'What! Disarm my regiment? I will answer with my life for the loyalty of every man!' On my repeating the order the poor old fellow burst into tears."

And so it was at Peshawar. At six o'clock on the morning of May 22,

Brigadier General Sydney Cotton, the Peshawar commandant, summoned the British commanders of four doubtful Indian regiments to his headquarters and told them that the troops would be disarmed in exactly one hour. On hearing this, the officers almost mutinied themselves. Even correspondence that Nicholson had seized, and which showed the sepoys up to their turbans in treason, failed to make an impression. According to Edwardes, it was "a most painful scene.... [The officers] unanimously and violently declared their implicit confidence in their men. One advised conciliation and another threatened us that his men would resist and take the guns." That of course was the problem. Even with British troops on hand, who could guarantee the meek submission that would inhibit a Pathan outbreak?

But Cotton had made his decision and the order stood. At seven o'clock sharp, the four regiments were ordered to fall in on the parade ground. Ammunition wagons had been brought up to carry off the surrendered weapons. Two British regiments, backed up by several field batteries, stood ready at both ends of the sepoy formation. Cotton strode to the center of the parade ground and snapped out the order to pile arms. The sepoys did not move. Cotton repeated the order. It was not obeyed. There was a stir in the British ranks and the rippling crack of 1,000 hands on musket slings as company commanders barked: "Volley firing . . . Ready! Present!" Sweat broke out on more than one British face. It looked as if there would be either a fight or a massacre. The British preferred the former. Firing in anger was one thing; few men relished the prospect of committing murder—even the murder of mutineers—in cold blood.

Then a sepoy stepped forward and placed his weapon in one of the wagons. He was followed by two or three more men, then a platoon, then a company, then an entire battalion. The British troops grounded their own rifles smartly on command as the surrender continued smoothly, although not joyously. "It was a painful and affecting thing," wrote Edwardes, "to see [the sepoys] putting their own firelocks into the artillery waggons—weapons which they had used honorably for years. The [Indian] officers of a cavalry regiment, a very fine set of fellows, threw in their own swords with those of their men, and even tore off their spurs. It was impossible not to feel for and with them."

But Cotton's prompt action had done more than just nip a Peshawar uprising in the bud. It had also brought an immediately visible bonus in a change of heart among the Pathans, who had previously hung back from joining the British. "As we rode down to the disarming," Edwardes later wrote, "a very few chiefs and yeomen of the country attended us, and I remember judging from their faces that they came to see which way the tide would turn. As we rode back friends were thick as summer flies, and levies began from that moment to come in."

Nor did they come in a moment too soon: the Nowshera mutineers had yet to be dealt with. On May 23, they were reported making a forced march on the 55th's permanent headquarters, thirty miles northeast of Peshawar at Mardan, where the rest of the regiment by then had also mutinied. Accompanied by Nicholson with a band of his newly enlisted Pathan levies, a British column marched out of Peshawar to head off the insurgents. An hour or so after sunrise on the 25th, Nicholson's telescope picked out about 500 of the mutineers. They appeared to be heading north of Mardan, to get through the Malakand Pass into Swat, whose mist-cloaked high country offered inaccessible positions in which they could re-form.

Already, the day was broiling hot. The pursuing troops had been on their feet or in the saddle for nearly forty-eight consecutive hours. Toward noon, the British commanding officer gave off the chase. Nicholson did not. At the head of his mounted tribal levies, he rode the fugitives down in the hills, flushing them out of villages, prying them from ravines, personally accounting for many with his own saber. Upwards of 200 sepoys were killed that day and 120 captured. Nicholson took the prisoners in chains to Peshawar, where they were immediately sentenced to be blown from the mouths of cannons.

When the commander of the 55th, Colonel Henry Spottiswoode, learned that his children had betrayed him, he put a pistol to his head and blew his brains across the floor of his tent. Just possibly, the suicide may have played a role in prompting the wrathful Nicholson to forbearance toward the captured mutineers. "Temper stern justice with mercy," he wrote Edwardes, ". . . spare boys scarcely out of their childhood, and men who were really loyal and respectful up to the moment when they allowed themselves to be carried away in a panic by the mass." Edwardes needed no persuading, nor did John Lawrence, who thought that making live ammunition out of all the prisoners would not be "justified in the eyes of the Almighty." One-third should suffice, he said.

And so it was done. On June 10, the entire Peshawar garrison stood to attention and thousands of Pathans thronged outside the Cantonment to watch as drummers beat a somber tattoo while forty prisoners—some soiling their breeches in terror—were lashed to the muzzles of forty siege guns. The drumbeat stopped and the order to fire was followed instantly by forty thunderclaps and a red deluge of shredded flesh and pulverized bone. Some of the rain splattered on the troop formations. "It was a terrible sight," wrote Roberts, ". . . likely to haunt the beholder for many a long day; but that was what was intended." The spine of the Frontier mutiny had been snapped.

Nicholson and Edwardes could now turn their full attention to recruiting and training the tribal levies—Yusufzais, Mohmands, Afridis, Mullagoris, Shinwaris, Khattaks, Orakzais, Wazirs, Mahsuds and other clansmen who were pouring out of the hills by the tattered, reeking, howling thousands. Rapidly, the tribesmen were assigned to fill the gaps in existing regiments, absorbed into the Movable Column or formed up as irregular units. Time permitted only the minimal formal drill, but no one had to be shown how to mount a horse, fire a musket or swing a saber. It was without doubt the least presentable army in British military history, and the British could not have cared less. Every able-bodied tribesman was needed to shore up the tottering foundations of the Punjab.

One reason for the Punjab's straits at this time was the drain on its own military manpower in answer to cries for help from other parts of India. For the Mutiny's showdown battles were taking place some 600 miles east of Peshawar, where strong sepoy forces were taking place in central India's key cities. Only 700 British and loyal Indian troops under Henry Lawrence were available to defend Lucknow against 15,000 mutineers. Lawrence himself was one of the first to buy it during the five-month siege, when splinters from an eight-inch shell shattered his left leg. (He still had enough time to say: "I forgive everyone. I forgive my brother John.") At Cawnpore, a 400-man force held out so staunchly against Nana Sahib's 6,000 sepoys that Nana Sahib finally offered the defenders—along with some 500 civilians—a safe conduct down the Ganges. Hardly had the offer been accepted than Nana Sahib ordered his artillery to open up on the river craft; nearly every man, woman and child in the refugee force drowned or exploded while Nana Sahib's army marched into Cawnpore and slammed the gates shut. Months would pass before they were pried open again.

The big fight, however, was taking place outside Delhi, where the main insurgent army had made its stand. In Delhi stood the palace of the Moguls' last living ruler, and the doddering Bahadur Shah had been talked into believing that if he lent his name to the revolution the old Mogul Empire would rise from its ashes and bask in the sun of a new Golden Age. As spring ended and the fearful Indian hot weather set in, Delhi became the focus and symbol of anti-British resistance. Its recapture by the British would mean the effective end of the Mutiny.

But Delhi was held by 40,000 sepoys, embedded solidly behind seven miles of massive, fortified walls that were three stories high and that mounted nearly 200 heavy field guns. British strength in central India came to fewer than 20,000 troops, of which nearly three-quarters of that number had to be deployed for the relief of Lucknow, Cawnpore and other cities to deal with roving insurgent armies and to guard communications. A force of barely 5,000 took up positions along a two-mile ridge north and west of Delhi and laid siege to the city.

It was a Mexican standoff. The mutineers could ill afford the risk of abandoning their strategic and psychological nerve center, while the besiegers could find no way to break in. The ridge was naked not only to artillery fire but to disease, and the eight-to-one odds facing the British rose rapidly as cholera, dysentery, malaria and heat cooperated with shell fragments in felling the troops. Pus, vomit and liquid feces further polluted the blood that spurted to the ground from amputated limbs. Field hospitals took up nearly as much space on the ridge as did the ragged tents of the dwindling number of men who remained fit to fight. Reinforcements were on the way from England, but the voyage could take up to four months.

Meanwhile, only the Punjab—known even then as the "sword arm of India"—could furnish anything like the immediate infusion of manpower and firepower needed to beat down the walls of Delhi. Hardly had the uprising begun in May than Canning, the Governor General, had sent off an urgent telegram to Lawrence in Lahore: Delhi was counting on the Punjab.

Lawrence responded with dispatch, siphoning troops from his own beleaguered province as swiftly as they could be mobilized. The crack Guides were among the first to go. Thy made a record-breaking forced march to Delhi, eating up slightly under 600 miles in twenty-one days—twenty-seven miles daily in heat brutal enough to poleax a caravan of Bactrian camels. The columns reached Delhi at sunrise on June 9; one onlooker later wrote that "they came in as firm and light as if they had marched but a single mile." Which was just as well. The sepoys were given thirty minutes to eat their morning rice and chapati rations and pull on their water bottles before being ordered into a counterattack against a massive rebel column that had begun to storm the ridge. In the wild fire fight that ensued, the mutineers were hurled back behind the Delhi walls, after which the Guides settled down to more than three months of uninterrupted skirmishing. In the process, they sustained over fifty percent casualties; their entire officer complement had to be replaced four times. Other Punjab contingents fared likewise. But their numbers were to make all the difference in the final outcome of the siege.

On the Frontier, a siege of a different sort was in the making. Early in June, Lawrence sent up a trial balloon—or rather dropped a bomb—when he wrote to Edwardes with a recommendation that Peshawar be handed over to Dost Muhammad.

On the face of it, this astonishing proposal seemed almost sound. At that time, Lawrence had become pessimistic to the point of despair over the prospects of recapturing Delhi. There were just not enough British troops and loyal sepoys, he felt, to bring it off. He warned Edwardes that "if disaster occurs at Delhi, all the native regulars and some of the Irregulars (perhaps many) will abandon us. We should, then, take time by the forelock." What that meant, Lawrence explained, was capitalizing on the friendship that Dost Muhammad had pledged in the 1857 treaty:

an arrangement ought to be concluded whereby the Amir would occupy Peshawar and other key Frontier positions as an ally, thus freeing every available fighting man in the Punjab for the all-crucial task at Delhi. "Peshawar would accomplish [Dost Muhammad's] heart's desire, and would do more to make the Afghans friendly to us than anything else," wrote the man who had once told Edwardes not to trust Afghans for the right time of day.

Edwardes' initial reaction was to think that overwork had finally got the better of Lawrence. It was known that Dost Muhammad's subjects had been begging him to exploit the crisis in India, to send his armies through the Khyber and simply expropriate the Frontier from the embattled British. Afghans "frequently came to him," wrote Roberts, ". . . throwing their turbans at his feet, and praying him as a Mahomedan to seize the opportunity for destroying the 'infidels.'" It was also known that Dost Muhammad had thus far resisted the pressure because of the treaty he had made with the Company. But how long would he hold out if Peshawar were actually offered to him on a platter?

Even for the accommodating Edwardes, Lawrence's proposal was too much. After a hurried conference with an equally aghast Nicholson and Cotton, he replied: "We are unanimously of opinion that with God's help we can and will hold Peshawar. . . . It is the anchor of the Punjab, and if you take it up the whole ship will drift to sea. . . . As for a friendly transfer, Dost Muhammad would not be a mortal Afghan—he would be an angel—if he did not assume our day to be gone in India, and follow after us as an enemy. Europeans cannot retreat—Kabul would come again."

But Lawrence saw it otherwise and continued to press for the evacuation of what, in a very real sense, was the key to the defense of the Raj. Obsessed by the close-border theories he had molded into policy, determined to throw up a wall between India and Afghanistan, convinced that the Frontier was a liability to British rule, he went on the attack through June and July with a barrage of letters to Canning. "Peshawar is not India" became his battle-cry. It was not until August, when he received a direct order by telegraph from Canning—"Hold on to Peshawar to the last"—that Lawrence finally abandoned his inexplicable scheme. Had he been heeded, the outcome of the siege of Delhi might not have mattered a great deal.

As August drew to a close, the British at last found themselves ready to take the offensive at Delhi. Some weeks earlier, Nicholson had been made a brigadier general and placed in command of the Movable Column with orders to march on the mutineer stronghold. It was hoped that the 8,000-man Punjab force would provide the besieging troops with enough muscle to carry the walls of the city, and Nicholson's own presence, when he arrived on August 14, proved a badly needed shot in the arm. Certainly the time for leadership was long overdue. Morale had gone rancid among the bullet-punctured, disease-flayed troops on the ridge. British generals at Delhi were the ossified product of a seniority system that had placed the likes of Elphinstone and Gough at the head of armies. The situation cried out for a man to take charge. That man seemed to be Nicholson. "The camp is all alive," wrote Major William Hodson of Hodson's Horse, "at the notion of something decisive taking place soon."

Something did take place. Approaching Delhi at this time was a huge British siege train—the heavy guns that were a sine qua non to a successful breach of the walls. During the last week in August, it was learned that a powerful sepoy column was making a forced march to place itself between Delhi and the siege train. On the 25th, at the head of 1,600 riflemen and 450 cavalry troopers, Nicholson rode out of Delhi to intercept the interceptors.

By then, torrential summer rains were hammering down; for eighteen hours, Nicholson's men slogged knee-deep across twenty-one miles of rock-garnished consommé before making contact with the enemy. Then they discovered that they were outnumbered by more than four to one. They were also drenched, famished and bone-weary, unable to move ahead another yard. Nicholson ordered an immediate attack. The men waded forward with bayonets fixed while the mutineer artillery contributed to the continuing deluge with a hailstorm of grapeshot. Finally, both sides collided and went at each other in twenty minutes or so of dirty fighting. Nicholson's swinging saber flashed dully above the melee and seemed to give his own men a second wind. When the riot ended, not a single mutineer remained alive.

The way had now been cleared for the siege train, and Nicholson had also come to be thought of as the de facto commander of the troops on the ridge. He lost no time in exercising that unofficial authority by calling for an immediate all-out assault on Delhi.

But not all of Nicholson's fellow-officers welcomed him. The hasty promotion to brigadier general of a thirty-four-year-old captain in the uncouth Company army was looked on as an affront by more than one holder of the Queen's Commission in such regiments as the 60th Rifles and 6th Dragoon Guards; some officers mockingly addressed the Movable Column commander as "Mister Nicholson." And least elated of all by the new arrival was the British commander-in-chief at Delhi, General Archdale Wilson. This man dreaded taking initiative only less than he resented the upstart Frontier officer's insistence that he do so.

Nor did Nicholson hold an exalted opinion of Wilson. "I have seen lots of useless generals in my day," he wrote, "but such an ignorant, croaking obstructive as he is, I have never hitherto met with." On September 4, when the siege train rumbled up to the foot of the ridge, Wilson continued to croak and vacillate while Nicholson stepped up the pressure of his demands. Clearly, one of the two men would have to give ground. Clearly, it would not be Nicholson.

Nicholson never had a more ardent admirer than his twenty-five-year-old aide, Lieutenant Frederick Roberts. As late as 1897, when Roberts had become a field marshal and a peer of the realm, he could still write of Nicholson as "the beau-ideal of a soldier and gentleman," who "impressed me more profoundly than any man I had ever met before, or have ever met since." And on September 6, Roberts felt both flattered and shocked when Nicholson confided in him "of his intention to take a very unusual step. . . . 'Delhi must be taken,' he said, 'and it is absolutely essential that this should be done at once; and if Wilson hesitates longer, I intend to propose at to-day's meeting that he should be superseded." When Roberts nervously pointed out that such a move would place Nicholson himself in command, Nicholson replied that he had already chosen another officer whom he would recommend for the post, "so no one can ever accuse me of being influenced by personal motives." What was vital, he said, was to get Wilson out of the way. But when the news of Nicholson's plan reached Wilson, it sufficed to galvanize the feeble-willed commander into ordering the long-delayed offensive. Wilson also placed Nicholson at the head of the storming force.

On September 14, after a few days of tactical probing and heavy bombardment, five British columns, each about 1,000 strong, drove in on the Delhi walls from north and west as the British siege guns shivered the earth and the rebel artillery vomited out a counterbarrage of forty-pound iron meteorites. Nicholson's column spearheaded the assault. His troops breached the northernmost gate and advanced along the inner wall, through clouds of musket fire, toward another gate that had to be forced open to admit a flanking column from the west. Halfway to the gate, the mutineers' enfilading volleys had almost by themselves become a wall; soldiers were thudding to the ground in clusters as the rebel small arms ground up their ranks. When some of the men began diving for cover, Nicholson raced to the head of the line to rally them. He was brought up short when a ball tore through his lungs. This had the effect of bringing the whole advance to a halt. "The fact is," wrote Roberts, "too much had been attempted. . . . The narrow strip of ground we gained had been won at severe loss."

Still, Nicholson had given the British a toehold, and a toehold was all they needed. Fatally wounded, Nicholson himself was out of the action and very close to the end of his life, but for more than a week the old rage continued to burn. He silenced throngs of uniformed Nikal Seyns who prayed clamorously outside his hospital tent by emptying his pistol through the tent wall. On learning that Wilson planned to withdraw from Delhi, where street fighting went on with mounting fury, he raised himself from his cot and gasped: "Thank God I have the strength yet to shoot him if necessary."

It did not prove necessary. On September 21, a Pathan orderly brought Nicholson the news that the Union Jack had gone up over the great red fort of Delhi's old Mogul rulers. Nicholson said: "My desire was that Delhi should be taken before I die and it has been granted." Even then, however, it took him three more days to expire.

Months of bloody mopping up also remained, but the fall of Delhi assured another nine decades of uninterrupted British mastery in India.

It would be an exaggeration to say that the Raj had been preserved by the men of the Northwest Frontier. It is not unreasonable, however, to ask how British supremacy over India's lesser breeds might have been affected had not Cotton moved so decisively to stamp on the sepoys at Peshawar, had not Edwardes and Nicholson raised the tribal irregular forces that filled the widening gaps in the loyal Punjab regiments, had not the Guides reached Delhi so swiftly, had a commander with less than Nicholson's infuriated singleness of purpose been placed at the head of the columns that stormed the Delhi walls. Although there is little doubt that Delhi would have fallen eventually, a negotiated surrender or even an extended siege could well have sapped British authority in the years to come. That did not happen. The defenses of Delhi crumbled under the blows delivered by a Frontiersman.

There is also the question of what might have been British India's fate had John Lawrence been given his way on Peshawar, and much more to the point, had Dost Muhammad not stayed his hand when the Company was on the ropes along the whole Frontier. "I am convinced," wrote Harry Lumsden, "that, had it not been that the minds of the Afghans were in a measure prepared for the Amir's non-interference, he could not have prevented a general rush down the passes." Roberts put it even more strongly: "Had [Dost Muhammad] turned against us . . . Delhi could never have been taken; in fact, I do not see how any part of the country north of Bengal could have been saved."

The Mutiny spawned a galaxy of British heroes. But a non-Briton—and a "native" to boot—may have kept British rule intact in India simply because he kept his word.

13

Crag Picquet and the Dunce Cap

THE MOST IMMEDIATELY visible result of the Mutiny was the overnight dismantling of the East India Company and the complete transfer of India's government to the Crown. The Company army was absorbed into the Queen's forces, while the workmanlike title of governor general gave way to the more grandiose office of viceroy. In 1877, Disraeli was to put a characteristically vainglorious cap on the whole thing by arranging for Queen Victoria to become Empress of India. At the Imperial Assemblage held in Delhi to solemnize the event, a 101-gun salute stampeded several dozen ceremonial elephants; they in turn scattered an immense gathering of maharajas and British generals. But the Old Queen was delighted.

Meanwhile, tranquility returned to the subcontinent as swiftly as did the switch of responsibility—except on the northwest frontier, which soon became the arena of a searing epilogue to the Mutiny. Although it was an insurrection of a somewhat different kind, it came within an ace of driving the British back across the Indus.

Autumn of 1863 seemed to be a time for mountain warfare. While Union and Confederate armies went at each other on Missionary Ridge and Lookout Mountain, soldiers of the Queen were caught up in an at least equally jolting set-to on more remote heights. The seeds of the conflict had been sown more than three decades earlier, by a circuit mullah named Ahmad Shah Brelwi, whose incendiary preachings against Sikh rule had taken fire among a number of Yusufzai tribal groups living

[136]

north of Peshawar in the aerie-like Graustarks of Swat and Buner. Ahmad Shah Brelwi may not have known what he started.

Although not even a Pathan, Ahmad Shah Brelwi was a notable figure in Pathan history, one of those rare rabble-rousers who could actually prevail on feuding clans to bury the hatchet and unite, at least temporarily, under a single leader. In 1830, vast numbers of tribesmen had responded to his exhortations and poured down from the hills on Peshawar, actually capturing the city from the Sikhs and occupying it for several months. In due course, Ahmad Shah Brelwi was killed, but many of his followers remained united and formed a hideout-colony in eastern Buner, nearly two miles up in the clouds. From this stronghold, they continued their forays against the Sikhs and later the British. During the Mutiny they added to their numbers by harboring and enlisting fugitive Muslim sepoys. Not surprisingly, the British dubbed them the "Hindustani Fanatics."

In 1858, a strong task force under Sydney Cotton had scattered the Fanatics and driven them from their main base, but within two years they had re-formed at another site. By the late summer of 1863, Fanatic raids on caravans and villages in the Peshawar Valley had reached the point that they could no longer be shrugged off as a tribal nuisance. Peshawar itself was too close for comfort. It was one thing for the Peshawar garrison to be struck by a Pathan reconnaissance-in-force, even by a Pathan army, but the onslaught of an entire Pathan quasi-nation—and a berserk quasi-nation at that—simply could not be permitted.

In the post-Mutiny era, the British tended to push the panic button at even the smallest display of cheek by their dusky underlings. Here, on the Frontier, they found themselves faced with open rebellion on a massive scale. After a flurry of staff meetings and exchanges of memoranda and telegrams between Calcutta, Lahore and Peshawar, a counterstroke was ordered. In mid-October of 1863, two Indian Army columns, numbering 6,000 troops supported by nineteen field and mountain guns—a larger force than that which had stormed Delhi—marched north from Peshawar to stamp out the insurgents for once and for all.

Influential elements of the military had opposed the expedition, among them General Sir Hugh Rose, the Indian Army Commander-in-Chief,* who had fought and won the last major campaign of the Mutiny.* The son of a British diplomat who had once served in Germany, Rose had learned his soldiering from Prussian officers and favored a methodical approach to warfare. He had urged that the offensive against the Fanatics be postponed until the following spring; the oncoming cold months, he argued, did not allow enough time to equip the force with adequate

* His antagonist was the Rani of Jhansi, a dainty young woman who may have been braver than Nicholson, a smarter politician than Palmerston and a greater patriot than Gandhi.

transport, stores and reserve ammunition. Brigadier General Neville Chamberlain,* who had been chosen to lead the expedition, did not even want to command, being down with malaria and still feeling the bite of wounds picked up in the Afghan War, both Sikh Wars, the Mutiny and an assortment of Frontier tussles. "If duty requires the sacrifice I cannot repine," he wrote his brother, "but . . . I have no wish for active service." What Chamberlain really hoped for, he said, was "to turn my sword into a shepherd's crook."

To the Indian Government, however, the Hindustani Fanatics presented too grave a threat to permit any delay in retaliation, or even a change of commanders. Chamberlain's leadership, moreover, was known to be of the highest order; he could be relied on to move his troops with the right kind of dash. Both generals were overruled.

The Fanatics' stronghold was a village called Malka. To reach it, Chamberlain had to negotiate the Ambela Pass, about sixty miles east and north of Peshawar. The last foreigner to make the attempt had been the Mogul Akbar in 1586; in the process he had lost nearly every soldier of an 8,000-man army. But the British anticipated little opposition at Ambela beyond that of the Fanatics themselves. The Pathan Bunerwal tribes living in the neighborhood were the spiritual subjects of a seventy-year-old sage known as the Akhund of Swat, who wielded more than the usual influence of Frontier holy men. It was an article of faith among Bunerwals that supernatural forces placed enough gold for the Akhund's daily living expenses beneath his prayer rug every morning. The Akhund had made it plain that he was out of sympathy with the Fanatics' cause, and the British had issued a proclamation declaring that their quarrel was with the Fanatics only. Accordingly, civil authorities in Peshawar had assured Chamberlain that the Bunerwals would not impede the army's advance.

But even without tribal resistance, the going was stiff. On October 20, the leading columns of the British force made camp at the summit of the Ambela Pass. They were alone and all but invisible in a vast shroud of mist. The narrow, rocky goat path that coiled almost vertically up the heights had proved a punishing challenge to man and beast. The infantry had become a corps of alpinists. Cavalry troopers had had to dismount and lead their continually shying, stumbling horses. Except for a handful of ammunition mules, no transport animals had even been able to start the ascent. Two days would pass before supplies—and the rest of Chamberlain's force—reached the summit.

And if the pass itself was not impediment enough, Chamberlain now learned that the Akhund of Swat had reconsidered his own neutral stance and that the Bunerwals had gone over to the Fanatics.

In effect, the Akhund's volte-face placed the British in a trap. The

---

* No relation to the future Prime Minister despite an almost photographic resemblance.

whole country was now up, not only threatening to sever Chamberlain's slender thread of communication to the rear but positioning a vast tribal phalanx across the line of his advance to Malka. For the time being, the British could only dig their heels in and go on the defensive, fortifying two strongpoints in the pass known as Crag Picquet and the Eagle's Nest. If either position were captured and occupied in strength, the expedition could reasonably expect to be wiped out to a man.

Now began a continuing series of frenzied mass assaults by the tribes that lasted an entire month. That amount of time alone was cause for concern: Pathan armies seldom carried food for more than three or four days, after which they would usually disperse. But a great deal was at stake at Ambela, as no fewer than 15,000 tribesmen tried to wrest Crag Picquet and the Eagle's Nest from the British. Through forests of bursting shells and the thick underbrush of massed rifle fusillades, the Fanatic and Bunerwal hordes drove in on Chamberlain's force in wave after ragged wave. They charged down and even up slopes. They rolled boulders from high ground and pelted the British with stones when ammunition ran short. They vaulted barricades and pitted tulwars against bayonets in toe-to-toe harpooning contests. Their green battle flags mingled with Union Jacks and British regimental colors like banners at a nominating convention. Attackers and defenders temporarily lost their hearing in the crack of tumbling boulders and the basso-profundo explosions of mountain guns that reverberated off the walls of the pass against an incessant chattering counterpoint of rifle and jezail fire. Both sides tried to out-thump and out-scream each other with their drums, pipes, war cries and cheers.

For hours, even days at a time, the Ambela action was also an Armageddon of blind men. Visibility was often reduced to a few feet, not only by the mist that hung over the pass like an immense downy quilt but by a shifting thunderhead of black powder. The screen once enabled a Guides lance-*daffadar* (corporal) leading three sowars to disperse a force of 300 Bunerwals by shouting commands at his men as if he were at the head of a regiment. And the fogbank continued to swirl and eddy as the desperate battle went on. Crag Picquet was captured three times, only to be retaken by the combined counterpunches of artillery barrages and massed bayonet charges. At least 2,000 Pathan, British and Indian corpses piled up around Crag Picquet; it was soon named *Kutlgar*, the place of slaughter.

The long engagement also proved to be something of a family affair. Many Pathans fighting on the British side of the Guides and other Frontier Force units had close relatives in the tribal ranks; more than one sepoy found the corpse of his father or a brother among the Bunerwal dead. Wounded tribesmen were treated in British army field hospitals and then sent back to their own lines to return to the line of fire. For their part, the tribesmen abstained from their usual practice of mutilating captured enemy soldiers. Banter among Pathans on both sides was continual. Roberts, who was there, remembered that "the enemy used to joke with our men . . . and say, 'We don't want you. Where are the *lal pagriwalas* (as the 14th Sikhs were called from their *lal pagris* [red turbans]) or the *goralog* (the Europeans)? They are better *shikar* (sport)?' The tribesmen soon discovered that the Sikhs and Europeans, though full of fight, were very helpless on the hill-side, and could not keep their heads under cover."

Yet despite the ties of kinship and the fact that the Akhund's influence had brought unusually strong religious overtones to the conflict, there was not a single Pathan desertion from the British ranks. And the climate of mutual respect continued to prevail on October 27, when Chamberlain called a cease-fire so that the Bunerwals could bury their dead. At this time, he also invited the tribal maliks to his camp, where he called a sort of informal British-Pathan jirga and tried to persuade the headmen that the continued Fanatic-Burnerwal offensive would be futile. "Their demeanour was courteous," wrote Roberts, "but they made it evident that they were determined not to give in."

In fact the tribal forces had not even begun to fight. On November 20, they launched their heaviest assault on Crag Picquet and occupied the position for the third time. To rally his own men, Chamberlain personally led the counterattack. He took a jezail ball in the arm but stayed in command, waving his pistol with his good hand as he labored up the slope at the head of the troops. Once again, the tribesmen were driven out, but by then it hardly seemed to matter. With casualties mounting, rations dwindling and Pathan guerrillas strangling the supply lines in the rear, it had begun to look as if the British were undone.

And if they were not, they had only to wait. It was also known at this time that a mission from Kabul had arrived in the Bunerwal camp. Dost Muhammad had died five months earlier, and, in the confusion of the scramble for succession to the Afghan throne, the peace treaty with the British had evidently been forgotten. At any moment, the tribes might be joined by an Afghan army numbering tens of thousands. Chamberlain therefore put in a call for massive reinforcements.

What he got instead, on November 26, was an order to withdraw the entire force. The Indian Government had panicked.

Providentially, the order was never implemented. General Rose, who had previously opposed an autumn expedition because he thought it premature, stepped in to warn that a pullback in the existing circumstances would place the British in an even less tenable position. Only the total rout of the force itself, he said, could be more calamitous than Government's loss of face among the tribes if the retreat were carried out. Retirement at this stage of the campaign would inevitably be seen as

Everybody's uncle had a bugle in his throat: rare photograph shows
Roberts (hand on knee) in rare moment of relaxation, while painting
by Louis Desanges finds him in more characteristic surroundings on
the march to Kandahar, August 1880. (*Radio Times Hulton
Picture Library*)

Abdur Rahman: "There were few of those before him who did not tremble."
(Photograph by Frank A. Martin, from his book, *Under the Absolute Amir*)

Junior Afghan officials "enjoy" dinner with Abdur Rahman. (Drawing by Frank A. Martin, from his book, *Under the Absolute Amir*)

Divine Service: *London Graphic* artist depicts Swat's Mad Mullah preaching to tribal congregation, July 1897. (*Culver Pictures*)

Donnybrook: Guides Cavalry and 11th Bengal Lancers collide with Pathans in first phase of Malakand siege, July 1897. Watercolor by E. Hobday, 1899. (*National Army Museum*)

"Like most young fools I was looking for trouble." Winston Churchill in battle dress of 4th Hussars, just before covering Malakand campaign, 1897. (*Radio Times Hulton Picture Library*)

Forward the Chowderheads. With bullets in both legs, Piper Findlater skirls away for Gordon Highlanders and Gurkhas as they storm Dargai Heights in Tirah campaign, October 1897. (*Historical Pictures Service, Chicago*)

Laying down the law: Political officers of Lockhart's staff read terms of submission to Afridi jirga during Tirah campaign, November 1897. It later turned out that the Afridis had not been listening. (*National Army Museum*)

"No one who has read a page of Indian history will ever prophesy about the frontier." Curzon (front, center) with his American wife, Mary, and members of staff. (*National Army Museum*)

Misguided do-gooder: Amanullah receives Doctor of Civil Laws degree at Oxford, 1928. This photograph, one of a number showing an unveiled Queen Souraya (second from left), helped pave the way for the Afghan monarch's overthrow a few months later. (*Underwood & Underwood*)

"The Frontier Gandhi." With four future recruits, Abdul Ghaffar Khan stands at head of Red Shirt regiment, Peshawar, 1931. (*United Press International*)

The lucky jungle uniform: Lord and Lady Mountbatten shortly after Peshawar confrontation with Frontier tribesmen, April 1947. (*United Press International*)

an admission that the Frontier was too hot to handle. It could encourage outbreaks of much greater mass and frequency, not only in Yusufzai country, but across the entire trans-Indus region. Not inconceivably, the financial outlay—and the cost in lives—needed to deal with continuing and mounting unrest might in due course cause Government to consider the evacuation of the Frontier itself.

This time Rose was heeded. A 7,800-man relief column under General Sir John Garvock was pushed up to Ambela, Garvock taking over command of the entire force from the wounded Chamberlain. By December 15, the British were ready to go on the offensive and force the pass.

To do this, they had to occupy a hill lying a short distance to the east of Crag Picquet; whoever held that position controlled all movement through the pass. The hill did not seem an easy nut to crack. It was shaped like a giant dunce cap and its steep sides were gay with the battle flags of nearly 4,000 tribesmen. But after a sustained working-over by British mountain guns, the flags could be seen to shift as the defenders' lines began to buckle. Bugles brayed and the riflemen of the Guides and three Indian infantry regiments began clambering up the conical slopes, well blanketed by their own artillery. Near the summit, the attack was halted briefly by a gale of bullets and stones, but the storm soon blew itself out under the walloping of the mountain guns, and the peak of the dunce cap was carried at bayonet point. By December 17, Garvock's troops held the Ambela Pass. To all practical purposes, the campaign against the Fanatics had ended.

There remained, to be sure, the task of destroying the Fanatics' "capital" at Malka, twenty miles to the east, but this was now seen less as a military operation than as a symbolic gesture of reprisal. The relative ease with which the Ambela Pass had finally been carried was due at least in part to the Bunerwals' absence from the fight. Pressure from the Commissioner of Peshawar, Colonel Reynell Taylor, and other political officers, reinforced by the arrival of Garvock's column, had at last convinced the tribal leaders that their alliance with the Fanatics had been a mistake. As Garvock prepared to march on Malka, a Bunerwal deputation came in and offered the tribe's services to the British in any capacity. Garvock then decided that the Bunerwals, rather than the Indian Army, should destroy Malka. Not only would the leveling of a tribal village by another tribe at British orders demonstrate the clout of the Raj that much more forcibly, but it would also keep the Bunerwals themselves from further mischief. On December 19, therefore, a handful of British officers led by Taylor set out with a small Guides escort for Malka, to watch the Bunerwals carry out their imperial mission of teaching the natives a lesson.

Soon, however, it began to appear that the campaign might not have ended after all. On arriving at Malka after a two-day trek in a slashing winter sleetstorm across an icy rock landscape that could have been painted by Doré, the British officers found themselves facing an almost solid wall of hostility. Although no resistance was offered when the Bunerwals began putting Malka to the torch, Roberts, who was with the party, observed that the villagers "did not attempt to disguise their disgust at our presence. . . . They gathered in knots, scowling and pointing at us, evidently discussing whether we should or should not be allowed to return."

That question was anything but academic. The Bunerwals had promised an escort of two thousand warriors, but only seventy men had turned up. At least thirty times that number of armed tribesmen now began converging on the tiny party of intruders as pillars of oily smoke climbed skyward from the blazing village. "The Native officers of the Guides warned us that delay was dangerous," wrote Roberts, "as the people were becoming momentarily more excited, and were vowing we should never return. It was no use, however, to attempt to make a move without the consent of the tribesmen, for we were a mere handful compared to the thousands who had assembled. . . . Our position was . . . extremely critical."

Things finally came to a head when Taylor decided there was no choice but to put a bold face on it and simply march out. This touched off an explosion. With a great roar, the tribesmen pressed swiftly in on the British party, and the officers drew their pistols for a last stand.

At that moment, the leader of the Bunerwal escort, an ancient malik named Zaidullah Khan, stepped forward. He was half blind, had only one arm and his trunk was crosshatched with the scars of long-forgotten battles. He faced the Malka tribesmen and stared them down with his single eye. Slay the Feringhis if you will, he said, but first you'll have to kill us Bunerwals, for we've taken an oath to protect these Sahibs with our lives, and you vomit of syphilitic camels know we'll keep our word. "This plucky speech had a quieting effect," wrote Roberts, "and taking advantage of the lull in the storm, we set out on our return journey."

The party was still not out of the woods. The entire length of the winding track back to the British camp was lined solidly on both sides with armed Pathans looking for the smallest excuse to attack. The officers plodded uneasily through a stream of abuse. Several times, groups of tribesmen blocked the path and conducted screaming arguments with Taylor. One banner-waving Fanatic actually rushed the party, hoping to draw its fire. "Fortunately for us," said Roberts, "he was stopped by some of those less inimically disposed; for if he had succeeded in inciting anyone to fire a single shot, the desire for blood would quickly have spread, and in all probability not one of our party would have escaped." The point was that the party did escape, for the real showdown had taken place at Malka, when the venerable Zaidullah Khan had called the bluff of the hostiles at the touchiest moment of their hair-trigger rage. No British proconsul could have dispersed a mob of "natives" with more cool. Writ small, Zaidullah Khan's act had helped the Feringhi as much as had Dost Muhammad's refusal to invade the Frontier during the Mutiny. Had he not pulled the claws of the Hindustani Fanatics when and as he did, the whole Fanatic-Bunerwal coalition could have re-emerged and returned to the warpath with no telling what consequences for the British. As it was, the Fanatics from that moment on ceased to be a threat on the Frontier.

But their sons and grandsons would remember. Thirty-four years later, the battle of Ambela was to bear bitter fruit.

PART THREE

Duel in the Sandbox

14

The Smile on the Face of the Bear

The position of [our government] in Central Asia is that of all civilised states which come into contact with half-savage, wandering tribes possessing no fixed social organisation. . . . In order to cut short . . . perpetual disorders we established strong places in the midst of a hostile population. . . . But beyond this line there are other tribes which soon provoked the same dangers. . . . The state then finds itself on the horns of a dilemma. It must . . deliver its frontier over to disorder . . . or it must plunge into the depths of savage countries. . . . Such has been the lot of all countries placed in the same conditions. The United States in America, France in Algiers, Holland in her colonies . . all have been inevitably drawn into a course wherein ambition plays a smaller part than imperious necessity, and where the greatest difficulty is in knowing where to stop.

T HIS BRITISH IMPERIAL MANIFESTO was written in 1864, by Prince Aleksandr Mikhailovich Gorchakov, the Foreign Minister of Russia, to explain his own country's manifest destiny in Central Asia. Its operative phrase, "the greatest difficulty is in knowing where to stop," pinpoints what may have been the crux of a century-long struggle between Russia and England for hegemony on the Asian land mass. Britain's objective was not further conquest—India sufficed. But Russian expansionism seemed a direct threat to India and had to be resisted at any cost. Thus the lines were drawn.

British statesmen and historians have called Anglo-Russian Central Asian rivalry the "Great Game," and indeed the behavior of the diplomats on both sides did at times suggest children disputing ownership of a sandbox. But the Great Game also brought the two nations to the brink of war at least twice—war that would almost certainly have drawn in all the other European powers. Red alerts seemed continually a-blink in Central Asia for at least six decades of the nineteenth century, as Russia's eastward imperial expansion went into high gear and triggered a prolonged spasm of paranoia among the shapers of British foreign policy. This seizure was reflected most dramatically on the extreme outer fringes of India's northwest frontier.

Of all the European imperial powers, Russia may have been able to bring to bear the most logic—or at any rate the least illogic—in her apologia for expansion. Britain, France, Portugal, Holland, Italy and Germany all sent their fleets scouring the farthest reaches of the planet to annex lands with which they had not the slightest geographic, ethnic, national, cultural, political or religious bonds. But except for Alaska, which Czar Alexander II was never separated from the motherland by any ocean. If Russia's ties to Central Asian peoples were frail and sometimes nonexistent, at least it could be said that master and subject shared the same land mass. Eastward expansion under the czars could be considered —and defended—as a natural extension of more or less natural land frontiers. This was sometimes acknowledged even by Britons. "The conquest of Central Asia is a conquest of Orientals by Orientals," wrote Lord Curzon, who was anything but a Russophile. "The expansion of Russia is the natural growth of the parent stem. . . . In Central Asia the Russians are residents as well as rulers. In India the English are a relief band of occupants."

And if the natural frontier rationale did not always wash, Russia could invoke, as did Prince Gorchakov, the need to guard her outposts of civilization against wild men. Gorchakov certainly appreciated the not dissimilar explanation that was being voiced concurrently on the other side of the Atlantic. He could hardly have felt otherwise. While American farmers, ranchers, railwaymen and soldiers busily expropriated 100 million square miles of tribal property west of the Mississippi River, the might of Russia was absorbing vast Central Asian kingdoms much as blotting paper soaks up ink.

Since the route of the Russian eastward-southeastward advance did not require ocean voyages (steamers usually crossed the Caspian and Aral seas in less than twenty-four hours), the task of subjugating Central Asia might have seemed easier than the British conquest of India. This was not so.

India was a fearfully hot country, crawling with disease, but Russian armies marching east from the Caspian had to cope with more than thirst, sunstroke and fever (although they had their share). The sandstorms of the man-killing Kara Kum and Kyzyl Kum deserts threw up almost insuperable obstacles during the torrid months, while in winter, screaming polar blizzards simply brought life itself to a halt. Of this region, the Russian General Mikhail Skobelev wrote that "if known to Dante, the Central Asian roads would have served as an additional corridor to hell."

There was also the matter of welcome. Under the Moguls and various Hindu rulers, India had attained to a high order of civilization that adapted tolerably, if not eagerly, to European institutions. But the Central Asian Khanates and their great cities of Khiva, Bokhara, Samarkand, Tashkent and Khokand, at one time jewels of Islamic culture and models of Islamic law, had fallen into anarchy since the dissolution of the Timurid dynasty in the fifteenth century. All of the country between the Caspian Sea and the Syr Daria (or Jaxartes) River had become the playground of nomadic bandit warlords and their armies: Uzbek, Tajik, Khirgiz, Khazak and other natural-born killer peoples whose lineage traced back to the hordes of Genghis Khan. Slavers and caravan plunderers by profession, the warrior horsemen who roamed north of the Hindu Kush were at least as truculent as the Pathans. Conceivably they were even more xenophobic.

Indeed, as late as the 1870s, the Hungarian linguist-explorer Arminius Vambéry could write that "Central Asia has had to endure the sad celebrity of being, in our time, the darkest point in the civilisation chart of the old world, owing to the wild barbarism of its inhabitants. . . . The very names of Khiva, Bokhara and Samarkand are so associated with danger and difficulty that no European who is not prepared to take his life in his hand can venture to visit them."

Vambéry rates a word of mention. Next to Alexander Burnes, he may have been the most celebrated of the handful of westerners who ventured alone into Central Asia during the first seven decades of the nineteenth century. In its own way, his journey through the great Khanates in 1862 and 1863 was as significant in drawing back the curtain on a terra incognita as had been Columbus' first voyage to the West Indies. But it was also much more hazardous. For the duration of the 1,500-mile trek, Vambéry affected the garb and character of a dervish, or mendicant holy man. He called himself Haji Reshid and made his way about in realistic dervish fashion, peddling knives, needles, thread, glass beads and other articles in bazaars and caravanserais. A massive Koran suspended from a cord round his neck and an eloquent fluency in Arabic and Persian rounded off an all but foolproof camouflage.

The make-believe was necessary, and Vambéry could never afford to drop his guard. Because of the nature of their missions, Burnes and one or two others could not conceal their identities; Burnes enjoyed almost miraculous good fortune—denied to Stoddart and Conolly—in being able to return from Bokhara intact. Even in disguise, however, an infidel traveling alone in Central Asia—particularly a white infidel—was a poor insurance risk. A European could be smoked out if he became uncomfortable while squatting; if he took a drink of water after, rather than before, coffee; if he used his left hand to eat; if his instep was arched from wearing Western shoes; even if the crown of his head somehow appeared too flat. When Conolly went to Bokhara to rescue Stoddart, he first tried to pass himself off as an Uzbek merchant, but was spotted at once because he paid directly for a melon in a bazaar instead of haggling over the price. The mistake cost him his life.

Thus Vámbéry was far from immune. In the introduction to his book about his journey, he acknowledged that the work probably contained errors, which he explained by asking his readers "not to forget that I return from a country where to hear is regarded as indulgence, to ask as crime, and to take notes as a deadly sin."

This was the mentality of the peoples who blocked the path of Russia's eastward expansion.

But the Russians proved equal to it. Like the British, they had the engines of modern warfare that could eventually smash up the resistance of any tribal force, however savage. Unlike the British, Russian generals and Cossack horsemen were more than a match—as will be seen—for Uzbeks and Tajiks when it came to barbarity in action. As for the tribesmen themselves, they did not enjoy the Pathan's tactical advantage of broken mountain country, but had to defend their homes on what amounted to a vast pool table. Once the Russian juggernaut began to roll, Central Asia's subjugation was only a matter of time.

The drive can be said to have begun in earnest in the mid-1840s, when Russian holdings on the east coast of the Aral Sea were consolidated with the building of forts along the lower reaches of the Syr Darya River. Within a decade, armed Russian stern-wheel steamers were plying the Syr Darya for nearly 300 miles of its length, well into Turkestan. By 1864, St. Petersburg's orbit had extended as far east as Lake Isik-Kul on the Chinese frontier, while a Russian army hovered some 90 miles above Tashkent, once a great layover point for merchants on the caravan route from Samarkand to Peking and still one of the strategic keys to mastery of Central Asia. It was at this time that Prince Gorchakov saw fit to issue his landmark circular, chiefly with a view to assuring Europe in general and England in particular that Russia had at last reached "the limits where interest and reason command us to stop."

But since the same memorandum also noted that "the greatest difficulty is in knowing where to stop," it hardly came as a surprise to Britain when, in June 1865, Russian troops occupied Tashkent and then formalized the annexation by creating the province of Turkestan. Samarkand had to be next. Three years later, the onetime pearl of Muslim

Central Asia fell to a Russian army. Its commander, General Konstantin Kauffmann, was shortly afterwards made Governor of all Turkestan.

Kauffmann was one of the most distinguished soldiers in the Czar's eastern frontier service. He also knew how to play the proconsul. No one was allowed to sit in his presence, and he had triumphal arches made for him whenever he entered a city with his 100-man mounted Cossack escort. It was sometimes said that the inhabitants of Samarkand knew only three great names: those of Alexander, Tamerlane and Kauffmann. Disraeli did not idly call him "the Russian Napier." (Caroe writes that Kauffmann's "name stinks in Central Asia to this day.") But mainly, Kauffmann was a fighting man. Hardly had the gates of Samarkand been forced in May 1868, than he marched his columns west to deal with Bokhara. In June, a Tajik army outside that city was battered into submission by Kauffmann's field guns and Cossacks. Although "Bokhara the Noble" was not annexed, the treaty that Kauffmann forced on its Amir made that ruler a Russian marionette. The long arm of St. Petersburg's influence could now be felt on the north bank of the Oxus.

And the pounding of its fist was heard in India.

Up to this time, the Russian advance had caused little stir in British diplomatic circles. But with the fall of Bokhara, Foreign Office officials began taking a long, careful look at the map of Euro-Asia—even though no more than a glance was needed to reveal how swiftly and dramatically the gap between British and Russian imperial possessions had narrowed. A century and a half earlier, some 4,000 miles had separated Russia's easternmost outposts of Orenburg and Petropavlovsk from East India Company holdings along the Bay of Bengal. Now, with the Punjab Frontier Force patrolling the trans-Indus hills and Cossack garrisons in Samarkand and Bokhara, the distance had shrunk to barely 400 miles—with Czar Alexander II as landlord of a Central Asian property more than twice the size of the continental United States.

Even more unsettling was the fact that the British had come to a halt on the eastern flank of the Frontier mountain chain, while the Russians showed no signs of stopping short of the Oxus or even the Hindu Kush. Afghanistan could well be the Czar's next objective. After that? Improbable and unrealistic as it may have seemed in some quarters, an invasion of India could never be ruled out entirely. At the very least, it was considered imperative that steps be taken to prevent the establishment of a contiguous Russian-British border in Central Asia.

Accordingly, there began a five-year series of conferences and exchanges of long-winded memoranda between London and St. Petersburg, as the two imperial powers—neither anxious for war with the other—sought to define a neutral zone between Russian Central Asia and British India. In January 1873, an agreement was finally hammered out by Gorchakov and Lord Granville, the British Foreign Minister. Although not specifying any neutral buffer area, it did define Afghanistan's northern border, of which the most important sector was the line of the Oxus. Both nations pledged themselves not to cross that line, and Gorchakov even went so far as to declare that Alexander II regarded Afghanistan as "completely outside the sphere within which Russia might be called upon to exercise her influence." It was not the most ironclad of treaties, but it did at least appear to have halted Russian southward movement. And much more to the point, it tacitly allowed Britain a free hand to manipulate Afghanistan.

This was not to say that the Granville-Gorchakov Agreement in any way appeased Russia's Central Asian land hunger. In the very same year that the bargain was sealed, an army under Kauffmann marched on Khiva, 300 miles northwest of Bokhara, capturing the place and indenturing its Khan to the Czar. This was hardly the sort of move designed to allay British anxieties that Russia at some future time might reverse direction and launch a thrust at India via Afghanistan. Realistic or not, the threat continued to loom very large and even seemed to grow.

Indeed, the years between the subjugation of Samarkand and Bokhara in 1868 and the conquest of Khiva on the heels of the Granville-Gorchakov quasi-treaty in 1873 witnessed a sweeping reassessment of Indian frontier geopolitics as a counter to further Russian expansion. Particularly noticeable was a mounting uncertainty over the wisdom of John Lawrence's close-border policy in the defense of the Raj.

When Lawrence stunned Indian officialdom with his plan to hand over Peshawar to Dost Muhammad at the height of the Mutiny, he was simply carrying his own close-border theories to what he regarded as their logical conclusion. Many advocates of "masterful inaction," impelled largely by a wish to prevent a repetition of the 1842 Kabul tragedy, believed it essential to avoid precipitating a showdown with Afghanistan. Incidents could be easily avoided, they maintained, simply if the Indian Government made a strict point of staying on its own side of the so-called administrative border of the northwest frontier. But Lawrence took a giant step further. Even after the Mutiny, he continued to see the entire Frontier region as a dangerous liability. It was his contention that British rule in India would be far more secure if Government simply acknowledged traditional Afghan claims and pulled her own northwest boundary line to the east bank of the Indus. In 1858 and 1859, he reintroduced the proposal to give Peshawar back to Dost Muhammad, explaining his reasons to Prime Minister Palmerston with blunt frankness: "Those who oppose this policy consider it a confession of weakness... To this it may be replied that our position in India is weak." The obvious inference to be drawn was that the position would be buttressed if British India divested herself of her trans-Indus albatross.

Palmerston shrugged off this logic as "an instance of the follies of the wise," and no more was heard of unloading Peshawar or falling back on the Indus. But owing to Lawrence's immense influence—not to mention his elevation to the peerage and appointment as Viceroy in 1864—the policy of masterful inaction on the Frontier itself remained intact. In 1867, when Harry Lumsden proposed annexation of the Kurram and Khost valleys southwest of Peshawar to stiffen British Frontier authority, Lawrence's veto was emphatic: "The Afghan will bear poverty, insecurity of life; but he will not tolerate foreign rule. . . The Afghans do not want us; they dread our appearance in their country." And that ended that.

But in 1868, when Russia's military engine rumbled in on Bokhara and Samarkand, a geopolitical assault was also mounted against Lawrence's isolationism from a highly influential quarter in England. Major General Sir Henry Rawlinson was not just another ex-soldier with a seat in Parliament. He had been Political Officer at Kandahar during the 1839–42 Afghan campaign, had subsequently served as British envoy to Persia, and also happened to be something of a Renaissance Man* who knew more about Central Asian affairs than any living contemporary. When he spoke, cabinets stopped their work to listen.

Rawlinson's response to the news of the Russian advances took the form of a semi-official memorandum that made three points. First, the Russian presence in Bokhara must inevitably be followed by a bid to establish diplomatic relations with Afghanistan. Second, Russian emissaries in Kabul could be counted on to foment intrigue in India with a view to triggering another nationwide insurrection. With chilling candor, Rawlinson acknowledged so intense a hostility among Indians toward their British masters that "it may truly be said that we are living upon a volcano in India, which at any moment may explode and overwhelm us." The third point came directly to the point: "With this prospect before us—with the knowledge that . . . if Russia were so disposed she might in the natural course of events be enabled severely to injure us, are we justified in maintaining what has been sarcastically . . . called Sir John Lawrence's policy of 'masterly inaction'?"

Obviously, Rawlinson's answer was "no." He saw it as Britain's "bounden duty," to "forestall" Russian moves toward Kabul by jettisoning the close-border policy and reestablishing a strong formal relationship with Afghanistan. What this meant, specifically, was a British envoy in

* As president of the Royal Geographical Society, Rawlinson would later belittle Stanley's search for Livingstone and send the Society's own man to Africa in a vain effort to reach Livingstone first.

Kabul, with all the risk that entailed. And risk there must be, since Rawlinson and his followers wanted not just a run-of-the-mill consul type in the Afghan capital, but a diplomat-politican who would actually work behind the scenes to shape Afghanistan's foreign policy in accordance with British needs. Yet "whatever the price," said Rawlinson, "it must be paid, of such paramount importance is it to obtain at the present time a dominant position at Cabul, and to close that avenue of approach against Russia."

Rawlinson's pronouncement did not instantly obliterate the close-border policy or its implementation, but the memorandum was the open-ing gun of what came to be called Britain's "Forward Policy" of Frontier and Afghan diplomacy, and Rawlinson himself won recognition as its architect. In 1875, he included the original memorandum in his monu-mental work, *England and Russia in the East*. This book was a showcase of his talents as a grandmaster of the nonstop sentence and marathon footnote—which could partially explain why the whole Frontier question became as bewildering as it did—but it was also the Bible of Forward Policy advocates. No other political document ever worked so revolu-tionary an effect on Britain's entire Central Asian stance.

From a superficial reading of *England and Russia in the East*, one gets the impression that Rawlinson wishes to stress two main points: (1) Russia will never attempt to invade India, and (2) she most certainly will. On closer examination, that contradictory position is likely to be confirmed. Britain, declares Rawlinson, need not fear "the immediate, or even proximate, invasion of our Indian empire. . . . What we really have to apprehend is, that an Asiatic Russia will arise to the north of the Hindu Kush, possessing within itself a germ of vitality and vigour that will . . . render it . . . a formidable rival to our Indian empire. . . . But the growth of such a Satrapy . . . will be a work of time—a work, perhaps, of ages." But then he says: "The continued advance of Russia in Central Asia is as certain as the movement of the sun in the heavens. . . . Russia will continue to push onward towards India till arrested by a barrier which she cannot remove or overstep. If this programme be correct, it means of course contact and collision . . . and such I believe . . . to be the inevitable result in due course of time."

These remarks are quoted from context with a vengeance. Rawlinson frequently said also that political leverage in Europe rather than the conquest of India was what Russia really sought from her Central Asian advances—and this probably came closest to being the truth. But Rawlinson would not have been worth his salt as an imperialist had he failed to voice a genuine concern for India's defense against a Russian invasion. *England and Russia in the East* fairly howls with siren alerts. Rawlinson even went so far as to map out, with the painstaking detail of a soldier, the line of advance that he was certain a Russian army must follow. The route is interesting because it sidesteps the Khyber Pass by 400 miles. Russian generals, in Rawlinson's opinion, would be compelled to choose the longer southerly approach through the Bolan Pass after a somewhat roundabout march from Herat to Kandahar, "where the roads are open and traverse districts that have been called 'the granary of Asia.'" The advantage of such a route was that it would eliminate the need for armies to negotiate "the sterile and difficult passes" of the north. Although Rawlinson of course did not consider the Bolan a six-lane freeway, he saw it clearly as offering the least difficult strategic entry to India.

Not that this route was Rawlinson's idea; nor was it even new, having been marched across by Alexander's hoplite columns twenty-two centuries earlier. And as late as the 1830s, British anxiety that a Russian army might follow in Alexander's footsteps had done a great deal to start the Afghan War of 1839–42. Even Keane's Army of the Indus had left India through the Bolan rather than the Khyber (although this was for reasons of political expediency and not strategy). But given the climate of near-panic that often dominated the Central Asian scene at the height of the Great Game, it is not entirely inaccurate to say that Rawlinson put the southerly route on the map. In any case, a march from Kabul through the Khyber was ruled out. Rawlinson saw Herat, the jumping-off place, as the "key to India," and that view came to be shared by all British military strategists of the time.

Whether that view was held also by Russian strategists is open to question. In 1881, when the contest was really beginning to heat up, a Russian-born English journalist named Charles Marvin visited St. Petersburg* and interviewed a number of top-ranking Russian staff officers. Almost to a man, they told him that they were at a loss to understand Britain's perpetual state of terror on the Indian frontier. General Mikhail Skobelev, the thirty-eight-year-old Commander-in-Chief in Central Asia, who dismissed British-Russian tensions as "all humbug," did not even believe an invasion of India feasible, or so he said. "I should not like to be commander of such an expedition. The difficulties would be enormous. . . . To invade India we should need 150,000 troops; 60,000 to enter India with, and 90,000 to guard the communications." Another general seconded Skobelev, except he said that 300,000 men rather than 150,000 would be needed. But an engineer officer may have hit the nail on the head most smartly when he mentioned Rawlinson's opinion of Herat as the main staging area of a Russian invasion: "You give so much attention

* For a moment, he thought he would not be allowed to return to his original homeland. Applying for a visa at the Russian Embassy, he said he represented the *Newcastle Daily Chronicle*, which evoked the chilly reply: "Ah, that is the paper to which the Nihilist leader, Prince Kropotkin, contributes." But his passport was stamped.

to the fact of certain centers being what you call 'keys,' that you altogether overlook the vast distances separating them from the places they are supposed to protect."

It will be seen presently that Russia was far from being as feeble or as innocent as the above disclaimers would suggest, but the fact remained that the Czar's diplomats and soldiers, except in rare instances, did not burn with an all-consuming passion to see Mother Russia embrace Mother India. Nor did Russian statesmen look to the security of their own Central Asian possessions with the near-hysteria that almost invariably characterized the shaping of British Indian policy. Marvin, like most adopted citizens of free countries, was a fervent British patriot, but he deplored "the indiscriminate wolf-cry of certain English writers on Central Asia [who have] done more harm than good to the cause they espouse." Yet room for suspicion of Russian motives definitely existed, while developments in Afghanistan during the last three decades of the nineteenth century gave the Forward Policy its greatest impetus.

And considering the tragic consequences of those developments, one might find room to wonder just how the Forward Policy could have served British interests—either in Afghanistan or India itself—in any way.

15

The Friends of Sher Ali

WHEN DOST MUHAMMAD DIED in 1863, he was succeeded by his forty-year-old son Sheri Ali, a man of no small dignity, who instantly found himself challenged by two older brothers, Afzal and Azim. The former was a practicing alcoholic, the latter a sadist whose excesses were a bit much even for an Afghan. Ordinarily, neither man should have caused Sher Ali much concern, but Afghanistan was Afghanistan and a five-year civil war commenced, during which one sometimes had trouble knowing who was fighting on whose side. In 1868, after battling and intriguing his way into Kabul, Sher Ali reinstated himself as firmly as any Afghan ruler could under the circumstances. Certainly the circumstances were not good. If the preceding half-decade of strife had not quite returned Afghanistan to its turn-of-the-century condition of anarchy, the country had at least become ripe for outside picking.

From India, the British had been looking on in some bewilderment; the civil war had seemed to them a violent game of musical chairs in which Sher Ali, Afzal and Azim each sat on the throne whenever he could seize it. But Lawrence, as Viceroy, had also maintained a strict neutrality. He laid it down that "our relations should always be with the *de facto* ruler"—a policy that was criticized for encouraging chaos and, worse, helping soften up Afghanistan for Russian intrigue. This may or may not have been true, but Russian proximity, at the very least, could no longer be gainsaid. When Sher Ali took up the shaky reins of government in 1868, Kauffmann's army seemed almost to be breathing down his neck from Samarkand and Bokhara.

Certainly the moment was opportune for Rawlinson to sound his warning against Russian designs on India via Afghanistan and to declare that the hour was at hand to deep-six Lawrence's isolationism forever. Britain, he insisted, must now play an active, assertive role, not only on the trans-Indus frontier, but in Afghanistan itself—through the influence exercised by an accredited British envoy. "It is a position which we must inevitably occupy sooner or later," he intoned, "unless we are prepared to jeopardise our Indian Empire."

To say the least, Sher Ali did not concur. Nor was he a man to abstain from outspoken dissent. Photographs show the very model of the Oriental potentate. Arched eyebrows, haughty Roman nose, flaring nostrils above a cascading black beard and an expression of sublime disdain from behind partly closed eyelids—all bespeak a soaring regal composure which was all too often belied by Sher Ali's other nature. Fraser-Tytler may be understating it in writing that Sher Ali "required careful and patient handling." For this man, much given to displays of rug chewing passion, was possibly the most emotional, high-strung and petulant amir in Afghanistan's history. And although he was also the least predictable, there was one issue on which he never wavered: the very thought of even a token British presence in his country could throw him into a boiling tantrum that verged on certifiability. Even three decades after the British occupation of 1839, the shame of that intrusion burned in his mind like a branding iron.

And yet, however repugnant the idea, Sher Ali knew that he could not disregard entirely Britain's policy dictates. Disunited, backward, feeble, Afghanistan had become the principal pawn in a no-quarter struggle between the world's two mightiest imperial powers. If he was to survive, Sher Ali had to align himself with one, and the prospect of turning to Russia was even more chilling than the thought of an accord of some sort with British India. At the very least, Sher Ali knew something about the British, who had been on the scene for three decades and who, despite their single wanton violation of sacred Afghan soil in 1839, had since remained stationary behind a self-imposed barrier. The same could not be said for the Russians, who seemed to show no signs of halting their southerly drive toward the Hindu Kush. If Allah willed it that defending Afghanistan's borders meant that Sher Ali must do Britain's bidding, so be it—up to a point.

Accordingly, one of the Amir's first acts on returning to the throne was to put out feelers for talks of some kind with the Indian Government. Partly because of the impact of Rawlinson's memorandum, partly because his own term as Viceroy was expiring, Lawrence wrote Sher Ali to say that such a meeting would not be unwelcome. Early in 1869, the Amir was formally invited by Lawrence's successor, Lord Mayo, to be guest of honor at a *durbar* in Ambala, India.

From the standpoint of pomp and circumstance, Sher Ali had every reason to be gratified with his reception: the British were nothing if not grandmasters in the art of choreographing twenty-one-gun salutes, full-dress parades, state dinners and all the other token gestures of obeisance to peanut royalty. The Amir also did well for himself materially, receiving a subsidy of £120,000 while the Afghan arsenal was expanded with four eighteen-pound siege guns, two eight-inch howitzers, a battery of mountain guns and some ten thousand assorted rifles, muskets and smooth-bore pistols. And at the personal level, Sher Ali found a genuine friend in Mayo. The new Viceroy was a stout, sunny-faced, warm-hearted Irishman possessed of an empathy and patience ideally suited to dealing with the temperamental Amir. Despite the language barrier, the two men conversed easily with interpreters, Sher Ali even unbending to the point of a small joke. During a ceremonial march-past of the kilted Gordon Highlanders, he turned to Mayo and remarked that "the dress of the Scotch is beautiful, and indeed terrific, but is it decent?"

The treatment seemed to have the desired effect. In his bread-and-butter letter to Mayo, Sher Ali pledged that "if it please God, as long as I live, or as long as my Government exists, the foundation of friendship and good-will between this and the powerful British Government will not be weakened."

In fact, however, the Ambala summit paved the way for the collapse of Anglo-Afghan relations.

Sher Ali's main reason for meeting with Mayo was to win a firm commitment of British aid should Russia attack Afghanistan. In the earlier treaty with Dost Muhammad, the Indian Government had merely promised not to interfere in Afghan affairs; the war with Persia had been fought in British rather than Afghan interests. At Ambala, Sher Ali quickly learned that although the isolationist Lawrence was no longer on the scene, his views continued to dominate Indian policy. Britain's refusal to make a formal pledge of aid did not simply disappoint the Amir; it embittered him deeply. And it also had the effect of stiffening his back against subsequent British bids for diplomatic representation in Kabul.

Accommodation could have been reached by both parties. Had Sher Ali yielded on the envoy issue, the risk of Afghan foreign policy coming under Whitehall's control would have been offset at least in part by the removal of the Russian threat, and it was certainly in Britain's interest to back the Amir against the Russians. But Sher Ali's fear of British designs effectively dashed any British hopes for gaining a policy wedge in Kabul. Sher Ali's anxieties had at least some foundation; Britain's behavior made less sense. Although she had everything to gain from a formal commitment of aid to Sher Ali, three decades of a close-border philosophy produced a knee-jerk response in a righteously—and militantly—antiexpansionist Gladstone Government. So there the matter rested, or rather simmered.

But in February 1874, the whole edifice of masterful inaction came tumbling down and the Forward Policy at last became official policy when Gladstone and his Liberal party were ousted by Disraeli and his unashamedly imperialist Conservatives in the British general elections. Rawlinson's views were mirrored by the new Tory cabinet and particularly by Lord Salisbury, the Secretary of State for India, who made it known that "England would be impelled by her own interests to assist [Sher Ali] in repelling the invasion of his territory by a foreign power." Salisbury backed this up by authorizing the newly appointed Viceroy, Lord Lytton, to make the Amir "a promise, not vague . . . of adequate aid against actual and unprovoked attack."

There was even to be a bonus: British recognition, long sought by Sher Ali, of his favorite son, Abdullah Jan, as the rightful heir apparent. Gladstone's Government had leaned toward Abdullah Jan's older brother, Yakub Khan, whom the Amir at least once called "my dutiful son, the ill-starred wretch," and who was then languishing in prison for plotting to seize the throne. Now, with the pretender repudiated and what appeared to be a no-strings aid commitment in the offing, Sher Ali's fondest dreams seemed realized at last.

And they might well have been realized had it not been for Lytton. A far cry from the compassionate Mayo, the new Viceroy was to characterize Sher Ali as "a savage with a touch of insanity," and if that judgement was not wholly inaccurate Lytton was hardly the man to make it, being, in his own way, a personality at least as impetuous as the Amir. A son of the novelist Edward Bulwer-Lytton, he himself was a poet of no small gifts, and enhanced that image with curly locks, soulful eyes and such Bohemian mannerisms as smoking cigarettes at the dinner table. But his lyrical flights of Victorian fancy were more suited to the politics of vainglorious imperialism; at times, it seemed almost as if his mouth watered at the prospect of painting all Central Asia red.

It must be said also that Lytton was a born executive with an uncommonly keen mind and a refreshing gift for cutting through red tape. Many of his administrative ideas were progressive and farsighted. Among other things, he drew up a set of detailed reforms for Frontier government that were to be adopted, almost to the letter, a quarter of a century later. But the only reason why these changes were not put into effect during Lytton's own incumbency was that they had to take a back seat to events he himself set in motion with a program of expansionism that was mind-boggling in its ambition. As one of Rawlinson's most ardent disciples (Rawlinson had, in fact, suggested his appointment as Viceroy to Salisbury), Lytton was to formulate a nearly science-fictional blueprint for putting the master's basically defensive theories into aggressive practice.

And in the process, he was to totally demolish the last hopes of friendly relations between Britain and Afghanistan.

But first things first. On arriving in Calcutta early in 1876, Lytton embarked on his viceroyalty by disembarking on the wrong foot. Without delay, he sent off a letter to Sher Ali informing him that a veteran British diplomat, Sir Lewis Pelly, was already proceeding to Kabul "to discuss with Your Highness matters of common interest." It was almost as if Lytton was deliberately seeking to touch Sher Ali's rawest nerve. The Amir scotched that plan, however, with a frigidly courteous refusal to receive Pelly, and a year-long exchange of barely civil correspondence followed. Sher Ali became so fed up with it that at one point he discussed with his ministers the pros and cons of launching an anti-British jihad. Nothing came of it.

During this period, the Amir was also feeling some diplomatic pressure from Kauffmann in his capacity as Governor General of Russian Turkestan, while Lytton, for his part, was showing his own very reasonable side by implementing Salisbury's instructions to offer a formal alliance. But since a British envoy remained the condition of military assistance, and since Lytton had probably overplayed his hand in trying to force Pelly down the Amir's throat, as it were, even a temporary emissary in Kabul would have been less welcome to Sher Ali than a crate of scorpions. All that could be achieved was a sullen compromise. At the end of 1876, Sher Ali finally agreed to send his most trusted minister and confidant, one Said Nur Muhammad, to meet with Pelly in Peshawar and discuss a draft treaty. Everything really remained up in the air.

And the talks never got off the ground. Sher Ali had always at least tried to couch his anti-British feelings diplomatically, but Said Nur Muhammad made no attempt to conceal his own undiluted loathing for the infidel giant to the east, and his mood at Peshawar was further soured by an illness in its terminal stages. He opened the meeting by announcing to Pelly that Sher Ali had "a deep-seated mistrust of the good faith and sincerity of the British Government." He then went on to declare that Sher Ali expected British aid as a natural right, and further laid it down that British diplomatic representation in Kabul was absolutely out of the question. Then he dropped dead. When Sher Ali received the news in Kabul, he was said to have gone literally wild with grief and rage, rending his garments, pouring dust on his head and screaming hoarsely that he must now declare war on England. His outburst was only a momentary lapse, but it contributed nothing to the equanimity of either party.

And as if this were not enough, the British next learned that Sher Ali had been discussing military matters with the Russians and that he was also encouraging a tribal jihad on India's northwest frontier. The reports were either grossly exaggerated or downright false, but they were all the hot-headed Lytton needed. He promptly broke off all negotiations, informing Sher Ali that Britain no longer considered herself under any obligation to Afghanistan beyond the rudimentary terms of the earlier treaty with Dost Muhammad. Unless the Amir gave some ironclad assurance of future good behavior, he could expect no further British commitments or even efforts on his behalf.

Sher Ali proved surprisingly accommodating. He offered at once to accept any terms the British might include in a treaty, Lytton replied with a surprise of his own: resumption of the talks, he said, would no longer serve any useful purpose.

This appalled not a few of Lytton's advisers. It had come to look as if the Viceroy was totally incapable, or unwilling, to make allowances for Sher Ali's capricious temperament. Lytton himself insisted that he had not really locked the door on further negotiations. It was merely his intention, he said, to "let the Amir (if I may use a coarse but expressive phrase of Prince Bismarck's) stew for a while in his own gravy." But by then it was beginning to seem to a growing number of diplomats in India and England almost as though Lytton were seeking an open breach —if not open war—with Afghanistan.

The recess also enabled Lytton to antagonize Sher Ali further by concentrating on another Forward Policy matter. In accordance with Rawlinson's theory that a Russian army would strike at India through the Bolan, rather than the Khyber Pass, the Frontier's southern flank in upper Baluchistan was being secured at this time with the establishment of a major garrison at Quetta, the town guarding the western entrance to the Bolan. Perhaps more than anything else, that move hastened the deathblow to Anglo-Afghan relations.

The background to Quetta's occupation requires a quick detour into earlier Frontier happenings. Although the British had recognized Quetta's strategic value ever since Keane's Army of the Indus had marched through the place en route to Kabul in 1839, policy had dictated that it be left alone. The flyblown slum of mud hovels belonged to a sort of gray area known as the Khanate of Khelat, whose ruler claimed to be independent even though the region was part of Baluchistan and had been tributary to Kandahar ever since the reign of Ahmad Shah Durrani. Rather than provoke Afghanistan on the issue, the Indian Government under Canning and Lawrence had swiftly shot down proposals that Quetta be occupied as a defense outpost. But the annexation of Sind had brought the British too close to Quetta to forget its fortress potential. In 1866, a long stride toward commandeering the town was taken when a Frontier official anticipated Rawlinson by openly violating the precepts of masterful inaction.

This man was Captain Robert Sandeman, the Deputy Commissioner of the Dera Ghazi Khan district adjoining the Khanate of Khelat on the west bank of the Indus. Khelat's inhabitants were predominantly non-Pathan: Baluchis, Brahuis, Bugtis, Marris and other tribes known to be more obedient to their chiefs than were the Frontier clans—although they were not a whit less truculent. In fact, when Sandeman took up his post in 1866, he found Dera Ghazi Khan reeling under a continual fusillade of raids from Khelat. He was the right man to handle them. One of the few nineteenth-century British Indian frontier soldier-administrators not distinguished by a lean and hungry look, Sandeman actually went to stoutness, and his benevolent, even jolly, countenance seemed to reflect his belief in amiable discourse rather than military kung-fu as a means of managing subject peoples. He put this belief into action when he set about dealing with the Khelat raiders.

What he did, instead of mounting a punitive expedition, was simply to enlist a few Baluchi guides and hike across the border, carrying nothing but a revolver and high hopes. The former was not needed and the latter were realized when Sandeman sat down with a group of local chiefs and haggled with them until he won their agreement to blow the whistle on the banditry. Despite the relative tendency to obedience of the Baluchi tribes, it was a signal achievement, not to mention Sandeman's first major stop toward fame as British master of Baluchistan.

But what mattered for the moment was that Sandeman had extended the Queen's writ into forbidden territory and, in so doing, had made the occupation of Quetta a foregone conclusion. In 1877, with Lytton's blessing—and in complete disregard of Afghan claims—Sandeman concluded a treaty with the Khan of Khelat whereby Quetta and its environs came under the Union Jack on a rental basis.

A side effect of the agreement was to soften up the rest of Baluchistan for subsequent British annexation, but in the meanwhile Sher Ali saw the troop buildup at Quetta as a spear pointed directly at Kandahar. Perhaps at this juncture he remembered the Pathan saying that "a good enemy is better than a bad friend."

For the British move on Quetta did not merely cause Sher Ali even more anxiety than did the stirrings of the Russians in the north. It also changed his mind about who Afghanistan's real allies ought to be.

It was also at this time that the Russians made their boldest move on Afghanistan. They did so by declaring war on Turkey.

Strategically, the Russo-Turkish conflict turned on control of the Dardanelles, Russia's long-sought outlet to the Mediterranean. And the Dardanelles came within an ace of drawing Britain into the war, since

British statesmen thought of Russian naval access to the Suez Canal as an even greater menace to India than Sher Ali considered the British presence at Quetta a threat to Afghanistan. Five thousand Indian troops were sent to Malta on the swiftest transports available. For six months, British and Russian fleets faced each other on the Bosporus with gunports open. The word "jingo" was coined during the crisis.

And the diversion of British military resources and manpower from India also served as an opportunity for Czar Alexander II to put on a muscle-flexing exercise for Sher Ali's benefit. Following Turkey's defeat in the spring of 1878, a diplomatic mission, headed by Major General Nikolai Stolietoff, was sent to Kabul with a view to impressing the Amir with Russia's vastly elevated influence as a world power. At the same time, three columns under Kauffmann marched from Tashkent toward the Afghan border.

If Sher Ali was alarmed by the approach of the mission, he was no less impressed—and probably even more unsettled—by the British seizure of Quetta. He therefore made a virtue of necessity and received Stolietoff on the outskirts of Kabul with the traditional escort of palace guardsmen and gaudily caparisoned elephants on which the Russians entered the city as royal guests. On reaching the Bala Hissar, Stolietoff presented Sher Ali with a letter from Kauffmann, suggesting that Afghanistan's "union and friendship with the Russian Government will be beneficial to the latter, and still more so to you." With Kauffmann's troops less than ten marches from the Oxus, Sher Ali took the hint seriously. In all likelihood, he also welcomed it.

Then Stolietoff had the rug pulled out from under him. Largely at Britain's instigation, the major European powers had met in Berlin and forced a modification of the harsh peace terms that Russia had imposed on Turkey. Stolietoff learned of this blow to his country's prestige in a letter from Kauffmann, who called the news "melancholy" and advised that a softening of Russia's tone was in order.

But as far as Lytton was concerned, the damage had already been done. By its mere presence in Kabul, the Stolietoff mission had openly and flagrantly violated Russia's pledge that Afghanistan lay outside her sphere of influence. In a memorandum to the India Office, the Viceroy warned that "it is almost absolutely certain that in the ordinary uncorrected, and probably incorrigible, course of events . . . we shall . . . find ourselves conterminous with Russia along the North-West Frontier." He hardly needed to mention that this would enable Russian armies to control the western entrances to the Frontier passes.

Lytton also had a solution to the problem. He proposed to Disraeli that Afghanistan no longer be regarded as a sovereign state, and that it submit to dismemberment.

What the Rawlinsonian visionary had in mind was the Rawlinsonian credo in its most brazen manifestation; Fraser-Tytler has called the blueprint "the high water mark of the British Forward Policy." In Lytton's view, the mountain chain marking India's northwest frontier was a "hopelessly bad line" for a political boundary, especially with impending Russian access to the Khyber and Bolan passes. It was his intention, subject to London's approval, to create a new and more secure borderline by pushing the frontier right up to the northern slopes of the Hindu Kush, which he called "the great natural boundary of India." At a time when the expression "scientific frontier" was very much in vogue, the proposal could be seen as not totally insane. There was even a precedent: at one time, the Hindu Kush had marked the outer reaches of India's Mogul empire. No one could accuse Lytton of a lack of imagination.

The thing would not be quite an outright annexation—even Lytton had to draw the line there. But he thought it could be brought off by formal negotiation, which really amounted to gunboat diplomacy. The first act of his scenario, he wrote, should be the dispatch of a mission to Kabul, which "whilst instructed to use every endeavour to conciliate and convince the Amir, will be armed with a formidable bill of indictment against His Highness." The British envoy would also hand down a set of terms and make Sher Ali "distinctly understand that, if he rejects them, we shall openly break with him altogether" and "contemplate with great reluctance" overt military action to "conquer and hold so much of Afghan territory as will . . . be absolutely requisite." In effect, Lytton was urging that the stage be set for a repeat performance of the 1839 piracy.

But he was given the green light, and, on August 14, 1878, he wrote Sher Ali to inform him that a mission under Neville Chamberlain was proceeding to Kabul to discuss "matters of importance" relating to "the welfare and tranquility of [Afghanistan and India], and for the preservation of friendship between the two Governments." Lytton had chosen the commander of the 1863 Ambela expedition because of Chamberlain's personal acquaintance with the Amir. He also felt certain that Sher Ali could hardly refuse to receive the British Envoy with a Russian mission already in Kabul. But the letter could not have been more badly timed. It reached Sher Ali on the same day that his favorite son Abdullah Jan died. On learning of the coincidence, Major Pierre Louis Napoleon Cavagnari, a veteran Frontier officer with close contacts in Afghanistan, told Lytton he suspected that the heir-apparent's death might have temporarily deranged Sher Ali once more. If nothing else, it did give the Amir an excuse to put off a reply to Lytton.

At this time also, Sher Ali sought Stolietoff's advice on whether or not to receive the Chamberlain mission. Stolietoff voiced the opinion that the simultaneous presence in Kabul of Russian and British diplomats might cause embarrassment. He also made no offer to withdraw his own mission.

But with or without a reply from the Amir, Chamberlain set out for Kabul. On September 21, he and his party reached the dreadnaught-like bulk of Fort Jamrud at the entrance to the Khyber Pass, and Sher Ali moved to head them off at the pass.

The showdown took place the following day. Cavagnari, the commander of Chamberlain's military escort, rode ahead with twenty-four Guides troopers to arrange a safe-conduct through the Khyber with local Afridi chiefs. Ten miles inside the pass, near an old water mill shaded by mulberry trees on the banks of the Ali Masjid stream, a band of Afridis materialized. Their headman told Cavagnari that a large body of Afghan infantry and cavalry was massed only a mile or so ahead; he also said that this force had orders to open fire if the British party proceeded any further. The Afridis themselves began fingering their jezails. It was time to turn back.

Cavagnari dismounted instead. Presently a burly Pathan in the uniform of an Afghan Army general rode up, splashed across the stream and approached the British party. Cavagnari recognized Sirdar (general) Faiz Muhammad Khan, commander of Sher Ali's Khyber forces. The two men salaamed, saluted, shook hands and sat down beneath one of the mulberries. Chamberlain's military secretary, Lieutenant Colonel F. G. Jenkins, later described their exchange.

The Sirdar never flinched from first to last, but gave us distinctly to understand that he would oppose the passage of the mission by force, and that it was a waste of time to argue with him.

Major Cavagnari then said to the Sirdar—

"You are a servant of the Amir, and you take upon yourself to stop a Mission . . . from the British Government, with which he has long been on friendly terms. How do you know that the Amir himself will not be very angry with you for doing this?"

The Sirdar replied—"What friendship is there in what you are doing now? . . . You have come here on your own account. . . . You are setting Afridis against Afridis and will cause strife and bloodshed in this country and call yourself friends!"

The Afridis who were standing round us applauded this speech; and it would not have been prudent to have continued to converse in this tone. Therefore Major Cavagnari said to the Sirdar—"We are both servants—you of the Amir of Kabul, I of the British Government. It is no use for us to discuss these matters. I only came to get a straight answer from you. Will you oppose the passage of this mission by force?"

The Sirdar said—"Yes, I will; and you may take it as a kindness and because I remember friendship, that I do not fire upon you for what you have done already." After this we shook hands and mounted our horses: and the Sirdar said again—"You have had a straight answer."

"The first act has been played out," Cavagnari later told Lytton. Meanwhile, however, he reported back to Chamberlain, who in turn wrote the Viceroy: "Nothing could have been more . . . humiliating to the dignity of the British Crown and nation. . . . We must either sink into a position of merely obeying [Sher Ali's] behests on all points or stand up on our rights and risk rupture." Although Lytton hardly needed to be told this, he echoed Chamberlain's sentiments in a dispatch to London: "The repulse of Sir Neville Chamberlain by Sher Ali at his frontier while the Russian emissaries are still at his capital . . . has deprived the Amir of all claim on our further forbearance."

At about the same time, Sher Ali was throwing another match into the powder keg. In October, his reply to Lytton's original communication of August 14 finally reached the Viceroy. The Amir declared himself "astonished and dismayed" by what he called Lytton's "harsh expressions and harsh words, repugnant to courtesy and politness, and in tone contrary to the ways of friendship and intercourse." Actually, Lytton's letter had been studiously deferential, if cool, but Sher Ali's reply hardly warranted the Viceroy's next move. Three British columns had already been massed on the Frontier. Lytton now told his Government that the time had come to take off the gloves and order the troops to march on Kabul.

London was less hawkish. Salisbury, now Foreign Secretary, had been applying pressure on the Russians, who had assured him that the Stolietoff mission was only temporary and would be withdrawn shortly. Lytton was therefore told that Anglo-Afghan differences could yet be resolved if Sher Ali were given one more chance to mend his ways. All he need do was apologize and receive the Chamberlain mission. Accordingly, on October 30, Lytton wrote the Amir and extended the olive branch. It took the form of an ultimatum: if a reply was not forthcoming in three weeks at the latest, Sher Ali could consider himself the declared enemy of Great Britain.

This could hardly have surprised the Amir, who had become increasingly receptive to Russian overtures and promises. Even as St. Petersburg was assuring Salisbury of the absence of sinister motives in the Stolietoff mission, Sher Ali was pondering the draft of a treaty drawn up by the Russian envoy. It stipulated, among other things, that "if any foreign enemy attacks Afghanistan, and the Amir . . . asks the assistance of the Russian Government, the Russian Government will repel the enemy." Stolietoff himself was busily fomenting Anglophobia in the Bala Hissar. "You should be as a serpent," he wrote the Amir's wazir; "make peace openly, and in secret prepare for war. . . . It will be well, when the [British] Envoy . . . wants to enter the country, if you send an able emissary, possessing the tongue of a serpent and full of deceit, to the enemy's country, so that he may with sweet words perplex the enemy's mind and induce him to give up the intention of fighting with you.''

It was immaterial that Afghans, of all people, hardly needed lessons in guile. What mattered was that Sher Ali had now switched his allegiance. He knew he was in grave trouble with the British; nothing short of abject capitulation would appease Lytton any longer, and even that might be too late. Like Auckland and Macnaghten four decades earlier, Lytton had driven Britain's potential Afghan ally into the camp of Britain's worst enemy and seemed determined that he should stay there. Sher Ali's reply to Lytton's ultimatum was unacceptable. He accused the Viceroy of bullyragging him and stated flatly that Chamberlain had been halted out of fear "that the independence of [Afghanistan] might be affected" had the mission been allowed to proceed. The letter also arrived two weeks after Lytton's deadline. Early in December, Stolietoff prepared to leave Kabul for Russian Turkestan, and Sher Ali also decided to depart. Releasing Yakub Khan—his son, the wretch—from prison and appointing him Regent, the Amir joined the Russian party.

In going to Russia, it was Sher Ali's intention not just to secure a commitment of Russian troops but personally to plead Afghanistan's cause in an audience with Alexander II. Shortly after quitting Kabul, he wrote to "the Officers of the British Government," declaring that "if you have anything in dispute with me . . . you should initiate and establish your case at St. Petersburg.'' Nothing could have made Sher Ali's new allegiance plainer.

But the Russians had their own ideas about that, and Sher Ali might even have expected an unpleasant surprise. Shortly before his departure, he had received a letter from Kauffmann, who said: "I urgently request you not to leave your kingdom . . . because your arrival in Russian territory will make things worse.'' And Kauffmann made the point even clearer when the Amir crossed the border: "I have received an order from the Emperor to the effect that it is impossible to assist you with troops now.'' The Czar had found it expedient to pull in Russia's horns, at least for the time being. And since the bridge to conciliation with the British had already been burned, Sher Ali could no longer look to either power for support. Disillusioned, bewildered and by now critically ill, he made his faltering way through the snows back to Afghan Turkestan. Early in 1870, his party reached the town of Mazar-i-Sharif in the province of Balkh, once the center of the ancient Graeco-Bactrian Empire. It was a fitting place for kings to die. On February 21, 1879, Sher Ali did so.

Meanwhile, Lytton had got his war at last. Finding no reply to his ultimatum on November 20, 1878, he had ordered the army to march on Afghanistan and so informed London in a telegram. "*Jacta est alea!*" he exulted—the die is cast.

16

The Magpie's Omen

T HE FORCE THAT LYTTON UNLEASHED on Afghanistan was twice as large as the army that Auckland had fielded in 1838: 30,000 troops and 144 guns, divided into three columns thrusting forward along a 300-mile front. On the left, moving out of the new base at Quetta, were the 12,000 men of the Kandahar Field Force under Major General Sir Donald Stewart. Frederick Roberts, now also a major general, led the center column, which had been designated the Kurram Field Force for the valley marking its route. On the right, headed for Jalalabad via the Khyber Pass, marched the Peshawar Valley Field Force, 15,000 strong, commanded by Major General Sir Samuel Browne, who had won a Victoria Cross and lost an arm in the Mutiny and had since devised an odd shoulder belt to carry his sword and pistol. Following relatively familiar routes, neither Stewart nor Browne met with serious resistance. Stewart had a long and wearying tramp to Kandahar, but it was almost equally uneventful. Browne's men got into a vicious but brief dustup when they captured the Ali Masjid position in the Khyber, but that was all; on December 20, the troops virtually coasted into Jalalabad.

The same could not be said for Roberts' column. The cedar- and boulder-laced high country of the upper Kurram Valley, which debouched into the Afghan Khost Province, was terra incognita to the British. Roberts, moreover, was heading up his first independent field command (the rank of major general was local; in his own regiment he remained a major), and the force itself was the smallest of the three columns, mustering only 3,200 men. Roberts later wrote that the "people in Kuram did not care to disguise their belief that we were hastening to our destruction. . . . When they saw the little Gurkhas for the first time, they exclaimed: 'Is it possible that these beardless boys think they can fight Afghan warriors?'"

That question did not, of course, trouble Roberts, but he experienced "a feeling akin to despair" as he considered his situation. The Afghans not only outnumbered his force by six to one, but blocked the only route of advance into Khost, from defenses 9,400 feet up in the sky, at the summit of a pass called the Peiwar Kotal, where they had gouged out a maze of deep entrenchments reinforced by breastworks of heavy felled logs. From this position, wrote Roberts, "an overwhelming fire could be brought to bear" on the British, and the Afghans, for a change, had artillery to spare. The Peiwar Kotal had been made into an aerie of enraged eagles.

And as if the Afghans were not bothersome enough, Roberts at this juncture had his first run-in with a war correspondent—the breed having just begun to emerge as a British institution. The reporter in question was evidently an inventive type and had been filing copy that Roberts described as "founded on information derived from irresponsible and misinformed sources." Since the effect of these lurid stories was "to keep the public in a state of apprehension regarding the force in the field, and, what is even more to be deprecated, to weaken the confidence of the troops in their Commander," the Commander finally sent the correspondent to the rear. Roberts probably wished he could dismiss the Afghans from the Peiwar Kotal just as easily.

After poring over a sheaf of worthless maps, Roberts presently decided that the only way to crack the Afghan defenses would be by a feint combined with surprise. One thousand British and Indian troops, with strong artillery support, would launch a direct frontal assault on the Peiwar Kotal; it was expected to throw the Afghans off balance, opening their left flank and rear to a blow delivered by the 2,200 men of the main British body. Led by Roberts himself, this force would get into position under cover of night in absolute secrecy; tents were not to be struck, cook-fires would be left burning just as if the troops were in camp, rather than beginning their end run up a lofty, broken hogback that was held by only a small enemy detachment. British Frontier soldiers had learned that Afghans tended to cave in when hit from behind, and Roberts' plan had the virtue of simplicity. The chief problem was that the terrain could barely be negotiated by mountain goats.

Roberts did the goats one better, although the flanking advance ran into trouble from the moment the troops formed up on the night of December 1. In anticipation of an unusually stiff climb, the sepoys and British soldiers had been ordered to wear summer uniforms, which swiftly proved almost fatal in zero temperatures and winds that sliced down like razor blades from the glacial heights. Baggage animals continually skidded on the ice-coated ground; some lost their footing completely and plunged hundreds of feet to splattering death on frozen stream beds. The elephants carrying several mountain guns eventually had to be left behind. At one point, the whole force's cover was nearly blown when several disloyal Pathan sepoys from a Punjab infantry regiment fired off their rifles. And all the while, the units found it almost impossible to keep contact in the blackness.

Even when the sun finally rose on December 2, the route of march remained anybody's guess. For a good part of the day, the men of a Highland and Gurkha regiment stumbled blindly through a jungle of frost-rigid cedars and refrigerated boulders trying to find Roberts, while Roberts for his part sent officer after officer in search of the missing regiments. The officers failed to return.

And yet, Roberts pulled it all together. As the Afghans on the Peiwar Kotal met the British frontal feint with a massive infantry-artillery over-reaction, Roberts and the main body were able to work round to the rear of the entrenchments. Roberts also managed to bring up enough mountain guns for a concerted pasting that soon had the defenders in full flight westward. The Peiwar Kotal action was Roberts' first small step on the road to fame. By January 1879, he had secured the entire Khost region, and the three-pronged British force was in position to converge on Kabul without further delay.

The advance proved unnecessary. In February, when the Regent Yakub Khan learned of his father's death, he acted at once in his capacity as the new Amir, writing Lytton to sue for peace, or, as he put it, to assure that "the friendship of this God-granted state with the illustrious British Government may remain constant and firm." Having taught the Afghans their lesson, Lytton was prepared to negotiate.

In fact he had little other choice. The reenactment of the 1839 campaign had stirred up a hornet's nest in Parliament. The big guns of the Liberal Opposition were thundering righteously against the vainglorious and arrogant subjection of helpless Asiatic peoples. Gladstone and a Greek chorus of back-benchers lambasted the actions that had thrown Britain's only real ally against the Russians into the embrace of the Russian bear. In the House of Lords, John Lawrence inveighed against the scuttling of the close-border policy and was backed up by Viscount Halifax, who reminded fellow peers that "the old policy gave us thirty years of peace; thirty months of the new has plunged us into war." More than one Liberal seized on Lytton's earlier declaration that England had no quarrel with Afghanistan, only with its ruler; if that was so, cried the Opposition, why occupy Afghanistan at all now that Sher Ali has been removed from the scene? Why alienate the Afghan people beyond redemption? If the military offensive continued, Disraeli might soon face downfall in a general election.

So Lytton offered terms. Yakub Khan, who also had not much choice, accepted them. Moreover, this unprepossessing fellow seemed the type who would prefer acquiescence to the sweaty work of eyeball-to-eyeball negotiation. Some years earlier, Arminius Vambéry had met Yakub Khan while the latter was Governor of Herat, and recalled that "the young prince . . . would sit, most of the time, in an arm-chair at the window; and when wearied with the great number of petitioners which it was his official duty to receive . . . would order military drills . . . to be executed on the place below his window and inspect them from there." And so it was in the peace talks with the British. On May 26, 1879, near the site of the 44th Foot's last stand at Gandamak, the new Amir, after registering barely audible objection, signed a treaty.

Its provisions were clear enough. Yakub Khan was to be granted an annual subsidy of £60,000, in return for which he would place the administration of the Khyber Pass, the Kuram Valley and a sizable portion of Baluchistan in the hands of the Indian Government. It was a thumping concession.

But what the Amir really gave away was his country's freedom. He did this when he approved—albeit with great reluctance and his only real show of stubbornness—the clause which specified that a permanent British envoy be received in Kabul. Quite correctly, Sher Ali had always feared that "British envoy," when applied to Afghanistan, was a euphemism for "foreign minister," and now his son had opened the gates to such a back-room manipulator. Control of Afghan foreign relations, which meant de facto control of Afghanistan, was on its way to becoming a function of Whitehall. The transfer of responsibility would be invisible, and gradual rather than rapid—that was the British way— but Yakub Khan had in effect signed over his sovereignty, and Lytton's dream of a British Indian frontier on the Hindu Kush seemed about to come true.

Observing that Yakub Khan had submitted to his castration with a minimum of fuss and even a show of good grace, Lytton could hardly fail to feel that he had brought off a great triumph. Disraeli seemed to share this view and congratulated the Viceroy: "Whatever happens," he wrote, "it will always be to me of real satisfaction that I had the opportunity of placing you on the throne of the Great Mogul." In any event, the Treaty of Gandamak formally ended what was now being called the Second Afghan War. There is no record of anyone quoting to Lytton the old Pathan proverb that war in the Afghan hills begins only after peace has been concluded.

To fill the post of envoy, Lytton chose Sir Louis Cavagnari, who had just been knighted, not only for past service but to give his new office the proper aura of dignity. A French-Irish officer whose father had been one of Napoleon's generals, Cavagnari bore a slight resemblance to Robert E. Lee. He had served on the Frontier for thirteen years, was a veteran of seven punitive expeditions against the tribes and had run a taut ship as Deputy Commissioner of the Kohat district south of Peshawar. More recently—and more significantly—he had shown himself to be a gifted negotiator when he played a key role in prevailing on Yakub Khan to desist from balking at the envoy clause in the Treaty of Gandamak. That in itself seemed at the time worthy of a knighthood.

Cavagnari's qualifications as an ambassador were another matter. Chamberlain thought he had "more of the Nicholson style than any man I know," which was only partial praise in context: "I should say he is more the man for facing an emergency than one to entrust with a position requiring delicacy and very calm judgement. . . . If he were left at Cabul as our agent, I should fear his not keeping us out of difficulties." Obviously, however, Lytton did not share this opinion, nor, of course, did Cavagnari, who, like his predecessor Macnaghten, was a pathologically sanguine personality. He was also totally without physical fear, and it was characteristic that he had volunteered to head up the Kabul mission. To John Lawrence's dour prediction from England that Cavagnari and his staff "will all be murdered—every one of them," the Envoy replied: "If my death sets the red line on the Hindu Kush, I don't care."

Lawrence was not alone in his gloomy outlook. Roberts probably spoke for the majority of officers on the Frontier when he voiced the opinion that both the treaty and the mission were premature. The Afghans, he believed, "had not had the sense of defeat sufficiently driven into them . . . and therefore . . . a peace made now, before they had been thoroughly beaten, would not be a lasting one, and would only end in worse trouble in the near future."

Roberts also knew, however, that Lytton was under political pressure from England and that nothing could be done but put the best possible face on the thing. On July 15, 1879, therefore, Roberts and several others accompanied Cavagnari's party to the Shutargardan Pass, just north of the Peiwar Kotal, where the mission was to meet its Afghan escort. At dinner in the British camp that evening, Roberts was called on to offer a toast; "but somehow," he wrote, "I did not feel equal to the task; I was so thoroughly depressed, and my mind was filled with such gloomy forebodings as to the fate of these fine fellows, that I could not utter a word."

Next day the mounted Afghan escort rode up, its troops uniformed in a shabby imitation of British dragoons. The Afghan commander was all hospitality, ordering carpets spread on the ground and serving the British curds, lamb kebabs, sherbet, Russian tea with cardamon and black coffee laced with opium. But Roberts remained uneasy, and his mood seemed catching. At one point, he wrote, Cavagnari noticed a magpie, and "begged me not to mention the fact of having seen it to his wife, as she would be sure to consider it an unlucky omen." When the time came to part, the two men shook hands and walked away from each other. Then, as if by some ESP signal, both turned around simultaneously and shook hands again.

The British mission numbered eighty-one men, including Cavagnari; his political assistant Jenkyns; Dr. A. H. Kelly, the medical officer; and Second Lieutenant Walter Hamilton, commanding a Guides detachment of fifty-two sowars and twenty-five sepoys. When they reached Kabul at the end of July, the Europeans were given the standard VIP welcome, riding to the Bala Hissar in the gilt-and-silver howdahs of two royal elephants while nine Afghan regiments lined the street and presented arms, two batteries of eighteen-pounders banged out a ragged salute and several bands tried to play "God Save the Queen." Cavagnari then presented his credentials to Yakub Khan in the throne room, and the two men chatted stiffly but cordially on a broad range of trivialities. The Envoy later wrote to Lytton that Yakub Khan "showed a fairly good knowledge of French affairs, and said he supposed the republic would have a good chance of lasting." No mention was made of Afghanistan's chances.

Yakub Khan had also arranged quarters for the mission inside a walled courtyard that adjoined the Bala Hissar. In addition to stables, barracks for the troops and houses for servants, a large two-story lath-and-plaster building did double duty as Cavagnari's official headquarters and accommodation for the other Europeans. Cavagnari found the compound and buildings overcrowded, although he told Lytton that "we . . . have a better residence than the Amir himself." At the same time, however, he began to draw up plans for permanent quarters, not unlike the replica of Jefferson's Monticello that he had built for himself in Kohat. What he called "European principles of comfort and sanitation" would, he knew, enable his wife to join him.

The Embassy quickly settled into a smoothly functioning, if dull, routine. There was little to occupy the junior officers' time apart from riding, partridge shooting and drilling the Guides, so they used their leisure in efforts to create a climate of goodwill. Dr. Kelly worked on plans for a local dispensary, and Afghans were invited to join the mission staff in the time-honored British Army pastime of tent-pegging. The offer met with limited success. The Afghans seemed to look on the sport as practice for more realistic skewering of their countrymen.

Cavagnari was just slightly busier. He had regular meetings with Yakub

Khan on matters of inconsequence and received Afghan court officials when they made formal calls on the Residency—although he refused to emulate his subordinates by mingling with the people, who saw him only on his morning or evening rides to the city. He also sent daily reports to Lytton over the new telegraph line that had been strung from Peshawar to Kabul. The communiqués, like those from Macnaghten to Auckland thirty-eight years earlier, were almost uniformly upbeat, and, with only a few exceptions, far less informative. "Cholera has occurred during the last four days," and "violent earthquake last night," were typical items of hard news.

A less supremely self-assured man might have had more to say and a great deal more to keep his eye on. For nearly four decades, no Englishman had set foot in Kabul, and the previous British visitors to the city were not remembered fondly. Dr. Kelly understated it in a letter to his father: "We are treated with every consideration by the Amir, who insists upon our being his guests. . . . The people are, however, rather fanatical, not yet accustomed to our presence, so we always go about with a troop of cavalry on our rides." Despite the facade of Anglo-Afghan amity and the surface tranquility in Kabul, it was not hard to sense a certain electricity in the air.

Cavagnari chose not to notice any storm warnings. Early in August, six Afghan regiments were transferred, as a matter of routine, from Herat to Kabul. Far removed from the fighting of the previous winter, these troops had sustained no defeats at the hands of the British; their arrival in Kabul, with bands playing and crowds lining the streets, had all the aspects of a victory parade, and the Heratis themselves made no attempt to conceal scorn, if not overt belligerence, toward the Embassy and its staff. It was one thing for Cavagnari to disregard sullen stares, even Afghans spitting on the ground, while riding through Kabul; it was something else to ignore being cursed loudly as the wet excrement of a seven-legged pig, to shrug indifferently as hands went to jezail locks and tulwars were hefted by brawny soldiers spoiling for a fight. But Cavagnari's reaction was an almost languid aloofness.

The Heratis in fact were on the verge of mutiny, having gone without pay for nearly a year, and their very fractiousness provided Cavagnari with a golden opportunity to score a diplomatic coup when Lytton offered an advance on Yakub Khan's subsidy to liquidate the wage debt and remove the threat of revolt. Cavagnari opposed immediate payments, however, and although he did acknowledge to Lytton that, as a result, he had been "strongly advised not to go out, for a day or two," he continued to take his daily constitutional rides. Even when a retired Pathan Guides officer went to him with well-founded information that the Heratis were plotting an attack on the Residency, he smiled and observed that barking dogs did not bite. "Sahib," replied the Pathan, "these dogs *do* bite."

It has been said that Cavagnari felt himself obliged to turn a deaf ear and a blind eye to the reports and visual evidence of mounting unrest because going on an alert could have been construed as an improper act on the part of a friendly embassy. He also believed that no organized anti-British faction existed in Kabul, although he was aware, and said so in a letter to Lytton, that Yakub Khan's power was rapidly crumbling because of his capitulation to the government that had inflicted the British mission on his country.

And there were even grounds for suspicion that the Amir himself might be less than amicably disposed toward his guests. Shortly before the Treaty of Gandamak had been signed, at a time when Yakub Khan was proclaiming his wish for "constant and firm" friendship with the British, Indian authorities had intercepted a proclamation of a different kind from the Amir. Addressed to the Khugiani Pathans near Jalalabad, it outlined Yakub Khan's intention of launching a jihad against the British and exhorted the Khugianis to do likewise; "the whole of [the British] will go to the fire of hell for evermore," wrote the Amir; "Therefore kill them to the extent of your ability."

And now Cavagnari was receiving further warnings from many quarters that Yakub Khan might well play his allies false in an emergency. He paid the reports no heed. "I have been quite bewildered sometimes," he wrote Lytton on August 30, "with the stories that have been brought to me hinting that no trust should be placed in Yakub Khan, and that he is only temporising with us. Although he is not to be thoroughly trusted, any more than any other Oriental, still if he has any game in hand I must confess to having not the slightest conception as to what it can be. . . . Notwithstanding all people say against him, I personally believe Yakub Khan will turn out to be a very good ally, and that we shall be able to keep him to his engagements."

In the same letter, Cavagnari made passing mention of his disappointment with *The Times'* failure to cover the mission's arrival in Kabul; "I am afraid there is no denying the fact," he wrote, "that the British public require a blunder and a huge disaster to excite their interest." Three days later, on September 2, Cavagnari telegraphed Peshawar: "All well in the Cabul Embassy." He never sent another report.

Even as Cavagnari's telegram was singing along the wire to Peshawar, welcome news was circulating among the Herati regiments: on the following day, they would receive their back wages in full from the Amir. Shortly after dawn on September 3, the troops entered the Bala Hissar and massed eagerly outside the palace. Presently, the palace gates opened and an officer came out to announce that only one month's pay would be forthcoming. A whoop of rage went up. Quickly, the gates were drawn shut as the Heratis began moving on the palace. Then someone shouted: There's gold at the house of the Feringhis, let's take it. A wave of hoodlums surged toward the Residency.

The British were caught napping. Cavagnari had just returned from his morning ride outside the city and was sitting down to breakfast with Jenkyns. Hamilton and Kelly were supervising some grass cutters near the stables. The Guides cavalrymen were tending to their horses; a few of the infantry troops were standing sentry duty, but the rest idled about in the courtyard, waiting to be assembled for drill. When the Heratis burst into the compound, they at first displayed little more than unruliness. Only a handful carried weapons. The mob jostled several of the Guides troopers, made as if to seize a few saddles and sabers. The irruption seemed almost an improvisation of crude conviviality.

But suddenly there was a fist of black smoke and the ringing thump of an Afghan musket. Three or four more shots banged out. The Guides raced to the barracks for their rifles. Cavagnari and Jenkyns appeared on the Residency veranda, the Envoy buckling on his pistol. Hamilton had hurried up from the stables and was barking out orders. Then, as quickly as it had materialized, the threat of violence seemed to have passed: the Heratis were forming up in rough order and marching off.

But Cavagnari now realized that the regiments were only going for their own weapons and would be back. At least, however, the breather allowed him to have the compound gates swung shut while Hamilton deployed the Guides in defensive positions, which were not good. The Residency buildings stood out like sore thumbs, wide open to musket fire from taller structures all around them—especially a five-story house less than 300 feet from the walls. Except for a low parapet atop the main building, there was no protection on any of the roofs. It had not been thought necessary to put up sandbags, even to loophole the walls; now, the British could only drag chairs, tables and other furniture to the windows and prepare to fire from behind those frail emplacements. It was quite clear that without reinforcements, the mission stood no chance whatever of holding out.

Cavagnari therefore wrote a hasty SOS, which was delivered by a sepoy to Yakub Khan. After a few minutes, the sepoy returned and told Cavagnari that the Amir had torn his beard, ripped up his robes and wept on receiving the message. This seemed an encouraging sign—if the Heratis' treachery had moved Yakub Khan to such a display of emotion, he would send relief that much more swiftly. Nearly half an hour went by and the reinforcements did not materialize. Nor would they.

In four decades of dealing with Afghan rulers, British diplomats had made a wondrous botch of things. But they knew how to die. Some of the various eyewitness accounts of the events in Kabul on September 3, 1879, have probably been embroidered, but hundreds of people—including Indian and Afghan servants inside the Residency itself—saw what happened, and their recollections, while inevitably clashing on minor points, have dovetailed consistently on the broad lines of action and the conduct of the antagonists on both sides. The siege of the Kabul Residency was the Alamo writ small.

The Heratis returned. At least 2,000 strong, they surrounded the compound and commenced laying down a ragged but continuous barrage of musket fire, their best marksmen cracking away from the roof of the five-story house. Cavagnari was among the first to buy it. Taking up one of the new breech-loading Martini-Henry rifles, he had climbed to his own roof and picked off four of the besiegers before the splinter of a ricocheting jezail ball plowed a furrow across his forehead. Half senseless with pain and almost blinded by a rag of bleeding scalp that hung over his eyes, he had yet to be put out of the fight. Staggering down the stairs and into the courtyard, he rallied some sepoys and led a bayonet charge against a clutch of Heratis who had managed to climb the wall. But when the Heratis had been dispatched, Cavagnari could no longer stand. Kelly helped him inside to the cot where he died.

Now Hamilton took charge of the mission. The commander of the Guides detachment was barely old enough to shave, but he had won a Victoria Cross with Sam Browne's column in the Khyber action the previous winter. Now, his immediate task was to repel a direct assault on the section of the main building that lay against the compound wall. By this time, the Heratis had brought up scaling ladders and were swarming to the roof under heavy covering fire. Hamilton ordered a platoon of Guides to the roof. They blasted into the brown of the Heratis until their ammunition pouches were empty, then went to work with bayonets and rifle butts. But the sepoys were outnumbered by at least thirty to one; after only a few minutes they had to give way. The Heratis then poured down the stairs, hurling flaming, oil-soaked rags in front of them, shouting the Sunni Muslim war cry, *"Yar Charyar!"* Then, suddenly, they began thudding to the floor in screaming, writhing bunches as the squad of Guides, with fresh ammunition and a few reinforcements, rushed out of a doorway and opened up on the solid mass of robes at point-blank range. Three or four surviving Heratis just managed to scurry back up the stairs and down the tottering ladders.

By this time, however, the defenders had come under fire of a different kind, for the Herati rag bombs had done their work well. Thick fingers of flame were crawling up the walls and along the rough wooden ceiling beams of the main building. Hamilton could do little to quench the spreading blaze. He had already lost about one-quarter of the Guides;

the others could not be spared from their improvised firing points at the windows. Coughing and retching began to punctuate rifle and musket reports. Heavy wood smoke thickened the fog of black gunpowder.

But at least, Hamilton could try getting a second message to Yakub Khan. Somehow, one of the Residency servants was able to reach the palace undetected. This time the Amir responded with reinforcements. They consisted of his eight-year-old son, the boy's tutor and several Afghan army officers. The group approached the mob and the tutor on the mutineers to disperse. He was greeted with laughter and a shower of stones. Now General Daud Shah, the Amir's commander-in-chief, rode up with a squad of Afghan cavalrymen. They were promptly dragged from their horses and stoned, while the tutor had the Koran kicked from his hand. Prince, tutor, general, officers and troopers beat a hasty retreat to the palace.

The Heratis had begun their siege at about eight o'clock in the morning. By noon, the Union Jack was still drooping over the Residency, but the defenders' strength had been whittled down to three Britons and about thirty Guides who remained fit to fight. Those casualties not already dead or dying were comatose from Kelly's dwindling supply of laudanum as the overworked medical officer treated at least two dozen assorted gaping bullet holes and bone-deep knife gashes. Kelly had no time for walking wounded. Nor could the walking wounded be spared: at any moment, the Heratis might force the main gate or scale the walls again—against proportionately feebler resistance. The end was only a matter of hours, possibly of minutes.

A third appeal went out to Yakub Khan. The messenger this time was a Guides sowar named Shahzada Taimus. *Shahzada* means "prince," and the courier was in fact a member of the Afghan royal family, distantly related to the Amir himself. He also carried Hamilton's letter with fittingly regal bearing, making no attempt to conceal himself as he climbed the wall and strode directly into the thick of the Heratis, reminding them, at the top of his lungs, that they would incur eternal disgrace and everlasting agony if they so much as nudged him. Caught off balance by this bold act, the Heratis allowed Shahzada Taimus to enter the palace, for whatever good that did. Yakub Khan had now taken refuge in his harem, where he kept declaring, to anyone who would listen, that assistance was no longer in his power. Possibly this was true.

Back inside the Residency, Kelly suddenly felt the floor jam upwards at his feet as a shattering explosion seemed to hoist the main building several inches above the ground, literally hammering Kelly and others to their knees. The Heratis had now brought up two field pieces and were shelling the main building and walls from barely seventy-five yards off. Normally, artillery could never have been taken in so close. Had not the chair and table emplacements at the Residency windows begun to burn, driving the Guides to even less suitable firing positions, their rifles would have picked off every Afghan serving the two guns.

As it was, Kelly had to leave his patients. Hamilton had ordered a charge on the guns. If even only one could be captured or spiked, the Residency might hold out for another hour or so. Every able-bodied man in the mission, including the noncombatant doctor, was needed to carry out the rush or cover it with rifle fire.

What happened next is usually seen only on late-night television. Led by Hamilton, Jenkyns and Kelly, twelve Guides crossed the courtyard on the run and opened the main gate, firing from the hip as the Heratis let loose a hemorrhage of lead. But every Afghan shot went wild; the besiegers had been caught off guard momentarily, and the vest-pocket British assault team reached the guns intact. Berserk with desperation, they shot and slashed and thrust about them until the Heratis drew back. Then all fifteen men threw themselves on one of the gun carriages and began dragging it toward the main gate. A renewed hailstorm of musket fire was too much for them. After Kelly and six Guides had been chopped down, Hamilton, Jenkyns and the remaining six Guides had to fall back on the Residency, just barely managing to hold off the Heratis at bayonet- and sword-point. As the men gasped to recover their breath, Hamilton formed them up for another charge on the guns.

They had not advanced twenty feet before a slug tore off half of Jenkyns' head, but Hamilton and half a dozen Guides succeeded in dodging through the smoke and zinging lead to gain their objective. Once more they heaved and strained on the ponderous gun carriage. Once more they had to give it up as the Heratis engulfed them. Once more they brought off what can only be called a miracle as they held the Afghans at bayonet's length and reached the cover of the Residency again. But the cover by then was no cover at all. The flames had gone completely out of control. As walls and sections of ceiling collapsed around them in an almost solid packing of black smoke and powdered plaster, the remnant of Cavagnari's escort—fewer than two dozen men—was forced below ground level into the building's brick bath, where breathing was possible, but only just.

Right, said Hamilton, between spasms of coughing, here's what we'll do. You six men will come out with me to the gun. When we reach it, you three harness yourselves to the carriage with your belts and bring it in. Never mind me—I'll hold off the swine myself. . . You, you and you: back me up with your rifles. Use your bayonets if you haven't time to reload. The rest of you, form up at the gate and give us covering fire. This time we'll have that gun. Understood? Very good. Let's be off, then.

Out they came for a third time, racing head-on at the Heratis with the second wind of insanity. They reached the gun while the Heratis momentarily gaped at them, unbelieving. Three Guides unbuckled their belts, hitched them to the carriage. The Heratis opened up again. One of the sepoys was somersaulted twenty feet to the side as several bullets simultaneously caught him full in the stomach. But the other two men threw their weight forward, veins bulging from their foreheads. *Shabash! Good work! Grand! Keep at it!* screamed Hamilton, emptying his revolver into the now-advancing mass. Then he disappeared beneath the human wave, although the blade of his saber could be seen for two or three seconds, decapitating that many Heratis before it too vanished. Only the momentary diversion of Hamilton's death allowed the five remaining Guides to abandon the gun and rejoin their comrades in the trap of the Residency bath.

It was all over. Both sides knew it. The Heratis called out to the dozen still-living Guides to surrender. Your Sahibs are dead, they shouted; we have no quarrel with you. Come out and you can return to your homes. The men looked to their remaining officer, Jemadar Jewand Singh. So be it, brothers, said Jewand. Ordinarily, no Sikh would have called a Pathan dog a brother, but this was not an ordinary situation. So be it, he said; we must go out if that is their wish. But we must go out fighting. They did, and within five minutes they were dead. So too were 600 Heratis, who had been slain in the eight hours it had taken to overwhelm fewer than seven dozen Guides.

Hamilton got his second Victoria Cross posthumously. Double pensions went to the widows and children of the dead Guides. The regimental colors thenceforth carried the legend "Residency, Kabul" among its battle honors. An arch and pool were built at the Guides' Mardan headquarters in memory of the escort. The plaque on the arch can be read today: "The annals of no army and no regiment can show a brighter record of devoted bravery than has been achieved by this small band."

But those tributes would be paid later. More urgent matters had to be dealt with first. Queen Victoria's emissary to the court of an allied potentate had been gunned down in broad daylight by soldiers of that ruler's army, while the ruler himself had simply looked on, perhaps condoning the act if not, as many believed, actually being party to it. To Britons riding the crest of their Forward Policy wave, there could be only one response to the outrage. Manipulation of Afghanistan through an obedient amir was no longer enough. Although his hands seemed far from clean, Yakub Khan might be allowed to remain the de jure monarch, but the country itself must be brought under direct British rule—by force of military occupation.

Lytton could hardly contain his elation at the prospect, although he was at pains to seem appalled as he somberly wrote Disraeli: "I do not disguise from myself that we may now be forced to take in hand the permanent disintegration of the national fabric it was our object to cement in Afghanistan." But lest this imperial burden should appear too heavy to the archimperialist of the nineteenth century, the Viceroy also hastened to add the good news: "Still, the renewed, and perhaps extended, efforts now imposed upon us *can* have no other result, if rightly directed, than the firmer establishment of the undisputed supremacy of the British Power from the Indus to the Oxus."

Lytton was even more explicit in his instructions to Roberts, who had been placed in command of the avenging British army: "You can tell them we shall never again altogether withdraw from Afghanistan."

Inadvertently, Yakub Khan echoed Lytton. "I have lost my friend the Envoy," he said in a telegram to Roberts, "and also my kingdom."

PART FOUR

The Queen's Amir

17

Bandy-Legs and the Fragrance of the Universe

IT WAS IN NO SMALL PART because of his success in forcing the tricky Peiwar Kotal a year earlier that Frederick Roberts had been chosen to lead the army that would bring Afghanistan to its knees for the second time in four decades. But an equally important reason was the fact that his Kurram Field Force happened to be the only one of the three British columns invading Afghanistan that had not been disbanded. Thus, it can almost be said that Roberts rose to the heights by a fluke.

In 1879, at the age of forty-seven, Roberts had not yet become Britain's greatest military hero since Wellington—even in army circles he was only another major general—but his abilities and character were beginning to make themselves felt. A diminutive, red-faced, bandy-legged gamecock with the bearing of a lightning rod, he had steel-blue eyes (only one of which worked) that almost seemed to skewer and they reflected his well-deserved reputation as a slap-leather disciplinarian. Kipling would write of him:

> He has eyes all down his coat,
> And a bugle in his throat;
> And you will not play the goat—
>   Under Bobs.

But any ferocity in Roberts' expression was cancelled out by a reflective half-smile and a fine set of Balaclava whiskers that made him look like everyone's uncle. If he was not a Napoleon or a Moltke, whatever he may have lacked in military genius was compensated for by other gifts. Long service as a quartermaster officer had given him a clerk's grasp of minutiae, but he had also won a Victoria Cross in the Mutiny and had later shown on the Peiwar Kotal that he knew—it might be said he knew by instinct—how to improvise on the grand scale, which meant everything in actions against unpredictable mountain irregular fighters. He was possessed of an unsinkable self-confidence as well, while his unswerving belief in the Forward Policy and the sublime rightness of the British civilizing mission was remarkable even for a Victorian soldier.

What really set Roberts apart, however, was a quality that has never been adequately explained or even clearly defined. For want of a better term, psychologists, historians and writers (including the author of this book) are forced to fall back on the word "leadership," which actually says very little, for that same word is genuinely merited by only a handful of the uncountable men and women who have ever been placed in positions where leadership has been essential. The best one can probably do is shrug and suggest that Roberts may have been born, rather than taught, to give orders that were never questioned, even obeyed with a willingness bordering on joy. Including even Montgomery, no British general ever commanded quite so much loyalty and personal devotion as did "Bobs."

That this should be so might seem slightly puzzling. Roberts' behavior —and the literary style of his autobiography—sometimes suggest a caricature of Colonel Blimp, although his occasional harrumphs are always low-keyed and gentlemanly. He was not without humor but he was not a humorous man. He frowned on drinking by British troops and actively promoted soldiers' temperance societies in an age when gin-swilling was one of the army's most popular pastimes. He thought of Indian soldiers as magnificently brave but "lacking in the qualities that go to make leaders of men." But despite these things it is not extravagant to say that his men—British and Indian alike—loved him. Today, Roberts would be a paternalistic anachronism, possibly a figure of fun. In the last three decades of the nineteenth century he was the right man in the right place at the right time.

The advance on Kabul began at the end of September 1879, along a route over a trackless mountain wilderness west of the Kurram Valley. Roberts' command, fittingly designated the Kabul Field Force, numbered 7,500 men and twenty-two guns—"none too large for the work before it," he wrote in what was to prove an understatement. At least 1,500 of these troops were automatically ruled out of the actual invasion, being assigned to guard the badly exposed lines of communication that wound through the Frontier passes. Even under British command, an effective fighting strength of 6,000 would face uphill going against numberless Afghan hordes.

Mobility and striking power were further sapped by a vast insufficiency of transport. After the Treaty of Gandamak, the Indian Government had ordered the disbanding of most of the army's pack animals. Roberts now found himself with half the number he needed, and those elephants, camels, bullocks, horses and mules that his transport officers were able to round up proved mainly swaybacked. Many were too sick to walk, let alone carry loads. Underfed battery mules ate each others' blankets and tails. During one stage of the march, Roberts actually had to commandeer the mounts of his three cavalry regiments to bring up food supplies from the rear. The result of all this was that the Kabul Field Force could not move with anything approaching the speed essential to the delivery of a paralyzing blow against the Afghans—and a swift strike was vital if organized Afghan resistance were to be prevented.

Perhaps the only consolation Roberts could find was in the morale of his troops. "A splendid spirit pervaded the whole force," he wrote. "The men's hearts were on fire with eager desire to press on to Kabul, and be led against the miscreants who had foully massacred our countrymen, and I felt assured that whatever it was possible for dauntless courage, unselfish devotion, and firm determination to achieve, would be achieved by my gallant soldiers." Henty could not have said it better.

But then Roberts found himself obliged to cope with Yakub Khan, who was still Britain's ally despite a growing belief that he intended to play his allies false. The Amir had already sent personal messages to Roberts, as well as more formal communications to the Indian Government, declaring himself "terribly grieved and perplexed" by Cavagnari's murder. But the British had also received reports that Yakub Khan had hinted to the Heratis that they would get their back pay in full if they attacked the Residency. Further intelligence indicated that Yakub Khan was now inciting the Frontier Ghilzais against Roberts' force, so as to delay the advance on Kabul and buy time to organize a full-scale resistance. This seemed borne out—although impossible to prove—in a brief but rattling fire fight between some 2,000 tribesmen and a 400-man detachment of the 3rd Sikhs and 21st Punjab Infantry in the narrowest part of the Shutargardan Pass at the western end of the Kurram Valley. Although the Ghilzais were scattered, the very fact that they had attacked did not sweeten Roberts' disposition toward Yakub Khan.

Nor did his temper improve when, after negotiating the church-size boulders in the cloud-hidden heights of a pass known as the Gate of Hell and descending into a valley called the Land of Delight, he learned that the Amir had come down from Kabul to greet him. Like it or not, the charade of welcoming Britain's ally into the British camp had to be carried out.

In personal appearance and bearing, the thirty-two-year-old Yakub Khan did not command awe. He was almost chinless, his head came to a point and he could not look anyone straight in the eye. To Roberts, all this "tallied exactly with the double-dealing that had been imputed to him." A few days earlier, the Amir had written Roberts, urging him to hold up the British advance just long enough to enable him, Yakub Khan, to punish Cavagnari's murderers and restore order in his own country. Roberts had declined with hypocritical deference, explaining that he felt "sure the great British nation would not rest satisfied unless a British army . . . assisted Your Highness," but now Yakub Khan repeated the request even more urgently. Courteously curt, Roberts replied that a delay would not be possible, whereupon Yakub Khan became "much chagrined." Nonetheless, the Amir decided to stay on with the British force, and Roberts observed protocol by turning out a cavalry squadron in full-dress uniform, "ostensibly to do him honour, but in reality that I might be kept informed as to his movements. Unwelcome guest as he was, I thought the least of two evils was to keep him now that we had got him."

Roberts probably came to regret this decision. On October 5, the army marched into Charasia, an orchard- and garden-embroidered village at the foot of a towering range of hills about twelve miles south of Kabul. Thanks partly to continuing tribal interference on the march, but even more to the baggage animal shortage, a lightning blow at the Afghan capital was no longer possible. From one of Cavagnari's Indian servants who had managed to slip out of the city and reach the British lines, Roberts learned that preparations for massive resistance were well under way. He was also certain that the Afghan commanders in Kabul were being given full details of his own strength and dispositions by Yakub Khan. Mounted messengers from the city were now continually riding up to the Amir's tent, then galloping back to Kabul. Roberts could not stop them without affronting his country's "ally."

And adding to his unease was Yakub Khan's "change of manner, which, from the first a mixture of extreme cordiality and cringing servility, became as we neared Kabul distant, and even haughty." Clearly, the situation did not bode well for the Kabul Field Force. Even more obviously, Yakub Khan was enjoying Roberts' discomfiture to the hilt. But it was too late for Roberts to rid himself of his royal guest. He had no option but to attack Kabul without delay.

At dawn on October 6, the need for haste became obvious. The hills to the north literally bristled with Afghan army regiments and huge irregular formations beneath a long, gaily snapping clothesline of battle flags. The rising sun also glanced off the barrels of field guns—British scouts were able to count sixteen—a far cry from the days when artillery was the scarcest commodity in the Afghan arsenal. Roberts later learned that the force opposing him numbered about 15,000. This gave the Afghans a nice four-to-one edge, since one British brigade was cut off by a tribal roadblock some miles to the rear and could not be expected to arrive in time. If Roberts waited for the brigade, the Afghan numbers would only increase proportionately. After a hasty cup of coffee, Roberts deployed his columns for an assault on the hill positions.

The main Afghan force was concentrated along a jagged, boulder-crenellated ridge whose lowest point reared up to at least 1,000 feet above the advancing British formations. Providentially, however, the men of the Kabul Field Force were anything but newcomers to rock-climbing. At the head of the column, amid clusters of bursting shells, clambered the kilted clansmen of the Seaforth Highlanders, their pipes snarling shrilly above the crack of their Martini-Henry rifles, which they fired coolly and steadily from the kneeling position. Momentarily checked by Afghan musket fusillades from a hidden strongpoint, the Seaforths were swiftly beefed up by more Highlanders: two companies of the 5th Gurkhas, grinning, doll-sized murderers from the Himalayas, and 200 Pathan hill tribesmen of the 5th Punjab Frontier Force Infantry. Although almost comically outnumbered, these troops were nonetheless in their element on heights, and the Afghans could not stand up indefinitely to their fire discipline. Soon, the impregnable enemy line began to bend. Then it broke. By midafternoon, with twelve of their field guns captured, the Afghans were streaming down the reverse slope in disorder and Roberts held the entire ridge.

It was a moment for gloating that he could not resist. "Throughout the day my friend (!) [Yakub Khan] had been watching the progress of the fight with intense eagerness, and questioning everyone . . . as to his interpretation of what he had observed. So soon as I felt absolutely assured of our victory, I sent an Aide-de-camp to His Highness. . . . It was, without doubt, a trying moment for him. . . . But he received the news with Asiatic calmness, and without the smallest sign of mortification, merely requesting my Aide-de-camp to assure me that, as my enemies were his enemies, he rejoiced."

Although Kabul had yet to be taken, the Afghan commanders now decided to follow the example that had been set by Dost Muhammad's army in the summer of 1839, when it had slipped away from the city to await a better opportunity. As the sun rose on October 9, every Afghan soldier of the defending army had vanished. Next day, the Kabul Field Force marched into Kabul.

The entry was impressive, as Roberts had meant it to be, for nearly all of Kabul's 50,000 inhabitants were his audience, and they had to be shown what stuff their conquerors were made of. In full-dress uniform, the entire force lined the road up the hill to the Bala Hissar: the riflemen of the 5th Punjab Infantry in their glowing scarlet tunics; the 5th Gurkhas, a dull blaze of bottle-green, every sepoy wearing his bellboy cap at a dangerous angle over his right ear; the Seaforths, decked out in trews; the Gordons with their green plaid kilts and pipe-clayed crossbelts; the prancing horsemen of the 14th Bengal Lancers and 5th Punjab Cavalry; Royal Artillery and Indian mountain gun crews at attention beside the glittering barrels of their pieces; literally scores of other foot and mounted units. Regiment after regiment came to a crashing present-arms as Roberts and his staff rode by to the citadel's main gate. Rifle barrels, bayonets, sabers, polished brass buttons, red turbans, plumed helmets, regimental colors and pennons were an orderly but angry bonfire in the morning sun.

Suddenly a barked command cut across the crisp autumn air and the Union Jack was slowly run up over the battlements while a thirty-one-gun salute thundered out and the band of the 67th Foot struck up "God Save the Queen." And hardly had the last echo of the salute rolled off into the Chardeh Valley west of Kabul than Roberts dismounted to conduct the ever-popular British ritual of reading a proclamation to a vanquished people.

It was a good performance. Roberts declared that because of Cavagnari's murder and because the Afghans had resisted the British advance, "it would be but a just and fitting reward for such misdeeds if the city of Kabul were now totally destroyed and its very name blotted out." Then he paused for effect and delivered his verdict: "But the great British Government ever desires to temper justice with mercy, and I now announce . . . that the city will be spared." If this drew a sigh of relief from the multitude, it was cut short when Roberts went on to declare a state of martial law, the imposition of a heavy fine on the entire city, the appointment of a military governor "to administer justice and punish with a strong hand all evil-doers," and an automatic death penalty for any Afghan found carrying a weapon inside the city limits. For the second time in forty years, Afghanistan had been made a de facto British protectorate.

And perhaps none too soon, in Roberts' view, since he "found Kabul more Russian than English." In his official report to the Indian Government, he wrote that the bazaars spilled over with Russian wares—"glass, crockery, silks, tea, and many other things that would seem to be far more easily procurable from India than from Russian territory." He noted that "a habit . . . seems to have been growing up among the Sirdars and others of wearing uniforms of Russian cut," and it struck him as a particularly "curious fact that the amount of Russian money in circulation should be so large. No less than 13,000 gold pieces were found in the Amir's treasure alone; similar coins are exceedingly common in the city bazaar." Above all, however, it was in Kabul that the British unearthed the secret correspondence and treaty proposals that had passed between Stolietoff, Kauffmann and Sher Ali. These documents alone may have played the largest role in Roberts' decision to impose what amounted to a dictatorship on the Afghan capital.

But other influences also shaped his policy, especially his instructions from Lytton, who reminded him that "it will probably be necessary . . . that you should assume and exercise supreme authority in Kabul, since events have unfortunately proved that the Amir has lost that authority, or that he has conspicuously failed to make use of it." Indeed, the Amir was no longer even in the picture. Just before the Army's entry into Kabul, Yakub Khan had gone to Roberts' tent and announced that he was abdicating. "His life, he said, had been most miserable," wrote Roberts, "and he would rather be a grass-cutter in the English camp than Ruler of Afghanistan." He added that the decision was final and irrevocable.

Despite his own personal loathing for the Amir—who had "showed himself to be, if not a deliberate traitor, a despicable coward"—Roberts all but begged him to reconsider. He knew well that even a powerless Yakub Khan on the Afghan throne would be a more useful instrument of the British will than no Yakub Khan at all. But Yakub Khan would not be swayed. In due course he was exiled to India. By default, as it were, Roberts had become British amir pro tem. In that capacity, he felt it mandatory that the Afghan people "understand . . that they were at our mercy."

His power, moreover, was absolute. With a promotion to lieutenant general, and with strong garrisons posted elsewhere in the country, Roberts now commanded an occupying force whose numbers totaled 20,000, enough to enforce whatever police state measures he might wish to take. And in some instances he was quite stern. The British ordered public hangings of several dozen Afghans found guilty by a military court of complicity in the massacre of the Cavagnari mission. (Among them was the mayor of Kabul, who had been seen carrying the Envoy's head through the streets on a pole.) Roberts also commandeered all state-owned grain for his troops "as our right," and ordered large sections of the Bala Hissar pulled down or blown up to furnish building materials for wood fuel and barracks. Roberts had decided against quartering any troops in the Bala Hissar, mainly because there was not enough room for the entire force, which would have had to be separated. But he also thought that the demolition of the great citadel, "the symbol of the power of the Afghans and their boasted military strength," would be a more fitting punishment for treachery and insult than any other we could inflict."

Yet Roberts also showed scruple and a lively sense of fair play. He issued a proclamation of amnesty to all Afghans not involved in the attack on the Residency—which meant virtually the entire population of Kabul. With his approval, thousands of sick Kabulis received free treatment from British doctors in a special army hospital and dispensary. For every bushel of government-owned grain that he expropriated, he saw to it that at least three bushels were bought from private growers "at a price the avaricious Afghan could not resist." This was not, however, entirely an exercise in prodigality or even generosity: Roberts felt that a sweetening of the pot was necessary, since many Afghans feared retribution from their fellow-countrymen after the British departed—if and when they did depart—for collaborating with the enemy.

Roberts was also continually haunted by the knowledge of how another British army of occupation had come to grief through callous indifference to the sensibilities of a conquered but proud race. Uppermost in his mind was the fuse of rage that had been touched off in 1839 by the casual acquisition of Afghan mistresses. Even before the capture of Kabul, he had issued a general order to the army forbidding fraternization, which, he said, would almost certainly "arouse the personal jealousies of the people . . . who are, of all races, most susceptible as regards their women." During the army's entire second sojourn in Afghanistan—well over a year—not a single Afghan woman registered a complaint of mistreatment by any British or Indian officer or enlisted man. And there were numerous outlets, official and otherwise, for the airing of such grievances. If Alexander Burnes had accompanied Roberts to Kabul, he might just possibly have been court-martialed and dishonorably discharged.

But Roberts was far from blind to the extent of the humiliation he had inflicted by his mere presence in Afghanistan: "The prolonged occupation . . . the capture of . . . vast munitions of war, which had raised the military strength of the Afghans to a standard unequalled among Asiatic nations; the destruction of their historic fortress . . . and, lastly, the deportation to India of their Amir . . . were all circumstances which united to increase to a high pitch the antipathy they naturally felt towards a foreign invader." Roberts' chief of staff, Colonel Charles MacGregor, put it more plainly: "We are thoroughly hated and not enough feared."

Symbolizing MacGregor's remark was an oddity of interior decor found in the Bala Hissar, a primitively rendered painting by an Afghan artist, depicting Akbar Khan's humiliation of Elphinstone's army in 1842. The correspondent of the Allahabad *Pioneer* noted that Akbar himself was shown astride a splendid charger, wearing rich gold-braided robes and "an expression of haughty contempt." At the horse's side scampered a dog, "abnormally developed in some particulars," and apparently exulting in "his master's triumph."

What that triumph is, has yet to be told: on the flank of the horse, and so close as to be in danger of its heels, is the figure of a British officer . . . crouching in the most abject fear. . . . He is at the double to keep up with the horse, and the artist has cleverly depicted in figure and expression the humiliation he is undergoing. Nothing could be finer than the contrast between the black-bearded Afghan, with his enormous pouting lips . . . and the smooth boyish face, full of timidity, of the unlucky Briton he is leading captive.

The painting, said the reporter, had become "a standing curiosity in camp." He did not add that it was also an unsettling reminder that the shame of defeat, rout and subjection was far from being an Afghan monopoly in Afghan dealings with British armies.

Because of all this, there was special cause for concern over Roberts' choice of permanent quarters for the Kabul force. The area, generally known as Sherpur, was the exact site of the ill-fated Cantonment of 1839—42.* Roberts himself had decided on the place with misgivings, picking it only because it was well situated for the concentration of troops in the event of an attack. Whether an attack would actually take place he had no way of knowing, but he was aware that the chances would increase with the onset of winter, when relief columns from India, and even from garrisons in Kandahar and Jalalabad, might not be able to reach Kabul if they were needed. Roberts did not relish this prospect, but neither could he rule it out.

And by early December, as army elephants began to topple over and die from the cold—"much to the annoyance of the olfactory nerves of all passers-by"—and as the ink froze in Roberts' pen even while he wrote out orders, the possibility of a major uprising suddenly became very real.

For two months, a nonegenarian mullah named Mushk-i-Alam—the Fragrance of the Universe—had been on a circuit preaching tour of Afghanistan. Carried on a bed by his *talibs*, or pupils, he had not over-looked a single mosque in the country, and in each of these places he had been inciting packed congregations to jihad. Now, the Fragrance of the Universe had finally reached Kabul, and he busily reminded the citizenry of how their fathers and grandfathers—true men, not skulking pi-dogs—had driven the thrice-accursed Feringhi camel entrails from their country's capital in disgrace. To arrest Mushk-i-Alam would have been risky, but his sermons grew more frenzied with each day. Sir William Macnaghten would probably have been delighted by the performance; Roberts was not amused. On December 8, he telegraphed for the entire Corps of Guides as reinforcements.

The message was flashed out none too soon. That very day, an Afghan army took the field against the British.

Its strategy seemed clear enough. From the remains of the Bala Hissar, three massive troop concentrations could be seen plowing up the snow in the Chardeh Valley to the west as they converged from three separate directions on the range of hills forming a rough semicircle around Kabul's western outskirts. Roberts immediately perceived that the objective of the Afghan commander, a battle-wise artillery officer named Muhammad Jan, was to occupy those heights and then enter Kabul itself through a

* Today it is the site of Kabul's international airport.

wide defile called the Deh-i-Mazang. Once inside the city, the Afghan numbers would swiftly multiply as forbidden weapons came out of hiding places and at least 10,000 Kabulis, egged on by Mushk-i-Alam, joined Muhammad Jan for the final assault on Sherpur.

There was only one way to stop Muhammad Jan: to defeat each of his three columns in detail and thus keep them from combining. While aware that he was outnumbered, Roberts had no doubt that his own smaller but far better disciplined force was equal to the task. His army had already disposed of a phalanx four times its size in October.

He later wrote that he had "but a very imperfect idea of the extent of the combination, or of the enormous numbers arrayed against us."

The next six days witnessed some of the most violent, inconclusive and confused skirmishing in the history of British arms as Roberts' columns drove into the Chardeh Valley to blunt and smash the Afghan trident. But by December 13, the weight of the Afghan numbers had begun to make itself felt. Even though the Guides had arrived and plunged directly into the thick of it, Muhammad Jan had managed to occupy the Asmai Heights, which commanded the Deh-i-Mazang defile. Asmai was really the key to the door of Kabul. Its possession enabled Muhammad Jan to start pushing advance columns toward the Deh-i-Mazang while other Afghan contingents began moving on the skeleton of the Bala Hissar from a spur below the defile. Desperately, Roberts telegraphed Jalalabad for another brigade and prepared to launch a massive counterattack against Asmai.

Actually, "massive" was a relative word; the British and Indian troops who stormed the slopes on the morning of December 14 numbered barely 1,500. But they were also the cream of the Queen's forces in India: the Guides, the 14th Bengal Lancers, the 5th Punjab Infantry and the wild Scottish tribesmen of the Seaforth and Gordon Highlanders. Under the shuddering blanket of a steady barrage laid down by field and mountain batteries, the men drove their way upward, firing rapidly from behind what little cover they could find, and there was precious little to be had. Their progress could be measured in inches, but when they finally reached the Afghan outer perimeter, they rose as one man to the yelp of bugles and bore in with fixed bayonets, carving a ragged furrow through a stubborn but gradually buckling wall of resistance. Shortly before noon, a heliograph winked out to Roberts from the summit: Asmai reoccupied.

Roberts' elation was short-lived. As he swept the heights with his telescope, he saw what could not be seen from the crest: several thousand Afghans massing beneath a broad rock ledge to strike back at the now-spent Indian and British troops. At the same moment, he also received what was probably the most accurate estimate yet made of total enemy fighting strength when another heliograph officer signaled that "the crowds of Afghans in the Chardeh remind me of Epsom on the Derby Day." A moment of truth was at hand: "I realized, what is hard for a British soldier, how much harder for a British commander, to realize, that we were over-matched, and that we could not hold our ground. . . . The Afghans by force of numbers alone [had] made themselves masters of the situation."

If confirmation was needed, it came almost at once: "My heart sank within me, for . . . I only too plainly saw our men retreating down the hill." With Asmai back in Afghan hands, Muhammad Jan's columns were not only beginning to pour through the Dehi-i-Mazang in a great river of poshteens, but were threatening to cut off the British troops on the heights. Roberts now had to issue an order for the unthinkable: a general retirement on Sherpur.

At least, however, he took comfort from watching the men bring it off without a hitch:

It is comparatively easy for a small body of well-trained soldiers, such as those of which the army in India is composed, to act on the offensive against Asiatics. . . . But a retirement is a different matter. [The enemy] become full of confidence . . . and if there is the smallest symptom of unsteadiness . . . a disaster is certain to occur. . . . The ground was all in favour of the Afghans, who, unimpeded by impediments of any kind, swarmed down on the mere handful of men retreating before them, shouting cries of victory and brandishing their long knives; but our brave men . . . were absolutely steady; they took up position after position with perfect coolness; every movement was carried out with as much precision as if they were manoeuvring on an ordinary field day. . . . As each regiment and detachment filed through the Head-Quarters gateway I was able to offer my warm congratulations and heartiest thanks to my gallant comrades.

But if congratulations were in order, so too was concern. Before the sun went down, the Afghans had taken possession of their capital once more and the British army of occupation was cooped up behind the defenses of Sherpur. Roberts now found himself in exactly the same state of siege that had been imposed on Elphinstone thirty-eight years earlier.

There were, however, at least three differences. One was that Roberts had not neglected to stiffen the Sherpur defenses. A partly finished wall along the western perimeter was shored up with massive logs and glued tight with an entanglement of felled holly-oak trees and barbed wire. A soft spot on the northwest corner became a solid shield of gun limbers and gun-carriage wheels. And above all, the weakest sector had been transformed into the stoutest when Roberts extended the perimeter line to embrace the Bemaru Heights; he knew that "to have given up any part of [Bemaru] would have been to repeat the mistake which proved so disastrous to Elphinstone's army." The whole Bemaru Ridge now was

198

firmly protected by a line of deep trenches and tall rifle towers. The gossamer defense works of the 1841 Cantonment had become the British hollow square, expanded and reinforced a thousandfold.

The second difference was the troops, a far cry from the gallant but dispirited derelicts of Elphinstone's doomed force. Although nowhere nearly as gaudy—khaki tunics, breeches and puttees and Wolseley helmets had become standard issue for Indian service—neither were they an assemblage of jailbirds transformed into robots. A combination of reform bills in England and the scandals of the Crimean War had wrought a small but significant revolution in the conditions of British military service and the character of the British fighting man. The purchase of commissions and promotions had been abolished; officers advanced on merit alone. By the late 1870s, most of the rank and file could read and write, but they could no longer be flogged (Roberts had a hand in the outlawing of this punishment) and were also spoiled with small pay raises, shorter terms of enlistment, canteens, organized games and other sissified indulgences. The effect of this pampering had been to instill in the Kabul Field Force a gung-ho esprit that was worlds apart from the heroic fatalism that had pervaded Elphinstone's ranks. There were no croakers at Sherpur in the winter of 1879.

Finally, Roberts was not Elphinstone. The Afghan offensive had surprised him—even had momentarily dismayed him—but it had not caught him unprepared. Hardly had the Sherpur gates been swung shut than he sent out what he knew would be his last telegraph message to India before the Afghans cut the wire. He found it "a satisfaction to be able to assure the authorities . . . that there was no cause for anxiety as to the safety of the troops." This was almost an understatement: enough ammunition, food, medical supplies and firewood had been stocked to carry the force through the winter and, if need be, well into the summer.

Nor did Roberts emulate Elphinstone when Muhammad Jan sent an Afghan officer to Sherpur under a flag of truce with a guarantee of safe-conduct back to India. Roberts simply gave the messenger a Victorian version of McAuliffe's reply to the Germans at Bastogne. Then he sat back to await Muhammad Jan's attack.

An uneasy quiet settled over Sherpur. All British intelligence estimates pointed to an Afghan strength of at least 100,000, giving Muhammad Jan an eight-to-one edge over Roberts, but the Afghan commander seemed in no hurry to launch his onslaught. Roberts himself grew increasingly apprehensive as the days went by without word from the second brigade he had requested. The tension also reached the troops; forced laughter greeted forced jokes, such as one rifleman's remark that "this is the first time I ever 'eard of a bleedin' general bein' confined to quarters." But even poor attempts at humor at least measured the army's morale.

On December 18, a galloper finally brought news from the relief brigade mired down at Jagdalak, thirty miles to the east. Its commander, Brigadier General Charles Gough, wrote Roberts that his 1,400-man force was under attack by heavy Pathan concentrations on front, flank and rear and that he did not think the brigade strong enough to reach Kabul. Roberts scribbled a reply which he gave to the officer: "Order Gough to advance without delay. This order is imperative, and must not be disobeyed."

On December 21, a heliograph signal told Roberts that the brigade should reach Sherpur the following day, but that it had been forced to drop most of its cavalry to hold off the tribesmen in the rear. Roberts accordingly reinforced the reinforcements by sending them his own 12th Bengal Lancers—an act that he may have come to regret almost at once.

For on the next day, December 22, the relief column was nowhere to be seen and Roberts' scouts reported to him that the Afghans had set their H-hour for the following morning. At dawn, he was told, Mushk-i-Alam would light a beacon fire at the crest of the Asmai to signal the commencement of the onslaught against Sherpur. The Afghans had chosen a symbolically fitting date. December 23 was not just the last day of the religious feast of Muharram, which brings Muslims to a high emotional pitch; it also happened to be the thirty-eighth anniversary of Macnaghten's murder.

That night, the British and Indian regiments shivered at their posts, too cold to be afraid as they listened to the songs and war cries of the Afghans, who slowly and invisibly approached Sherpur beneath a quilt of starless sky that was blacker than black. After nearly twelve hours, some of the men were starting to doze on their frostbitten feet when a fat gobbet of yellow flame erupted at the summit of Asmai. Seconds later there was a sustained, ragged crashing of musketry as an ocean of Afghan soldiery rolled in on the Sherpur walls from east and south. Almost simultaneously the blanket of night was torn from the attackers when the burst of several star shells threw the entire force into a blinding bath of spectral green. Now, the British began loosing their own volleys, regiment by regiment, and even before the sun came up the frozen ground beneath the walls was littered with twisting bodies. Roberts had not been caught napping.

But still the Afghans came on. Muhammad Jan seemed to have a bottomless box of them. Even as four British batteries opened up and their shells began to tear gaping, bloody channels in the attacking columns, more Afghans surged forward like liquid cement to plug the holes. By seven o'clock in the morning, scaling ladders were being thrown up along the southeastern wall. Again and again, Ghazi suicide squads reached the top rungs, only to be spitted on the bayonets of the Gordons. By ten o'clock, the Afghans could almost scale the defenses on the heaped-up corpses of their comrades. Only the artillery and the relatively rapid fire of the Martini-Henrys kept them from doing so.

At about that time, however, Roberts noticed that the onslaught had begun to lose a little of its impact. So too, apparently, did an old Muslim orderly, who came up to remind Roberts that his bath was becoming cold. Both men were mistaken. By eleven o'clock, the Afghans had got a second wind and were smashing away at the fortifications with renewed fury. Not even heavier shellfire could slow down the human avalanche; at any time, it could start pouring over the walls. But Roberts was being paid to stop it, so he attacked.

As attacks went, it was a modest one, being carried out by seven officers and 325 sowars of the 5th Punjab Cavalry under the covering fire of only four guns. But an attack—especially from an unexpected quarter—was the last thing Muhammad Jan had taken into account. For Roberts had sent the Punjabis north and east, over the wall of the Bemaru heights. His blow was delivered against the least protected sector of the Afghan rear.

The surprise—indeed, the very idea of any British offensive move—had the desired effect. From that moment on, the assault on the southern defenses could be seen to flag visibly. By one o'clock in the afternoon, the Afghan tide was receding, and the withdrawal swiftly became a rout when Roberts ordered three Indian cavalry regiments out of Sherpur in pursuit. On the following morning, when mounted Guides patrols began probing into Kabul, not a single soldier of Muhammad Jan's army could be found in the city or the surrounding hills. Once again, the Afghans had brought off their spooky vanishing act.

On the same day, advance units of the relief brigade rode into Sherpur. The brigade might just as well have stayed in Jalalabad.

18

The Wooing of the Marionette

With the rout of Muhammad Jan's legions and the beginning of the year 1880, tranquility of a sort returned swiftly to Kabul, but not to Roberts' mind. For the military dictator now had to devote full-time attention to the two-pronged political question of Afghanistan's future: "What was to be done with Afghanistan now we had got it? and, who could be set up as Ruler with any chance of being able to hold his own?" The decisions, of course, were not Roberts' to make, but he was the man on the spot, and his views would carry great weight in India and Britain.

The first question took priority. Should Afghanistan remain a single nation or become a loosely-knit confederation of autonomous provinces? Roberts urged balkanization, not only because Lytton favored it and because it was what he himself called the country's "normal condition," but also because if Afghanistan stayed united, even under a pro-British amir, "there would always be the danger of [his] . . . turning against us for some supposed grievance, or at the instigation of a foreign Power"—meaning, of course, Russia. As for the second question, Lytton and Roberts were primarily interested in a ruler of Kabul, which was still the seat of power. Such a man had to be not only acceptable to the people of that city but submissive to the British will. Although there were those who found it hard to imagine the Afghans welcoming any amir who had Britain's blessing, Lytton endorsed Roberts' plan.

He also prepared to evacuate Afghanistan.

For the man whom Disraeli had likened to the Great Mogul, withdrawal back to India must have been as welcome a prospect as going to the dentist, but Lytton perceived that he had no other option. Afghanistan had now become a political hot potato in England, where Gladstone's Liberal Opposition had recognized the whole issue as likely to hasten a general election that would probably unseat Disraeli and atomize the Forward Policy. Roberts had already been singled out and attacked for his summary hangings of Afghans implicated in the massacre of the Cavagnari mission, and had been required to submit to Parliament a formal explanation of his policies in Kabul. In some London circles it had even become fashionable to call him "Butcher Roberts." But this was only the tip of the iceberg.

For by now the very presence of British troops in Afghanistan had become odious to large, and ever-growing, numbers of the British electorate. Shortly after the army's occupation of Kabul, Gladstone had cast his eyes heavenward and exhorted the voters to "remember the rights of the savage, as we call him. Remember that the happiness of his humble home . . . the sanctity of life in the hill villages of Afghanistan, among the winter snows, is as inviolate in the eye of Almighty God as can be your own." Among Victorians, this kind of supercharged piety, especially when voiced by the Jehovah-like Gladstone, was raw meat. And Gladstone threw huge chunks of it to British voters as his campaign moved into high gear.

Lytton saw the handwriting on the wall. Perhaps prematurely, he also saw his dreams of a British frontier on the Hindu Kush going up in smoke. But even without an army of occupation, even with pressure for a British envoy temporarily in abeyance, the Viceroy still thought it would be possible for Britain to stay in control of Afghanistan. Provided, that was to say, that Afghanistan remained weak.

Accordingly, Lytton took steps toward that objective. The country would not just be broken up into a poorly united confederation; it would also be partially dismembered. Plans were set in motion to cede Herat to Persia or to make it an independent state ruled by Yakub Khan's brother, an ambitious warlord named Ayub Khan, whom one British writer has called "the Afghan's Prince Charlie." Kandahar, under a puppet Afghan governor, would be retained as a British military base. Kabul and its environs would be presided over by any prince who was strong enough to stay in power, and who would do Britain's bidding.

Under such an arrangement, it seemed to Lytton, the Forward Policy stood a not unreasonable chance of weathering a Liberal administration in England.

Lytton had even picked his candidate for Amir of Kabul. During the Afghan civil war of 1863–68, a grandson of Dost Muhammad named Abdur Rahman had at one time led an Afghan army in a victorious campaign to win brief incumbency on the throne for his own father, Sher Ali's brother Afzal. Although neither Lytton nor Roberts had had any previous dealings with Abdur Rahman, they knew him to be a man whose truck-driver physique complemented a violent temper and magisterially forceful personality; unlike Sher Ali and Yakub Khan, Abdur Rahman seemed potentially quite capable of imposing his will on recalcitrant subjects. But Abdur Rahman was also believed to be a realist, not likely to buck the fait accompli of British control, direct or otherwise. The consensus was that he would not only be acceptable to the military forces and civil populace of Kabul but receptive to British overtures. Roberts therefore began putting out feelers to the prospective puppet.

There was only one problem: how to reach Abdur Rahman. Twelve years earlier, he had exiled himself to Russian Turkestan. And although reports had come in that he had grown disenchanted with his hosts—another reason why Lytton smiled on him—he might just as well have taken up residence on the moon.

But then, early in February 1880, Roberts learned that Abdur Rahman had crossed the Oxus. A few days later, the prince's mother, who lived in Kandahar, went to General Sir Donald Stewart, commander of the British garrison in that city. She told Stewart that her son had been in communication with the pretender Ayub Khan, and that Ayub Khan had urged Abdur Rahman to join him in an anti-British jihad. Abdur Rahman had spurned the offer angrily, said his mother, and had also told Ayub Khan that if he had a grain of sense he would submit to British authority. The potential man of the hour seemed on his way to a rendezvous with destiny, or at least with Roberts.

Or so it seemed to Lytton. Early in March, Roberts was joined by the Secretary of the Punjab Government, one Lepel Griffin, whom the Viceroy had just appointed to the office of Chief Political Officer in Kabul. Griffin arrived in the Afghan capital staggering under the weight of detailed instructions from Lytton on the wooing and winning of Abdur Rahman. Lytton had also cabled Lord Cranbrook, the Secretary of State for India, requesting "early public recognition of Abdur Rahman . . . as sole means of saving [Afghanistan] from anarchy," and Cranbrook had immediately wired back his endorsement.

Cranbrook had also asked: "But where is he? And how do you propose to learn his wishes and intentions?"

A partial answer to that question was soon forthcoming; intelligence reached Kabul that Abdur Rahman had been busily consolidating his position, and presumably mobilizing some military strength, to the north, near the Afghan Turkestan town of Faizabad. In fact, Roberts observed, he "had made himself master of Afghan-Turkestan," and was also corresponding with influential Afghan leaders in Kabul. So at least there was now a way to reach him directly. On April 1, Griffin wrote and invited

Abdur Rahman to Kabul "to submit any representations that you may desire to make to the British Government."

Two weeks later, with Roberts looking over his shoulder, Griffin read the long-awaited word from the British candidate. After a winding, fulsomely Oriental preamble in which the prince informed his "honoured friend," that "throughout these twelve years of my exile . . . night and day I have cherished the hope of revisiting my native land," Abdur Rahman got to the point. "Now, therefore, that you seek to learn my hopes and wishes, they are these: that as long as your Empire and that of Russia exist, [Afghanistan] should rest at peace between them, for my tribesmen are unable to struggle with Empires . . . and we hope . . . that you will place [us] under the protection of the two Powers."

Abdur Rahman added that he was prepared to cross the Hindu Kush for further discussions, but this offer went all but unnoticed. The suggestion that Russia be given a share of an acknowledged British sphere of influence was tantamount to recommending that Prince Gorchakov be appointed British Foreign Secretary. An almost frantic Lytton instructed Griffin to tell Abdur Rahman that his proposal could under no circumstances "be entertained and discussed." But since Lytton had no wish to give Abdur Rahman second thoughts about throwing in his lot with the British, Griffin was further directed to give the candidate the not-so-subtle hint that "there are at present, in and around Kabul, personages not destitute of influence, who themselves aspire to the sovereignty he seeks." In short, it was in Abdur Rahman's own best interests to remain in the British corner and to "lose no time in proceeding to Kabul."

Meanwhile, in a shuffling of troop dispositions preparatory to evacuation, Stewart, the Kandahar commander, had been transferred to Kabul on May 5. Senior to Roberts, he now assumed supreme command in Afghanistan while Roberts remained in charge of the Kabul forces, and had more freedom to continue throwing out lines to Abdur Rahman. Although Roberts did not especially mind being superseded by a close personal friend, he had different feelings about the news that reached Kabul from England on the day of Stewart's arrival. The general election had taken place. Disraeli was out. Gladstone was back in. Lytton had resigned. "I dreaded," wrote Roberts, "a reversal of the policy which I believed to be the best for the security of our position in India."

Roberts' fears were not fully realized. For it quickly became evident that Gladstone, for all his anti-imperialist fulminations, had no more intention than did an even more celebrated successor at Number Ten Downing Street to preside over the liquidation of the British Empire. While Almighty God might have been moved to profound grief and terrible anger by the British occupation of Afghanistan, it did not follow that He would fail to appreciate the vital necessity of protecting British

India, or that He was unable to bestow His blessing on the idea that Afghanistan remain a British sphere of influence—not an occupied quasi-protectorate, of course, but simply a buffer state with a friendly king standing between India and Russia. Gladstone was prepared, even eager, to withdraw the British army, but not if that army were to be replaced by Cossacks. To keep the Russians out, an accommodating amir was a sine qua non.

So the flirtation with Abdur Rahman continued under Liberal sanction.

It also ran into a snag. Abdur Rahman did not intend to rule a truncated Afghanistan. Although nothing had come of Lytton's plan to divest the country of Herat (the city did, nonetheless, remain in Ayub Khan's control), and although it was now more or less tacitly acknowledged that Abdur Rahman's writ would not be confined to Kabul, the question of Kandahar suddenly surfaced, and threatened to scupper the entire British game plan in Afghanistan.

One of Gladstone's campaign pledges had been the evacuation of Kandahar and the return of that city to its rightful owners in the shortest possible time. Now, however, the British were showing no signs of even the slightest intentions to leave Kandahar, and Abdur Rahman was becoming restive. Losing Herat would be blow enough to him, but without Kandahar he could only have felt like an amputee. During the late spring of 1880, the British in Kabul intercepted many letters from Abdur Rahman to relatives and supporters, in which, said Roberts, "he had made it clear that he expected the whole inheritance of his grandfather, Dost Mahomed Khan . . . [and] that he was doing all he could to strengthen himself, even at our expense." As summer approached, the remote-control negotiations had become so bogged down that there was talk of installing Yakub Khan's openly hostile brother Ayub, or even reinstating Yakub Khan himself.

In June, however, Gladstone finally came through with a firm assurance to Abdur Rahman that Kandahar would be evacuated as swiftly as possible. While Abdur Rahman might have taken this pledge with a large grain of salt, it did seem to have the effect of bringing him to a more accommodating attitude. Besides which, he was by now becoming noticeably impatient to take the throne, apparently sharing the view of most Afghans that "the only chance of getting rid of us," as Roberts put it, "was by agreeing to any form of settled government we might establish." Since the British had stipulated expressly that any amir had to accept Whitehall's "advice" on foreign relations, and since Abdur Rahman had accepted this condition long before Kandahar had become an issue, there no longer seemed much concern that the amir-designate would continue to balk.

Also at this time, the British themselves had become eager to conclude all negotiations. In mid-July, they learned that Abdur Rahman was finally on his way to Kabul. Taking no chances, Stewart did not even await his arrival, but proclaimed him Amir on July 22. The occupation forces now prepared to evacuate the country. They were no longer needed. Britain had engineered—if not very deftly—a continuation of her indirect rule of Afghanistan.

Then the roof fell in.

19

Prince Charlie's Army

SHORTLY BEFORE HE was to lead his troops back to India through the Kurram Valley, Roberts gave himself a brief busman's holiday, riding eastward toward the Khyber Pass to satisfy a personal wish to follow the blood-stained path of Elphinstone's nightmare 1842 retreat. But at Jalalabad, while "wandering over the place where Sir Robert Sale in some measure redeemed the lamentable failure of the first Afghan war," his tour was brought to a halt as weird as it was abrupt. "Suddenly a presentiment, which I have never been able to explain to myself, made me retrace my steps and hurry back to Kabul." Dismounting from his sweat-lathered horse outside army headquarters, he discovered that his inexplicable hunch had not been a false alarm. Three hundred and fifty miles to the southwest, at a village called Maiwand near the Helmand River, barely a day's march west of Kandahar, a 2,500-man British force had just been all but totaled by an Afghan army ten times its size—and Kandahar's British garrison was now under siege.

It was much more than just the most shameful reverse sustained by British arms in Afghanistan since Akbar had chased Elphinstone out of the country. The Afghan army then investing Kandahar was threatening to smash to flinderation the entire machinery of Britain's buffer state.

The disaster had been in the making since spring, when Ayub Khan had gone to Herat and prevailed on that city's chiefs to submerge their differences under his leadership in all-out war against the British. Not merely an eager-beaver Anglophobic pretender to the Afghan succession,

[207]

Ayub Khan was also his country's most able field general. By mid-June, he had mobilized a ten-regiment force of 7,500 trained Afghan regulars, backed up by ten guns. He next commenced a 350-mile easterly drive on Kandahar, augmenting his numbers en route with tribal levies and Ghazis. Early in July, when the British in Kandahar finally learned that hostiles were approaching the Helmand River, Ayub was riding at the head of 25,000 well-armed fighting men whose discipline, for Afghan troops, was impressive. Ayub had also brought the weight of his artillery punch to thirty field pieces. Even with the tribesmen and Ghazis, this was no band of brave but disorganized guerrillas. It was something like a real army.

By contrast, the British column sent out from Kandahar to stop Ayub crossing the Helmand consisted of a single brigade and twelve guns. The troops were to reinforce a local army raised by Kandahar's tame Afghan governor, but the linkup never took place because the locals suddenly deserted en masse to Ayub. This made it all the more urgent that the Helmand be reached swiftly, but the British-Indian column, marching in 100-degree heat across a bone-dry crematorium of rock and sand, was badly hobbled by its 3,000 overladen baggage animals. Worse, the commanding officer, Brigadier General Burrows, had never led troops in action, with the consequence that he was continually harried by telegrams from Simla dictating his strategy and tactics. "Playing chess by telegram may succeed," wrote one of Burrows' officers, "but planning a campaign on the Helmund from the cool shades of Simla is an experiment which will not, I hope, be repeated."

That remark was made some weeks after Burrows and Ayub had collided at Maiwand. Undoubtedly befuddled by the telegraphic advice, Burrows was beaten from the very start—although even without Simla's kibitzing, defeat was probably inevitable. When advance British columns reached the outskirts of Maiwand on the morning of July 27, Burrows found that the Afghans had already crossed the Helmand and were dug in solidly behind commanding positions on high ground. Even as he deployed his force to attack, Burrows' left flank was almost instantly enveloped by a charge of 2,000 regular Afghan cavalrymen while his right wing buckled and came close to breaking under successive head-on assaults by at least 5,000 screaming mounted Ghazis. Numbed by the flanking blows, the British began feeling the full weight of Ayub's strength on their center as the thirty Afghan guns, served by Russian-trained artillery officers, opened up with a paralyzing half-hour barrage. When the fire lifted to allow a frontal assault by the main Afghan body, which burst through the fogbank of black powder in several huge waves, there was no way for Burrows' line to hold.

After four hours of confused retreat, Burrows tried to re-form and rally the survivors of his force in a walled garden enclosure. A hand-to-hand donnybrook ensued. With ammunition running short, British officers deflected two Ghazi onslaughts by hurling stones down on the attackers from the garden wall. Infantrymen and dismounted sowars swung rifle butts and sabers like baseball bats. Afghans were pulled into bayonets by their beards. Men who had lost their weapons strangled scores of Ghazis with bare hands. Burrows was everywhere. A sort of British Custer, he rode up and down his ragged lines, encouraging the troops and picking off Afghans with his revolver. Even after his second horse had been shot from under him, he personally saved the lives of three sepoys. It said something about the action in the garden that the Afghans later built a brick pillar at Maiwand to honor the British and Indian dead.

The last stand was also futile. When Burrows finally ordered a general retirement on Kandahar, the ensuing twenty-four hours became a hot-weather reenactment in miniature of the 1842 retreat from Kabul. By then, the shattered remnants of the brigade had degenerated into a panic- and thirst-crazed rabble of vagrants, staggering almost blindly across a twenty-five-mile frying pan of cracked earth as the Afghans continued to clout them with artillery, rivet them with rifle fire and vivisect them in knife charges. Incredibly, a substantial number of the troops managed to reach the Kandahar gates on the afternoon of July 28, but at assembly the next day, more than 1,100 officers and men failed to answer to their names at roll call. Burrows' brigade had lost half its strength and the remaining 1,400 troops seemed deprived of the will to resist as Ayub Khan surrounded Kandahar and prepared to invest the city.

The relatively small size of the force that Ayub Khan had trounced in no way cushioned the impact of the shock wave that rolled across northern Afghanistan when the news reached Kabul. Kandahar had been one of the sore spots in the British dealings with Abdur Rahman, and although that question had finally seemed resolved, Maiwand could reopen the sore. Abdur Rahman, to be sure, had been formally proclaimed amir, but he himself had yet to accept the office. "It was impossible to predict," wrote Roberts, "how the news [of Maiwand] would affect the recent agreements entered into with Abdur Rahman." The possibility even existed that despite the Amir-designate's known hatred for Ayub, he might in some way emulate the pretender with his own armed forces. Roberts expressed the opinion that "exaggerated reports of the Maiwand affair being rife in the Kabul bazaars, which were daily becoming crowded with armed Afghans from Abdur Rahman's camp . . . made it more than ever necessary to bring negotiations with the new Amir to a speedy conclusion."

Accordingly, Abdur Rahman, now encamped in the Kohistan hills—barely a day's march from Kabul—was invited to come to the capital and finalize all arrangements for his immediate accession. In his reply to Stewart, Abdur Rahman said that the Afghans advising him in Kohistan were "ignorant fools, who do not know their own interests, good or bad"; but he added that he was ready to sit down with the British, "irrespective of the opinion of the people." On reading this, Stewart decided to backtrack. Among other things, if Abdur Rahman were to come to Kabul at the bidding of the British on the very heels of a British defeat by an Afghan army, his puppet status would become far too transparent for comfort. The immediate personal conference was therefore postponed. Roberts and Stewart could only hope that Abdur Rahman's seemingly accommodating stance would not change.

Meanwhile, an equally urgent priority faced the British. Although momentarily localized in Kandahar, Ayub Khan's revolt was anything but an isolated demonstration. If immediate countermeasures were not taken, Ayub might well make himself master of Afghanistan. And that was not all. His revolt could also sweep up the Frontier, pour through the passes and vault the Indus to take fire among the Muslims of the Punjab. And whereas a jihad was strictly a Muslim affair, at least 200 million Hindus east of the Indus were quite capable of taking the hint from Ayub and staging a mass uprising of their own. Roberts noted that "throughout India the announcement [of Maiwand] produced a certain feeling of uneasiness . . . [among] those who remembered the days of the Mutiny." And no less important, of course, was the fate of the beleaguered Kandahar garrison. That soldiers of the Queen should be forsaken by their own while they faced extermination at the hands of savages was unthinkable.

To make it unmistakably clear that the British still had the final word—not only in Afghanistan, but across the entire subcontinent—a swift and decisive blow had to be delivered against Ayub Khan.

On July 30, therefore, with Stewart's endorsement, Roberts sent a personal and secret telegram to Simla: "I strongly recommend that a force be sent from Kabul to Kandahar. . . . It is important that we should now show our strength throughout Afghanistan. . . . You need have no fears about my division. It can take care of itself." Roberts was putting forward his own name because Stewart, as supreme commander, had to remain in Kabul. Four days later, the request was approved by Lord Ripon, the new Viceroy, and Roberts rolled up his sleeves to get his army on the march.

He faced a job of work, if for no other reason than his assurance, in the telegram to Simla, that the force would reach Kandahar within a month. Ordinarily this might not have been a specially difficult promise to keep, despite the 320-mile obstacle course separating the two cities. In 1839, Keane's Army of the Indus had hiked from Kandahar to Kabul in slightly less than five weeks and would have advanced more swiftly but for the time taken to capture Ghazni. But Roberts in fact was giving himself not a month but barely three weeks. This was because it would take him at least one week to organize a force of 10,000 troops, 8,000 followers, 18 guns and more than 10,000 animals. And a three-week forced march across some of the worst terrain on earth at the hottest time of the year was asking more than could be expected even of trained professional soldiers.

Mobility had to be the keynote of the operation. The maximum weight allowed for each British soldier's kit was thirty pounds, that of a sepoy twenty. The force would be expected, somehow, to live off the land. No food supplies were carried except for iron rations of bread, flour, *ghee* (clarified butter), preserved vegetables, tea, sugar, salt and rum. All guns had their wheels removed—wheels being useless in almost roadless mountain country—and were placed on the backs of camels. Accompanied by a medical officer, Roberts personally inspected the entire force, down to the last detachment and squad, weeding out every man judged physically unfit for the demands of a forced march. Stragglers would act as a brake on the army, and there was no way of knowing how long the Kandahar garrison could hold out.

Shortly before three o'clock on the morning of August 8, the populace of Kabul was awakened by the jabbing yip of several dozen bugles sounding "rouse" for the Kabul-Kandahar Field Force. Barely an hour later, the eight-mile-long British column was winding out of the city. And it became obvious at once that there would be nothing leisurely about the drive on Kandahar. At 5:00 A.M., when the troops had been marching for an hour, they stacked arms, lit pipes and pulled on water bottles as a halt was called. Ten minutes later they were stepping off again. They enjoyed another ten-minute break at six o'clock, another at seven; at eight, a full twenty minutes was allowed for breakfast. For the rest of the day, the end of each hour saw only a ten-minute breather. When camp was made at five o'clock in the afternoon, the men had been on their feet or in the saddle for nearly eleven consecutive hours.

And yet, on its first day, the force had covered barely ten miles, and after four full days of marching, when the troops bivouacked in the gentle valley of the Logar River, Kabul still lay less than fifty miles to the northeast. But the lagging pace was deliberate: "I thought it wise," wrote Roberts, "not to attempt long distances at first, that both men and animals might become gradually hardened." He knew that the army would not face its real test of endurance until it had passed Ghazni, where the badlands began.

Ghazni was reached on August 15, and the ensuing days proved the wisdom of Roberts' planning. The force had now entered a blasted, trackless boneyard of iron mountains and sightless desert. During the day, the sun failed the columns with such ferocity that the simple act of drawing breath was like a workout in a gymnasium. "If shadows could have been made saleable," wrote one officer, "they would have fetched any price, even the patch of shade under a horse's girth." At night, the men burned in a paralyzing cold. The dead chill was particularly trying on the Highlanders, whose kilts were an open invitation to frostbite in the most sensitive parts of the anatomy. Probably the Gordons felt the cold more than any other unit; their 650 troops had only 100 serviceable greatcoats, which had to be assigned to sentries on night guard duty.

And as if heat, cold and the task of placing one foot in front of the other were not burden enough, the troops also found themselves saddled with double duty. Two days out of Kabul, nearly all of the army's Afghan drivers had deserted, and the responsibility of looking after the baggage animals had to be shared by the fighting men. Roberts called it "fortunate that the soldiers had been practised in loading, leading and tending the animals," but "fortunate" was probably not the word the soldiers would have used.

Uppermost in everyone's mind was the matter of simple survival in a burned-out land. Oddly enough, Indian corn, grown by the region's few inhabitants, could be found in modest quantities, but the crops were not always sufficient to feed the army at the end of a day's march, since animals' needs had first priority. The same applied to water; scooped up in sandy lumps from dehydrating streambeds and strained into buckets or makeshift troughs, it was alloted more generously to cavalry mounts, ammunition mules and pack camels than to humans. The men could only stand and watch the animals drink. "The worst torment that pursued us was unquenchable thirst," an officer recalled. "Tantalus dreams of ruby-coloured claret cup, or amber cider, used to haunt my imagination till I felt I must drink something or perish."

The threat of fuel shortages also loomed. The country was virtually treeless. Camp and cooking fires had to be made from the finger-sized roots of a shrub called southernwood, which required long hours to scratch up and gather. When roots could not be found, the houses of tribal villages were sometimes pulled down for their few frail timbers. Along with the commandeering of corn crops, and sometimes of animals, these demolitions caused real hardship to the local populations who had the misfortune to make their homes in the army's path. But Roberts at least saw to it that all farmers and landowners received generous cash compensation on the spot. In this respect, the drive on Kandahar might have been likened to Sherman's march through Georgia with manners. Not all the tribesmen appreciated the fair treatment. Once beyond Ghazni, the army came under continual Pathan sniping and general harassment, and the troops of the rear brigade (which was changed every day) were fully occupied from dawn to dusk with the dangerous task of rounding up stragglers. "It was certain death," wrote Roberts, "for anyone who strayed from the shelter of the column; numbers of Afghans hovered about on the look-out for plunder, or in the hope of being able to send a Kaffir, or an almost equally-detested Hindu, to eternal perdition." Despite this, the demands of the march were such that many followers became indifferent to the tribal threat, being "so weary and footsore that they hid themselves in ravines, making up their minds to die, and entreating, when discovered and urged to make an effort, to be left where they were."

Roberts of course would have none of that, assigning badly needed pack animals to carry exhausted followers. A total of twenty-four stragglers was lost on the march, but all things considered, it was an extraordinarily low rate of attrition.

And so it went for fifteen days of seemingly interminable marching, with sandpaper throats and growling, near-empty bellies, with troops and followers coughing like a phalanx of tubercular patients in their own built-in pillar of dust while potshots zinged at them as if from a thousand disturbed beehives. For more than a fortnight, an entire army was completely cut off from the rest of the world; India and England could only hope that the columns had not been slaughtered to a man by tribal hordes, or that they had not simply been swallowed up by the desolation itself.

On August 23, the force staggered into a place called Khelat-i-Ghilzai, and Roberts finally called a twenty-four-hour halt. It was no more than the men deserved. They had maintained the pace set by their commander, averaging 15 miles daily and eating up a total of 225 miles since leaving Kabul. If they continued to step off in that fashion, Kandahar would be reached before the end of August.

The day of rest served its purpose. On August 25, the columns formed up again and flaunted their second wind by logging nearly fifty miles in the next three days. Although the performance was gratifying to Roberts, he was feeling less pleased with himself, having just been laid low by overwork, sun and a jolting attack of fever. "I had now to give in for the time being, and was compelled to perform the march in a doolie [litter], a most ignominious mode of conveyance for a General on service; but there was no help for it, for I could not sit on a horse."

At about this time, Roberts received a message by runner from Lieutenant General Primrose, the Kandahar garrison commander, informing him that Ayub Khan had raised the siege and was entrenching his troops in the hills outside the city. Although this meant that the pressure on Kandahar, to all intents and purposes, had been relieved, it did not mean that the relief force could slacken its pace. The Afghans were now in a position from which they could retire swiftly on Herat, and as long as the rebel army remained at large, British management of Afghanistan through Abdur Rahman would be a frail device, if not a mockery. Besides, Ayub Khan's troop dispositions suggested that he might have decided to take on Roberts and then resume the siege of Kandahar. It was if anything even more urgent that Roberts reach Kandahar on schedule.

Ayub did not try to interfere with Roberts. In fact, he seemed eager to bury the hatchet. On August 29, an Afghan officer came to the British camp under a flag of truce with a letter from Ayub, protesting that the Maiwand action had been forced on him, that "what was preordained came to pass"; this, said Ayub, was "the real truth." The Afghan leader also sought Roberts' thoughts on how "affairs might be settled in an amicable matter." Roberts advised Ayub that if he wished peace he need only surrender all his prisoners and "submit yourself unconditionally to the British Government." Although Ayub did not reply, neither did he attack. It began to look as if he planned a fast get-away to Herat. That had to be prevented at all costs.

On the morning of August 31, the Kandahar gates were thrown open and the garrison stood to attention as the ragged, dust-caked troops of the Kabul-Kandahar Field Force dressed their ranks and entered the city to the animated thumping and squealing of tenor drums and pipes. They had come 313 miles in twenty-three days, for a respectable average of slightly more than 13½ miles daily. Other forced marches had witnessed and would witness greater turns of speed, but seldom in country so thoroughly unsuited to organized movement of any kind. Roberts rode at the head of the column on his white Arab charger Vonolel. He was still too weak to stand, but would have resigned his commission before allowing himself to be carried in.

Yet whatever elation he may have felt over his achievement began to dissolve when he took a close look at the 4,000 British and Indian troops who had turned out to greet his own force. "I confess to being greatly surprised, not to use a stronger expression," he wrote, "at the demoralized condition of the greater part of the garrison." It reminded him of the siege of Agra during the Mutiny, where the beleaguered British had "never even hoisted the Union Jack until the relieving force was close at hand." But Roberts also remembered that most of the English at Agra had been women, children and male civilians, whereas the Kandahar garrison was composed of professional fighting men: "For British soldiers to have contemplated the possibility of Kandahar being taken by an Afghan army showed what a miserable state of depression and demoralization they were in." Their sagging esprit did not suggest that they would be of much use in the impending action against Ayub Khan. Not that this kept Roberts from placing the Kandahar troops under his command, or from deploying them with the entire force for an immediate attack on the morning of September 1.

The Afghan army was by then drawn up along a line of razorback hills running some five or six miles north and slightly west of Kandahar. Ayub Khan had concentrated his troops mainly on the steep escarpments of the Baba Wali Kotal, the principal pass through the heights, and in a village called Pir Paimal just north of the pass and west of the hills. With the help of scouting patrols and his own telescope, Roberts learned that the Afghans had thrown up stout defensive works on both positions, particularly Pir Paimal. Their strength had already been ascertained at about 10,000, indicating that the bulk of the irregular levies and tribal forces had dispersed in customary Afghan fashion. Scouts and spies further informed Roberts that at least 1,500 other Afghans, having learned of Abdur Rahman's rise to preeminence in Kabul, had offered to desert to the British if an attack on Ayub were launched. This meant that Ayub's effective fighting force came to about 8,500 against Roberts' 11,000 sepoys and 3,800 British troops.

But the British did not hold that much of an edge. The Afghans were on their own turf and, as seemed almost always to be the case, occupied all the high ground worth holding. Besides, the defections from Ayub's ranks had included no Ghazis, and one Ghazi tended to be worth about half a platoon. Ayub's artillery also remained intact; the Russian-trained gunners could be counted on not to waste ammunition but to serve the guns with clockwork precision and aim them with the eyes of falcons. Dislodging the Afghans from the Baba Wali Kotal and prying them out of the heavily barricaded Pir Paimal defenses could not be an effort of sheer muscle power alone.

Roberts' plan was the old reliable feint. He would throw Ayub off balance with an artillery-supported lunge by Primrose's Kandahar troops at the Baba Wali Kotal, while his own 1st and 2nd brigades, advancing on parallel lines, would swing round the lower foothills in a two-pronged drive on Pir Paimal. The deception went off smoothly. At 9:00 A.M. sharp, Primrose's batteries began lobbing forty-pound shells into the narrow confines of the Baba Wali Kotal, where several thousand tightly-packed Afghans found little cover from a million whistling shards of steel. As Roberts had hoped, the barrage forced Ayub to focus his attention on the pass and give less thought to the two brigades when they began their drive on the key position at Pir Paimal.

The brigades, however, did not move on jeweled bearings. Entering a village called Gundi Mulla, the 2nd Gurkhas and the Gordons of the 1st Brigade had to crawl through a maze of winding alleys under a steady drizzle of musket and rifle fire from loopholed walls and enclosures. Even when space was found to rush some strongpoint, the Afghans held on with suicidal fury, falling back on the next line of walls only after score upon score of their numbers had been spitted on bayonet points. Eventually, however, they were swept aside in a concerted bayonet charge as the Highlanders and Gurkhas literally raced against each other to clear out the last pockets of resistance.

The 2nd Brigade found the going even stiffer. It ran headlong into what seemed a dead end as it entered the larger village of Gundigan. Here, the Seaforths and 2nd Sikhs were jolted, checked, and sometimes even thrown back by furious headlong attacks of whooping Ghazis who poured from the concealment of vegetable gardens and irrigation canals. It was almost noon before the sheer weight of British numbers enabled the 2nd Brigade to sweep through Gundigan and link up with the 1st Brigade for the mass assault of cold steel that finally carried Pir Paimal.

But if the main Afghan position was now in British hands, the Afghans had yet to throw in the towel. Pir Paimal suddenly became almost invisible in cloudbursts of flying earth and shell fragments as Ayub Khan's artillery finally began pelting the British and Indians from the Baba Wali Kotal, while swarms of Ghazis formed up in rough array beneath gaudy battle flags atop the pass. A counterattack was in the making. It could be stopped only if the Afghan guns were silenced. Major George White of the Gordons shouted to his men: "Highlanders! Will you follow me?" In reply, the Gordons' pipes commenced squealing out "The Slogan" as the riflemen fixed bayonets. Almost simultaneously, the Gordons were joined by the 2nd Gurkhas, and the assault on the rocky escarpment began under sheets of Afghan musket fire and pillows of shell bursts from the Afghan guns. At least two dozen of the attackers were slammed out of the action as they clambered up the slope.

They were halfway there when the firing suddenly stopped. For once, the prospect of facing British bayonets and Gurkha *kukris* had proved too much even for the Ghazis. When the heights were crowned, the two regiments found nothing but abandoned guns and empty entrenchments. Then there was another race as White and Sepoy Inderbir Lama of the Gurkhas sprinted to the nearest gun. White won by a hair, but had the "victory" snatched from him when Inderbir leaped onto the breech of a twenty-pounder and shouted that it had been captured in the name of the Prince of Wales' Own Gurkhas. Later, Roberts told the two regiments: "The very last troops [the Afghans] will ever wish to meet again in the field are Highlanders and Gurkhas."

It was all over but the mopping up, and the British had little enough of that to do. In accordance with Afghan demobilization practices, Ayub Khan's beaten troops had either vanished into thin air or changed from their shabby uniforms to the even more threadbare garb of farmers; virtually no one could be identified as the enemy of a few hours earlier.

But the British did bury at least 600 Afghan bodies strewn out along the line of attack from Kandahar to Pir Paimal. Against those casualties, their own 41 killed and wounded seemed a relatively cheap price to pay for the restoration of Pax Britannica in southern Afghanistan.

The spoils of victory did not include Ayub Khan, who appeared to have quit the field early in the action and was now believed in flight to Herat, apparently with only the clothes on his back. But as a commander, the Afghan Prince Charlie had not lacked for creature comforts. When British troops entered his sprawling headquarters tent, they found silk tapestries on the walls, deep-piled Persian carpets, a king-size damask couch with a leopard-skin spread. Jezails with ivory-inlaid stocks and jewel-hilted tulwars hung from tent poles, while many leather-bound volumes of Persian poetry and several mandolins lay strewn about with a plentiful stock of British tinned foods—the last liberated at Maiwand. All that spoiled the opulence was the body of a youthful British artillery officer outside the tent; flies buzzed over the still-warm blood of his freshly-cut throat. He too had been captured at Maiwand, and his rescue by Roberts' force had been frustrated by some Ghazis, barely minutes before the battle ended. Queen Victoria later wrote Roberts that she had experienced a "thrill of horror" on learning of the murder.

That was practically the only sour note in India's and Britain's response to the march on Kandahar and the rout of Ayub Khan's forces. In autumn, when Roberts departed for England, his whole army turned out to bid him godspeed as he rode through the Bolan Pass. "As I parted with each corps in turn," he wrote, "its band played 'Auld Lang Syne,' and I have never since heard that memory-stirring air without its bringing before my mind's eye the last view I had of the Kabul-Kandahar Field Force. I fancy myself crossing and re-crossing the river which winds through the pass; I hear the martial beat of drums and plaintive music of the pipes; and I see Riflemen and Gurkhas, Highlanders and Sikhs, guns and horses, camels and mules, with the endless following of an Indian army, winding through the narrow gorges, or over the interminable boulders. . . . I shall never forget the feeling of sadness with which I said good-bye to the men who had done so much for me. I looked upon them all, Native as well as British, as my valued friends."

The send-off was just the beginning. Arriving in England, Roberts found himself "fêted and feasted to an alarming extent" in reward for having brought off his country's most decisive feat of arms since Waterloo. In due course he would be elevated to the Peerage as Earl Roberts of Kandahar, but he would never fully understand the honor. In his opinion, he had faced a much more difficult task, and infinitely heavier odds, in his march on Kabul a year earlier. The excitement generated by the Kandahar campaign, he felt, could be accounted for only by "the glamour of romance thrown around an army of 10,000 men lost to view, as it were, for nearly a month . . . and the corresponding relief . . . when that army reappeared to dispose of Ayub and his hitherto victorious troops."

But Robers did not spurn any of the kudos heaped on him by his countrymen. Nor was there any reason why he should have.

The victory at Kandahar also set the stage for Britain's departure from Afghanistan. Departure was now considered not only politically expedient but more or less safe. Fears that Abdur Rahman might be encouraged to mischief by Ayub Khan's uprising had been ill-founded; there was hardly anything the amir-designate would have welcomed more than a defeat of his chief rival by the British. On August 10, Abdur Rahman had finally been installed. Before the end of 1880, all British occupation forces in Afghanistan would have returned to India.

Except for the garrison at Kandahar, which opened a can of worms in England. Despite Roberts' victory, the Maiwand disaster had thrown a shudder of fear through certain Tory elements of the British body politic, and Gladstone's withdrawal pledge became the issue of prolonged and impassioned debate in Parliament. The Rawlinsonians fought a desperate holding action, guaranteeing that every imaginable calamity would overtake the Raj if Kandahar were left wide open to the Russians. They were not silenced when Queen Victoria announced, in her Speech from the Throne in January 1881, that she had been advised to recommend evacuation. That only inspired further cries of doom, balanced by Lytton's assurance that if Britain held Kandahar, "you may look on the permanent security of the North-West Frontier of India as a question practically closed."

But the die had been cast. Commons finally settled the question with a vote to withdraw, and by March 1881, Kandahar was back in Afghan hands. The Forward Policy had been laid to rest forever.

Anyone who thought so was mistaken. Although Gladstone's non-interventionist views had prevailed, in practice, nonintervention on the Indian frontier in the final two decades of the nineteenth century was to prove the reverse of isolationism. Even without a garrison at Kandahar, Britain's hold on the northwest frontier had been tangibly reinforced by the events leading to the Second Afghan War and by the war itself. Quetta had by that time been made into the Frontier's intimidatingly fortified southern anchor, and as such, it was believed, a very real inhibition to plans to invade India through the Bolan Pass. By the Treaty of Gandamak, not only the vital Khyber Pass but the strategically important Kurram Valley had been recognized as falling under effective British authority. Indeed, along a 400-mile front from upper Baluchistan to the hills north of Peshawar, Afghan control and influence had been visibly diluted. A real Indian frontier was beginning to take on something like shape and substance.

Just as significantly, Afghanistan itself, although no longer a British-occupied territory, could still be viewed in many respects not merely as a buffer to India's northwest frontier but as an appendage of the Empire itself. The key to Britain's support of Abdur Rahman had been the Amir's agreement not to enter into any agreement with other countries (namely Russia) without the consent of the Indian Government or the British Foreign Office. In short, Afghan policy was to be shaped and dictated by Whitehall, and Abdur Rahman would play dummy to the ventrilo-quism of the Viceroy of India.

Provided, of course, that Abdur Rahman would choose to honor his pledge. The security of the Indian frontier would hinge in great measure on the character of the stormiest petrel in the history of Anglo-Afghan relations.

PART FIVE

Genghis Khan in Chains

20

The Torturer at Home

T HE AMIR ABDUR RAHMAN KHAN once told an Englishman named
Frank Martin that during the course of his reign he had ordered the
execution of more than 100,000 Afghans. Martin served for some years
as Abdur Rahman's chief civil engineer, and the book he wrote about his
experiences with the Amir included a chapter entitled "Tortures and
Methods of Execution," whose subtitles read: "Hanging by hair and
skinning alive . . . Beating to death with sticks . . . Cutting men in pieces
. . . Throwing down mountain-side . . . Starving to death in cages . . .
Boiling woman to soup and man drinking it before execution . . Punishment by exposure and starvation . . . Burying alive . . . Throwing into
soap boilers . . . Cutting off hands . . . Blinding . . . Tying to bent trees
and disrupting . . . Blowing from guns . . . Hanging, etc." Martin also
noted that "there are other forms of torture . . but these cannot be
described."

The most revolting aspect of these barbarities was that they were
perpetrated in a good cause.

When Abdur Rahman took up the reins of Afghanistan's government in
1880, he found himself presiding over a state of unbridled anarchy. The
firm foundations of order and unity built by his grandfather Dost
Muhammad had begun to crack during the five-year war following the
Dost's death in 1863, had crumbled further under Sher Ali and Yakub
Khan, and had finally collapsed altogether in the Second Afghan War
and the British occupation. As in the decade before Dost Muhammad's
accession in 1826, Afghanistan had retrogressed to a mutilated balkaniza-

tion that had stripped it of any pretensions to sovereignty. Once again, murderers did their dark deeds in bright sunlight while highwaymen bushwhacked caravans across the length and breadth of the land so thoroughly that trade had all but dried up. To the extent that any administration existed, it was being eaten alive by a corrupt elite of semi-literate civil servants called *mirzas*, who feathered their nests by accusing other mirzas of swindling and then took huge bribes to withdraw the charges. It was always easy to make an indictment stick, said Martin, "for very few besides the mirzas can do more than count up to twenty."

Although the British had smiled on Abdur Rahman, he held even less power when he took the throne than had Dost Muhammad five decades earlier. Once again, the real rulers of Afghanistan were its tribal robber barons who held their provinces by duplicity and naked force, who mobilized huge armies against each other and kept the whole country in a state of perpetual vendetta. In such conditions, any amir who wished to restore order and assert a legitimate claim as de facto and de jure monarch could hardly be a stickler for parliamentary procedure. The task required a strong man. Abdur Rahman proved to be all of that.

His priority need was to smash the power of the tribal warlords. He had got off to an excellent start in that direction even before Lytton and Roberts had offered him the Afghan throne—indeed, while he still believed the British to be his foes. Early in 1880, tiring of his self-imposed twelve-year exile in Russian Turkestan and noting that the time might be ripe to depart, he gathered a handful of armed tribesmen and began the long ride home. It was interrupted on the north bank of the Oxus, at a caravanserai called the Inn of the Drunkards and Smokers, where Abdur Rahman received a message from the chief of Afghanistan's Badak-shan region. This man, one Shahzada Hassan, had once been a protégé of Abdur Rahman, but now he sent warning that if Abdur Rahman crossed the Oxus he would be slain.

It was no idle threat. Shahzada Hassan had 12,000 armed followers whereas Abdur Rahman's "army" numbered just over 100. "I knew that if I escaped this time," Abdur Rahman later wrote in his autobiography, "the people of Badakshan and Kataghan would kill me, and if I escaped them, I had to face the English army, so, considering all these dangers, I had little hope of living."

The prospect did not seem to upset him as he wrote a reply to Shahzada Hassan: "O idiot, O ungrateful coward, I brought you and your brothers up for many years . . . I have now discovered my mistake, and learned your true character. If I had feared death, I should not have come so far. Tomorrow will decide which one of us is the stronger, O coward." And the morrow proved more than decisive. Awed by Abdur Rahman's defiance, Shahzada Hassan's troops deserted en masse and went over to the bolder man. When Abdur Rahman crossed the Hindu Kush and approached Kabul, he had not only made himself a force to be reckoned with in the British camp but had dealt a staggering blow to the machinery of chiefdom in Afghanistan.

An even more crucial punch followed almost at once. Within a few weeks of his accession, Abdur Rahman further consolidated the monarchy with a surprise drive on Herat, where he ousted the semifugitive Ayub Khan and placed Herat itself under a firmer centralized rule than the breakaway city had ever known. Properly impressed by the swift trouncing of Abdur Rahman's most powerful and dangerous rival, other renegade chiefs soon began falling into line; over the years, all would submit to the authority of Kabul.

When they did not, Abdur Rahman struck like a tulwar. In 1888, his cousin Ishak Khan, whom he had appointed Governor of Afghan Turkestan, let his ambitions run away with him and proclaimed himself Amir, whereupon the real Amir took personal command of a punitive expedition on a forced march across the Hindu Kush. Ishak Khan did not even wait to see how his own army might fare in the showdown, but fled to Russian territory while Abdur Rahman's horsemen rode down the rebel troops and systematically cut them to pieces. Several thousand of the survivors were blinded with quicklime and Afghan Turkestan remained an integral part of the nation. When Abdur Rahman died in 1901, Afghanistan had been transformed from a henhouse of squabbling headmen into something like a sovereign state.

Abdur Rahman was no less diligent in his war on crime. Accurate records were never kept of the number of human hands lopped off with swords as punishment for theft, or of the deaths from shock when the blood-spurting stumps were plunged into boiling tar to prevent infection, but the figure probably ran into the scores of thousands. Executions were summary, although not always swift. A bandit caught waylaying a caravan could consider himself lucky if he was merely bayoneted to death or blown from the muzzle of Kabul's noonday gun. Just as often, he could count on having several square inches of his skin removed daily, for as many days as it took him to succumb. Or he might be hanged, but not from the conventional drop-gallows with its split-second snapping of the neck. The condemned man was simply hauled up and allowed to strangle at leisure.

Other executions lasted even longer. Travelers crossing the Lataband Pass on the road between Kabul and Kandahar rode beneath a huge iron cage suspended from a pole; in it lay the bleaching bones of convicted highwaymen who had been placed there to advertise Abdur Rahman's justice by dying of hunger, thirst, heat stroke, frostbite or all four. If the cage contained a still-living inmate, no one dared give him so much as a grain of millet or a drop of water. Minor offenses carried penalties that included the sewing together of upper and lower lips, rubbing snuff in the eyes, hanging by the heels for a week, nose amputations and whisker-plucking. The last was specially dreaded: a smooth-cheeked Muslim, unable to swear oaths by his beard, tended to feel like a quadriplegic.

The two most important things about these sentences was that they were carried out on a massive scale—unprecedented even in Afghan history—and that they were public. Although the lesson did not get across instantly—"the boast of the true Afghan," wrote Martin, "is that he can endure pain, even to death, without a sigh or sound, and some do so"—its impact was gradually felt and its results, in due course, became visible. By the 1890s, Abdur Rahman could write with a certain pride of the contrast between his highways, where caravans no longer needed armed escorts, and the Khyber Pass, "which the English have not been able to render safe for travellers, without a strong body-guard, even after sixty years' rule."

Of course, Abdur Rahman never eradicated crime completely; that would have been too much to expect among a people whose instincts for corruption, conspiracy and murder were a conditioned reflex. He was continually alive to potential insurgency in the highest councils of government and made it an article of policy to arrange for the secret garroting or throat-cutting of close advisers who seemed likely to emerge as rabble-rousers or plotters against him. He girded his person with an elaborate security apparatus, installing spies not only in every government department but in his own household. (Some close relatives had their own agents spying on the Amir.) Special guards stood round-the-clock sentry duty over his food and drink; at mealtimes, all dishes placed before him were first tasted in his presence by the palace cook. Once, when he had a toothache, his surgeon told him that the extraction would take only twenty minutes with chloroform, whereupon Abdur Rahman ordered that the tooth be pulled without anesthetic, shouting angrily that he could not risk being out of the world for twenty seconds.

But for all the imperfections of Abdur Rahman's system, no ruler of Afghanistan had ever united the country more firmly or given its people a stronger sense of national unity—or made it more unmistakably clear who was in charge. And in so doing, Abdur Rahman also made himself the most feared individual in Central Asia.

Certainly he looked the part. Even in his declining years, when he was racked by gout, wore badly fitting false teeth and dyed his huge beard black in accordance with Afghan custom, Abdur Rahman remained a bull-lion of a man. Martin described him as "very stout and broad, with a rather long body and short legs. His eyes were very dark, almost black, and looked out from under his heavy brows with quick, keen glances. . . .

[He] was always the king, and there was that about him which forbade any one taking advantage. . . . When roused to anger, his face became drawn, and his teeth would show until he looked wolfish, and then he hissed words rather than spoke them, and there were few of those before him who did not tremble when he was in that mood, for it was then that the least fault involved some horrible punishment."

There was another side to Abdur Rahman's character. He had a lively sense of humor and was a gifted raconteur who liked to tell jokes about himself. A favorite anecdote concerned his youthful affliction with a large intestinal worm, which no amount of therapy could dislodge until he put his own ingenuity to work. What he did, he liked to explain with elaborate gestures, was order a banquet laid out before him. The smell of the food tempted the worm, which then began to crawl up Abdur Rahman's throat, enabling him to reach into his mouth and draw the worm all the way out. When he told such tales, the throne room would quake with the thunder of his laughter.

Even his rages with miscreants could be tempered with whimsy. One of his generals, found guilty of some seemingly disloyal act, was cashiered and made to serve as a *batcha*, or palace dancing boy. When some gold was being counted in his treasury, Abdur Rahman noticed that a high-ranking cabinet minister had abstracted several coins and hidden them in his stocking. The Amir then made a deceptively casual remark about the mistaken belief among foreigners that Afghans were not white-skinned, and asked the embezzling official to explode the fallacy by baring his leg. The perpetrator had no choice but to obey. To his great good fortune he was merely thrown into prison.

A more or less model family man, Abdur Rahman was deeply devoted to his five sons, even though he suspected their political ambitions and often treated them as upper-echelon bureaucrats rather than the fruit of his loins. He was Afghanistan's chess and backgammon champion (possibly no one dared beat him), and his passion for flowers gave the royal palace in Kabul a resemblance to a scaled-up greenhouse even in winter. Music seemed to have charms that soothed the Amir's savage breast. He himself played the violin and rebab passably well, and bragged in his autobiography that "it must be therefore a luxury and pleasure for my officials to be in my presence to enjoy all the various pleasures I provide for them." Considering what else Abdur Rahman was capable of providing, the officials probably found the music more relief than enjoyment.

Abdur Rahman probably took his greatest pride in being a jack of all trades and master of some. Even as a child he had shown a mechanical aptitude rare among Afghans, teaching himself architecture, carpentry, blacksmithing and rifle-making before he began to grow whiskers. During his exile in Russian territory he continued his self-education, adding medicine, dentistry, watch-making, phrenology, gold-working and piano-tuning to his list of skills. He was a staunch upholder of the work ethic and often voiced contempt for the idle ways of other Asiatic princes. Even when prostrate with gout, he ran his country single-handedly. In 1894, Curzon visited Abdur Rahman in Kabul and wrote that "there was nothing from the command of an army or the government of a province to the cut of a uniform or the fabrication of furniture that he did not personally supervise and control." If there had been railways in Afghanistan, he would have seen to it that they ran on time.* He worked a twenty-hour day, disregarding the pleas of his hakims and his two or three British doctors** to follow a less demanding schedule. "As I am a lover of the welfare of my nation," he wrote, "I do not feel my own pains, but the pains and sufferings and weaknesses of my people."

His people may not always have appreciated this concern for their betterment, and Abdur Rahman himself often despaired of ever succeeding in his attempt to drag them out of the Iron Age. (His own private secretary had a sixth-grade knowledge of reading and could barely compose a letter.) But he never stopped trying, and his reforms were by no means exclusively punitive. To make Afghanistan less dependent on imports, he hired expatriate technicians who studied the country's mineral resources—particularly its gold, silver, copper, lead, tin, nickel and zinc. Other foreign specialists on his payroll laid the foundations of a rudimentary industrial system, training nomadic warriors in a variety of skilled trades. In Kabul's flourishing workshops, Afghan mechanics and craftsmen not only mass-produced guns and ammunition for the armed forces but minted coins and turned out furniture, leather goods, European clothing and a proliferation of metalware. Abdur Rahman also offered cash prizes as incentives to good work, and if an Afghan wanted to go into business for himself, he could usually count on a generous interest-free loan from the Amir's own pocket. It has been said that as many as 100,000 of Abdur Rahman's countrymen found gainful employment in some sort of modern manufacture or commercial enterprise.

Above all, Abdur Rahman made himself accessible to every class of the populace. "It was usual," wrote Martin, "for people to be allowed to present petitions when meeting him on the road, or returning from the musjid [mosque] on a Friday (the Mussulman Sunday), and this he encouraged, and even went so far . . . as to call all men, even sweepers, 'brother." At public durbars in the royal palace, the pleas and disputes of street beggars who came before Abdur Rahman received as much

* There were none because Abdur Rahman feared that they might expedite the movement of Russian or British troops if either power ever decided to invade. To this day, there is not a single foot of rail in Afghanistan.
** President Kennedy was not the first chief of state to have a woman physician; Abdur Rahman anticipated him when he hired Dr. Edith Hamilton from England.

attention and thoughtful adjudication as did the petitions of influential chiefs and wealthy merchants. Although some suppliants did not always have the few coppers needed to bribe the guards at the palace gate, no one was ever turned away deliberately by Abdur Rahman himself. It is quite possible that the fairness of the personal justice that he meted out may have compensated at least a little for his more barbaric excesses.

If Afghanistan's backwardness exasperated Abdur Rahman, his sorest trial was the accident of his own birth, which in terms of his pugnacious instincts came at least a century too late and denied him the opportunity to emulate Genghis Khan. Curzon wrote of him as "a man who, had he lived in an earlier age and not been crushed, as he told me, like an earthenware pot between the rival forces of England and Russia, might have founded an Empire, and swept in a tornado of blood over Asia and even beyond it." As it was, the Amir could only chafe at his status as the petty prince of an impoverished Third-World principality huddled in the shadow of the nineteenth century's two mightiest imperial behemoths.* His agreement to accept British advice—which meant orders —on foreign relations as a main condition of British support was an intolerable humiliation to a man who had been born to lay down the law. The rage of his frustration came as a surprise to the British, who did not realize at once that they had a tiger by the tail. Throughout his reign, he complained bitterly over his puppet role, and often tried to kick over the traces. One of these attempts was to come within a hair's breadth of sweeping the British from the northwest frontier of India.

As a rule, however, Abdur Rahman not only accepted the reality of his own impotence but perceived that his country's interests would best be served by being accommodating if not consistently friendly toward the British rather than the Russians. Even the hospitality he had received while in Russian Turkestan had not diluted a lively suspicion and fear of his hosts. He was never shaken from his belief that a priority article of Russian imperial policy was that "the Islamic kingdoms should be washed away from the face of the Asiatic continent." He thought Sher Ali had "talked like a lunatic" when he sought assistance from Stolietoff and Kauffmann. To be a pawn of London and Calcutta rather than a serf of St. Petersburg seemed to him the lesser of two evils. Abdur Rahman never quite left the British camp.

Correct or not, Abdur Rahman's theory of Russian Islamophobe

* As a conqueror, he had to content himself with the annexation of a small cluster of mountains called Kafiristan, the setting of Kipling's "The Man Who Would Be King." He also acquired the Wakhan panhandle on Afghanistan's extreme northeast frontier, although Wakhan was more or less forced on him by the British, who, oddly enough, did not want the icy outpost either.

objectives was reinforced mightily by that country's expansion along the northern Afghan frontier during the 1880s. It was also a period that caused the British no less concern, since it saw the Anglo-Russian Great Game heat up to a crisis that threatened a massive military invasion of India.

It also came within an ace of touching off World War I three decades ahead of schedule.

21

Bloody Eyes

Early in 1880, while Abdur Rahman was crossing the Hindu Kush on his way home from exile, a Russian army mobilized at the military base of Krasnovodsk on the eastern shore of the Caspian Sea and commenced a march across the Kara Kum Desert toward Samarkand. The troops of this force were unarmed; instead of artillery and rifles they carried picks and keying hammers. They were the work gangs and platelayers of Russia's Transcaspian Railway.

For fifteen years, the idea of such a line had been under consideration; reducing the travel time between St. Petersburg and Samarkand from six weeks to ten days would obviously be of incalculable benefit in consolidating Russia's Central Asian gains and developing the commerce of the region. And in terms of tightening imperial bonds, the Transcaspian Railway would be to Central Asia what the Suez Canal was to India. (At one point, in fact, the Russian Government had approached Ferdinand de Lesseps, the builder of the Suez Canal, to take charge of the railway project.) Certainly the British recognized this, and they began watching construction with particular interest when it was learned the first major stop on the line was to be a village called Geok Tepe.

This place was the capital of a large tribe of Turkmen bandits, the only people of Russian Turkestan who had not yet submitted to the Czar. Shortly before construction of the railway began, a Russian expedition against Geok Tepe had been soundly thrashed. But at the end of 1880, when another campaign was mounted to subdue the Turkmen, its objectives seemed less punitive than strategic. Geok Tepe happened to lie on the caravan road to the great Merv oasis, 130 miles north of Afghan territory. "Queen of the World" in the distant past, Merv was now beginning to reemerge as a geopolitical holy grail. Although not quite part of Afghanistan, neither did it come under Russian rule, but nineteenth-century British strategists tended to view it as the best jumping-off place from Russian Turkestan to Herat—Rawlinson's much-touted "key" to the invasion of India via Kandahar. Thus the almost simultaneous convergence of a Russian railhead and a Russian army on Geok Tepe was more than enough to set Britain's imperial watchdogs looking under their kennels.

The leader of the punitive force did nothing to dispel anxieties in London and Calcutta. General Mikhail Dmitreyevich Skobelev was the Czar's most able field commander in Central Asia and probably in all the Russias. During the Russo-Turkish War, the U.S. military attaché to the Russian Army had written: "I firmly believe that should [Skobelev] live twenty years more . . . history will then speak of him as one of the five great soldiers of this century, side by side with Napoleon, Wellington, Grant and Moltke." Skobelev never got the chance to make the prediction come true, falling into dissolution and dying in 1882 at the age of thirty-eight. But at the height of his career he was not a figure to be dismissed idly. Nor did the British do so.

Skobelev was a sort of Slavic Patton, both in personal style and martial philosophy. He fancied ivory white horses and gaudy white uniforms; one contemporary wrote of him that he rode into action "scented and curled like a bridegroom to a wedding, his eyes gleaming with wild delight." He also thought of war as mankind's loftiest occupation and made a point of transferring officers who believed in fair play toward a foe. The journalist Charles Marvin wrote of Skobelev's "winning smile" and "the kindliness of his eyes," but also quoted him as saying: "You must not publish this, or I shall be called a barbarian by the Peace Society, but I hold it as a principle that in Asia the duration of peace is in direct proportion to the slaughter you inflict upon the enemy." Not without reason, Turkmen called Skobelev "Bloody Eyes."

Skobelev was also Russia's foremost hawk. He has already been quoted as telling Marvin that he would shrink from an invasion of India, even with 150,000 troops, but that timidity contradicted his words in an official memorandum: "It will be in the end our duty," he wrote, "to organize masses of Asiatic cavalry and hurl them into India as a vanguard, under the banner of blood and rapine, thereby reviving the times of Tamerlane." This might have been no more than idle braggadocio had not Skobelev wielded enormous influence in the court of Czar Alexander II.

In January 1881, Skobelev staged what could have been considered a taste of things to come in India when he attacked Geok Tepe. Although his own 7,000-man force was opposed by at least 10,000 sharpshooting Turkmen riders, who also infiltrated the Russian lines at night and cut up sentries by the score, his sixty field guns more than evened the odds. Once the artillery had reduced Geok Tepe to a trash heap, Skobelev and his Cossacks rode into the smoking ruins to polish off the stunned Turkmen survivors. While doing this, they also ran their sabers through the bodies of some 10,000 women and children. And, with Geok Tepe now in undisputed Russian control, only the Merv oasis stood between Skobelev and the Afghan border.

At that point, St. Petersburg deemed it expedient to reassure London that Russia had no designs on Merv, much less on Herat. And indeed this had been quite true ever since the departure from Kabul of the Stolietoff mission in 1878 and the subsequent Second Afghan War. Russia had by then not only accepted the fair accompli of Afghanistan as a British sphere of influence, but considered it no more than a matter of time before Britain extended her Indian frontier right up to the Hindu Kush. Moreover, with a strong Indian Army occupation force in Kandahar, any southward advance by Russian columns would have been madness.

Barely a month after the capture of Geok Tepe, however, Russian diplomatic and military circles received a pleasant jolt when it was learned that the British had agreed to return Kandahar to the Afghans. This unexpected shift in policy—not to mention the evacuation of British troops from Afghanistan—suggested at the very least that a thrust toward Merv could well meet with minimal opposition.

Yet for the next three years, Russia showed no signs of any eagerness to seize Merv. If she had any designs on the place she was at pains to conceal them. Nikolai Karlovich Giers, the Russian Foreign Minister, periodically reassured Whitehall with disclaimers of further territorial ambitions on the Afghan frontier. So on February 14, 1884, when St. Petersburg announced the annexation of Merv, Britannia found herself caught with shield and trident down.

In London, reaction to the news was mixed. In some quarters it was pointed out that Merv, after all, was not Herat, that more than 200 miles of desolation separated the two places, that Czar Alexander II's successor Alexander III was abundantly aware of the diplomatic risks entailed in ordering Russian troops into Afghanistan. While Gladstone's cabinet met hastily to discuss possible countermeasures, a section of the press played up the Duke of Argyll's mocking remark that the Government was suffering from a case of "Mervousness." But Central Asian frontier tensions had been mounting for too long, and public opinion seemed to share the official view that the Great Game might be approaching critical mass. In Commons, a resolution was introduced that Russia be warned bluntly that an attack on Afghanistan would be considered "detrimental to the interests of this country." It was another way of threatening mobilization.

Russian diplomats seemed unruffled by the British panic. Lord Granville, the Foreign Secretary, was assured by the Russian Ambassador that the annexation of Merv had been anything but an act of aggression. Quite the contrary, he said, it was no more than an effort to solve a problem shared by England and Russia alike: that of ascertaining how far an empire must extend its frontiers in a land peopled by savages. But this paraphrase of Gorchakov's earlier statement that "the greatest difficulty is in knowing where to stop" was not reflected in the behavior of the Russian hawk community. Although Skobelev was no longer on the scene, his ghost seemed to continue wielding clout in the councils of the Emperor. Only a few years earlier, Skobelev had declared that if Russia sent a strong task force across the Hindu Kush, the Indian people would rise in revolt against their British rulers, and that the turmoil would keep British forces so occupied that they would be unable to guard the passes of the northwest frontier. Carried away by the prospect of Armageddon, Skobelev had even gone so far as to cite "competent English authorities" who conceded that a serious setback on the frontier might well touch off what Skobelev called "a social revolution in England." Now, with Merv in Russian hands, more than one of Alexander III's generals virtually frothed at the mouth to hasten that upheaval.

In all likelihood, Skobelev had placed little if any stock in his own predictions of bread riots in London and Manchester. But he had probably revealed the real purpose of his country's aggressive southeastward thrust when he said: "The stronger Russia is in Central Asia, the weaker England is in India and the more conciliatory she will be in Europe." Even Rawlinson often acknowledged European political leverage as the most realistic objective of Russian "threats" to India. And that goal now seemed to have been gained—at least in the sense that Gladstone was visibly recoiling from the thought of being drawn into a jingo war that would almost inevitably involve other European nations and erupt into a global explosion.

Besides which, having occupied Merv, Russia appeared satisfied not to push her frontiers or her luck any further, for the time being at any rate. No objection was raised in St. Petersburg to a British compromise proposal that the two nations send commissions to the region south of Merv to define a mutually acceptable Afghan-Russian borderline.

During the nineteenth century, European border commissions deciding on the extent of their respective imperial possessions in Asia and Africa seldom took into account the boundaries of indigenous states unless this happened to suit their own needs. On the northern Afghan frontier in 1884, it was very much in Britain's interest to insist on the territorial integrity of Abdur Rahman's kingdom. The area in question, a misery of desert less than half the size of Delaware, was in some respects a no-man's-land, not having been formally annexed either by Russia or Afghanistan. But since the Turkmen tribes of the region had always paid tribute to Afghan rulers, Abdur Rahman seemed to hold a slight edge. Britain backed his claim to the hilt.

Russia dissented. Merv proved to be not enough. St. Petersburg now had its sights set on a swamp known as the Panjdeh Oasis, lying 100 miles south of Merv within comfortable marching distance of Herat. The task of the Anglo-Russian border commission was to iron out the respective claims of Czar and Amir to this place, just as if either side was prepared to yield a square inch.

At the head of the British party was Harry Lumsden's brother, General Sir Peter Lumsden, who left England in the summer of 1884 to meet his Russian counterpart, General Zelenoi, in the disputed area. Arriving in November, Lumsden discovered that an alarmed Abdur Rahman had already dispatched a 2,000-man Afghan force to garrison Panjdeh, and that General Alexander Komarov, the local Russian commander, had countered by marching his own 4,000 troops to within almost point-blank artillery range of the Afghan lines. On the heels of this news came a note informing Lumsden that Zelenoi would be unable to meet him until the following spring. To Lumsden, the conclusion was inescapable: Russia had engineered an artificial delay to precipitate a showdown.

Komarov did not seem fitted for the role. In appearance and tastes, the fat, bespectacled general suggested less a fighting man than the scholar-antiquarian that he was. But he also proved himself an articulate if not eloquent letter writer when he sent a message to the Panjdeh garrison commander, General Ghaus-ud-din, calling him a coward and a liar. Not to be outdone, Ghaus-ud-din replied in kind, adding that Komarov was also a thief. If the correspondence continued in this vein, both generals would soon set aside their pens and reach for their swords. Hastily, Lumsden stepped between them, with a rebuke to Ghaus-ud-din for "imitating the impolite language of the Russian." There was not much else he could do.

Nor were reprimands at this stage of the game much more than meaningless. By mid-March of 1885, the situation had become so tense that Sir Edward Thornton, the British Ambassador in St. Petersburg, told Giers that any further southerly moves by Russian forces would have to be regarded as a declaration of war on England. Giers replied that he had no knowledge whatever of a contemplated advance on Panjdeh, much less on Herat. He appeared to be genuinely astonished that Thornton should even bring up the matter.

Early in the morning of March 30, Russian patrols reported to Komarov that Ghaus-ud-din had ordered his troops out of Panjdeh in extended formation toward a small stream that both sides considered a boundary of sorts. This seemed provocation enough, and Komarov's artillery promptly opened up to cover a full-scale infantry-cavalry attack. Armed mainly with venerable flintlocks, the Afghans stood little chance against the Russian breech-loaders, even less against a head-on charge of Komarov's war-whooping Cossack horsemen. Before the sun went down, the Afghans had been scattered like ants whose hill has been trodden on and Panjdeh was in Russian hands. Within a few days, an exultant Russian press was crying out for an immediate drive on Herat; one editor declared that the time had come for Russia to "pierce a window" looking south-eastward to India. H-Hour was at hand.

Even Gladstone knew it. Hardly had the news of Panjdeh reached England than he went before Commons to request—almost to demand—a £6.5 million credit for war purchases, telling the House that Russia had trampled on "the authority of a sovereign, our protected ally, who [has] committed no offense." The cables hummed between London and Calcutta as orders flashed out for the mobilization of two Indian Army Corps. If Alexander III was bluffing, his bluff had been called.

But owing to the customary transport shortage, the Indian Army columns were slow in reaching the Frontier; commanders feared they would not arrive in time to stem the tide of Cossacks pouring through the passes. Nor was British anxiety allayed by the attitude of the hill tribesmen. A political officer asked several Pathan maliks whose side they would take if the Russians invaded, and was told: "We would just sit here on our mountaintops and watch you both fight until one or the other was utterly defeated. Then we would come down and plunder the vanquished to the last mule. God is great!"

By a coincidence, Abdur Rahman happened to be in India when the Russians seized Panjdeh. He had been invited by the Viceroy, the Marquess of Dufferin and Ava, to a durbar in the Punjab city of Rawalpindi, in accordance with the British practice of buttering up the Amir whenever possible. Even before Abdur Rahman arrived, the British laid it on. During his three-day journey through the Khyber Pass, he was escorted by the 400 horsemen of the crack 1st Bengal Cavalry, while clouds of carrier pigeons winged ahead to Peshawar to convey the news of his every step. Hundreds of Indian Army sepoys and tribal militiamen stood guard over Abdur Rahman's camp at night. When his entourage reached Fort Jamrud at the eastern end of the pass, the guns of a half-battery crashed out a royal salute while the sowars of another cavalry regiment drew their sabers to the present. Some years later, during the visit to the Khyber of Prince Albert Victor, Queen Victoria's son was welcomed with more pomp than had been Abdur Rahman, but only a little more. The flattery was considered necessary if Britain was to maintain anything like peaceable control over the angry Amir. In the five years since his accession to the throne, Abdur Rahman had proved far more outraged —and cantankerous—over having been denied a real voice in his own country's foreign policy than the British had expected. The only way he could assert his "independence," it seemed, was through haughty and often high-handed behavior toward his allies. He had barred all British diplomats from Afghanistan. The Queen's only "ambassador" in Kabul at this time was a middle-echelon Muslim Indian civil servant whose house Abdur Rahman kept under twenty-four-hour surveillance by posting spies across the street in the garb of tea vendors. Letters to and from the "embassy" were always intercepted and read, not infrequently destroyed. Any Afghans suspected of trying to communicate with Britain's all but emasculated envoy were liable to prison sentences or worse. As a result, virtually no news of any value regarding developments in Afghanistan ever reached the Viceroy. Such an arrangement hardly suggested British management of anything at all in Afghanistan.

More than one Briton in India thought it dangerous policy to coddle Abdur Rahman. Roberts wrote that the Amir "mistook the patience and forbearance with which we bore his fits of temper for weakness, and was encouraged in an overweening and altogether unjustifiable idea of his own importance." The Indian Government's Foreign Secretary, Sir Henry Mortimer Durand, whose work brought him into something approximating contact with Abdur Rahman, found him "a troublesome and unsatisfactory ally [who] shows the utmost jealousy of ourselves. . . . If it were not for the fact that his fall would . . . give Russia an opening, I should not be sorry to see him driven out of the country." Even as the royal guest at Rawalpindi, Abdur Rahman maintained a certain iciness; Roberts remarked that "his manner was sufficiently courteous though somewhat abrupt."

Then a telegram arrived with the news of Panjdeh. As soon as Dufferin read it to him, Abdur Rahman could be seen to begin thawing. He unbent even further when the Viceroy reaffirmed Britain's pledge to support Afghan frontier claims even at the risk of war with Russia. And at a formal reception, on being presented with a jewel-studded ceremonial sword, Abdur Rahman melted altogether, slicing the air and crying out that "with this sword I hope to smite any enemy of the British Government."

But there was more to the sudden rapprochement than words. Lumsden had dispatched a team of army engineers to Herat to reinforce the city's defenses. Ordinarily, they would have been halted and perhaps detained at the border, but with Abdur Rahman's blessing they were cheered wildly as they passed through the city's gates. The Amir also welcomed further British material assistance in the form of ten brand-new field guns and twenty thousand breech-loading rifles for the Afghan Army. Humped over the Khyber Pass on the backs of elephants, the hardware was soon ready for action.

So too, in due course, was the pair of Indian Army corps on the northwest frontier. All that remained was for the shooting to begin.

Panjdeh seemed an unlikely casus belli. An isolated smear of damp ground oozing from the middle of a parched emptiness, it was hardly suited even to its function as a watering place for caravans. Possession of the site by Russia or Afghanistan would be more burden than benefit. Yet during the spring and early summer of 1885, Panjdeh nearly preempted Sarajevo. It had become the focus of world attention and anxiety mainly because British policy-makers, on the brink of hysteria over the alleged threat to Herat and India, had arbitrarily made it off limits to Russia. Should Alexander III decide to hold it, not just the Indian but the British Army would mobilize. Other European powers would then, almost certainly, be drawn into the conflict: Anglophobic France on Russia's side and Germany, Austria-Hungary and Italy, fearing a Franco-Russian alliance, entering the British camp. England's own posture of "splendid isolation" would go by the board. Only in the lineup of the potential antagonists did 1885 differ appreciably from 1914.

If the Russians had ever seriously considered going to war over an open-air sewer in a squalid corner of Central Asia—which was not totally inconceivable—they swiftly discarded the idea when it became clear that, even under Gladstone, Britain meant business. And that impression was reinforced in June 1885, when a general election returned the jingo Conservatives to power. Although Disraeli had died in 1881, the new Prime Minister, Salisbury, had none of Gladstone's lofty distaste for imperial brawls, especially when India was at stake. After a suitable interval, during which the ritual of exchanging diplomatic notes allowed Russia to climb down gracefully, Giers agreed to withdraw from Panjdeh, and a protocol was duly signed whereby the two powers accepted the general line of a northern Afghan border.

The agreement did not end the Great Game. Both Lion and Bear were to continue snarling and occasionally lashing out at each other from their respective sides of the uncertain boundary; at least one more incident would see the antagonists approach the brink. But Panjdeh is generally considered the high-water mark of the Russian "threat" to Afghanistan and India. And even more significantly, the peaceful resolution of the crisis put off World War I for another twenty-nine years.

It also did nothing whatever to alleviate the growing British migraine on the northwest frontier of India.

22

The Man in the Steel Corset

PROBABLY THE MOST IMMEDIATELY visible aspect of the 1885 Panjdeh incident, from the Afghan standpoint, was Britian's clear demonstration to Abdur Rahman that she could be relied on when the chips were down. To what extent Abdur Rahman appreciated this was another matter. If the 1880s and 1890s witnessed a reduction of pressure from the Amir's antagonists to the north, anything but the same could be said for his allies to the east.

Nor did Abdur Rahman say it. In fact, he made a point of writing that "though England does not want any piece of Afghanistan, still she never loses a chance of getting one—and this friend has taken more than Russia has!"

Which was quite true. By the Treaty of Gandamak and subsequent engagements, the Indian Government had gained control of the Khyber Pass, the Kurram Valley and other immense tracts along the vaguely defined Afghan-Indian border. But Abdur Rahman did not recognize these acquisitions. He considered himself the spiritual and de facto temporal leader of the Frontier Pathans and claimed the whole tribal belt—regardless of agreements—as "the hereditary property of Afghan kings." As neighbors, moreover, the British had a way of making him uneasy, especially in grey areas where title had not been established beyond question of legal doubt either by Amir or Queen. In 1891, when the Indian Government threw up a line of defensive works along the crest of the Samana hills overlooking the vales of Tirah, it could only seem to Abdur Rahman as though his infidel allies had further westward penetration in mind. Troop buildups against tribal provocation in Waziristan were considered necessary by the British; to Abdur Rahman, the same mobilizations appeared not much less menacing than a naked land grab.

Even in territory more or less acknowledged as their own, the British could alarm. The building of some narrow-gauge Frontier military railways may have seemed the worst threat of all. As Abdur Rahman saw it, the extension of the rail line from Quetta to Chaman—fifty miles west of the Bolan Pass and only half that distance from Kandahar—was "just like pushing a knife into my vitals."

Abdur Rahman did not simply sit back and place the Frontier's fate in the hands of Allah. In the numerous protests he lodged during the 1890s with the Viceroy, Lord Lansdowne, he was sometimes almost polite, with veiled threats suggesting that British border policy was self-defeating. "In your cutting away from me these frontier tribes, who are people of my nationality and my religion," said Abdur Rahman, "you will injure my prestige in the eyes of my subjects, and will make me weak and my weakness is injurious to your government." But the Amir could also warn openly: "If at any time a foreign enemy appear on the borders of India, these frontier tribes will be your worst enemy."

And Abdur Rahman would not have been Abdur Rahman had he confined himself to letter-writing. He also used his influence among the hill Pathans, which was not inconsiderable, to sow the seeds of anti-British discontent, which was not hard to do. "The Amir is behaving worse than ever," wrote Sir Mortimer Durand in 1892. "He tells us he is King of the Afridis, and almost admits that he has stirred them up against us." British counterprotests fell on deaf ears. "[Abdur Rahman] treats our envoy as a prisoner," said Durand, "... and he won't come to meet the Viceroy 'like an Indian Chief' ... I cannot see where it is to end."

Presently, however, Abdur Rahman seemed to have concluded that threats would get him nowhere. In the late summer of 1893, he astonished Lansdowne with a proposal that a conference be held in Kabul with a view to a formal, and final, delimitation of the border. This, of course, was agreeable to Lansdowne, who had found his plate full with Abdur Rahman's ongoing intrigues among the Pathans. Durand was appointed to head up the Indian Government mission, and although he wrote that he expected Abdur Rahman to be "extremely unpleasant," he added that "the thing must be done, and ... I think I shall be able to persuade him ... to be reasonable about our frontier."

Durand got a welcome surprise. Arriving in Kabul in early November 1893, "I looked in vain for my old acquaintance ... with his Henry the Eighth face and ready scowl. I suppose the scowl is ready still when wanted, but the Amir of today is a quiet, gentlemanly man; his manner and voice so softened and refined that I could hardly believe that it was really Abdur Rahman. I trust all his extreme pleasantness does not mean a proportionately stiff back in business matters."

Nor did it. Although Abdur Rahman took the precaution of hiding one of his ministers behind a curtain to write a verbatim account of the proceedings, the frontier dispute was swiftly and amicably ironed out. On November 12, perhaps to Durand's amazement, Abdur Rahman put his signature and seal on a treaty renouncing all claims to a band of territory extending from the Hindu Kush to the westernmost limits of Baluchistan. The area particularly included the Khyber and Bolan passes, together with the previously contested northwest frontier regions of Bajaur, Dir, Swat, Buner, Tirah, the Kurram Valley and Waziristan. The treaty formalized the emergence of the British Empire's longest land frontier next to the United States-Canadian border. It was a concession on a grand scale.

It was also not entirely explicable. With scarcely a demurral, Abdur Rahman had surrendered nearly all of the land in which the British presence had been stirring his anxieties and fury for years. At least one British historian has claimed that the agreement was signed under duress, and, although this cannot be ruled out, there is also reason to believe that the Amir may have been inadvertently bamboozled. "It is possible," writes Fraser-Tytler, "that in spite of Durand's careful and lucid explanations [Abdur Rahman] did not really take in all the implications of the line drawn on the map before him, but was too conceited to say so." Thus he simply may not have known how much he was giving away.

In any case, the Frontier question was settled at last. Durand returned to India with a bright feather in his cap.*

It hardly needs saying that the treaty created more problems than it solved. Although the 1893 boundary—commonly known as the Durand Line—has not changed to this day, it has come under continual and often severe criticism for its flaws. Fraser-Tytler calls it "illogical from the point of view of ethnography, of strategy and of geography," noting particularly that "it splits a nation in two, and it even divides tribes." This arbitrary amputation could barely be justified, even on grounds of geopolitical expediency. Despite the cantankerous independence of the Frontier Pathans, they were by history, tradition, race, language and temperament Afghans. If their allegiance to the Amir was spotty at best, they were even less suited to becoming subjects of the Queen; trying to absorb them and their lands into British India was like trying to graft a cactus spine to the trunk of an oak tree.

* He had a great deal more good fortune with Abdur Rahman than with another strong-minded chief of state. In 1905, he was recalled from his post as Ambassador to the United States at the instigation, it has been suggested, of Theodore Roosevelt, who was said to have found Durand too British for his tastes. Roosevelt preferred Durand's successor, Sir Cecil Spring-Rice, who was not exactly an Armenian.

And if Abdur Rahman had not initially understood the fine print—even the capital letters—of the treaty he signed, neither did it take him long to cry out that he had been robbed. His rage was to bear bloody fruit.

But even the loss of his eastern frontier provinces did not entirely shatter the foundations of Abdur Rahman's alliance with the British. In his worst moments of fury and frustration, he never abandoned his most cherished hope: "to bring nearer the moment when the Court of Afghanistan shall be permanently represented at St. James's." Abdur Rahman had for some time been considering a personal visit to London to win the Queen's approval of an Afghan ambassador. Indeed, it was partly with this goal in mind that he responded favorably to a letter from an Englishman who wrote him in the spring of 1894, requesting an audience in Kabul.

The Amir's petitioner was no run-of-the-mill diplomat or politician, but a budding proconsul-statesman whose star was shortly to rise over the Indian subcontinent. Wit, clubman and super-aristocrat, the thirty-five-year-old George Nathaniel Curzon, future Marquess of Kedleston, was also a scholar of almost intimidating credentials. Contemporaries thought of his three major works, *Russia in Central Asia, Persia and the Persian Question* and *Problems of the Far East*, as belonging among the most penetrating analyses of late nineteenth-century British Asiatic policy. Next to Rawlinson, he was Britain's foremost authority on Eastern affairs.

Much of Curzon's knowledge had been gained on the spot. A compulsive traveler with two round-the-world trips under his belt, he had ridden 2,000 miles across the almost roadless wastes of Persia. He was one of the first Britons allowed by the Russians to make the journey to Bokhara and Samarkand on the Transcaspian Railway. Just before visiting Afghanistan, he had crossed the Pamir Mountains on foot and discovered the source of the Oxus, or at least became the first European to see it. None of these wanderings was inhibited by an incurable curvature of the spine, which forced him to be strait-jacketed almost perpetually in a steel corset; few days of Curzon's adult life went by without his experiencing pain that could border on the excruciating.

What may have helped him get through it were his aspirations as a political animal. In 1894, Curzon stood on the threshold of a public career that promised to match Gladstone's and Disraeli's. Many Britons saw him as a future prime minister, and he concurred. Meanwhile, however, he had set his sights on becoming Viceroy of India, an office to which he believed himself virtually destined. It could almost be said that he had been rehearsing for the viceregal appointment since he first debated Indian affairs at Eton in 1877. In 1891, he had seemed to take a long stride toward his objective when he was made Parliamentary Under-Secretary of State for India. A devout disciple of Rawlinson, Curzon also saw the northwest frontier as a bastion of Empire at least as important as Gibraltar and the Suez Canal. Thus, Afghanistan loomed large in his plans for the day when he would have to deal with the man he called "the stormy and inscrutable figure who occupied the Afghan throne."

The only trouble was that Afghanistan was the one major Asian nation Curzon had never visited. In 1893, Gladstone's government had turned down his request to accompany the Durand mission to Kabul. Gladstone's Liberal successor, Lord Rosebery, and his Viceroy, Lord Elgin, also shrank from the idea of a Rawlinsonian in Abdur Rahman's court. So Curzon went over their heads with a personal letter to the Amir.

He took no chances on being spurned, appealing to Abdur Rahman's mountainous ego with what he called "more than oriental hyperbole." It was his "principal and incessant desire," he wrote, "to be permitted to visit the dominions of Your Highness; so that I might . . . offer my salaams to the powerful and liberal-minded Sovereign of whom I have so often written and spoken. . . . Khorasan I have seen and visited; I have been in Bokhara and Samarkand. I have ridden to Chaman. . . . But the dominions of Your Highness, which are situated in the middle of all these territories, like unto a rich stone in the middle of a ring, I have never been permitted to enter, and the person of Your Highness, which is in your own dominions like unto the sparkle in the heart of the diamond, I have not been fortunate enough to see."

And even though this eyewash was more than enough to soften up the Amir, Curzon took further steps to put his best foot forward in Kabul. Since formal British diplomatic uniforms struck him as drab, he decked himself out in a gaudy cocked hat, a pair of glittering Wellington boots and an enormous jewel-studded curved sword. He also rented several oversize medals and orders from a London costumer ("I think that they belonged to some of the smaller states of Eastern Europe") and rounded off the getup with a pair of gold epaulettes not quite as large as frying pans. Abdur Rahman later ordered a duplicate pair made by his own tailor.

The two men hit it off at once. Abdur Rahman found his guest "a very genial, hard-working, well-informed, experienced, and ambitious young man," Curzon for his part was fascinated and impressed with "this monarch, at once a patriot and a monster . . . this terribly cruel man [who] could be affable, gracious and considerate to a degree." Only one gesture of hospitality was declined. When Abdur Rahman offered to repair Curzon's broken watch personally, Curzon managed somehow "to save it from the hands of the illustrious amateur." But Curzon also had ample opportunity to study the Amir's personality. During his two-week stay in Kabul he met with Abdur Rahman daily, and their conversations lasted for hours, since "the Amir would talk discursively about almost every topic under heaven." Curzon took specially admiring note of his host's "manner of unchallengeable dignity and command," and remarked that "for stating his own case in an argument . . . the Amir would not easily find a match on the front benches in the House of Commons."

But Curzon also got his own oar in, since Topic A was Abdur Rahman's proposed visit to England. The Amir in fact had already received a formal invitation through Elgin, but "with calculated rudeness," said Curzon, he had not yet replied; "I had good reason for thinking he was postponing his answer until I arrived in Kabul, and he could hear from me personally what sort of reception he would be likely to meet with in London." It took Curzon the entire length of his visit to assure the Amir of a warm welcome, but Abdur Rahman finally gave him a personal letter of acceptance, wrapped in violet silk, to Queen Victoria.

On only one aspect of the impending visit did Abdur Rahman and Curzon differ. This concerned Roberts, "against whom the Amir cherished an overweening, though entirely unfounded prejudice," based mainly on the summary hangings of Afghans during the 1879–80 occupation. Abdur Rahman had a plan for revenge on Roberts, which he described to Curzon at length. Curzon recorded it verbatim:

A. I understand that there is in London a great Hall that is known as Westminster Hall. Is that not so?

C. It is.

A. There are also in London two *Mejilises* (*i.e.* Houses of Parliament). One is called the House of Lords and the other is called the House of Commons.

C. It is so.

A. When I come to London, I shall be received in Westminster Hall. The Queen will be seated on her throne at the end of the Hall, and the Royal Family will be around her; and on either side of the Hall will be placed the two *Mejilises*—the House of Lords on the right and the House of Commons on the left. Is that not the case?

C. It is not the usual plan; but will Your Highness proceed?

A. I shall enter the Hall, and the Lords will rise on the right, and the Commons will rise on the left to greet me, and I shall advance between them up the Hall to the daïs, where will be seated the Queen upon her throne. And she will rise and say to me, "What has Your Majesty come from Kabul to say?" And how then shall I reply?

C. I am sure I do not know.

A. I shall reply: "I will say nothing"—and the Queen will then ask me why I refuse to say anything; and I shall answer: "Send for Roberts. I decline to speak until Roberts comes" . . . and when Roberts has come and is standing before the Queen and the two *Mejilises*, then will I speak.

C. And what will Your Highness say?

A. I shall tell them how Roberts paid thousands of rupees to obtain false witness at Kabul and that he slew thousands of my innocent people, and I shall ask that Roberts be punished, and when Roberts has been punished, then will I speak.

"It was in vain," wrote Curzon, "that I indicated to the Amir that things in England and in London were not done exactly in that way. . . . Nothing could convince him." At least, however, Curzon was later able to dine out on the anecdote, and noted that "the only person in England who, when I recounted the story, failed to find it at all amusing—and this perhaps quite pardonably—was Lord Roberts himself."

But even if the British penal code had suited Abdur Rahman's plans, the opportunity to carry them out was denied him, for he did not make the visit after all; apparently he concluded, as Curzon put it, that "had he left the country, the chances were that . . some less fierce and dreaded occupant would be installed upon the Afghan throne." Abdur Rahman even decided against sending his eldest son and heir apparent, Prince Habibullah, in his stead, acknowledging "fear of anything happening to me during his absence." In the end, the Amir chose a younger son, Prince Nasrullah, to plead his cause.

But Nasrullah's qualifications for the mission seemed to cause his father some uneasiness. Before the prince departed in 1895, Abdur Rahman wrote him a detailed guidebook on the rudiments of diplomacy and etiquette. Among other things, Nasrullah was instructed not to discuss politics under any circumstances and to voice noncommittal astonishment at possible references to the Amir's cruelty. He must tip hotel servants, but not British soldiers ("Only praise them for their discipline and good order."). At social functions, he was to shake hands with gentlemen on being introduced, "but with the ladies you must only take a bow." And Nasrullah was particularly enjoined to "take care . . especially when ladies are present . . not to spit and not to put fingers into your nose."

The high point of the visit, of course, was to be Nasrullah's audience with the Queen, during which, after a rambling, fulsomely Oriental introduction, the duly memorized pitch for the ambassadorship would be delivered: "His Majesty the Amir has made only this one request, that always one of his trusted servants should remain in London as his agent, to communicate the happy news of Your Majesty's welfare and that of your Royal Family and your Government to my father personally here, and from Your Majesty, who are most gracious and kind like our own mother, I have every reason to expect the acceptance of this request, so that I should return with the joy and honour of having . . succeeded in my mission."

Nasrullah may have returned to Afghanistan with joy, but he did not bring with him the honor of the ambassadorship. Abdur Rahman attributed the failure of the mission to jealous British politicians who saw to it, he said, that Nasrullah's request "was not put before the House of Commons in a proper light." Most Britons saw it differently. According to Colonel A. C. Yate, a veteran Frontier political specialist, Abdur Rahman "could have selected no more unsuitable instrument for securing the consent of the British Government to the maintenance of an Afghan Envoy at the Court of St. James'." At any rate, there the matter rested. It would not be until twenty-one years after Abdur Rahman's death that his dream of diplomatic representation in England was realized.

Meanwhile the rebuff stood. It is hard to know the extent of its effect on the explosion that was about to rock India's northwest frontier.

PART SIX

Jihad

23

Abdur Rahman's Sermon

JULY 26, 1897, was what the British would call a devilish hot day—
devilish hot even in the cedars of the high country around the
Malakand Pass, some forty miles north of Peshawar. But the drilling rays
of the early afternoon sun failed to keep the officers of the tiny Malakand
and Chakdara garrisons from riding off to the nearby village of Khar for
their weekly polo match. Nor did the sweltering heat discourage an
unusually large turnout of local spectators, an attendance that could
easily have gone unnoticed by the players, since Pathans were enthusiasts
for any sort of mounted competition. But when the game ended and the
sun began casting long shadows across the polo field, a number of villagers
approached one of the officers and warned him to expect an attack on
Malakand and Chakdara that night. A very holy man, they said, had been
preaching jihad in the surrounding hills; thousands upon thousands of
tribesmen were already on the move.

The officers lost no time spurring their horses into a fast canter
through the swiftly gathering darkness to Malakand. Lieutenants Minchin
and Rattray of the Chakdara garrison had a slightly longer ride to the
toy fort that guarded a rope bridge over the Swat River. Suddenly they
reined in. The rough dirt track ahead was blocked by a solid mass of
armed Pathans. But the tribesmen made way for the riders and even
greeted them in Pushtu. May you not be tired! they shouted, and the
officers called back the traditional reply: May you never be poor!
Cheering an enemy before smiting him was a custom not entirely
unknown in the hills.

But the two garrisons did not know what lay in store for them. When the attack came, less than three hours later, it signaled the commencement of a mass tribal rising that was to sweep across almost the entire Frontier, a holy war aimed at driving the Feringhis from the Pathan homeland forever. The British in India were facing their gravest crisis since the Mutiny.

The 1897 revolt was the boiling point of troubles that had been simmering ever since the annexation of the Punjab in 1849. During those forty-eight years, the Indian Government had mounted approximately as many punitive campaigns to deal with acts of defiance by the hillmen. One three-year period in the 1870s had seen ten major expeditions into tribal territory—or one campaign for every 100 days. The Second Afghan War and subsequent British Frontier annexations had done nothing to sweeten the Pathan disposition toward the Raj; Not even in Ireland was a conquered province of the British Empire quite so overripe for insurrection as India's northwest frontier in the last two decades of the nineteenth century.

From a certain perspective, however, the situation might not have seemed desperate. During the 1880s and 1890s, as it became increasingly clear that the British had no intention of leaving the Frontier, some tribal elements actually tried to adjust to the unwelcome presence. Their attitude even suggested that harmonious relations might some day be achieved. Two diametrically opposed British institutions in particular helped nourish that misguided belief.

Military service remained the best instrument of rapprochement. Attracted by uniforms, regular pay, camaraderie and the license to kill, tribesmen continued to enlist in the Guides and other regiments of the Punjab Frontier Force, and, more significantly, in the Border Military Police and various locally raised militias. During the 1880s and 1890s, the militias in particular grew in importance. Commanded by British officers, they generally kept an eye on troublemakers from posts scattered across the hills. A militia fort could be an intimidating stone citadel with a powerful garrison; more often, it was a crude mud structure punctured by a few loopholes and manned by perhaps two dozen sepoys. But by its very presence in a district it prevented more than one tribal outbreak that might otherwise have occurred. Service under the Union Jack in the post-Mutiny years helped cement whatever goodwill the Pathan could muster toward the man who tried to be his master. It was not uncommon for bandit parties to refrain from ambushing militia detachments simply because some member of a gang who happened to be an ex-sepoy or sowar recognized a former British commanding officer.

Among the militias, the model of uniformed loyalty to the Crown was to be found in one of the least likely spots on the Frontier—where the

350 sepoys of the Khyber Rifles kept a semblance of order among their turbulent fellow Afridis. Geopolitics had given birth to this force. During the thirty years between 1848 and 1878, the Khyber door had been sealed tight, both by Afghan suspicion and John Lawrence's close-border policy. Only on the rarest occasions—such as the visits of Dost Muhammad and Sher Ali to India in 1857 and 1869—had Briton and Afghan risked utilizing what both considered literally a warpath. It was not until 1879, when the Forward Policy reached its apogee, that the Khyber resumed its historic role as the main corridor between India and Central Asia. But as always, that corridor had to be guarded against its own inhabitants, and the best men for that job, in the view of the Indian Government, were the inhabitants themselves. For nearly twenty years, the Khyber Rifles fully justified the confidence that had been placed in them.

Formed shortly after the Treaty of Gandamak placed the security of the pass in British hands, the Khyber Rifles were originally designated the Khyber Jezailchis—for the matchlocks the men carried, and furnished themselves, until the issuance of standard army rifles. Afridis also called the troops the *Sur-Lakkais*, or red tails, because their first uniforms were no more than pieces of red cloth stuck in their turbans. But this rag was worn as proudly as the red hackle of the Black Watch, and khaki uniforms and British discipline further hastened the transformation of armed hooligans into a crack regiment. Besides policing the pass, the troops also fought in two major punitive campaigns outside their own territory and returned with chestfuls of medals. Only to the Guides did the Khyber Rifles take a back seat as the Frontier's *corps d'élite*.

One reason why they performed so well may have been their not too distant blood kinship to their commanding officer, Colonel Sir Robert Warburton, a grandnephew of Dost Muhammad by virtue of his father's marriage to the Dost's niece during the British occupation of Afghanistan in 1839.* But Warburton did more than just lead his sepoys. For eighteen years he doubled as Political Agent of the Khyber district, and in that capacity very much changed the face of the pass. To expedite troop movements and protect caravans, Warburton supervised the widening and extension of the serpentine road from Peshawar to the Afghan border and was instrumental in having strongpoints and Beau Geste forts built or reinforced to cover favorite ambush spots. The most imposing forts were at Ali Masjid and Landi Kotal, especially the latter, where a complex of armories and barracks lay inside elephant-thick two-

* The other side in the 1839–42 conflict was represented in the Khyber Rifles by its second-in-command, Lieutenant Colonel Sir Aslam Khan, whose father had been Shah Shuja's Wazir. According to Caroe, "old Sir Aslam was the best-known figure in Peshawar in his day, and his portrait used to look down with eagle eye upon the revelries in the Peshawar Club." His son later became a brigadier general in the Indian Army.

story loopholed walls with rifle towers commanding each corner. If these defense works gave travelers an inflated sense of security, they at least offered something better than no security at all.

Warburton's most conspicuous accomplishment in the Khyber may have been his organization of a traffic control system that allowed westbound and eastbound caravans to move through the pass, with a certain degree of safety, on a twice-weekly schedule. Escort duties were shared by Afghan army detachments and units of the Khyber Rifles, meeting at the border to exchange the camel and mule trains they had conveyed up from Kabul and Peshawar. While a caravan's passage through the Khyber remained a hairy proposition, the point was that the journey could be made. If a narrow-gauge railway had not been built between Peshawar and a point near the border in 1925, Warburton's system might still be operative today.

As a half-Afghan, Warburton proved particularly well suited to the task of paterfamilias in a large, unruly and intuitively disobedient household. His success, to be sure, was only partial—no human on earth could have stamped out tribal feuding and raiding entirely—but over the long haul he kept the peace. Even feuding clans recognized him as a sort of mobile DMZ, it "being understood by the tribesmen," he wrote in his autobiography, "that wherever my camp was in their hills, the greatest enemies might resort to it with perfect safety." Not a few clans were also openly hostile to Warburton himself, but he never hesitated to enter their villages, with or without armed escort. A sort of Nicholson without Nicholson's bloodlust, the deadliest weapon he ever carried was a walking stick.

His permanent home was a spacious, well-appointed bungalow near Landi Kotal, where he lived with his wife, but he was often absent for long periods. One could usually find him hiking about on the escarpments of the pass—surveying a road, supervising the digging of a well or the laying of a pipeline, handing out sweets to Afridi children, hearing the grievances and petitions of scores upon scores of tribesmen. His favorite campsite was the crest of the 5,600-foot Tor Sappar peak, where the sun had its fangs drawn by subalpine airs, where he could look down over the entire length of the Khyber and beyond, sometimes even making out dust clouds raised by caravans as they departed from Kabul. The Tor Sappar encampment also attracted Afridis like flies. They brought Warburton roast chicken, lamb kebabs, coffee and the special sherbet that was freshly made from ice that had been collected in the hills during winters and stored. Here, too, wrote Warburton, "we had great gatherings of the tribesmen. . . . [They] gradually opened their hearts to me regarding their joys and sorrows, and I on my part tried to explain various things to them, amongst others the mystery which greatly puzzled them of what became of the sun every night. . . ."

The chance for a mountain tribesman to become a soldier of the Queen was not Pax Britannica's only asset on the Frontier during the 1880s and 1890s. Visible if not spectacular headway against Pathan xenophobia was also being made by that indefatigable trail-blazer of the British Empire, the Christian missionary.

It said something about evangelist tenacity that any progress was made at all. While the church enjoyed certain advantages over the Frontier's military-administrative complex in that it was neither official nor coercive, missionaries seeking converts had to work with the very worst material in the world. There was something almost comical about extolling the virtues of turning the other cheek among a people whose most cherished article of faith was two eyes for an eye. The missionary who spread the Word in the Frontier hills or in the bazaars of Peshawar did not necessarily run the risk of being gunned down or cut up—although that risk was always present—but he could count on being heaped with ridicule, and was. "Oh, Padre Sahib," tribesmen enjoyed asking in tones of mock respect, "what is the use of your offering us the New Testament? If you desire to convert us, bring us gold." But the missionaries were nothing if not thick-skinned and patient. Their work could be seen, in time, to be making inroads, and even some converts.

Whatever success they enjoyed came largely because the Frontier was a sick man's country and because the thrust of Christian endeavor among the tribes was probably more clinical than it was theological. Since Herbert Edwardes' earliest proselytizing work in the early 1850s, upwards of a half dozen sizable mission stations had taken root in trans-Indus soil. The most conspicuous feature of each was its hospital, run by an ordained minister of the gospel who was also a licensed physician. Assisted by a staff of qualified nurses and attendants, this man treated malaria, smallpox, tuberculosis, malnutrition, cataracts, bone diseases, tumors, marrow-deep knife gashes, gas gangrene from bullet wounds and a galaxy of other endemic afflictions. A single mission doctor might perform as many as eighteen operations and amputations daily. The mission hospital was literally a medical assembly line.

Not every patient could be cured, but the recovery rate was high enough to attract a continual flow of sick Pathans. Nearly twenty-five percent of all tribesmen had eye ailments of one sort or another; it was not uncommon to see a long procession of blind or partially blind men arriving at a mission, each with his hand on the shoulder of the man in front of him, after groping their way for fifty or one hundred miles across the hills. Not a few walked home, their sight fully restored. Some tribesmen with maggot-writhing leg ulcers from bone infections that had crippled them since childhood literally crawled on hands and knees to the hospital. Innumerable victims of knife or gun fights were sewed up neatly, amputees fitted with artificial limbs, which were highly coveted as status symbols. There was a great deal of cosmetic surgery. Pathans brought in their daughters for the removal of smallpox scars from the girls' faces so that their bride price would not be devalued. Even noses and ears lost in knife duels were often replaced, although at least one such transplant aborted when a rubber Caucasian nose sent from England had to be stained walnut and then began to streak in a rainstorm.

Some tribal elements found the Feringhi doctor less than welcome. He was seen as a clear and present threat by the mullahs, fakirs, hakims, barbers and blacksmiths who for centuries had enjoyed lucrative medical practices with their primitive and often barbaric therapies. Dr. Theodore Pennell, the dean of Frontier medical evangelists—his Bannu mission hospital was the largest in tribal country—often found himself frustrated when he tried to vaccinate patients against smallpox. The main road-block, he wrote, was the "widespread superstition that [authorities] are really seeking for a girl, who is to be recognized by the fact that when the vaccinator scarifies her arm, instead of blood, milk will flow from the wound; she is then to be taken over to England for sacrifice."

Yet most Pathans managed to overcome such fears and felt little hostility toward the British doctors—if they felt any at all. At one time during the later 1870s, when a Wazir lashkar carried out a commando strike against the embryonic administrative center of Tank, the leaders placed a special guard over the mission hospital to keep it from being leveled with the rest of the town. Nearly all of the raiders were out-patients.

When not healing the sick the Frontier medical missionary doubled as a schoolmaster. Teen-age Pathans were beginning to see new horizons opened to them in the relatively high pay offered by the Indian Government to clerks and other apprentice civil servants who could graduate from Punjab University. To meet matriculation standards, boys* were given courses in elementary English, science and mechanics at the missions. English games, including football and cricket, were also part of the curriculum. Pennell once took his tribal football eleven on a tournament circuit across nothern India; the sports editor of the *Sindh Gazette* may have been surprised to note that the young Pathans played "altogether without roughness." They also won the match.

Besides their regular schoolwork, pupils of course were introduced to the Scriptures—a subject that could touch off riots. Tribal leaders might grudgingly permit boys to study the three Rs; being infected with the poison of the Feringhi creed was something else. Mullahs not infrequently issued *fatwas*, or decrees, that parents who sent their sons to mission schools would be excommunicated, as would the boys themselves. The threat was every bit as dire to devout Muslims as to Roman Catholics.

---

* Not quite the word; many fourth and fifth formers had wives and children.

But the fatwas sometimes backfired. Such was the case at Bannu, where a number of prominent and relatively enlightened Pathan families were not only alive to the material advantages of Western education, but also scorned the notion that infidel preaching would rub off on their children. Their open defiance of the edict forced the mullahs to give ground and permit attendance, although most of the pupils made a point of wearing special charms to protect them against contamination by heresy.

One reason for this victory was the progressive outlook of the Bannu mission head. Pennell never objected to pupils studying the Koran in tandem with the New Testament. He even encouraged the practice, maintaining that the leap from one religion to another could not be made overnight and that it was "a terrible thing to take away a boy's faith, even though it be a faith in a mistaken creed." Pennell's realistic approach to tribal child psychology helped him win a respectable number of converts. It did not trouble him unduly to know that some might have become Christians only to spite relatives, and he no doubt felt at least partly compensated when several mullahs began sending their own sons to the Bannu school.

Pennell wrote a book about his sixteen years on the Frontier. It reveals a man whose Victorian sanctimoniousness never quite stifled a deep human compassion and a large fund of horse sense. It was his view that, although the medical missionary had an edge over the conventional evangelist in that the latter had to seek his flock while the former needed only to wait for his clientele to come to him, no conscientious Frontier doctor would ever anchor himself to his mission hospital. Instead, he would go out into tribal country, not only to treat the men, women and children unable to reach the mission, but to get to know the clans and win their trust. Pennell practiced what he preached, walking across hundreds of miles of mountain and desert, living for weeks and months at a time in the squalor of isolated hill settlements. With his ragged rifle-toting tribal escorts, with his own splendid Victorian beard set off by a turban, pajamas and patched Afghan robes, all that distinguished him from a Pathan were his Bible and patent leather doctor's bag.

His example was followed by his many colleagues, although they often had to overcome a great deal of suspicion and even some open hostility. Sick people greeting a mission doctor on his arrival in a village would be accompanied by at least one mullah and his retinue, prepared to discredit the Feringhi hakim by engaging him in a theological debate loaded with semantics and other trickery. (A favorite ploy was to ask the missionary to define the shape and color of faith, which mullahs themselves could do.) If the visitor managed to avoid being drawn into the trap, the holy man would then warn the villagers that if they fed the unbeliever, whatever eating and drinking vessels he touched would become defiled. Incitement to violence could be brought to bear as a last resort, and showdowns called for a cool head. Pennell once learned that a notorious tribal bandit was waiting to kidnap him. He therefore made a point of spending that night in a lonely and conspicuously exposed spot. No abduction took place, and as a result, said Pennell, "the people . . . spread the idea that . . . there was an angel protecting the *Daktar Sahib*."

As often as not, however, the Daktar Sahib's reputation had preceded him. Despite the continual abuse and threats he received from the mullah faction, there would almost invariably be found in every community an influential, tolerant and amiable malik who threw open the door of the village's mud-walled *hujra*, or guest house. Other townspeople then came forward with kebabs, tea, coffee and sometimes even sherbet—and the ice would be broken. Pennell and others occasionally even enjoyed the hospitality of no less a personage than a mullah who also happened to be a decent and good-natured man.

In their capacities as preachers who were also physicians, Pennell and his colleagues sometimes became amateur lawyers, especially when they crossed the administrative border into tribal territory. There, they might well be approached by Pathans who claimed to have been unjustly accused or convicted of crimes, and who sought redress through the missionaries' good offices. Even the undisguised tribal outlaw trusted the evangelist to plead his cause with impartiality before British judges and political agents. It is hard to say whether any convictions were ever over-turned or even reconsidered as the result of missionary intercession, but in the person of the Frontier doctor-parson, the tribesman knew he had a friend in court. Nor would it have been inaccurate to call the missionary in tribal territory his country's ambassador without portfolio.

The examples set by compassionate soldier-administrators like War-burton and churchmen like Pennell could not fail to encourage. But this brighter side of the Frontier coin did not reflect several serious flaws in the British effort to pacify the Frontier. Had these errors of commission and omission been avoided, the 1897 revolt might never have taken place.

First off, there was the simple and inexplicable fact of the Frontier's having been placed under the jurisdiction of the Punjab. One of Britain's worst blunders in India was her failure, for many years, to acknowledge, or even to realize, that the northwest frontier was not part of the Punjab—much less indeed of India itself—and never had been and never could be. Ethnically, culturally and politically, the Punjab and its peoples belonged to the Indian subcontinent, whose civilization for nearly three centuries had demonstrated a capacity to absorb at least some Western values. But the Frontier was Central Asia, where another set of rules came into play. A framework of laws and customs just barely acceptable to Indians, whether Hindu or Muslim, was unremittingly and joltingly repudiated by wild Afghan hillmen whose only statutes were written in blood, and for whom being flayed alive might have seemed less distasteful than submission to any authority, including their own. As an ungainly administrative appendage of a Punjab with which it had nothing in common, the already arid Frontier was beginning to crackle loudly in the 1890s.

The Punjab Government itself was adding fuel to the fire by its consistent failure or refusal to show the tribes that they stood to gain any material benefits from their subject status. Such things as military service, a few low-echelon clerical jobs, clan allowances and the occasional irrigation project or camel road certainly did not suffice to convince the Pathan that he had a real stake in British India. In the years following the Mutiny, Punjab authorities devoted decreasing amounts of time, thought and funds to the barren Frontier region, which itself yielded only a trickle of revenues and cried out to have its economic pump primed. This disregard of the popular welfare had a great deal to do, if only indirectly, with the growing adversary relationship between the Frontier tribesmen and the British provincial officials who sought to shape their destinies.

Paradoxically, however, while the Frontier's human needs went neglected, the tribes received far too much attention as what might be called bureaucratic guinea pigs. Sometimes it seemed as if Lahore was trying to strangle the hills with red tape. Market towns were governed by fat volumes of municipal codes. Taxes were levied in accordance with a revenue act that could almost have been drawn up for England. But these burdens of complexity were mild alongside the farce of equal justice. Freighted down with bewildering legalisms, the machinery of Frontier jurisprudence creaked along on an endless conveyor belt of appeal that few, if any, hillmen could comprehend, but which was tailor-made for shysters. One Indian Government official has written that "the British judicial system with its tribe of lawyers, mostly Hindu, and the Chief Court at Lahore as its apex . . . [was] utterly unsuited to half-civilized tribesmen."

This may have understated it. One of the typical, and most important, Frontier district courts was situated in the picturesque town of Kalabagh on the Indus River. Here the district judge presided over trials beneath the shade of vast banyan trees. Fruit and tea vendors moved among the spectators, water pipes were smoked and a general atmosphere of friendly informality prevailed. But when any small peasant with an open-and-shut case against some wealthy land-grabbing malik saw the defendant arrive on the scene in the company of several smartly dressed lawyers from Lahore or Delhi, he knew at once what the verdict would be. It was not a way to make friends out of Pathans.

The bureaucratic mentality also handcuffed Frontier officials in the field. Indeed, during the 1880s and 1890s these men sometimes seemed less the satraps of a conquered province than the indifferent janitors of slum buildings tenanted by muggers and junkies. "Few officers," writes Caroe, "were left long enough in frontier posts to gain the confidence which alone would weigh against the difficulties that beset them. Lahore was far away and seems to have treated the frontier as something of a side-show. . . . Officers had not time enough to learn the frontier language or the ways to the heart of the Pathan."

The standard practice, in fact, was to avoid grass-roots contacts and assign the vital tasks of paying allowances and generally dealing with a tribe's or clan's jirga to *arbabs*, influential elders who acted as middlemen. This proved a windfall to the arbab, who often lined his pockets with the money intended for his fellow tribesmen and blamed the British for defaulting on their obligations. The system played directly into the hands of the Anglophobic faction of any tribe. Typical abuses were seen in the monkeyshines of an arbab known as the Khan of Hangu. In 1890 and 1891, this man not only withheld allowances from the Tirah Orakzais among whom he was supposed to keep the peace, but urged them not to pay fines and encouraged raids into the settled districts. It took two punitive expeditions and the building of a line of forts along the Samana range on the southern edge of Tirah to repair the damage.

Nobody did anything about the arbab system, but there was hardly a single knowledgeable official in the hills who did not think of it as the most direct cause of tribal discontent. "After spending about twenty-nine years of my service on the . . . Frontier," wrote Warburton, ". . . my firm and solemn conviction is that the majority of wars and fights between the British Government and the independent tribes of the Punjab border were due to the evil intrigues and machinations . . . of the middle-men who had been employed by us to do our work."

Working hand in glove with arbab abuses was the chaos that reigned in the belt of so-called tribal territory beyond the administrative border, where the fiercest of the frontier clans remained pretty much a law unto themselves. Even after the Treaty of Gandamak—when much, if not most, of the no-man's-land was recognized as falling under British jurisdiction, if not direct British rule—the Punjab Government had made little initial effort, partly because of the expense, to extend the arm of its authority into the region. For thirteen years, only the Khyber Pass enjoyed official status as a Political Agency—not a District, the term applied in "settled" areas—under Warburton, and even Warburton could not exercise absolute control over the Afridis. Between 1892 and 1895, the British did seek, rather belatedly, to consolidate their treaty gains by designating the other main tribal areas—notably the great Pathan duchy of Waziristan—political agencies. The most noticeable effect of this sudden irruption was to antagonize the tribes even further; six major punitive campaigns were needed to counter an infuriated Pathan response across the entire 200-mile borderline.

But the sheer weight of Indian Army manpower and metal had to tell, with the second result that an incomprehensible complacency took hold in the collective mind of Punjab officialdom. By 1895, it was honestly believed that the Queen's Peace, at long last, had been imposed forever on the turbulent marches beyond the Frontier's settled districts. Two whole years would go by before that myth literally went up in smoke.

But even without the nuisance of large Indian Army troop concentrations on the Frontier, the Durand Line alone might well have sufficed to create a revolutionary army. The sight of surveyors with their theodolites, of mapmakers laying down contour lines, of work gangs erecting boundary beacons, all seemed to justify the Pathan saying: "First comes one Englishman, as a traveler or hunter; then come two and make a map; then comes an army and takes the country. It is better, therefore, to kill the first Englishman." And although that initial opportunity had long been lost, the mappers of the Durand Line soon shaped up as fair game. Even though British boundary survey parties were protected by heavy armed escorts, border incidents, and not a few killings, began to occur after 1894.

Not surprisingly but no less disturbingly, tribal hostility to the Durand Line received every encouragement from the Amir of Afghanistan. Although Abdur Rahman had signed the Durand agreement of his own free will, he had not yielded up the personal conviction that the Frontier Pathans were his own subjects. The new boundary, moreover, had probably stirred anew his suspicions that the British might have even further encroachments in mind. Some Britons even acknowledged that these fears might not be entirely groundless. "The Amir well understood," wrote an Indian Army officer, "what a wonderful power of absorption the British possess. . . . We, of course, on our side, have always repudiated any idea of advance or annexation . . . but circumstances have often been in the past, and will be no doubt in the future, too strong for us. . . . By whatever name we may describe them, the result is the same: we advance, we absorb, we dominate, we destroy independence." Thus, there was little reason for Abdur Rahman to have hung back from trying to halt the reluctant juggernaut.

His camouflage in this endeavor was a heightened religious enthusiasm. It was also his weapon, since he well knew how the common bond of Islam could reinforce his standing with the fanatically devout hill Pathan. During the early 1890s, he assumed the title of *Zia-ul-Millat wa-ud-Din*, the Light of Union and Faith, and adopted the habit of referring to himself in correspondence as "King of Islam." It did not bother him that nearly all Muslims, himself included, looked on Turkey's Sultan

Abdul Hamid II as their real spiritual leader. Nor was Abdul Hamid himself put out. In the spring of 1897, he sent one of his most trusted lieutenants to Kabul, ostensibly to exchange courtesies with Abdur Rahman, actually to advise and assist in disseminating anti-British propaganda among the Frontier Pathans.

Concurrently, Abdur Rahman's new image as spiritual mentor was being enhanced further by the publication of a book called *Taqwīm-ud-Dīn*, which the Amir had written for Frontier consumption. Purportedly no more than a religious catechism, it dealt almost exclusively with the indispensable role of jihad in the Muslim way of life and was distributed to every mullah and fakir in the hills of the British tribal belt. Dutifully, the holy men treated the work as if it were the Koran, quoting its most inflammatory passages at great length to their congregations, who in turn were worked into the hoped-for frenzy by the exhortations to mayhem against the British infidels. And in the early summer of 1897, on the heels of the Turkish envoy's visit, Abdur Rahman invited several dozen leading Pathan priests to Kabul for a theological seminar which in fact was a series of impassioned anti-British tirades.

From the tribal standpoint, Abdur Rahman could not have chosen a better moment for the meetings. In 1897, British prestige in the Muslim world had reached its lowest ebb, thanks mainly to Gordon's murder at Khartoum in 1885 and Britain's failure, in the following twelve years, to drive the Muslim armies of the fanatical Khalifa from the Sudan. Conversely, 1897 saw militant Islam at its nineteenth-century apogee. The Turks had just followed up a resounding military victory over Greece with a wholesale massacre of Christians; British support of the Greeks and an abusive attitude toward Abdul Hamid had backfired badly. Through a telescope from so remote a vantage point as the northwest frontier tribal belt, Turkey's seeming ascendancy and Britain's apparent humiliation could easily be magnified far beyond their actual proportions. Never did the time appear more ripe to strike a paralyzing blow at an already crippled infidel tyrant.

Returning to their villages after Abdur Rahman's forum in Kabul, the inflamed Pathan mullahs began writing letters to maliks and other tribal leaders, spreading the word of Britain's enfeeblement and exhorting them to an uprising across the entire Frontier. The American colonial committees of correspondence could not have performed their task to better purpose. A typical letter reported that Abdul Hamid had captured Aden and the Suez Canal from the British and leased the canal to Russia, thereby preventing British troop reinforcements from reaching India in less than six months. "The Sultan, the Germans, the Russians, and the French," added the holy man, "are all in arms against the British. . . . In short, the British are disheartened nowadays."

Once having inspired these fish stories, Abdur Rahman then counseled against immediate action. But the Amir had his own interpretation of delay. At least one letter quoted him as advising: "You should wait a few days, so that I may hold a consultation . . . and decide what steps should be taken. I will then either come myself or send to you my son for *jehad*, with our victorious troops. . . . I will, with the greatest pleasure, make exertions in the way of *jehad*." He also issued a pamphlet to the tribes that declared that anyone who hung back from enlisting in the holy cause "shall draw on himself the indignation of God, and his abode shall be hell: an ill-journey shall it be thither!" In short, it was now just a matter of standing by for the signal.

Actually, Abdur Rahman was far too astute to give the tribes any green light against his British allies, let alone join them in open revolt. Not long afterwards, in fact, he went so far as to rebuke the very mullahs, fakirs and maliks whom he had encouraged, for highly improper behavior. In a letter which he took care to see that the British also read, he declared to the tribesmen that he had "entered into an alliance with the British Government," and that he would "never, without cause or occasion, swerve from [this] agreement." He then added: "What you have done with your own hands you must now carry on your own backs. I have nothing to do with you."

But it was quite enough that Abdur Rahman had got the tribes fighting mad in the first place. Somebody else could always start the actual revolution.

Somebody else already had.

24

Captain Blood and the Mad Mullah

CURIOUSLY, THE GREAT Pathan uprising of 1897 stemmed from a minor affray with the one tribal group on the Frontier that was not Pathan. A word about the role played by these people is in order.

Nearly 150 miles north of Peshawar and more than 4 miles up in the sky, the microkingdom of Chitral stands in refrigerated isolation among the loftiest peaks of the Hindu Kush. In the 1890s, Chitral was almost another planet. The only roads leading out of its capital, also called Chitral, petered off into glaciers and trackless snowdrifts after a few miles; to reach Chitral, the skills of an alpinist came very much in handy, even in summertime. The British knew that the kingdom's 80,000 inhabitants were of Mongol-Chinese-Tatar stock, and that although they had recently converted to Islam, they tended to keep aloof from the Pathans of Bajaur, Dir, Swat and Buner to the south. Chitralis were also said to have invented polo, but there was room to wonder how the game had ever managed to find its way out of a country that, since time immemorial, had been not much less remote from the world than Tibet.

Although Abdur Rahman had once laid vague claims to Chitral and although the country also had ties of a sort to the British Empire through a treaty concluded with the Maharaja of Kashmir in 1878, Chitral was really independent. At the same time, however, the British tended to look at Chitral as the northernmost bastion of the northwest frontier, if for no other reason than its proximity to Afghanistan and Russian Turkestan—and in disregard of its virtual inaccessibility to both of those countries and British India as well. British preoccupation with Chitral heightened during the Panjdeh crisis in 1885; even though Panjdeh lay some 600 miles to the west, the Indian Government appointed a temporary political agent to Chitral just in case.

Further embroilment began in 1892, with the death of Chitral's incumbent and long-reigning monarch, a sage known as the Great Mehtar, who left sixteen sons to scramble for his throne. The next two years witnessed a violent game of loaded poker dice, highlighted by several assassinations and some wondrously complex plotting that even brought a neighboring Anglophobic Pathan warlord named Umra Khan into the act. These intrigues hastened Britain's full involvement in Chitrali affairs. Early in 1895, having pledged his country's support to one of the princes, the harassed temporary British agent requested an Indian Army garrison. With minimal delay, 400 Sikhs of the Kashmir Infantry under Surgeon-Major George Robertson made the punishing climb from the almost equally isolated outpost of Gilgit, about 150 miles to the east.

And hardly had the sepoys caught their icy breath than Robertson found his plate full as another pretender made an alliance with the Pathan Umra Khan and laid siege to the tiny Chitral fort.

Now began one of those forgotten epics from which the stuff of Henty yarns was woven. Outnumbered by at least fifty to one, Robertson's troops occupied a blockhouse about eighty yards square, exposed on all sides to jezail fire from the upper branches of tall firs well within range of the walls. Each sepoy had barely 300 rounds for his Martini-Henry. There were only enough supplies to last ten weeks, provided the garrison went on half rations. Continual massed assaults on the fort were interrupted only long enough to allow the attackers to offer impossible truce terms, shout threats and try to burn down the fort. Sikh bucket brigades worked around the clock to put out fires in driving storms of snow and lead.

But Robertson was able to retaliate with a trick borrowed from the besiegers: "fireballs" made of dried pine chips and straw were soaked in kerosene, lighted and tossed from the walls at night to illuminate the ground and provide targets. After a while, the snow round the fort began turning pink with Chitrali and Pathan blood.

All that was lacking to complete the picture of British defiance was a Union Jack; for some reason, Robertson had not brought one with him. He rectified the oversight, however, by collecting enough scraps of red, white and blue cloth to be stitched into the proper pattern by a sepoy; there was only the briefest delay when the man sewed in a crescent and crossed swords, which had to be removed. If relief arrived too late, the garrison would at least go down with the flag flying.

But the British did not send a relief column. They sent two. By early March, news of the siege had filtered down through the snow-choked passes to Peshawar. Less than two weeks later, 15,000 troops of three infantry brigades, together with 28,000 pack animals, were ready to move on the command of General Sir Robert Low. At about the same time, a 600-man flanking force—supported by two mountain batteries—under Colonel J. G. Kelly was preparing to advance on Chitral from Gilgit in the east.

It was hard to say which column faced the heaviest going. Low's troops had to hack a path northward across broken, unmapped uplands that had never been penetrated in force, and which swarmed with massacre-bent tribesmen loaded for infidel bear. The advance was a 150-mile running fight. Mountain guns gave the British an edge, but the Pathans made expert use of their own natural artillery. Crossing the Malakand Pass against the concerted musket fire of at least 10,000 tribesmen, the British came under a thundering barrage—almost an avalanche—of boulders that were rolled down from the heights on signal. It was only the first of many rock bombardments.

Low also had to cope with the elements. Reaching the Swat River, his troops found a raging torrent in full flood from the already melting snows of the Hindu Kush. Engineers managed to throw up a shaky makeshift bridge for guns and pack animals, but most of the men had to ford the river, armpit-deep in water that froze their uniforms to boards. A few miles farther on, the Panjkora River could not be forded at all. A rickety footbridge of logs and telegraph wire allowed the Guides Infantry to reach the opposite bank, where they were promptly cut off when the bridge collapsed. Artillery cover barely enabled the Guides sepoys to hold off onslaughts by more than four times their number of tribesmen for the eight hours it took to build another bridge. Somehow, though, Low managed to keep his men plodding forward.

At the same time, Kelly's Gilgit force was plowing across a fifty-league ocean of chest-deep snow. Frostbite and snow blindness became endemic among the men. Detachments regularly stumbled off and vanished for hours and days in drifts larger than cities. During the ascent of the 12,400-foot Shandur Pass, riflemen blunted their bayonets trying vainly to chop footholds in the granite-hard ice that coated the narrow track to the summit. At a place called Chokalwat, Kelly had to order an advance under well-concealed Chitrali rifle fire along a path that coiled several miles beneath frozen crags ten times the height of the Eiffel Tower. After the column had forced its way through, it faced an even stiffer test in the pass of Nisa Gol, where Chitrali sharpshooters were protected by eighteen rock sangars climbing the white slopes that soared perpendicularly for a mile above both banks of the Mastuj River. Kelly's men also put Nisa Gol behind them, but not swiftly. The average distance logged daily was two miles.

The wonder was that any advance at all could be made by either of the two columns. But advance they did, reaching Chitral almost simultaneously in mid-April and quickly scattering the besiegers. As a feat of endurance, the relief of Chitral easily matched—if it did not surpass—Roberts' achievement in the march to Kandahar.

But the real significance of the episode was that it put Chitral on the political map. In the eyes of the Indian Government, the Foreign Office and both houses of Parliament, the frozen Graustark on the roof of the world had drawn attention to itself once more as a possible Russian objective. It was therefore decided in the summer of 1895 to guard the northernmost flank of the Frontier with a permanent British agent and a regular garrison in Chitral.

Such an arrangement, however, required an all-weather line of communication with British India. And that was the hitch. The only practicable route ran north from Peshawar, over the Malakand Pass and directly through the heart of the Bajaur-Dir-Swat-Buner region, an explosively hostile Pathan mountain stronghold that was British in name only—as Low's troops had learned on their relief march. This meant that not only Chitral, but the road itself, had to be protected.

Accordingly, after considerable negotiation, agreements were concluded with tribal maliks and other leaders, who pledged that in return for special allowances, their people would refrain from attacking the proposed British fort guarding the road at the key Malakand position. It was further agreed that the tribes would carry the mail, keep the telegraph line open and make any necessary repairs on the road itself. And it was only a matter of time before all these engagements were broken.

Actually, this did not happen for two years. But stationing a small British garrison to cover the trap of the Malakand was like placing a gunpowder charge in an oven.

The man who finally threw in the lighted match was a Swati religious leader named Sadullah, who had joined other prominent Frontier holy men on the aforementioned pilgrimage to Abdur Rahman's capital in the early summer of 1897. In keeping with their tendency to look on "native" antagonists as unhinged rather than patriotic, the British invariably referred to Sadullah as the "Mad Fakir," or the "Mad Mullah,"* and he was no doubt as crazy as a fox. On returning to the Frontier from Kabul, he embarked at once on an intensive preaching tour of the craggy countryside north of Peshawar. His parishioners were encouragingly responsive. Not a few tribesmen still lived who had stormed the British-held Crag Picquet thirty-four years earlier during the fight for the Ambela Pass, barely a day's hike east of the Malakand. Many descendants of the

* In Somaliland, on the "horn" of Africa, another "Mad Mullah" had British armed forces climbing the wall in frustration for the first two decades of this century.

Hindustani Fanatics also lurked on the slopes of the nearby Black Mountain; punitive expeditions against them in 1888 and 1891 had met with very limited success. And Low's intrusion en route to Chitral was fresh in every Pathan mind. The whole region was ripe for insurrection.

And so it was that a small following of a few dozen tribesmen rapidly swelled to 5,000 and twice that number as the Mad Mullah proclaimed in hoarse screams that the Prophet had given the word at long last for the long-awaited moment to strike down the Feringhi. He swore on his ragged beard that British bullets would turn to water, that the muzzles of their rifles and cannons would be stoppered up by a simple wave of his hand, that he would throw stones into the Swat River and they would become artillery shells to fling back at the infidel. It was a measure of the Pathan's superstitious naiveté that all this crap was implicitly believed.

But the not-so-mad Mullah had more going for him than carny-show magic. As he cried out for jihad in mosques and bazaars and on dusty goat paths, he always made a point of introducing his companion, a thirteen-year-old boy who he said was the last surviving heir of the Mogul dynasty. He did not need to add that the youth personified the Frontier Muslim's opportunity to restore the true faith to its rightful place in Delhi.

Nor was the Mad Mullah alone in choreographing holy war. Inspired not only by his success in Swat but also by Abdur Rahman's exhortations, colleagues were emulating him in nearly every other trouble spot on the Frontier. Just to the south, a priest known as the Hadda Mullah had begun to rouse his Mohmand congregations to a fever pitch of Anglophobia. In the Khyber Pass, the Mullah Sayyid Akbar was mobilizing thousands of Afridis for a night of the long knives. Mahsud tribesmen in southern Waziristan were rallying to the battle cry of the Mullah Powinda, who was to spend the next sixteen years as the sharpest Frontier thorn in the British hide.

There was even an open clash. In June, a political officer visited the north Waziristan village of Maizar with a strong escort of troops. After being properly salaamed as honored and welcome guests by the Wazir tribesmen, the British party suddenly came under heavy attack; all its officers were wiped out in the first jezail volley. Only the steadiness of their Pathan officers and several thick curtains of rifle fire enabled the sepoys to bring off a precarious withdrawal. As soon as possible, Punjab authorities were alerted.

The authorities disregarded the warning. In official eyes, the Maizar outburst was little more than an isolated tribal tantrum. So too were the storm clouds making up elsewhere in the hills. Even as seasoned a hand as Warburton thought that Abdur Rahman's intrigues among the tribes amounted simply to "carrying out an old pastime." Warburton, it is true, was now becoming extremely concerned over Afridi unrest in the Khyber Pass, but he himself later admitted to being unaware of the extent of the influence wielded by the Mullah Sayyid Akbar. The Punjab Government's confidence in the security of the Frontier at this critical moment was only less absolute than it was inexplicable.

Least troubled of all, it seemed, were the officers of the Malakand garrison in the heart of the Mad Mullah's territory. They had shrugged off reports of an uprising brought to them by their own sepoys days before the attack was launched. On hearing the rumors, Major Harold Deane, the Political Agent of the Malakand district, had ordered extra security precautions, but Deane himself—one of the more knowledgeable officials in Frontier history—tended to look on the alerts as a false alarm. On July 26, the weekly polo match went off as scheduled. Even when the Pathans struck the Malakand and Chakdara forts that night, no officer of either garrison seemed to realize at first that he was caught up in something bigger than a momentary display of tribal high spirits.

The attack came at ten o'clock sharp, with at least 10,000 tribal warriors pouring in from all sides against fewer than 1,000 Sikh infantrymen behind the Malakand fort's low perimeter earthworks. At almost the same moment, another Pathan force hurled itself at the even more frail defenses of Chakdara, where the odds against that garrison were in the neighborhood of one hundred to one. Only the pitch blackness— not much relieved by the winking of rifle fire—kept the attackers from overrunning both positions. The commanders at Malakand and Chakdara exploited this small advantage to telegraph for reinforcements, pull in their lines and hang on desperately until relief arrived the next day.

It arrived none too soon. The Guides covered the thirty-six miles from their headquarters at Mardan in a dust-burning sixteen hours. On their heels rode the 400 sowars of the 11th Bengal Lancers. But even with this beefing up, the garrisons were far from being out of the soup. By now the Pathan ranks had swelled proportionately and their mass onslaughts were seen to grow increasingly determined. The Guides' Lieutenant P. C. Elliott-Lockhart later wrote that "bands of *Ghazis*, worked up by their religious enthusiasm into a frenzy of fanatical excitement, would charge our breastworks again and again, leaving their dead in scores after each repulse, while [others] would encourage their efforts by shouting, with much beating of tom-toms, and other musical instruments." The tribesmen even had their own bugler, a former sepoy, who further confused the defenders with a continual blare of standard Indian Army calls—including mess call. If the British had not been armed with breech-loaders, and had they not had land mines, which they set off with devastating effect, the Malakand and Chakdara garrisons would probably have been swept away like twigs in a flood. At last, it began to dawn on the British officers that something big was on, that their own situation was not critical but grave.

Simla finally reached the same conclusion. On August 30, after four days and nights of sleepless, last-ditch resistance by both garrisons against a relentless pounding surf of banzai charges, the Viceroy, Lord Elgin, ordered massive retaliation. Three full brigades under General Sir Bindon Blood were to march on Lower Swat without delay.

Blood's mini-army was officially designated the Malakand Field Force, and the name had a stirringly euphonious ring for newspaper readers in England; during the late nineteenth century, even a minor tussle with Pathans tended to make headlines in the British press. Indeed, the entire northwest frontier, as an arena of rousing dust-ups properly romanticized by Kipling, had become a magnet not only for ambitious army officers but for action- and fame-hungry journalists.

Among those sensing a scoop in the Malakand was a pushy young half-American subaltern of the 4th Hussars named Winston Churchill, who had already been blooded as a war correspondent in Cuba. Although Churchill's regiment was then stationed in India, it was not sent to the Malakand, so he wangled leave and used his mother's influence to arrange an assignment to cover the campaign for the London *Daily Telegraph* at £5 per column. The sum was anything but small change in those days, especially to a cub reporter who, despite his illustrious lineage, already had to depend on writing for his livelihood.

But Churchill's real incentive was the adventure that beckoned. Nor was he let down, either by his own side or the enemy. The Pathans could hardly have proved a more suitable foe for the exuberant youth: "Every influence, every motive, that provokes the spirit of murder among men," exulted Churchill, "impels these mountaineers to deeds of treachery and violence. . . . To the ferocity of the Zulu are added the craft of the Redskin and the marksmanship of the Boer." The tribes also had a worthy adversary in Blood, "a striking figure in these savage mountains and among these wild, rifle-armed clansmen." Sir Bindon took enormous pride, said Churchill, in his direct descent from "the notorious Captain Blood," an upper-class Restoration bandit, who had once come within an ace of stealing the Crown Jewels from the Tower of London. Only half in jest, Churchill remarked that if Blood could have told the Pathans the story of his lawbreaking ancestor, they "would have completely understood the incident in all its bearings, and . . . it would never have been necessary for three brigades with endless tails of mule and camel transport to toil through the mountains and sparsely populated highlands in which my next few weeks were to be passed."

Churchill did more than just admire the contenders and grind out dispatches. "Like most young fools," he wrote many years later, "I was looking for trouble," and he was no doubt delighted to find it in an ambush from a "deserted" tribal village on a hill. His recollection of the episode is worth quoting at some length.

There was a ragged volley from the rocks; shouts, exclamations, and a scream. . . . One man was shot through the breast and pouring with blood; another lay on his back kicking and twisting. The British officer was spinning round just behind me, his face a mass of blood, his right eye cut out. Yes, it was certainly an adventure.

It is a point of honour on the Indian frontier not to leave wounded men behind. Death by inches and hideous mutilation are the invariable measure meted out to all who fall in battle into the hands of the Pathan tribesmen. . . . We all laid hands on the wounded and began to carry and drag them away down the hill. . . .

. . . I looked around to my left. . . . Out from the edge of the houses rushed half a dozen Pathan swordsmen. The bearers of the poor Adjutant let him fall and fled at their approach. The leading tribesman rushed upon the prostrate figure and slashed at it three or four times with his sword. I forgot everything else at this moment except a desire to kill this man. I wore my long Cavalry sword well sharpened. After all, I had won the Public School fencing medal. I resolved on personal combat *à l'arme blanche*. The savage saw me coming. I was not more than twenty yards away. He picked up a big stone and hurled it at me with his left hand, and then awaited me, brandishing his sword. There were others waiting not far behind him. I changed my mind about the cold steel. I pulled out my revolver, took, as I thought, most careful aim, and fired. No result. I fired again. No result. I fired again. Whether I hit him or not I cannot tell. . . . I looked around. I was all alone with the enemy. . . . I ran as fast as I could. . . . I got to the first knoll. Hurrah, there were the Sikhs holding the lower one! . . .

We fetched up at the bottom of the spur little better than a mob, but still with our wounded . . . while the tribesmen, who must have now numbered two or three hundred, gathered in a wide and spreading half-moon around our flanks. . . . The Colonel said to me, "The Buffs are not more than half a mile away. Go and tell them to hurry or we shall all be wiped out." . . .

But meanwhile . . . I heard an order: "Volley firing. Ready. Present." Crash! At least a dozen tribesmen fell. Another volley, and they wavered. A third, and they began to withdraw up the hillside. The bugler began to sound the "Charge." Everyone shouted. The crisis was over, and here, praise be to God, were the leading files of the Buffs.

Many such tight squeezes were experienced by the Malakand Field Force; the tribesmen of Lower Swat, Dir, Bajaur and Buner fought with more than their customary fearlessness and dash. But there was no way for the Mad Mullah's disciples to withstand the walloping inflicted by the field and mountain guns with which Blood covered his foot and mounted advance. Although the fighting lasted for more than three weeks, it could almost be said to have ended in the first engagement. And once the Malakand and Chakdara garrisons had been relieved—in a matter of barely forty-eight hours—it remained only for the Malakand Field Force to blast its way into the even loftier mountain fastnesses of Upper Swat. By the last week in August, it was all over but the mopping up. In fact it had hardly begun.

Punjab authorities seemed unaware of this, returning to their ivory tower as the storm signals continued to go up. Even while the thunder of Blood's artillery was shivering the escarpments of the Swat Valley, tribal concentrations were on the move against the forts of the Khyber Pass, and against Peshawar itself. On August 17, Sir Richard Udny, Commissioner of the Peshawar Division, was informed that the Mad Mullah had evaded capture in Swat and was now conspiring, in the Khyber Pass and the adjoining Bazar Valley of Tirah, with the Afridi Mullah Sayyid Akbar. Udny responded to this report by echoing Macnaghten's "All quiet from Dan to Beersheba" and Cavagnari's "All well in the Kabul Embassy" with a reassurance of his own. "Everything quiet," read Udny's telegram to Elgin in Simla.

Within hours of the telegram's dispatch—even while the Peshawar Vale Hunt rode in full cry after its jackal quarry—news reached Udny that Sayyid Akbar was marching through the Khyber without opposition at the head of a 10,000-man Afridi lashkar.

At that point, there was probably only one Briton who might have prevailed on the Afridis to return to their villages and who, if the Afridis had not heeded him, might have been able to lead the Khyber Rifles against their fellow tribesmen. But Warburton was in Lahore on leave before departing for England, his mandatory retirement having just come due at the worst possible moment. Warburton had left his post with grave misgivings. In June, a month before the eruption in Swat, he had warned the Punjab Government of a possible tribal rising, only to be told in reply that "our political success . . . has broken the back of Mullah fanaticism forever." But when Sayyid Akbar struck the Khyber in mid-August, Warburton received a telegram from Simla, asking if he would consider a return to emergency duty. He wired back at once: "Ready for any Government service if required." More than a week went by before he received his orders.

The orders arrived at least a week too late. By this time, wrote Warburton, "we were in for what I had laboured all my years and by every means in my power to avert—a great Afridi war."

Warburton did not exaggerate. Between August 22 and August 25, Sayyid Akbar's Afridi army ants had overrun and captured Landi Kotal and poured eastward, leveling smaller defense posts and putting to the torch the fort at Ali Masjid. The vacuum of Warburton's absence had also proved too much for the Khyber Rifles; as one man, they had mutinied and gone over to Sayyid Akbar. Some idea of that mullah's charisma had come across during the attack on Landi Kotal, when a Khyber Rifles sepoy turned to a tribal elder and said: "Here is Sayyid Akbar; let me shoot him and end this business for good and ever," to which the elder replied: "Would you destroy the light of Islam?"

At any rate, as August drew to a close only Fort Jamrud stood between the insurgent lashkar and Peshawar. After eighteen years, the British had lost the key to the northwestern door of India in less than half a week. "My mind is very heavy," wrote a shattered Warburton to a friend in England, "over this hideous disaster, which I feel could have been staved off even up to the day of mischief. It makes me feel quite sad to think of how easily the labour of years—of a lifetime—can be ruined and destroyed in a few days." Shortly after Warburton's death barely two years later, the same friend wrote: "It is no exaggeration to say that [the Khyber uprising] broke his heart."

Drunk with victory and flying on bhang, the rebels followed up their capture of the Khyber positions with an ultimatum to Peshawar from Sayyid Akbar: Without delay, all Government forces must withdraw from Swat and also evacuate the line of forts along the Samana range on the southern border of Tirah. Even before this message was received, Tirah's Orakzai clans joined the Afridi revolt and launched attacks on the Samana posts. Some Orakzai lashkars were even reported penetrating the Kurram Valley to the south. By then, there seemed very little the British could do about it.

But of course they could do a great deal, if ever they were jolted from their complacency. And that finally happened with the loss of the Khyber and the concurrent Orakzai rising. It now became clear that if the Orakzais were not contained, their raids into the Kurram from the north would be emulated in much greater force by the Wazirs and Mahsuds from the south, even clearer that unless the Afridis were pried out of the Khyber, they might well seize Peshawar. At long last, both the Punjab and Indian governments recognized that they were not dealing with a few brushfires of discontent, but with a conflagration that was about to set the whole Frontier ablaze. Sparks could even fly east across the Indus.

At the eleventh hour, the British moved to stamp out the flames.

25

The Trashing of Shangri-la

THE 35,000-man force that was mounted to deal with the runaway Pathan uprising in the early autumn of 1897 was the largest British army to take the field in India since the Mutiny. It was also the best equipped. Infantry regiments carried the Lee-Metford rifle, the first bolt-action weapon ever used by British forces. There were ten field and mountain batteries, totaling sixty guns, and one of the first machine gun detachments ever brought to bear against the hill tribes.* Engineer and ordnance units had their own large field parks to facilitate construction, maintenance and repair work. For the sick and wounded there were three general hospitals and twenty-seven wheeled aid stations, while the force's 30,000 horses, ponies, mules, bullocks and camels had a sizable veterinary field hospital. The medical corps even boasted one of the new x-ray cameras, which had never before been taken into a campaign, and which inspired the doggerel for a marching song called "The New Photographee":

> The inside of everything you see,
> A terrible thing, an 'orrible thing
> Is the new photographee.

The objective of the army's commander, General Sir William Lockhart, was the Afridi-Orakzai homeland of Tirah, partly because the Frontier insurrection centered in this region, partly because an invasion

---

*During the assault on Kabul in October 1897, Roberts had a pair of Gatling guns, which had proved useless.

of Tirah would contain the rebellious tribes and discourage further outbreaks to the south, particularly among the Wazirs and Mahsuds of Waziristan. Tribal strength in the Tirah region was uncertain, but the Afridis and Orakzais had combined temporarily and estimates gave them between 40,000 and 50,000 fighting men. Besides this apparent numerical edge, the tribes also enjoyed the customary advantage of defending their own ground; that alone was no small handicap to the British.

It was hoped and expected, however, that other factors would even the odds. The Tirah Expeditionary Force (much too big to be a common field force) was not just a superbly equipped juggernaut; it was also trained to a fine fighting edge. Few of its regiments had not seen Frontier action. General esprit, moreover, soared as seldom before under the spotlight of front-page coverage by every major daily in England. And it was a time when such things as a personal message from the Queen could work wonders with morale. According to the force's Colonel H. D. Hutchinson, who also doubled as a correspondent for *The Times*, "the feeling that Her Majesty is watching the progress of events on this wild frontier, as attentively and anxiously as any of her subjects, animates every soldier in this force." If Tirah was not to be a full-scale Peninsular Campaign, it would do until the Boer War came along.

Above all, undiluted confidence was reposed in Lockhart. A rather colorless, deadpan, ramrod product of the Victorian military mold, he was also a savvy, experienced Frontier fighting man who had already led two punitive expeditions into the hills. One, in fact, had been carried out against the Orakzais themselves and had led to the building of the fortifications along the Samana range, which marked Tirah's southern border. No other British officer in India had a more intimate knowledge of the battleground to which the force was marching.

Which may not have meant much in the circumstances. To the British, Tirah was the least known of all the Frontier regions, since the tribes had always held most of its hills and valleys literally sacred and had forbidden entry to any and all outsiders. Before 1897, the Punjab and Indian governments had found no special reason not to respect Tirah's "purdah"; even in 1891, the army had never penetrated any farther than the Samana range. Now, in effect, Lockhart would be leading his columns into a void.

Yet his three-phase strategy was not complex. First, the army would enter Tirah from the south, over the hump of the Samana. The country itself would then be subjugated, step by step, in a northerly and easterly advance; "the objective of the expedition, the hub and heart of the Afridi nation," wrote Hutchinson, "could be reached in four or five easy marches." Phase three was to be a move farther east and north, culminating in the recapture of the Khyber Pass, which itself was separated from Samana by only about thirty miles. Even taking into account the expected ferocity of tribal resistance and the fact that the British would be advancing more or less blindfolded, most officers believed the whole thing would be over and done with well inside of ten weeks.

Militarily, Lockhart's plan was sound, but it almost failed to get off the ground. On October 18, the campaign opened. With cover from several mountain batteries, a battalion of the Gordon Highlanders spearheaded the British drive on the Samana by scaling a 5,000-foot ridge called the Dargai Heights. Having seized the objective after a furious but brief fire fight, the Gordons withdrew at once; thanks to a sunburst of somebody's logistical incompetence, no pack animals were available to bring up the ammunition and rations needed to hold the position. Lockhart and his staff could only gaze upward in impotent rage and watch the declining sun throw into silhouette the battle flags of the several thousand tribesmen who had reoccupied the Dargai. Two days passed before enough mules could be driven forward to support a second try.

By then, however, the Pathans had planted themselves firmly on the heights, behind endless hundreds of boulders that looked for all the world like giant lumps of rock candy. Even an extended, brain-scrambling bombardment by the mountain guns failed to budge them from their lofty cyclone cellars. The Gurkha regiment leading the assault along a narrow spine near the summit became pinned down under a curtain of rifle fire that was unusually accurate even for the hawk-eyed tribesmen. Many Afridis and Orakzais were armed with breech-loading Sniders, Martini-Henrys and even some Lee-Metfords, stolen or captured in earlier affrays. Most of the best marksmen had two or three rifles each, plus assistants who served as loaders to speed up the rate of fire. Gurkhas began pitching down from the skinny ridge in clusters. The Dorset and Derbyshire regiments fared no better when they moved up in support. It began to look as if Tirah's purdah might just remain inviolate.

But the British still had the Victorian secret weapon of chowderheaded valor. Continuing to smart from their needless reverse on the eighteenth, the Gordons now fixed bayonets and went in again behind the regimental bagpipes and drums, to the high-pitched snarl of "Cock O' the North." Everywhere, their riflemen could be seen spinning in their tracks and thumping to the ground like sacks of meal as the Pathans poured volley after tattered volley into the kilted ranks. But still the Highlanders came on, stepping gingerly round the prone figure of Piper Findlater, who continued to play just as though bullets had not plowed through both his legs. There was even an air of nonchalance about the attack, at least to judge from one exchange that Hutchinson recorded: "Colonel Mathias, no longer quite in his first youth, was somewhat short of breath, and said to Colour-Sergeant Mackie . . . 'Stiff climb, eh, Mackie? Not quite—so—young—as I was—you know,' 'Never mind, sir!' answered the gallant Sergeant, giving his C.O. a hearty slap of genuine admiration on the back, which almost knocked his remaining wind out of him—'Never mind, sir! Ye're gaun verra strong for an auld man!'"

As the Gordons reached the crest, the artillery intensified its hammering while Gurkhas, Dorsets and Derbyshires moved forward again, with a Sikh regiment in support. Presently the tribal fire became less heavy. Suddenly it ceased altogether, and when the Union Jack was finally raised atop the Dargai, the heights were as empty of Pathans as if a giant vacuum cleaner had just swept by.

But the logistic headache did not go away. It now became a migraine. Somehow, transport officers had been unable to feed and water the baggage animals. Mules, camels and bullocks died in droves. The entire expedition had to be halted for more than a week while 3,000 more or less fresh camels were assembled to bring up 600 tons of supplies and ammunition in several trips. This was barely enough to allow the advance on the next objective, the 6,700-foot crest of the Sampagha Pass. And it may have been Lockhart's good fortune that the Pathans decided, for some reason, not to defend this position in strength.

Indeed, as October drew to a close, the British began to wonder uneasily what the tribes were up to. The Tirah Expeditionary Force was now approaching the heart of Tirah, but it was encountering no real resistance. Descending into the Mastura Valley, the troops found themselves in a picture-postcard Shangri-la. Cultivation proliferated on the valley floor; clean terracing lay like contour lines on the gently rolling hillsides. The leaves of walnut trees and well-tailored apricot orchards whispered in the light Indian summer airs that floated down from the cedar-carpeted upper slopes. The countryside was dotted with tidy, white-plastered houses of stone and baked mud; with their balconies and high rifle towers they looked much like improbable crossbreeds of sailless Dutch windmills and Chinese pagodas. In sheds adjoining the houses were found large harvests of maize, barley, beans, potatoes, onions and walnuts—more than enough to feed the army for weeks.

The tribesmen did not even try to stop the British from seizing these supplies. That was because there were no tribesmen to be seen. With their wives, children, flocks and herds, they had vanished into the hills. Hutchinson could inform his *Times* readers: "We have the valley to ourselves. . . . It has been the proud boast of the Afridis from time immemorial that no enemy of whatever race or creed has ever attempted to cross the mountain barriers which shut them in. . . . Well, we have changed all that."

This was undeniable. All that remained for the British was to get out of Tirah.

Early in November, Lockhart began sending messages to the clans in the hills, summoning their jirgas to the British camp where the terms of their surrender would be read to them. The tribal reply was to launch a campaign of long-range guerrilla harassment. Supply convoys were bushwhacked at night. Patrols and foraging parties came under fire from boulders, rock overhangs, crevices, dry watercourses and even the cover of thorn clumps. Other priority objectives were the survey parties whose work was all-important in an unmapped land. The telegraph line was cut daily, but not just snipped: miles of wire were also carried off so that repairs would take that much longer.

Above all, sniping began with a vengeance, particularly at campsites after sunset, and with special, preselected targets. The tribesmen, said Hutchinson, "not only easily recognise our officers by their conspicuous head-dress and gallant leading, but they well know their value. . . . It is extremely unpleasant, this whizz and spatter of bullets. If you have got to be shot leading your men in action, it is all right, and a proper and honourable way of being shot. . . . But to be potted in the dark is *autre chose.*"

The British could do absolutely nothing about it. Warburton, who accompanied the force as a political officer, wrote that "We . . . had no conception where the bullets came from or what quarter the . . . marksman fired his rifle. This is one of the advantages of your rifle with the smokeless powder falling into the hands of Jack Afridi, to be used against you in his own highlands. You are made to feel the bullet long before you hear the crack of the rifle."

It was not long, however, before Lockhart retaliated with a vest-pocket scorched earth campaign. The captured crops were not destroyed, of course, but nearly everything else was. Task forces carried out sorties in strength. They leveled entire villages with dynamite charges. They trampled fields and filled wells with rocks. They felled orchards—after picking the fruit—or ringed the trees so that they would die in a few months. They looted freely, collecting armloads of old jezails and tulwars and hubble-bubbles and other souvenirs; occasionally, a lucky pillager would come up with an almost priceless hand-written, illuminated Koran. Special pleasure was taken in pulling down and plundering the house of the army's *bête noir,* Sayyid Akbar. But the troops left his mosque untouched, nor was any damage done to other places of worship, in accordance with British codes of religious tolerance. The tribesmen, however, may not have appreciated fully these occasional acts of forbearance.

And certainly Lockhart's official program of vandalism was not implemented without opposition. Snipers continued to pick off targets from marching columns and skirmish lines. Larger bands lashed out at rear guards evacuating villages. During one British retirement to base after a day of demolition, a newly arrived infantry regiment found itself trapped between the walls of a broken ravine; the green troops took a terrible mauling from Afridi rifles and knives before a Sikh detachment could bring them out. Hutchinson called the ambush "so unfortunate that the term disaster may almost be applied to it."

In due course, however, the razing of the countryside seemed to make itself felt. As Lockhart well knew, the tribes could not survive the approaching winter in their hill hideouts, and jirgas began trickling in to the British headquarters camp. On November 11, Lockhart had a windfall when the maliks of the entire Orakzai nation arrived to consider the surrender terms. These elders, said Hutchinson, were "nearly all venerable old graybeards [with] nothing either warlike or truculent in their bearing or demeanour." He added that "they are our guests while with us." Squatting in a large semicircle outside Lockhart's tent, the guests listened without expression as they were told that their people must restore all arms taken from the British, hand over 300 of their own breech-loaders, pay a fine of 30,000 rupees (about $10,000) and forfeit all subsidies and allowances. It was no slap on the wrist.

Still, Lockhart and his officers felt confident that the terms would be accepted, or at the very least, that the Orakzais would end their resistance, since the maliks showed visible relief on learning that their country was not to be permanently occupied. And once the Orakzais submitted, almost identical terms would be imposed on the Afridis, thus bringing the campaign to a successful conclusion.

"But," remarked Hutchinson, "there is no reliance whatever to be placed on the word of an Afridi."

In fact, no word at all was forthcoming from the Afridis for nearly three weeks, during which time Lockhart's forces sustained at least 500 casualties in continual skirmishes and rear-guard actions. Following British custom in extended punitive operations against Pathans, the invaders were by then discussing the enemy in the same tones later used by American troops when evaluating the Viet Cong. Hutchinson's dispatches to his readers in England said many things the army already knew well: "They have absolutely nothing to learn from us, these Afridis. Contrariwise, their dashing and bold attack, the skill with which they watch for a favourable moment, and their perfect marksmanship—all these qualities have again and again won our admiration."

And to their guerrilla expertise the Afridis added a professional working knowledge of British field tactics, gained during service in the Indian Army and Frontier militias. Among the most common souvenirs picked up in deserted houses were British drill instructions and musketry regulations printed in Urdu.

But toward the end of November, as the cold began to set in, the jirgas of several large Afridi clans apparently decided that further resistance would be futile, and they came in to accept the British terms.

Their submission also owed a great deal to Warburton's presence on Lockhart's staff; even the most hostile Afridis knew that the man sometimes called the "uncrowned King of the Khyber" would see to it that his "subjects" got a fair shake. A sort of Frontier Kissinger, Warburton had been in continual touch with tribal leaders. For one brief period, he had even prevailed on an Afridi clan to protect a British detachment against ambush. (And he probably went so far as to agree when an elder told him at this time that "with the exception of your field guns, which we have not, man to man we are as good as any of you.") Now his diplomacy paid dividends as the Afridi maliks sat down to talk in an atmosphere that could almost have been called friendly. Not a few members of the delegation were even recognized as ex-Indian Army sepoys by their former British commanding officers. One elder wore four medals on his robe, including a decoration for the Egyptian campaign of 1882.

Still more conspicuous at the meeting was the absence of the tribe's two most obstinate and truculent sections, the Zakka Khels and the Kuki Khels. Even Warburton called the Zakka Khels "the greatest thieves, housebreakers, robbers and raiders among all the Khyber clans, their word or promise never being believed or trusted by their Afridi brethren without a substantial security being taken for its fulfilment." In effect, the refusal of the Zakka Khels and Kuki Khels to meet Lockhart meant that the Afridi surrender was anything but unconditional.

But with or without full tribal submission, the time had come for the British to depart; even in the valleys, the army would face wipeout by a Tirah winter. Lockhart accordingly issued a proclamation to the still-defiant Afridi clans, declaring his "intention to attack you in your other settlements during the winter," and adding that "the Afridis attacking the English is like flies assailing a lion." Then, on December 9, the columns began their final easterly thrust, through the forty-mile-long Bara Valley, toward the Khyber.

Hutchinson called this phase of the campaign "the sternest work and the stiffest trial the force has had yet." The troops struggled forward into a barely yielding wall of sleet and snow. Seldom able to see more than a dozen yards ahead, not a few soldiers and followers wandered off into the frozen holocaust and never found their way back. The crazily meandering Bara River retarded progress because it was not quite frozen over and there was no ice to support the weight of even a single man. The troops had to wade across it, often up to their chests, at least ten times for every mile covered. "The spray from the water, splashed up by wading, froze as it fell," wrote Hutchinson, "while moustaches became mere blocks of ice, and the horses' tails as they swished them about in the stream were covered immediately with long spiky icicles." So-called dry land was no better. Rice paddies on the river bank had become belts of near-icy bog into which many of the 12,000 remaining transport animals sank girth-deep. Only a few could be dragged out; the others had to be shot. By now too, nearly all of the force's tents had been lost, and campfires continually hissed out on ground that had been stamped into slush. At night, greatcoats and even poshteens offered only a little more warmth than mosquito netting.

And all the while, Afridi rifles continued to crash away from the valley's upper slopes. Although Churchill had not been able to talk his way into an assignment with the Tirah expedition, he learned that the march down the Bara "looked more like a rout than the victorious withdrawal of a punitive force." Many clans that had submitted now rejoined the Zakka Khels and Kuki Khels to harry the already reeling invader. Egged on by their mullahs, they not only stepped up the rate of their mass sniping but sometimes closed with isolated units. Once there was a daylight assault on the rear guard, which carried most of the force's wounded. The attack spread pandemonium among the stretcher-bearers, who had to be restrained at bayonet and pistol point from dropping their burdens and bolting. It cost the rear guard the better part of a day, at least 100 troops and followers, and nearly all its pack animals and supplies to make contact with the main body. On several occasions, only the British mountain guns kept the Afridis from pouring down the valley walls and methodically annihilating the Tirah Expeditionary Force.

But the tribesmen also took casualties, and by mid-December the British-Indian troops, their uniforms starched with ice, at last managed to haul themselves out of the Bara Valley trap. Lockhart could now turn his full attention to the Khyber Pass, where the Afridis had to stand or fall.

They fell. At last outside the lost world of Tirah, Lockhart was able not only to plan his tactics on familiar terrain, but also to make use of those still-intact forts that his troops recaptured. Moreover, as the British columns advanced slowly but steadily westward toward Landi Kotal, a new kind of hardship was inflicted on the Afridis. Besides burning villages to the ground, the British were able, at last, to seize the all-important tribal flocks and herds that had been moved beyond their reach in the Tirah hills. The rounding up of dozens of thousands of sheep and goats may well have hurt the Afridis at least as sorely as did their mounting human losses. By the time the snows began to melt in late March of 1898, the clansmen had come to perceive, as Hutchinson put it, "that to prolong the struggle was only to prolong their own misery." By April, even the Zakka Khels and Kuki Khels had accepted the British terms of submission.

It had taken Lockhart not ten weeks but more than five months to overcome the Afridis and Orakzais, but the great Pathan revolution had finally ended. For the first time in their history, the Frontier tribes had been beaten to their knees.

In many ways, however, the fruits of the British victory hardly seemed worth the price. In life and limb alone, the invasion of Tirah had cost 1,150 British and Indian soldiers killed, wounded and missing. Of the financial penalty, Churchill wrote: "There was no doubt who had the punishment, or who would have to pay the bill. Thirty-five thousand troops hunting, and being hunted by, Afridis . . . with twenty thousand more guarding their communications make a nasty total when computed in rupees." Earlier, at the end of the Swat campaign, after watching one clan hand over its breech-loaders, Churchill had also observed that "the rifles as they lay on the ground were a bitter comment on the economic aspect of the 'Forward Policy.' These tribes have nothing to surrender but their arms. To extort these few had taken a month, had cost many lives, and thousands of pounds. It had been as bad a bargain as was ever made."

Others thought it no bargain at all, perceiving that in its forcible demonstration of who was master on the Frontier, the Indian Government had only stirred the embers of an implacable hatred and nourished the old thirst for a day of reckoning. "Where a family residence, house or fortress has been destroyed," wrote Warburton, "and some of the male members killed in protecting their lives and property, or where their wives and children have been brought to death by exposure to cold, frost and snow, feelings of revenge will be cherished, and be remembered when the time comes for paying off the Power who has been the cause of these wrongs."

This view was seconded by no less a soldier than Roberts, who deplored the policy of "punitive expeditions which have already cost such a vast expenditure in blood and money, and inflicted such cruel misery on the innocent families of the delinquents. Burning houses and destroying crops, necessary and justifiable as such measures may be, unless followed up by some sort of authority and jurisdiction, mean starvation for many of the women and children . . . and for us a rich harvest of hatred and revenge."

It was all a way of saying that the real losers in the 1897 uprising had been the British. If Lockhart's troops and big guns had done nothing more than sow dragons' teeth, then the British must have been doing something very wrong on the Frontier for half a century. There were those who asked if the entire approach to tribal administration was not based on fallacies, whether drastic changes might not be in order. The changes were about to be made.

PART SEVEN

The Birth of a Graustark

26

The Wisdom of Chairman Curzon

SEVERAL WEEKS before the initial outbreaks of the 1897 Pathan uprising, George Curzon had launched an offensive of his own. He had begun openly electioneering, if that word can be used, for appointment as Viceroy of India before his fortieth birthday. The post, he knew, might well hold the key to the door of Number Ten Downing Street.

And the key to the Viceroy's house, in the meanwhile, was the incumbent Prime Minister, Lord Salisbury.

Accordingly, with an immodest candor not often found in junior British statesmen, Curzon wrote Salisbury two long letters of self-advertisement as the man to uphold the will of the Queen-Empress in India. He made a special point of flaunting his credentials as an expert on the politically sensitive northwest frontier: "If I have written books about . . . frontier problems—no doubt a risky venture—the views or forecasts I have been bold enough to express have I think on the whole turned out to be right; and I do not think, though my first book came out 8 years ago, I would cancel a single page in any one of them."

This assertion contradicted one of Curzon's better-known remarks: "No one who has read a page of Indian history will ever prophesy about the frontier." But at the time when Curzon was wooing Salisbury, the whole trans-Indus country seemed to be going up in smoke, and the Prime Minister recognized that few if any other Britons on the Indian scene could claim Curzon's grasp of the role played by the Frontier in imperial geopolitics. Like many United States ambassadors, viceroys could sometimes be political appointees with minimal interest in, and frequently less knowledge of, the country to which they were sent. But 1897 and 1898 did not seem the right moment for India to become a patronage plum. In 1898, Salisbury decided that Curzon was his man.

And hardly had Curzon donned the viceregal robes in January 1899, than he turned his eyes northwest and embarked on a program designed to change the entire face of the Frontier.

He was going to do that by a fairly simple administrative act. The Frontier would be removed from the jurisdiction of the Punjab, and its status elevated from that of oversize county to full Indian province under a Chief Commissioner reporting directly to Curzon himself. To more than one pillar of the Indian Civil Service, the scheme seemed not much less radical than handing India over to the Indians.

It was no such thing. It was a farsighted and eminently sound idea. Curzon knew the difficulties that stemmed from trying to manage a region that was no more than a neglected administrative stump of the Punjab. The Frontier was simply too big, its peoples too turbulent and, above all, its whole way of life too alien to remain subordinate to a provincial governor who had neither the time nor the inclination—and least of all, the ability—to deal directly with its tribal peoples. In effect, the Pathans had to become the responsibility of the Viceroy himself.

To be sure, Curzon's concern for the tribes was less compassionate than it was political, although he did have unbounded personal admiration for them. "I am never so happy as when on the Frontier," he wrote a friend in the Cabinet. "I know these men. . . . They are brave as lions, wild as cats, docile as children. . . . It is with a sense of pride that one receives the honest homage of these magnificent Samsons, gigantic, bearded, instinct with loyalty, often stained with crime." But "stained with crime" was the operative phrase; so long as the Pathans continued dissatisfied and unmanageable, so too would their homeland remain vulnerable to Afghan—and, indirectly, to Russian—intrigues, thus leaving open a cavernous hole in the wall of India's defenses. Relations with the Frontier clans were connected directly to the security of India. And who, if not the Viceroy, was ultimately held accountable for that security?

As things stood, however, it was almost impossible for the Viceroy to make a swift decision on any matter west of the Indus. Everything had to go through the channel of Lahore before reaching Calcutta or Simla. "The Government of India," wrote Curzon in a minute to the India Office, ". . . has placed between itself and the Frontier the Punjab Government which for twenty years has been an instrument of procrastination and obstruction and weakness. . . . I venture to affirm that there is not another country in the world which adopts a system so irrational in theory, so bizarre in practice, as to interpose between [itself] and its most important sphere of activity the barrier . . . of a subordinate government." Clearly, the only solution lay in removing that barrier.

Provincial autonomy for the Frontier was far from being Curzon's brainchild. As early as 1877, Lytton had drawn up a blueprint for a separate Frontier province, to be administered by Roberts; only the outbreak of the Second Afghan War had prevented the plan from becoming reality. Roberts himself had often urged provincial status as the means of ending "futile blockades and inconclusive reprisals," and of "turning the wild tribesmen from enemies into friends." Warburton too had seen an urgent need to rid the hill country of its Punjab anchor. "Many frontier questions," he said, "require an expert hand and speedy action to save future complications. They often necessitate an immediate visit to the locality, which the Lieutenant-Governor* cannot always undertake, and a knowledge of the Pushtu language, which no Lieutenant-Governor that I know of has yet acquired. . . . The only way to prevent future wars on the frontier and to create a friendly impression on the wild man of the independent hills, is to alter the system which has proved useless for thirty-five years."

If Curzon's proposed reforms were not without precedent, neither did they lack opposition. Many British Indian officials were scandalized by the notion that so squalid an outdoor slum as the Frontier might be raised to an equal footing with the Punjab and other legitimate provinces. Sir Mackworth Young, the Punjab's Lieutenant Governor, had no intention of handing over so much as a square inch of his fief. He and his supporters argued that provincial status for the trans-Indus districts would deprive the Punjab of badly needed revenues, that Calcutta was far too distant to exercise proper authority over the Frontier, that the Indian Government had not a sufficiently large cadre of trained civil servants to manage a newly created province. Above all, Young declared, no men in India had more practical experience in dealing with the Frontier tribes than his own Punjab officials.

Young also took the proposal as an affront to himself and Queen Victoria. "You have not cared to consult me," he complained to Curzon, "about forming a new Administration out of the territory which I have received a commission from Her Majesty to administer." And at the very least, Young had good reason for taking umbrage as the new Viceroy began to sweep his objections aside in a series of minutes to the India Office that were only less disdainful than they were compelling. "I cannot work under this system," wrote Curzon, "I cannot spend hours in wordy argument with my Lieutenant-Governors as to the exact meaning, purport, scope, object, character, possible limitations, conceivable results, of each

* At that time, only three of India's provinces had a full governor.

petty aspect of my Frontier policy. If they deliberately refuse to understand it, and haggle and boggle about carrying it out, I must get some fairly intelligent officer who will understand what I mean and do what I say."

Curzon also dealt with Young's arguments specifically. He pointed out that most Punjab officials were generally assigned only to the briefest terms of Frontier service, which was quite correct; and he further noted that the great figures of the region—men like the Lawrences, Nicholson, Edwardes and Warburton—had almost literally given their lives to the hills. This also was true, but misleading, since those officials had all been members of the Punjab administration. Nonetheless, Curzon drove ahead relentlessly. Taking up the Punjab's territorial, financial and demographic losses from the creation of a Frontier province, he observed that these would come to one-fourteenth of the area, one-fifteenth of the revenue and one-eighteenth of the population. Young's argument that Lahore was closer to the Frontier than Calcutta was dismissed as "a mere geographical plea . . . which itself breaks down when it is remembered that for five months in the year the supreme and local governments are located in the same spot, Simla." Whatever Young put forward, Curzon bowled over.

In London, his eloquence and logic had the twin effect of an artillery barrage and a dueling pistol. On November 9, 1901, the North West Frontier Province came into being. Four years later, Curzon would resign from the viceroyalty—a sour, embittered man, his political career in a shambles after a series of long and unbecoming petty squabbles with members of his staff and the home government. But the Frontier would not be an issue. The Punjab had lost a stepdaughter and British India had gained a legitimate son.

Although the Frontier now became the direct responsibility of the Viceroy through its Chief Commissioner, the organization of the new province differed little in certain ways from its makeup under the Punjab Government. The curious division of the country remained in effect, with "settled" and "tribal" areas fenced off from each other by the administrative border. As in the past, the "settled" districts east of the line were in the charge of deputy commissioners, while political agents continued to exercise a somewhat less firm rule over the so-called "independent" tribesmen occupying the hill country areas to the west. But there were also real and important changes—among them the most immediate, visible and telling being the discontinuation of indirect dealing with the tribes through their own middlemen. This was possible because of an infinitely more important development: the emergence of a new breed of Frontier official.

This man was not as colorful a figure, perhaps, as Nicholson or

Edwardes or even Warburton, but he was every bit as dedicated and just possibly more competent. Curzon's system encouraged the recruitment of administrators not just from the Punjab but from all parts of India. Anyone with an aptitude for laying down the law to hostile tribesmen—and, more to the point, for making friends with them—became likely material for a Frontier post, provided he was ready to roll up his sleeves and dive into the work. Abbreviated tours of Frontier duty were replaced by long-term assignments that often became lifetime careers. Steady advancement to the highest levels awaited the capable official toiling west of the Indus. The North West Frontier Province was to produce the cream of the Indian Civil Service.

Embodying this expertise and enthusiasm was the Chief Commissioner, Sir Harold Deane, whom Curzon appointed over the heads of several vastly senior officials. Deane had been the ranking political officer of the Malakand Agency since its founding in 1895. The respect and trust that he enjoyed among the people of that volatile area earned him a jesting rebuke many years later, when Churchill wrote his reminiscences of the Malakand campaign. "We had with us," he recalled, "a very brilliant political officer, a Major Deane, who was much disliked because he always stopped military operations. Just when we were looking forward to having a splendid fight and all the guns were loaded and everyone keyed up, this Major Deane—and why was he a Major anyhow? so we said—being in truth nothing better than an ordinary politician—would come along and put a stop to it all. Apparently all these savage chiefs were his old friends and almost his blood relations. Nothing disturbed their friendship. In between the fights, they talked as man to man and as pal to pal."

Which of course was what it was all about. It is probable that even the half-Afghan Warburton did not enjoy as full a measure of tribal trust and affection as did the tall, soldierly, blue-eyed Deane and his burly, hot-tempered successor, Sir George Roos-Keppel. Deane knew how to use not only his brains but a gently sadistic sense of humor. He once prevailed on a stubborn malik to accept some regulation by discussing it with him on a long hike through the hills. He knew that the malik had, for some inexplicable reason, just bought and was wearing a pair of patent-leather shoes, which had not yet been broken in. After ten miles, Deane got what he wanted. Roos-Keppel, who took office in 1908, was looked on by the tribes, according to Caroe, with "a regard that fell not short of adoration."

Both Deane and Roos-Keppel, along with many of their subordinates, were veterans not just of the Frontier but of the explosive tribal area beyond the administrative border that separated the men from the boys. But the men, wherever they might be stationed, were easy to recognize. If a new official was not revolted and disenchanted, and thus defeated, by

Pathan treachery and barbarity, if he could recognize those things in their context as elements of a virile and purposeful way of life, he would presently come to think as a tribesman, to understand and even share tribal aspirations. He would never lose his first loyalty to the Crown, but he would also become a sort of super-malik. As such, no one was better fitted to reconcile the differences between Pathan and Briton.

This, too, was part of the idea of Curzon's Frontier face-lifting: to bring the hillmen closer to India's socio-political-economic mainstream, to show the Pathan that Government had his interests at heart, to plant the seeds of a new kind of national identity, which, it was hoped, might begin to dilute the tribesman's traditional suspicion of his Feringhi over-lords. Even with the barrier of the administrative border, the hill warrior might presently come to realize that the Raj looked on him less as a savage placed in quarantine from the rest of British India than as a member in relatively good standing of that imperial community.

As the years went by, Curzon's reforms, and the men who implemented them, could be seen to bring dividends with a slow but steady wind of change. Irrigation schemes were to open up previously barren lands to cultivation and grazing. Useful agricultural skills would be imparted to tribesmen in a growing complex of Government primary and high schools. 1908 was to witness the opening of Islamia College—later the University of Peshawar—which would play Cambridge to Edwardes College's Oxford in turning out a Pathan aristocracy of civil servants and political leaders. Practically the only building on the Frontier that never had to be locked, Islamia was founded by the joint effort of Roos-Keppel and his close friend and alter ego, Sahibzada Sir Abdul Qayyum, one of the most distinguished officials ever to serve in the trans-Indus region. In many ways, it could be said that the Frontier was entering the twentieth century. "Not entirely consciously," writes Caroe, "Curzon had provided a focus for Pathan self-esteem, and so done much to consolidate a firmer frontier."

A by-product of the Frontier's elevation to provincial status was the stiffening of its defenses in a drastic reorganization of the Indian armed forces. Curzon was well known as a Rawlinsonian Russophobe; when he took office, it was believed in many quarters that his views would be reflected in a new spasm of Forward Policy aggressiveness. But although Curzon was never to lose sight of the Russian threat, his stewardship witnessed the revival of a sort of modified close-border policy.

In 1899, some 10,000 troops of the Indian Army were stationed on the far side of the administrative border along a winding, 200-mile perim-eter from the Malakand Pass to Waziristan. Although their presence was due mainly to the need for temporary occupation forces in the wake of the 1897-98 uprising, the Indian Government at that time was also considering proposals to build more forts in tribal territory with a view toward the establishment of permanent regular garrisons. Curzon filed those plans in the wastebasket as he initiated the policy that came to be known as "withdrawal and concentration."

This meant what the words said: all regular troops were to be withdrawn from tribal areas and concentrated in garrisons behind the administrative border. The tribes themselves would assume the chief responsibility for the defense of their own homes. That was the key to the change; as one Frontier army officer once put it, "it has always been the case that the less . . . the tribes saw of us, at any rate across the border, the more they liked us."

So the militias were built up again—on a much greater scale. Delinquencies of the 1897 revolt were forgiven, if not forgotten, as the Khyber Rifles were reconstituted and beefed up to a strength of two battalions. Tribesmen also patrolled the hills in the tattered uniforms of the Tochi Scouts, the Kurram Militia, the South Waziristan Scouts, the Samana Rifles and other jauntily named military and paramilitary units; even Chitral had its gang of ragged but falcon-eyed riflemen. By 1904, the King's Peace in the King's remotest domains was being upheld by vest-pocket legions of the King's least manageable subjects, and the idea seemed to be working nicely.

Curzon realized, however, that the militias could not be expected to hold back a full-scale Russian or even Afghan invasion, and that they could be relied on only to a point against any major rising of fellow-tribesmen. Hence, the "withdrawal and concentration" of regular Indian Army units as a reserve-in-force in the settled districts, together with a crash program of road, bridge and narrow-gauge railway building so that regulars could move up swiftly to deal with Cossack armies or insurgent Pathan lashkars or both. Massive retaliation was always within arm's length on the west bank of the Indus.

The regular forces, too, were restructured—even more so than the tribal militia. This overhauling may have been the most far-reaching domestic accomplishment of Curzon's stewardship.

Curzon could take only partial credit for it. Shortly after becoming Viceroy, he had requested a new Commander-in-Chief for the Indian Army, as he held his own generals in the lowest esteem. "Few of them read or study," he wrote. "Military science as such seems to be beyond them. A battle in their eyes is only a game of football. What is the good of heroism when you are being picked off by an enemy three miles away? . . . God forbid that we should ever have a war with such men at the head of affairs . . . we want a Kitchener to pull things together. If he is not available, I do not know whom to name."

General Lord Horatio Herbert Kitchener was no doubt the man for the job. He had restored British prestige and rule in the Sudan with his rout of the Mahdists at Omdurman in 1898. First as Robers' Chief of Staff, subsequently on his own, he had waged a scorched earth campaign in South Africa that had snapped the spine of Boer resistance. But he may have faced his greatest challenge when he arrived in India in 1902.

Apart from a handful of crack regiments, the Indian Army had been going steadily to seed since the 1897 uprising—indeed, since the Second Afghan War. Discipline was lax. Morale sagged. Curzon was troubled and enraged by a growing number of ugly racial incidents involving British troops and Indian civilians; he wrote that he would "not be a party . . . to the theory that a white man may kick or batter [an Indian] to death with impunity simply because he is only a 'd——d nigger.'" In a different respect, the sepoys were not much better. Few of them had ever fired or heard a shot fired in anger. Many units, raised from what Roberts once called "the effeminate peoples of the south," had acquired such bad reputations that British officers literally considered themselves disgraced if assigned to one. Roberts himself had recognized the dry rot more than a decade earlier: "I knew that nothing was more sure to lead to disaster than to imagine that the Indian Army, as it was then established, could be relied on in time of war."

Kitchener found all these things to be true. He did not merely second Curzon's outrage with racism, condemning "the idea that pervades every-one in India . . . that the Army is intended to hold India against the Indians." What was even worse for a soldier, Kitchener recognized at once that there appeared to be no rational organization or deployment of the force; he found it "scattered higgledy-piggledy all over the country, without any system or reason whatever." Clearly, a drastic shakeup was long overdue.

Three main tasks faced Kitchener. He had to achieve maximum striking power, put the troops back into fighting trim, and position the whole army so that it would face not imaginary internal threats but slightly less imaginary external threats. Under the system he had inherited, only four divisions were available to him, although the army had the man-power for more. After reshuffling all regiments and drawing up a new table of organization, Kitchener was able to field nine full divisions of standard strength.

In making this omelet he broke some eggs. Among other things, he drew heavy fire from outraged traditionalists when he disbanded the Punjab Frontier Force (including the Guides) and reassigned its officers and men to regular units. He also fell out with Curzon himself on a minor jurisdictional issue that was to become a principal cause of Curzon's resignation. But when the smoke cleared, India found herself with a twentieth-century fighting machine.

This was due largely to the deployment of the army, which in turn was related directly to the building of esprit, in the only logical place for any military force in British India. That place, of course, was the only vulnerable sector of the country's 4,000-mile land boundary. Kitchener arranged that at least three divisions were always stationed on the North West Frontier, where the ever-present threat of invasion or tribal insurgency would inevitably tighten the reins of discipline and bring all units to a high state of combat readiness. Frontier tours of duty were rotated, so that the entire army benefited from training on the world's most difficult obstacle course. Thanks largely to the rigors and demands of Frontier service—where conventional maneuvers could easily turn into the real thing without warning—the Indian Army was virtually the only army in the British Empire that had achieved anything like preparedness when the First World War broke out.

This was not all. From the standpoint of Indian border security, the most heartening feature of Curzon's administration may have been the final winding down of the Great Game in Central Asia. While Curzon himself played anything but the principal role in this development, and although the détente was not actually formalized until two years after he had left office, the simple fact of his presence on the scene was of considerable value in a rapprochement that threatened at first to be a war.

For the Great Game ended not with a whimper but a near-bang. In 1900, exploiting Britain's growing loss of international face from her embroilment and reverses in the Boer War, St. Petersburg made it known that Russia intended to open diplomatic relations with Afghanistan. The news jolted the Foreign and India offices, not to mention the Viceregal Palace. Although the proposed contacts with Kabul were to be purely commercial (so the Russians said), they openly violated the earlier pledges that Afghanistan lay entirely outside the Russian sphere of influence. Curzon of course was quick to recognize the obvious significance, and threat, of the ploy; even a Russian trade mission, he said, would assure that British "control of Afghan foreign relations . . . would disappear. . . . The Amir would attribute the concession to our weakness."

London was no less alert to the gravity of the move: a Russian presence in Kabul must almost certainly upset the entire Asian balance of power. Salisbury feared that "if Afghanistan is unprotected [Russia] can force us to give way in China by advancing upon India. She won't try to conquer it. It will be enough for her if she can shatter our government and reduce India to anarchy." Despite heated protests and warnings from Whitehall, Russian diplomats carried on a lengthy correspondence with Afghan officials. By 1903, it seemed as if there might be no way, short of another mobilization on the North West Frontier, to keep Russian armies out of Kabul—and just conceivably, Peshawar.

Then, almost without warning, the tide of crisis began to ebb swiftly as Russia found herself mired down in another Oriental bog. Staggering defeats at the hands of the Japanese Army and Navy, coupled with Anglo-Japanese treaties in 1902 and 1905, served to shift the Asiatic balance of power heavily in Britain's favor. In 1907, more than a century of Central Asian border tensions came to an abrupt and final end when the two nations signed an agreement in St. Petersburg whereby Russia reaffirmed her recognition of Afghanistan as a British sphere. At long last, the specter of Cossacks pouring through the Khyber Pass had been exorcised forever.

But why? Ever since the Granville-Gorchakov agreement of 1873, Russia had been continually pledging hands off Afghanistan and then breaking her word. What made the St. Petersburg Convention all that binding? The answer, simply, was the presence of a new specter. The thrashing Russia had taken from Japan was seen in many diplomatic circles as little more than a love tap when compared with what the German Army might do. Germany's swift rise as a world power, moreover, had become a source of mounting uneasiness, not only in St. Petersburg but in London. British and Russian diplomats were beginning to perceive that Anglo-Russian friendship in Europe had to make more political sense than Anglo-Russian saber-rattling over a rock collection in Central Asia. More than anything else, it was fear of German military might that ended the Great Game.

Berlin certainly saw it that way. After reading the text of the St. Petersburg Convention, Kaiser Wilhelm II noted drily on the margin: "Yes, when taken all round it is aimed at us."

The political squabbles and personal jealousies that led to Curzon's resignation, and that sabotaged his chances of becoming prime minister, have no place in this book; but shortly before Curzon returned to England in 1905, he was able to console himself with one achievement in India. Addressing the United Service Club in Simla, he said that he was "content with the simple facts that for seven years we have not had a single frontier expedition, the only seven years of which this can be said since the frontier passed into British hands; and that, whereas in the five years 1894–99 the Indian taxpayer had to find four and a half million pounds sterling for frontier warfare, the total cost of military operations on the entire North West Frontier, in the last seven years has been only £248,000."

This was not just a well-earned self-tribute. It was also an unintentional but astounding misstatement of fact.

Curzon had shown real farsightedness in granting provincial status to the Frontier, staffing it with compassionate and capable administrators and policing it with its own people. But none of those reforms could have been expected to make the hill Pathan into a pacifist. Nor did they. To the extent that Curzon's innovations took hold, they were almost entirely inside the administrative border, where most of the tribesmen could have been called at least partly domesticated. West of the line it was another matter; Fraser-Tytler has said that "the Curzon policy advanced our relations with the trans-border tribes not one whit," and this is altogether correct. If Curzon deserved every credit for seven years without a punitive expedition into the hills, the peace he wrought was deceptive at the very least.

In many ways it was not peace at all, but open war.

27

The Pestilential Priest

WAZIRISTAN HAS SOMETIMES been called "the Frontier Switzerland," but not because its two principal tribes, the Wazirs and Mahsuds, are cuckoo-clock manufacturers. Although the British could never agree which of the two was the fiercest of all Pathan peoples, no other group —not even the Afridis—was ever in the running for the palm. Caroe once tried to describe each tribe. "The nearest I can get to it," he wrote, "is to liken the Mahsud to a wolf, the Wazir to a panther. Both are splendid creatures; the panther is slier, sleeker and has more grace, the wolf-pack is more purposeful, more united and more dangerous." During the early years of the twentieth century, the Mahsud wolves almost had the British lion on the run.

A word of background is in order. In 1893, when the Durand Line was drawn and Waziristan officially came under the Union Jack, the Wazirs and Mahsuds were given a British political agent. This man, Richard Isaac Bruce, had seen long and honorable service in Baluchistan and, like nearly all Baluchistan administrators, he was a disciple of the great Robert Sandeman, whose record of peaceful rule over Baluchi, Brahui and Marri tribes was held up as a model for the whole Empire. The Sandeman system worked not because Baluchistan tribes were in any way gentle folk—for sheer orneriness and bloodlust they gave the Pathans a close race—but simply because they obeyed their chiefs. It was a habit all but unthinkable to any self respecting Mohmand, Afridi, Orakzai, Wazir or Mahsud.

Owing to this law-abiding tendency, the British under Sandeman had been able to penetrate Baluchistan with roads and strengthen their own arm with forts, at a time when no more than a token British presence could be said to have existed on the northwest frontier. By working through the chiefs, Sandeman and his subordinates, who were under the Bombay rather than the Punjab government, had succeeded in establishing an exemplary framework of law and order in Baluchistan. In some respects it was the ancestor of the system known as Indirect Rule, which came to be adopted in many parts of British Africa. And nothing on earth could have been less suited to the Pathans, particularly the Mahsud wolves of Waziristan.

Bruce thought otherwise. On taking up his post, he made it known that thenceforth, Pax Britannica in Waziristan would be upheld through the tribal maliks. The almost knee-jerk response to this fiat was expressed by a powerful Mahsud leader who told a British official: "Let it be field [war] and blow us all up with cannon, or make all eighteen thousand of us Nawabs!" On the heels of that challenge came the murder of a British Public Works Department official, followed shortly afterwards by the gunning down of five Indian Army sepoys. Bruce managed to smoke out the murderers and actually bring them to trial in full jirga, where they received long prison sentences. And hardly had the verdicts been handed down than three of the principal maliks involved in the trial had their throats cut, two others were terrorized out of the country and the remaining members made to understand that it was only a matter of time before their numbers came up as well.

Since this sort of thing was not done in Baluchistan, the Indian Government decided to put teeth into its presence with the permanent military occupation of a Waziristan hill town called Wana. Although this place actually lay outside Mahsud territory, it was nicely situated, at 4,500 feet above sea level, to dominate the tribe. But the tribe had its own ideas about that. Just before dawn on an autumn morning in 1894, 2,000 Mahsuds attacked Wana and slashed a bloody path through the streets and alleys to the very edge of the British lines. An Indian cavalry regiment finally scattered the tribesmen, but the damage had been done. At long last, a punitive expedition had to be mounted. It was led by Sir William Lockhart, who dealt as sternly with the Mahsuds as he would with the Afridis and Orakzais in the 1897–98 campaign. In fact, the swath of scorched earth that Lockhart's troops cut across Mahsud country may have had something to do with the fact that Waziristan almost miraculously stayed out of the 1897 rising. But the Mahsuds bided their time. As Curzon took office, they looked to their own leader.

The Mullah Powinda was a tall, well-muscled illiterate who conferred on himself the title of *Badshah-i-Taliban*, "King of Knowledge-Seekers," although the British preferred other sobriquets, such as "the Evil Genius of Waziristan" or Kitchener's label, the "Pestilential Priest." Evelyn Howell, a turn-of-the-century political agent in Mahsud country, was sometimes able to take a less emotional attitude toward the Mullah Powinda, even to pay him a backhanded compliment. "Given more malleable material to work upon than the Mahsuds," Howell once wrote, ". . . and a more fortunate setting in time and space, he might well have ranked with many who are accounted great men." But Howell also described the Mullah Powinda as "a sinister combination of priest and politician of style not unknown in medieval European history, whose intrigues were at the root of most of our troubles in the southern half of the Province from 1892 to the time of his death in 1913." An adversary, in short, not to be despised.

Among other things, the Mullah Powinda had instigated the attack on Wana, although he himself, according to a British journalist, had "remained unheroically in the rear, beating a drum, while his yelling accomplices rushed headlong in." This was a disservice to a very brave and resourceful leader. With the exception of the Swati Mad Mullah and one other man who would emerge three decades later, also in Waziristan, no other Pathan did as much to make the northwest frontier the worst liability of the British Empire.

It was all the more remarkable, therefore, that the tribes of Waziristan had not taken part in the 1897 uprising; but from 1898 onwards, the Mullah Powinda seemed bent on atoning for that dereliction. If the Mahsuds did not become the most dangerous men of the Frontier bad-lands it was not because they did not try. During the first two decades of the twentieth century, the hidey-holes of their jagged rock tenement-fortresses were the launching pads of endless harassment against the adjoining settled districts to the east. The Frontier historian C. Collin Davies—once also a Frontier army officer with the Gurkha Rifles—has likened the position of the Mahsuds' neighbors at this time to that of the early French settlers in Canada, "who always moved about in constant dread of the Iroquois tomahawks."

This was partly because the victims had no tomahawks of their own. Thanks to a masterwork of bureaucratic illogic called the Indian Arms Act, it was a criminal offense for the inhabitants of the settled districts to own weapons of any kind; a man could go to jail if he was found carrying a kitchen knife. But the act did not apply on the far side of the administrative border, giving rise to the belief that the Mahsud, as Davies puts it, "was a privileged person whom even the British wished to propitiate rather than offend."

That notion was reinforced by the impotence of local authority. Raids on villages, farms and caravans were usually so swift that the Mahsuds had vanished by the time the militia arrived on the scene. When border forces did overtake the marauders, they often found themselves outmatched: not only illegal arms channels but generous government allowances enabled the Mahsuds to buy modern breech-loading rifles with accuracy and firepower superior to the weapons carried by the official posses.

Nor was it only a matter of inadequate hardware. British officers commanding tribal militia and constabulary units could never be certain that their troops would exercise real force against their own flesh and blood. A district official in the region at this time wrote that over a period of two years, "not one Mahsud was ever killed or even wounded by the Border Military Police. . . . It was well known that no Border Military Police sepoy would shoot a Mahsud. He would fire, but be careful to miss."

Such noncooperation did not always stem from the bonds of kinship alone. According to Davies, "the police were useless from fear; rare were the occasions on which even notorious raiders were arrested." And on these rare occasions, the police never dared even to handcuff their prisoners.

Since the Mullah Powinda seldom lost an opportunity to humiliate his infidel rulers, Mahsud lawlessness was by no means confined to the civilian populace. Tribesmen regularly ambushed militia and police detachments on the march, robbed the mail, captured ration convoys, picked off sentries guarding wells, cut telegraph lines and then scattered repair crews with rifle fire. One war party launched a frontal assault on a militia fort and wiped out the garrison. A Border Military Police post was looted without interference, its sepoys having fled after their British commanding officer took a bullet between the eyes. The political agent at the district headquarters of Wana came within inches of being gunned down on the veranda of his own bungalow. Officers playing golf on Wana's nine-hole course were always preceded by armed patrols to flush out ambushes in the sand traps.

The first major countermeasure against the Mahsuds was taken in November 1900, when the tribe was fined a lakh of rupees (£10,000), the largest sum ever imposed as a penalty on the Frontier. The fine was to be paid within two weeks, but it was ignored. Government then moved to starve the Mahsuds into submission by placing them under military blockade. Within three weeks of the clampdown, the first installments had come in, and W. R. Merk, the Commissioner of the Dera Ismail Khan district adjoining Mahsud territory, reported to Curzon "a complete cessation of raids, robberies and thefts along borders." Three weeks later, the Mahsuds suddenly withheld payments as their rifles began drilling passageways through the blockade wall. By the autumn of 1901, a frustrated Merk had to tell Curzon that "a feeling of insecurity prevails

. . . and a growing belief that Government is unable to protect its subjects." So there was nothing for it but for Curzon to order the unthinkable: a punitive expedition.

It was not called that, nor, strictly speaking, was it a bona fide expedition. But it was punitive in every sense of the word. For nearly four months, Indian Army combat teams gave the Mahsuds a taste of their own medicine in a series of surprise strikes against tribal villages. By early March of 1902, having sustained upwards of 400 casualties, the Mahsuds submitted and paid the fine in full. Merk then sent Curzon another sanguine report, but having been burned once, he closed with the rider: "The native opinion on the border is definitely that the Mahsuds . . . cannot be reformed and induced to relinquish their old ingrained habits of murdering, raiding and thieving by anything short of permanent occupation of their country."

For more than two years, however, it seemed as if Merk had overestimated the Mahsuds as they settled into a state of almost drowsy tranquility and the Mullah Powinda became a model of obedience to the Raj. But an accommodating Mullah Powinda was a Mullah Powinda bearing gifts, and the gifts proved to be fragmentation bombs. The first went off in the early autumn of 1904, when the political agent of the district, one Captain Bowring, was murdered in his sleep by a sepoy of the South Waziristan Militia. Authorities recognized the killing for what it was—a political assassination engineered by the Mullah Powinda. But they seemed unprepared for the next explosion. Bowring's successor, Evelyn Howell, later wrote an account of what happened for fellow old boys of Cambridge's Emmanuel College. Some of it is worth repeating.

Howell took up his new post in January 1905, being received by a number of Mahsud leaders. They were "hawk-faced, trim-bearded, hard-bitten ruffians, but well-mannered and very pleasant-spoken. . . . I remember that as the two leading Mahsuds were shaking hands with me—let it not be forgotten that it was a Mahsud who had killed poor Bowring only a few months before—one of them, with a charming smile, remarked, 'We are so glad that a new Political Agent has come. For when there is no Political Agent, we are as orphans!' However, they seemed to bear their affliction lightly."

Howell, of course, felt more at home among fellow-Britons in the officers' mess at Wana, especially when the Emmanuel College lion on his dinner jacket was recognized by another Cantabridgian, Lieutenant Colonel Richard Harman, the commandant of the South Waziristan Militia. And the club atmosphere could not have been more convivial on the night of February 11, 1905.

Only four of us came to dinner that night. . . . The three military officers at mess were in uniform. I was in mufti. . . . We were all unarmed in accordance with our policy of confidence. The meal pursued its normal pleasant course and we were just approaching dessert, with the accompanying ritual customary in all messes on Saturday nights, when suddenly there was a sharp tinkle of broken glass. . . . I looked up at the sound and saw standing in the doorway a young Sepoy of the Militia, in uniform. . . . In his hands was his rifle with the bayonet fixed and the muzzle sloped upwards. . . . There floated through my mind a recollection of what someone had told me of a recruit who came into the mess ante-room one evening and explained, on enquiry, that he had come to see the tamasha (show). I thought that this lad was the victim of some similar hoax.

It was no hoax. But there was a victim.

As I stood by the table the man lowered his rifle barrel, but did not raise the butt to the shoulder. . . . The next thing I saw was Harman dashing round the foot of the table towards the man. . . . Simultaneously the man stepped backwards into the comparative darkness of the pantry. . . . I saw Plant struggling with the Sepoy for the rifle and Harman standing by the opposite wall. Turner and I rushed to Plant's assistance. The Sepoy was quickly over-powered and disarmed and we began to truss him up hand and foot with his own turban. . . . Harman called out, "Is any one hurt?" I looked round at the others and answered, "No; are you, Colonel?" He said, "I think I am," and while speaking slowly collapsed on his knees and sank to the ground. . . . The doctor came across at once in his dressing-gown and knelt down by Harman. Just as he did so Harman spoke again, for the last time, "they've got me," he said, "I knew they would." . . . The doctor then made a further examination and found that life was extinct. Harman had received a bayonet wound right through the heart.

The trouble had only begun. The sepoy was a member of a Mahsud detachment then on duty in the Wana fort's keep, and it was decided that these troops must be disarmed at once. With several officers, Howell approached the keep, "thinking my evening dress, especially the pumps on my feet, a very unsuitable costume." The sepoys were then ordered to come out and stack their weapons, "but, for what seemed a long time, nothing happened. . . . It might very well have been a trap. . . . I have never liked anything less in my life. . . . Then to my enormous relief the men began to file out . . . [They] formed up in two lines [and] laid their rifles down in the snow."

As Political Agent, Howell had the responsibility of trying the sepoy who had killed Harman. Following a quick guilty verdict, the man was hanged, although he "met his death in a resolute spirit. Indeed he was exultant and spent his last half-hour in the cell blackening his eyelids with collyrium, as young bucks do among the Mahsuds, to adorn himself for the Houris of Paradise."

But the trial had not been conducted too hastily for certain facts to emerge. The murderer, it transpired, had been "a mere tool" of the Mullah Powinda and was part of "an elaborate plot. . . He went into the mess

. . . expecting to shoot and the sound of shooting there was the signal for which his fellow-conspirators in the keep were waiting. They were at once to have attacked the quarter-guard, seized the magazine and treasure, and having killed all the British officers and let pandemonium loose . . . turn the resultant situation to the best advantage."

Yet even though the plan had miscarried, the situation remained tense, for "we could not know . . . what effect our drastic action would have on the local political situation—how the Mahsuds would stomach the affront. . . . It seemed quite on the cards that we should find ourselves, with greatly depleted strength everywhere besieged by swarms of infuriated tribesmen."

That this did not happen was due only to a call for reinforcements and the swift arrival at Wana of a regular Indian Army battalion. And, despite the Mullah Powinda's obvious role as mastermind of the entire conspiracy, the evidence against him was not considered legally admissible. Besides which, wrote Howell, "Lord Curzon . . . did not think the occasion opportune to break openly with the Mulla Powinda—which would have meant yet another Mahsud expedition."

So the Pestilential Priest continued to keep the district aflame. Another officer was murdered at the Mullah Powinda's instigation several months later. Howell became an almost perpetual target for Mahsud snipers; although they always missed him, they did manage to pick off his bearer and an Indian clerk, taking time out to vivisect the latter. Transborder guerrilla raids were also stepped up, to the point that by 1908, further military reprisals had to be ordered. Again they were not quite punitive expeditions, but they served the same purpose with the capture of nearly 400 Mahsuds and more than 1,800 of the tribe's sheep and goats. In 1910, when the Mullah Powinda failed to sabotage a jirga called by the political agent, many officials saw this as a sign that the Mahsud leader was losing his clout. In 1913, he died, and a great sigh of relief went up from the British on the Frontier.

It was wasted breath. The Mullah Powinda had dictated a farewell letter to be read to the whole Mahsud people at his funeral. The letter exhorted them to intensify their resistance to the Raj. The manner in which they obeyed over the years was to speak volumes about the effectiveness of the Curzon reforms on the far side of the administrative border.

Waziristan was not the only part of the Frontier where Curzon's policy found hard sledding. Across the length of the Khyber Pass—indeed, as far east as Peshawar itself—the first decade of the twentieth century became known to Frontier soldiers and administrators as the period of "weekend wars." The label understated the duration but not the intensity of what in fact was a seemingly endless continuation of the 1897 uprising.

A single Afridi clan was responsible for the state of emergency. In 1898, the maliks of the entire Afridi nation had placed their marks on the British terms of submission that ended the uprising, and the Afridis subsequently honored the pledge with a good faith that was only less gratifying that it was surprising. This did not apply, however, to the Zakka Khel clan. That group had been the last to cave in under Lockhart's guns, and it became the first to go back on the warpath. In the Zakka Khel view, the 1897 revolt had never really ended, and the clan was determined to revive it. Zakka Khels felt confident that continual raids and atrocities would throw the neighboring settled areas into such turmoil that the British would eventually be forced to retaliate. This in turn, it was hoped, would drive the other Afridi clans into the Zakka Khel camp, thereby setting an example of defiance that might well be emulated by more Pathan nations. It was a bold and ambitious strategy, and it almost worked.

Like the Mahsuds, the Zakka Khels were inadvertently aided and abetted by the British. Thanks to the Indian Arms Act, villagers in the settled districts chose submission or flight as the better part of dismemberment when the raiders began a long series of strikes in 1904. Tribal militia and constabulary were not much of a deterrent. Most Zakka Khel forays were launched beyond the reach of the Khyber Rifles—in districts guarded by the Border Military Police, who seemed under the ban of the Indian Arms Act themselves. Their thirty-eight-year-old Snider rifles proved not much better than water pistols against the brigands' Martini-Henrys and Lee-Metfords.

Almost as antiquated were the police and militia sepoys themselves; at least twenty-five percent of them had reached retirement age a decade earlier. Corruption and minimal incentives further reduced Government combat effectiveness. Native officers and NCOs in border constabulary forces were often promoted not on merit but because they had land-owning relatives, while the ordinary sepoy received so little pay that he found it hardly worth his while to go into action. The Zakka Khels could have been forgiven if they thought Government had issued them a license to raid.

Interestingly, the stiffest opposition to the Zakka Khels came from other Afridi clans, whose leaders had tired of war and genuinely wished to fulfill their engagements to the British. More than once, lashkars marched into the Zakka Khel home in the Bazar Valley of Tirah to carry out their own punitive campaigns against the outlaw clan. Fortified rifle towers were sometimes pulled to the ground. Whole tribal villages were burned. One band of raiders was actually expelled from the Bazar Valley. But such measures left no lasting impression on the largest, strongest and meanest of all the Afridi peoples. The Zakka Khels always re-formed and rallied to the exhortations of their own Mullah Powinda, one Khawas Khan, who held what could almost have been called a hypnotic influence over his people. At least, they did not seem to mind that some years earlier he had bilked them out of 50,000 rupees in Government allowances.

And if Afridi maliks failed to discourage the Zakka Khels, the very audacity of Zakka Khel aggression presently began to win the admiration of a growing number of unreconstructed tribesmen in the more peaceable clans. One act of particular cheek was not only typical but crucial.

In 1907, the jirgas of all the Afridi clans gathered at Landi Kotal in the Khyber Pass to receive their annual Government allowances. All clans, that was, but the Zakka Khels, who had long been labeled renegades and had thus forfeited any payments. So Roos-Keppel, then the Khyber Political Agent, could do little more than gape when the gates of the fort were swung open to admit an uninvited Zakka Khel delegation. Exploiting the conditions of unwritten truce and the element of momentary astonishment, Khawas Khan strode directly up to Roos-Keppel and thrust a paper into his hands. What Roos-Keppel read, among other things, was a demand that fines no longer be deducted from the allowances of any clans, and a pronouncement that thenceforth, the Zakka Khels would neither surrender prisoners nor interfere with raiders from other clans who passed through the Bazar Valley. The latter clause, of course, was redundant.

Before Roos-Keppel could collect his wits, the Zakka Khel jirga marched out of the fort and vanished into the hills. Khawas Khan had delivered what amounted to a declaration of independence.

And by way of putting teeth into their manifesto, the Zakka Khels then sent a party of raiders into Peshawar to kidnap an assistant commissioner. Although they failed to bring it off, the kidnappers themselves evaded capture easily, and the very fact that the attempt had even been made reflected an almost majestic insolence. To make certain, moreover, that this defiance would not go ignored, the Zakka Khels added injury to insult. In January 1908, a commando of eighty clansmen in stolen police uniforms entered Peshawar, broke down the door of a Hindu banker's home and walked off with a lakh of rupees.

That was the last straw. As thousands of Peshawar Hindus demonstrated angrily outside the Chief Commissioner's headquarters, the realization began to take hold among the British that the Zakka Khel fire had to be stamped out if it was not to spread. Already, said Roos-Keppel, the outlaws were being looked on as "the crusaders of the nation; they depart [on raids] with the good wishes and prayers of all, and are received on their return . . . with universal rejoicings and congratulations." It seemed perhaps only a matter of time before other Afridi clans began copying the Zakka Khels. Nor might a rising necessarily be confined to Afridis alone. By now, reports were coming in of growing unrest among the Mohmands and Orakzais who flanked the Khyber on the north and south. And how long might it be before alerts were sounded from the Malakand and Waziristan?

So at last the gloves came off as the British mounted a full-scale punitive expedition. It was short, swift and sure. Within two weeks, an Indian Army force under Major General Sir James Willcocks had so thoroughly chewed up the Bazar Valley with its mountain guns that the Zakka Khels staggered under casualties higher than those sustained by the entire Afridi nation during the five months of the Tirah campaign. At the end of February 1908, Zakka Khel headmen surrendered unconditionally and the Indian Government secured a willing pledge from the other Afridi jirgas to hold the delinquent clan on a short leash in the future. The Zakka Khel capitulation also had the effect of quashing other tribal ideas of concerted uprising. Order had once more gained the upper hand on the Frontier.

But the British had prevailed only by naked force. Curzon's reforms had nothing to do with it.

Probably the main reason for Mahsud and Zakka Khel Afridi successes during Curzon's "peaceful" administration was a quantum leap in the buildup of the Pathan arsenal. This development was largely the fruit of an illegal arms industry. It was so extensive and so uncontrolled that for several years, Frontier militia and constabulary forces, sometimes even regular Indian Army units, were literally outgunned by the tribes.

The gradual replacement of collector's item jezails—at first with British muskets, later with rapid-fire breech-loaders—had actually been in progress ever since the British first came to the Frontier. Whenever an action was fought with the tribes, a few rifles would usually be captured, but more were stolen. Parties of Pathan cat burglars made a regular practice of slipping past sentry lines into British bivouacs at night and gathering up as many as a dozen or more Sniders, Martini-Henrys or Lee-Metfords—sometimes from between the legs of sleeping soldiers. Barracks, guardhouses and arms depots in the settled areas yielded up larger hauls; rifles lifted from these places were often packed into coffins and carried across the administrative border on oxcarts or even in railway goods wagons. At the turn of the century, Warburton wrote that "the audacity with which thieves in the Peshawar Valley broke into cantonments and carried off property, chiefly rifles, baffles all description. This applies not only to the old days of our occupation but to very recent dates." It went farther than that; as late as the outbreak of the Second World War, the British had found no effective way to halt Pathan rifle theft.

Not long after the 1897 uprising, the tribal arms depot grew even bigger with the emergence of the Pathan rifle "factory," which turned out near-perfect copies of standard British Army rifles and pistols. Using primitive hand-operated machine tools, trans-Indus gunsmiths became highly skilled in fashioning bolts, rifling barrels and turning stocks. The finished products even carried British factory trade marks and the Army's official "V.R." or "E.R." stamping. There were several such "arms plants," the most important owned and operated by the Adam Khel Afridis near the Kohat Pass south of Peshawar.* All violated the Indian Arms Act. All were allowed to remain open. Government signed political "conventions" with the Adam Khels and other rifle-making clans, whereby safe passage on certain major Frontier roads was guaranteed in return for noninterference with manufacture. It was simple blackmail.

The British sought to rationalize their policy with the arguments that rifle manufacture might reduce rifle theft, and that it was safer for the tribes to have inferior weapons. The latter point at least made some sense, for the Pathan copies were far less reliable and durable than the real thing. Rifling tended to erode after a few hundred rounds, bolts often jammed, sights could be very inaccurate. Even so, the counterfeits were in great demand. A Kohat Pass Martini-Henry could fetch at least 100 rupees—about $33—an astronomical sum among Pathans, and the Adam Khels became the richest clan on the Frontier. Yet the price was not considered exorbitant among tribesmen receiving Government allowances. There is no way of knowing how many of these weapons were sold, but the total may have run well into five figures.

Theft and manufacture, however, were a drop in the bucket alongside the main source of Pathan arms supply: gun-running from the Persian Gulf. This industry was a combined effort of shrewd tribesmen, less scrupulous French and German arms dealers and quasi-piratical shipowners. Bulk weapons cargoes, offloaded from tramp steamers at the Arabian port of Muscat, were transferred to dhows and other small craft for the short run across the Persian Gulf or Gulf of Oman to any number of secret landing places on the desolate coastlines of Persia and southern Baluchistan. Concealed in sun-whipped moonscapes of baking boulders, Pathan caravans waited to take the arms on the final stage of their journey to the Frontier. When gun-running began, in the last year or so of the nineteenth century, its volume was little more than a trickle, but in less than five years the tribesmen had what amounted to a rifle conveyor belt.

Arms smuggling wrought a revolution in the hills. During the 1897-1898 Tirah campaign, the British estimated that one Afridi in ten owned a Martini-Henry; a decade later, one Afridi in ten did not, and the proportion was roughly the same elsewhere on the Frontier. By 1910, some tribesmen were even trading in their Martini-Henrys and Lee-Metfords

* One or two continue in business today.

for the brand-new .303 caliber Enfield, which had been made the standard infantry weapon of the British—but not yet the Indian—Army. The river of rifles became so large that the Adam Khels eventually closed down their factories and sank all their capital into gun-running caravans.

The British seemed helpless to halt the traffic. Vainly, they sought French agreement to the abrogation of treaties that permitted Muscat dhow skippers to fly the French flag, thus protecting them from search and seizure by the Royal Navy. Equally ineffective were military expeditions to southern Baluchistan, which only diverted the caravan stream into more westerly channels through Afghan and even Persian territory. After 1907, it was a rare year that did not see at least 15,000 or even 20,000 rifles arriving in the trans-Indus hills. One of the biggest, and most baffling, hauls at this time was a shipment of 30,000 Martini-Henrys that had been discarded by the Australian and New Zealand armies. "It boots not," the British journalist Arnold Keppel commented drily, "to inquire into the Homeric wanderings of these rifles from the date of their departure from the Antipodes and the date when the first of them reached . . . the North-West Frontier."

Late in 1909, the Indian Government finally called for help. There was nothing for it but to bring in the Royal Navy and carry out a simple exercise in gunboat diplomacy by sealing off the main rifle entrepot at Muscat with a blockade.

It worked. Within six months, more than 200,000 rifles and at least 3 million rounds of ammunition were coated with dust and crawling with scorpions as they lay undelivered in Muscat godowns. The price of rifles on the Frontier climbed almost overnight from 130 to 500 rupees, and the tribesmen fumed. The Adam Khels actually demanded compensation from the Indian Government for their losses; when this was refused, the clan went into a tantrum, carrying out several raids into the Peshawar district and robbing the mail in the Kohat Pass. But the British could still congratulate themselves: the rifle cornucopia had dried up. It would never flow again.

Government had also locked the barn door at least ten years after the horse had been stolen. In 1910, it was acknowledged that the weapons of Frontier militia and constabulary forces were dangerously inferior to those in the tribal arsenal. At the turn of the century, large Pathan raiding bands had often been dispersed by British and Indian patrols little more than a dozen strong; now, detachments of up to five or even ten times that number were sometimes needed to cope with even smaller tribal parties. A swift rearming of the Frontier forces was set in motion, and by 1914, the tribes no longer held the upper hand. But they still had a very modern and very formidable weaponry. It could and would be used when the proper time came.

That time, moreover, might well be determined by the Amir of Afghanistan. Even with the Russian threat removed, Afghanistan remained a limpet bomb clinging to the northwestern wall of India. If Britain thought of Afghanistan as her private sphere of influence, the Amir for his part continued to look on the northwest frontier as de facto Afghan territory. And in 1914, he was also continuing to smart from an affront. By neglecting to seek his views in any meaningful fashion on the Anglo-Russian détente of 1907, Britain had made it abundantly clear that she still considered the descendants of Ahmad Shah Durranī to be no more than the crowned office boys of the Viceroy of India. There was every reason why the Amir should keep an eye open for some sort of crisis in India, an opportune moment at which he might, at the very least, cause inconvenience to the Raj. Not inconceivably, such a moment might even give him the chance to reassert his sovereignty over the land and peoples that had been made part of the British Empire only by the drawing of an artificial line on a map.

With the outbreak of the First World War, that day of reckoning seemed at hand.

28

The Saber-Toothed Poodle

WHEN CURZON was campaigning for Salisbury's endorsement of his candidacy for the viceroyalty, he had been at pains to remind the Prime Minister of one of his strongest qualifications: the unique friendship he could claim with Abdur Rahman. Curzon added that he would be the right man to have in Calcutta in case Abdur Rahman did not live forever: "Trouble again must come when the Amir dies: it comes often enough while he lives. . . . [But] I also know Habibulla, his successor. I think that while the father lives I could get on well with him, and that should he die while I was out there, there might be a little less chance of trouble with his successor."

This prediction was neither more nor less accurate than could have been expected in the circumstances. In 1901, the old torturer-statesman died.* While it was a tribute to the cast-iron clout he had wielded that his eldest son Habibullah became the first amir to succeed to the throne without the interference or aid of a palace coup—or in the throes of an invasion—the succession itself did not necessarily signal a betterment of Anglo-Afghan relations. Like Abdur Rahman, the new Amir was equally at home in the role of Britain's friend and Britain's foe. For thirteen years, nobody could be certain which was the real Habibullah.

* According to Frank Martin, "it was said that his feet were dead a few days before, and the stench from them was such that no one could stop long in the same room with him."

Primogeniture never meant much in Afghanistan. Habibullah succeeded Abdur Rahman not because he was the Amir's eldest son but because he was the Amir's favorite son and always had been. Whenever Abdur Rahman had to be absent from Kabul, he had made a point of leaving Habibullah in charge, even while the Prince was barely old enough to walk. "He was only a little boy," wrote Abdur Rahman of Habibullah's first temporary stewardship, "yet he did a great thing in going among the soldiers and speaking in my behalf to the chiefs; he was neither nervous nor afraid." During Abdur Rahman's two-year campaign in Afghan Turkestan against his insurgent cousin Ishak Khan, Habibullah had to put down a concurrent uprising in Kabul. According to Abdur Rahman, Habibullah had "acted most bravely on this occasion, riding alone into the midst of the rebellious soldiers without showing any fear of their injuring him." More than anything else, it may have been Habibullah's icy courage that won him Abdur Rahman's favor.

Physically, Habibullah was a sort of Abdur Rahman in miniature: a bulky, five-foot six-inch, bearded medicine ball. Like his father, he knew how to make the most of his leisure time. He had one of the biggest harems in the recorded history of the Orient and was said to have begat at least 200 princes and princesses. Other hobbies included cooking— a popular pastime among male Afghans—tennis and cricket. One of Afghanistan's first photography buffs, he was the proud owner of a stereopticon and several thousand slides; when a British friend gave him a movie projector, he held a special show for the royal household, charging ten rupees per seat. Habibullah also shared with Abdur Rahman a passion for machinery of all kinds and was even more familiar with combustion engines than his father, although that may not have been much to brag about.

There were differences, to be sure. In public, Habibullah was an ice cube —stiffly formal, incapable of unbending, totally without Abdur Rahman's thundering merriment or paralyzing rages. By Afghan standards of the time, he was also a progressive, and Abdur Rahman might have spun in his grave when his son created Afghanistan's first parliament. As legislatures went, it was something less than representative or even deliberative, consisting of thirty hand-picked department heads who had very little voice and no vote. Yet one finds it hard to imagine Abdur Rahman taking even so faltering a step toward democratic institutions.

On Afghanistan's most burning political issue, however—the disgrace of forced alliance with Britain—father and son might have been identical twins. Habibullah yielded nothing to Abdur Rahman in his belief that India's northwest frontier and its Pathan tribes were Afghan soil and Afghan people stolen by a British thimblerig. And possibly even more than his father, he could not look on his country as a sovereign state in any meaningful sense so long as its foreign policy was dictated by the

British Foreign Office and the Viceroy of India. He lost no time in making this position clear when, shortly after his accession, he courteously but firmly declined Curzon's invitation to visit India. Sending his regrets was tantamount to disobeying orders.

Habibullah's views on the British, however, were by no means one-dimensional, and other influences guided his conduct toward the Indian Government. As it happened, he admired the British way of life and numbered many Britons among his personal friends. Moreover, while he might have felt that Abdur Rahman's concessions to the Raj had been extorted, he was nonetheless a man of honor and tried hard to respect the treaties, even though he did not always try hard enough. Above all, he had the sense to recognize real advantages in staying in the good graces of a powerful neighbor, and the risks of trying that neighbor's patience too far.

Thus in 1904, when Curzon sought again to bring him into line, Habibullah did not object to the visit to Afghanistan of a British diplomatic mission headed by Sir Louis Dane, the Deputy Commissioner of Peshawar. While Dane's party was in Kabul, Habibullah even signed a treaty reaffirming earlier agreements reached with Abdur Rahman. And in 1907, without even being asked, he paid a personal call on Curzon's successor, Lord Minto, in Simla.

The summit meeting went off to everyone's satisfaction. Minto brought a great deal of personal charm to bear on his royal guest, who in turn was duly impressed by the Indian Government's customary red-carpet deference to Afghan monarchs. The walls of Simla's Viceregal Lodge all but reverberated with Habibullah's professions of goodwill. "At no time," he told Minto, "will Afghanistan pass from the friendship of India. So long as the Indian Empire desires to keep her friendship, so long will Afghanistan and Britain remain friends."

And as the years went by, the British found ample reason to think of these words as diplomatic moonshine.

It was not that Habibullah took pleasure from treading the thin ice of increasingly strained relations with the British. It was simply that he was first and foremost an Afghan patriot. Despite the climate of harmony that had prevailed at Simla, Habibullah soon came to feel a mounting and burning resentment over the British Government's refusal to allow him an equal role in the negotiations with Russia that culminated in the St. Petersburg Convention—in the same year that Habibullah visited Minto. The Amir, of course, had been kept informed of developments, but that was all. With good cause, Habibullah fumed over this cavalier treatment. Satellite or not, Afghanistan was a sovereign nation. Its monarch had the right to expect something more from an ally than reports on diplomatic conferences in which the monarch himself should have participated.

And even if Habibullah had been content to accept his role as the

Viceroy's poodle—and he was not—he could never have disregarded the almost incalculable influence wielded by Afghanistan's so-called Anti-British Party. Had he opposed this faction, his reign would have been short.

Afghanistan's extremists—which was to say at least ninety-nine percent of the population—rallied around three leaders. The principal figure, perhaps not surprisingly, was Habibullah's younger brother Nasrullah, who had not forgotten Britain's rebuff during his visit to London in 1895. Nasrullah was almost certifiable in his Anglophobia; many Afghans would have preferred him as amir. The party's ideologue, one Mahmud Tarzi, enjoyed a well-deserved reputation as a satirist. Exiled by Abdur Rahman, who feared his barbs, Mahmud Tarzi had lived for some years in Turkey, where he had been converted to the modern ideas and revolutionary politics of Mustapha Kemal's "Young Turks." He returned to Afghanistan at Habibullah's invitation and, with the Amir's blessing, founded the country's first newspaper, which was really not so much a news organ as an anti-British propaganda sheet. Mahmud Tarzi also exercised an almost hypnotic influence over the third member of the triumvirate, Habibullah's own son Amanullah, who became Afghanistan's foremost champion of modernization after marrying Mahmud Tarzi's Western-educated daughter Souraya. Amanullah also absorbed his father-in-law's militant nationalism like a sponge. It was hard to say which of the three men was more rabid in his loathing of anything and everything British.

One of this trio's priority objectives was to stir up border unrest by fomenting acts of terrorism among the Pathans on the British side of the Durand Line. Tribal mullahs regularly went to Kabul to ask for, and get, aid from the three men. Among Nasrullah's guests was the Mullah Powinda, who received funds and the guarantee of a Mahsud sanctuary in Afghanistan. Another visitor was the Mullah Powinda's Zakka Khel Afridi counterpart Khawas Khan; thanks to his representations, Nasrullah paid generous allowances to the Zakka Khels and, in 1907, arranged to expedite a large illegal arms shipment that enabled the clan to step up its assaults across the administrative border. Without this kind of material assistance and moral support, Frontier insurgency would probably have been far less troublesome to the British during Habibullah's reign.

That is, had Habibullah himself taken steps to discourage such intrigues. But Habibullah was very much party to them, either for patriotic reasons or to pacify the extremist trio or both. The Indian Government believed him personally responsible for the activities of the so-called Hazarnao Gang, a band of Afghan guerrillas who often backed up Zakka Khel raids by filtering through the Khyber Pass and carrying out strikes of their own in the Peshawar area. He also allowed his country to become an official hideout. According to a British report, Zakka Khel kidnappers made a practice of taking their captives into Afghan territory, "where, under the patronage of the local Afghan Governor, who shares their profits, they can hold British subjects to ransom for many months."

And in the controversial Durand Line, Habibullah had an instrument of unrest on which he played with the skill of a concert violinist. In particular, the country of the Mohmands just north of the Khyber offered him limitless opportunity for mischief. Not only did the Durand Line literally split the Mohmands in half as a tribal nation, but the line's precise location in this area had never been completely ascertained. Minto could not have been overly surprised when Habibullah refused to cooperate in a clearer demarcation of the border. As things stood, Habibullah was actually able to allow one of his frontier governors to order several punitive expeditions into British territory, on the pretext that the Afghan troops were simply dealing with unruly Afghan subjects.

Thus it was that in 1911 the journalist Arnold Keppel could write: "Many would say that [Habibullah is] honestly anxious to fulfil his treaty obligations with the British, but that he [has been] debarred from doing so in an open manner through fear of the loss of influence with his subjects." But Keppel also had to hedge: "A smaller number would tell you that this [is] merely a pretext for a more far-seeing policy which aims at the complete independence of the Afghan kingdom. . . . Many circumstances point to the idea that the Amir is contemplating a coup of some sort in the near future."

Grudgingly loyal but helpless ally? Sworn enemy of the Raj? Perhaps Habibullah himself did not know, any more than did the British. Three years later, both Habibullah and the British would find out.

On August 8, 1914, Habibullah received a telegram from Minto's successor, Lord Hardinge, informing him that Britain had gone to war with Germany. Habibullah replied at once, thanking the Viceroy for keeping him advised, and adding that Afghanistan "will, please God, remain neutral. . . . Your Excellency may rest assured in this respect."

If Habibullah had declared war on Germany he would not have demonstrated more forcibly and convincingly his policy toward the British. Had he chosen to make himself a national hero by joining the Central Powers, or even by voicing sympathy for the German cause, he would have forced Britain to tie up most of the Indian Army—desperately needed in Europe—on sentry duty along the northwest frontier. By proclaiming his country's neutrality, he automatically freed nearly one million crack Empire troops for service on the Western Front. At long last, Habibullah had shown his true colors.

His countrymen thought so too; they now saw him as an Afghan Quisling. To the overwhelming majority of the Afghan people, the outbreak of hostilities in Europe was a heaven-sent opportunity to strike a blow at England. The war even took on the character of a jihad when Turkey's Sultan Muhammad V entered the lists on the German side. To hang back from the struggle joined by the Caliph of Islam himself was a dereliction bordering on heresy. Worse, it was a betrayal of national aspirations. Afghanistan's siding with Germany would mean Afghanistan's real independence from Britain, a final scrapping of the shameful treaties that had been forced on her almost at gunpoint. By failing to take up arms against the infidel oppressor, Habibullah had all but committed treason. It was a small miracle that Afghanistan's militant clique did not have him assassinated instantly.

But for four years, Habibullah stood alone against the nation. He became estranged from his son Amanullah and was barely on speaking terms with the rest of his family. There were continual shouting contests in the royal palace; Habibullah once stalked from the throne room in a cold fury when Nasrullah told him he must disregard the will of Allah and abide by the wishes of the people. In 1915, a rebellious group of Indian Muslims calling themselves the Army of God visited Kabul to urge war on Britain. Labeling Habibullah "a religious traitor," they were welcomed warmly by Nasrullah and Amanullah, who allowed them to establish an Indian government-in-exile. Habibullah had them thrown into prison. Mahmud Tarzi's press attacks on the British became so venomous that Habibullah had several issues of the newspaper confiscated and once threatened to kill Mahmud Tarzi with his own hand.

Sometimes he had to yield, or seem to. By 1916, public opinion against the British had become inflamed to the point that Habibullah agreed to receive a German-Turkish diplomatic mission. The delegates got him to sign a treaty and even to declare war on Britain. They also accepted several of Habibullah's own conditions, including a £10 million gift and the dispatch of 100,000 Turkish troops to Afghanistan, terms so unrealistic that the Amir's signatures on the treaty and war declaration might just as well have been forgeries. He also reassured the British Agent in Kabul by informing him that "I am not a double-dealer."

In his cheerless isolation, Habibullah probably found solace in the infrequent words of encouragement he received from his allies. One such message read: "I have been much gratified to learn . . . how scrupulously and honourably you have maintained the attitude of strict neutrality which you guaranteed. You will thus still further strengthen the friendship I so greatly value." So wrote King George V from Buckingham Palace.

One wonders how King George might have viewed that friendship had he known of Habibullah's long-range intentions. While honoring his treaty obligations to Britain, he remained no less determined than Nasrullah, Amanullah and Mahmud Tarzi to gain Afghanistan's independence by junking the earlier agreements that denied him a voice in his own country's foreign policy. But he meant to reach that goal peacefully and legally, and, in fact, Afganistan's nonbelligerence was the major element in his strategy. "It is I," he said, "who have caused India to be swept away of its armies to be able to fight in France, in Europe and in Egypt." —and he knew that so important a contribution to the Allied war effort would not go unrewarded. As the war drew to a close and Habibullah's position became clearer, so too did the Afghan people begin to wonder if he was all that much of a leper. There were even those who thought him an Afghan hero.

But toward the end of 1918, when Habibullah submitted a request to the new Viceroy, Lord Chelmsford, that Afghanistan be represented at the Versailles Peace Conference, he found his allies less appreciative of his loyalty than he had expected. "The demand is, of course, preposterous," minuted Chelmsford.

Naturally, Chelmsford did not say this to Habibullah, but the courteous diplomatic gibberish of the British reply amounted to the same thing. Habibullah therefore took a stronger tone. Early in February 1919, he wrote Chelmsford to ask for "a written agreement recognizing the absolute liberty, freedom of action and perpetual independence of the Sublime Government of Afghanistan." If this were not forthcoming, he said, Britain's ingratitude would be aired before the world at Versailles by an uninvited Afghan delegation, which would also "obtain, God willing, a written agreement according to their own desire under the signature of the Peace makers there."

While Britain pondered that challenge, Habibullah took a few days off to rest and hunt near Jalalabad. On the night of February 19, while he slept in the royal camp, someone entered his tent and blew off the top of his head with a rifle. The perpetrator was never discovered.

Events now began to move swiftly. One of the first to learn of the assassination was Nasrullah, who by coincidence had accompanied Habibullah on the trip, and who lost no time in having himself proclaimed amir. He was challenged at once by Amanullah, who happened to be in Kabul, where the power was. Within two weeks, Nasrullah had been charged with Habibullah's murder and had abdicated in favor of Amanullah, who then sentenced his uncle to life imprisonment. The assumption of innocence before proof of guilt was a prohibitive indulgence in Afghanistan.

The new Amir was twenty-seven years old, a chubby fellow of pleasant countenance and engaging manner who played a first-rate game of tennis. He considered himself a man of the people and made a practice of disguising himself in shabby robes so that he could listen unobserved to conversations in teashops and thus learn his subjects' true thoughts and wishes. As a prince, he had won enormous popularity, not only for his militant Anglophobia but because he had often gone behind his father's back to free prisoners who had been sentenced by royal edict. On taking the throne, however, Amanullah found his position none too secure. Habibullah had become a martyr, and many Afghans suspected his son of complicity in the murder, at the very least. Kabul was tense. Other claimants to the succession began mushrooming. Amanullah would have been greatly relieved by any sort of development that might focus public attention elsewhere.

In April, the British unwittingly created that diversion.

At this time, India seethed in a state of unrest even more highly charged than Afghanistan's, owing mainly to postwar Government legislation curtailing the civil liberties of a people who had spilled millions of gallons of blood for the Empire. The noisiest expressions of protest centered on the Punjab, particularly in the city of Amritsar, where a Gurkha force under Brigadier General Reginald Dyer was sent early in April to maintain order. Dyer knew how to deal with "natives." On April 13, as thousands of townspeople observed a Hindu holy day in defiance of a Government order banning public assembly, the Gurkhas advanced on the center of the multitude and Dyer ordered them to open fire. Ten minutes later, the smoke lifted on 379 corpses. At least 1,200 other men and women lay wounded and twisting on the ground. Thousands more were given the choice of being flogged or crawling through the streets on hands and knees. The outrage shocked the world and would shortly end Dyer's career. It also marked the beginning of Gandhi's rise to power and the beginning of the end of British rule in India.

And Amritsar was a gift on a silver platter for Amanullah. It mattered little to him that few of Dyer's victims had been Muslims; British tyranny, after all, was British tyranny, and the new Amir needed something to secure his own position. Summoning a special jirga, he wept as he called for jihad against England. "Gird up your loins," he told the members. "The time has come!"

Public response may have exceeded his expectations. A cordon of troops had to be thrown round the house of the British Agent in Kabul to protect it from rock-throwing students, who also hurled anachronistic imprecations at Queen Victoria and the East India Company. Proclamations urging holy war were posted in mosques across the country. Mullahs went into the Frontier hills to arouse the Pathan tribes. On their heels, at Amanullah's orders, marched the Afghan Army.

And Amanullah himself began to grow uneasy.

For he had not the slightest wish to go to war. His call to arms, the street rallies, even the mass troop movement were all part of a bluff on the grand scale, a stab at wringing concessions from a Britain sick unto death of war, however puny the antagonist. But Amanullah was not long in perceiving that by throwing down the gauntlet on the

Frontier he might have carried his bluff too far. For all his impassioned waving of the bloody shirt, he was an intelligent young man, and he knew that Britain was not going to cave in when one of the Empire's most sensitive nerve-ends came under threat.

Quite the reverse, in fact. Amanullah must have wished he had a more reliable army, but he had no such thing. He had only just promised the troops an increase in pay, but was not sure that he could raise the money. And even if he could have, he knew that Afghanistan's badly trained, shabbily equipped forces would be no match for the modern weapons and tactical skills of an Indian Army hardened by four years on the Western Front—even though that army's ranks were shrinking daily with demobilization. Clearly, war had to be ruled out.

It was easier said than done, however, for the Afghan people would not applaud an ignominious retreat, and Amanullah himself could ill afford a loss of public support while the foundations of his rule remained unstable. The best he could do at this juncture was simply hold the army on its own side of the Durand Line and wait for some chance to withdraw gracefully.

He was to have that chance and not take it.

One of the uncertain sections of the Durand Line was a shabby patch of cultivation called Bagh (garden) lying in the Khyber Pass just west of Landi Kotal. Neither India nor Afghanistan occupied Bagh, but both claimed the place, since it was situated on high ground and its proximity to Landi Kotal gave it a certain tactical value. On May 1, Afghan Army scouts observed a British officer and four sepoys making what seemed to be a reconnaissance of Bagh. Instead of disregarding what was probably no more than a routine patrol, Amanullah inexplicably became agitated over what he called an "encroachment of our boundary," and ordered that countermeasures be taken.

The order was obeyed by General Saleh Muhammad, the Commander-in-Chief of the Afghan Army, who also had field command of Amanullah's forces in the Khyber sector. Saleh informed Abdul Qayyum, the British Political Agent at Landi Kotal, that he was going to build a fort at Bagh. With a courtesy bordering on deference, Abdul Qayyum replied that Saleh was probably unaware that this would be trespassing on British Indian soil. He then added, less politely: "But if it is intentional, you will be responsible for any trouble which may arise."

Saleh's response came on May 3, when he occupied Bagh with 150 infantrymen. That same night, a band of Shinwari Pathans, led by a tribesman named Zar Shah, crept up on the camp of an Indian work gang near the disputed hummock and picked off five coolies with their rifles. Zar Shah then sent word to Abdul Qayyum that he had carried out the raid on Saleh's orders. He also began circulating copies of an anti-British proclamation that he said had been written by Amanullah.

Even then, the British held their fire. No less anxious than Amanullah to avoid war, Chelmsford sent the Amir a personal message virtually pleading with him to disavow the proclamation and arrest Zar Shah. But Amanullah may have thought it too late to back down. He may also have felt emboldened; at that time, Landi Kotal was garrisoned by fewer than 500 sepoys of the Khyber Rifles, while Saleh's force consisted of 5 infantry battalions supported by at least 6 field guns. For the moment, at any rate, the Afghans seemed to have a strong upper hand in the Khyber. Amanullah replied to Chelmsford with a reproach for Britain's refusal to recognize Afghan independence. On May 5, the Indian Government announced the formal commencement of hostilities against Afghanistan. The extended skirmish known as the Third Afghan War had begun.

29

The Bolshie Brigade and the Krupp Guns

IN DECLARING WAR on Afghanistan, the British had acted not so much to repel the Afghan Army as to counter the threat of a new and serious Frontier-wide tribal rising. Due in great part to high wartime prices for farm produce and increased wages for labor and soldiers' remittances, the trans-Indus hills had enjoyed a period of almost unprecedented quiet since the outbreak of the European conflict. Early in 1919, Roos-Keppel, Deane's successor as Chief Commissioner, was able to report buoyantly that during the previous twelve months it had been "curious and pleasing that the North West Frontier has [had] no history." But an Afghan offensive would change all that.

In the environs of the Khyber Pass alone, Amanullah's aggressive stance had already caused at least 20,000 Afridis, Orakzais and Mohmands to begin making menacing noises. If Saleh's Afghans consolidated their position at Bagh and moved on Landi Kotal, there would be every incentive for the Pathan lashkars to join the jihad. Further storm signals went up on May 7, when a rash of desertions broke out among the Afridi sepoys of the Khyber Rifles. Several days later, Roos-Keppel ordered the whole force disbanded and replaced by regulars. But this was only a way of anticipating a mass defection—if not an open mutiny.

Tension also mounted in Peshawar, as Afridi mobs gathered in the bazaars to hear speakers read Amanullah's anti-British propaganda. This material was delivered directly from Kabul to Peshawar, where an Afghan post office enjoyed a curious diplomatic immunity owing to the postmaster's status as Afghan Political Agent. Roos-Keppel worried about breaking up the meetings forcibly; he knew that "the cry which Afghans would have had . . . that their brothers in blood and religion were being slaughtered would have appealed . . . in a way that the misfortunes of strangers like the Sikhs certainly does not." It was not until May 9 that the British closed the post office and arrested the postmaster along with twenty-two other conspirators. On the same day, British and Indian troops barricaded all of Peshawar's sixteen gates, for whatever pacifying effect that may have had. By then, Afridi meetings inside the city had taken on a life of their own, and the proportions of a major riot.

British combat readiness, moreover, might have been better described as unreadiness. Thanks to demobilization, the Indian Army was dangerously below strength. Many if not most of its new recruits had not even fired on the rifle range, while few of their newly arrived British officers knew much of Indian—let alone Frontier—service. The Afghan Army, to be sure, was little more than a mob of bandolier-festooned ragpickers, and did not seem a formidable antagonist with its nonexistent discipline and generally rusty hardware, but its troops were at least inspired by jihad, and—what counted even more—they had every reason to expect the massive and fanatical support of large Pathan lashkars.

Contrariwise, the only backing the green sepoys could expect was from a few British regiments that had sweated out the war in various parts of India; the ranks of some of these units bristled with convicted felons who had been given the choice between prison sentences and military service. Officers and men thought of nothing but their imminent return to "civvy street" in England. When they learned that they were needed in an obscure but dirty Frontier campaign, their already flaccid morale simply collapsed. The spirit of Kipling, to be sure, still lived, but the British troops probably tended to think only of one of his verses:

When you're wounded an' left on Afghanistan's plains,
An' the women come out to cut up your remains,
Just roll to your rifle an' blow out your brains,
An' go to your Gawd like a soldier.

In a thickening climate of insubordination, a rumor spread that the orders to march might actually be disobeyed. Justifiably alarmed, the high command tried to sugar-coat the pill by asking the troops if they would volunteer. They naturally refused to a man, protesting that they had jobs waiting for them in England and could not expect their employers to remain patient while they stayed on in India of their own free will. They would "volunteer," they said, but only if the Army camouflaged the act by ordering them to the Frontier. The arrangement satisfied no one, but with their jobs at least protected, the men sullenly boarded troop trains for Peshawar.

Then some officer, considering the cover-up not only awkward and foolish but unpatriotic, informed newspaper correspondents that everyone had actually volunteered. The result was that for a while it looked as if a white man's Indian Mutiny was in the making. At least one outbreak did occur, in a contingent commanded by a Brigadier General O'Dowda. In open defiance of his orders, the men detrained en masse and pitched their tents alongside the track to wait for a train going in the opposite direction. They became known as "O'Dowda's Bolshie Brigade."

But somehow a force was mustered, and with a speed surprising under the circumstances, a grab-bag of infantry, cavalry and artillery units reached Landi Kotal. They even managed to conceal their presence as they moved up the Khyber Pass: all troop lorries were covered with tarpaulins, and for several days the tribesmen thought the vehicles carried only ammunition. Sometimes the British also fooled themselves. The Somerset Light Infantry's Captain G. N. Molesworth, who later wrote an account of the campaign, recalled that three real ammunition trucks were found to be loaded with casks of beer and that the rations of at least one regiment sank beyond recovery in a quagmire of paperwork. Other services proved not much better; Molesworth described the military map of the sector assigned to his own unit as "little more than a mis-leading diagram, contoured by someone with a vivid imagination."

Such logistic-administrative snarls, however, were to be expected. The main thing was that by May 7, two days after the declaration of war, a combined Gurkha-Sikh-British striking force under Brigadier General G. D. Crocker—Molesworth called him "a very gallant, but impetuous man"—had reached Landi Kotal. Shortly after sunrise on May 9, the troops began fanning out west of the fort and advancing across a con-fusion of steep, rock-littered hills to recapture Bagh.

Afghan resistance proved stiff; it was not until May 11 that Crocker could order the final assault. At best, the drive toward Bagh was faltering despite certain obvious enemy weaknesses. For some reason, Saleh had brought up only a single field piece—and an arthritic one at that—but its crew was well trained, and even though the gun's ancient shells seemed almost unwilling to burst, they served nicely in keeping British and Indian heads down. The old noisemaker was particularly troublesome because it fired from the mouth of a cave and could hardly be seen; only a freak direct hit by a British mountain gun finally put it out of action. British artillery also knocked out a museum-piece Nordenfeldt machine gun, although that weapon had been anything but intimidating. "The range was much too long," wrote Molesworth, "for it to do any damage, but its solemn rate of fire and the cloud of smoke it raised caused much merriment among the troops."

Otherwise, the troops had little to be merry about. Saleh had thrown up his main defense line along the crest of a sort of natural broken spinal column, where his own men, snug behind rock sangars, had clear fields of fire against attackers who could seldom see anything to aim at. British and Indian infantrymen sweated out long waits between short rushes from one protective spur or hillock to the next.

And always, Crocker's men kept an uneasy eye on their exposed rear. At the summit of a vaulting ridge just south of Landi Kotal, the sun glinted off a forest of Afridi rifle barrels. The tribesmen made no hostile gestures; beneath their battle standards they might have been spectators at a football match. And in fact they were awaiting the outcome of the contest. If the Bagh positions were not carried, Saleh could probably count on being reinforced by several thousand guerrilla sharpshooters, while the British line of retreat to Landi Kotal might even be cut off by the tribesmen. Nervously, Molesworth looked over one of his rifle company's Pathan guides, decided the man was "fairly reliable," and then "took the precaution of having him strapped to a Lance Corporal, with orders to shoot if he tried to bolt."

Crocker could only hope that the Afridis had not moved down in the predawn blackness of May 11, when the first assault on the Bagh defenses began. Afghan machine-gun and rifle fire became heavy during the stiff, groping climb up the shaly heights; for several hours, there was not even any way to carry wounded soldiers back to the British field dressing station. British machine gun mules stumbled and fell so often that their guns and ammunition belts were removed and humped up the slope on human backs. But the British-Indian guns were also busy, and when the men of the North Staffordshire Regiment finally reached the crest, a curtain of covering fire from the Somersets enabled them almost to stroll forward and lob hand grenades into the Afghan sangars. By noon, Bagh was in British hands, the Afghans were in full retreat and—what really mattered—the Afridi grandstand had stopped rooting for Saleh's team. Had the assault miscarried or even stalled, the Khyber might well have been inundated in a renewed tribal offensive.

Even so, the Afridis were still there and the British remained alert. Roos-Keppel reported to Chelmsford that the Afghans had "fought better than I expected, with great bravery and tenacity," but he added that the Pathans were "the greater danger . . . that they have not risen against us is extraordinary." Fatigue parties combed the Bagh position for unexpended cartridges—"a wonderful gift for the tribes to throw back at us," said Molesworth.

The capture of Bagh completed the first stage of a step-by-step advance on Kabul. The next objective was the village of Dakka, about five miles to the northwest. To soften up this position, a Royal Flying Corps squadron bombed the Afghan lines. The "bombers" were BE2C fighters, a type that had proved among the least airworthy of Allied or German planes on the Western Front, and they performed no better on the northwest frontier. Their pilots could not get enough altitude to take them over the Khyber Pass, so they flew through it, with the result that Afridi riflemen on the escarpments became the first and only antiaircraft gunners in history to fire down at targets.

And the bombardment itself accomplished little, beyond causing Amanullah to declare war officially, which he had somehow neglected to do thus far. The proclamation was no starchy, formal ceremony. In a Kabul mosque, Amanullah cried out against "the treacherous and deceitful English Government [which] . . . plunged their filthy claws into the region of the vital parts of our dear country. . . . May thousands of curses and imprecations be upon the English! After this dropping of bombs without any justification by the unstable airplanes on those who were pursuing the path of right, it became incumbent on your King to proclaim jihad. . . . God is great! God is great! God is great!"

Meanwhile, the war continued. On May 16, when Crocker's troops took up positions outside Dakka, the Afghan force, at least 3,000 strong, looked down at them from a 2,200-foot hill, which the British nicknamed "Stonehenge Ridge" for the circle of rock slabs forming a Muslim ziarat, or altar, at the summit. It was the one piece of high ground worth holding. Saleh also counted on help from hundreds of Mohmand snipers, as Crocker learned when he called a meeting of staff officers on a tiny exposed hillock. It was "somewhat like a picture of Napoleon directing his Marshals," wrote Molesworth, adding that "how no one was hit during this conference was a miracle."

This time, too, Saleh was making better use of his artillery, although the attackers were deceived at first by a diminutive pony-drawn field gun. Molesworth said that its shells "bounced along the ground before exploding like a child's firework and caused much amusement. . . . One cricketer clubbed his rifle in the hope that he might hit one for six, but he was not successful." The entertainment ended, however, when Saleh brought up seven modern Krupp guns, which effectively slowed down the advance of two Sikh regiments leading the British assault on the Stonehenge defenses on the morning of May 17.

But then the British artillery opened up with a counterbarrage. Molesworth had "no doubt that . . . if our own guns had held their fire, [the Sikhs] would have gained the summit."

As it was, the assault was stopped dead in its tracks, and became further mired down by Mohmand sniping. The tribesmen fired clay-filled expanding bullets, which made roomy caverns in whatever part of the body they exploded. It was not until strong reinforcements arrived from Landi Kotal that the crawl up Stonehenge Ridge could be resumed. The position was finally taken, but with 22 British and Indians killed and 157 wounded. It was a high price of admission to a Punch-and-Judy brawl.

The British then made camp at Dakka and settled down to await the order for the next advance—although "settled" was not really the word. "We existed," wrote Molesworth, "in an atmosphere of dust, stench and myriads of flies." The dust worked its way into everything, jamming rifles and machine guns, layering food and water, mixing with human sweat into a thick, itching paste. Temperatures inside the tents averaged 117 degrees. Several times the water supply approached boiling point inside its metal tanks. Rations consisted mainly of tinned beef that had already started going rancid; "the gentleman who produced it," said Molesworth, "had, rashly, put his portrait on the tins and many people kept these labels hoping that, in the future, they might meet him."

The stench to which Molesworth referred was mainly the jolting odor of death. Even after burial or burning, there was no escape from the everpresent pong of animal corpses, which decomposed swiftly in the heat. Molesworth wrote that "the vultures did a good deal to help," but that "this did not mitigate the smell." Human cadavers offered greater unpleasantness. Although a fair number of troops were killed in action, more succumbed to disease. Owing to the suddenness of the war, few of the men had been inoculated against cholera, which was running wild. So too was dysentery. The flies and the terrible heat did not permit the gloomy dignity of the British military funeral, with its files of troops carrying weapons reversed, with a gun carriage bearing a coffin swathed in a Union Jack, with a bugler lingering over the strains of "Last Post." There was time only for the briefest of prayers before the corpse was dumped into a hole.

Even this ceremony did not always proceed according to form. Officiating at the burial of several King's Dragoon Guards who had been worked over expertly with Mohmand knives, the chaplain twice interrupted his reading of the service to vomit.

Certainly the Mohmands added an element of real danger to the troops' misery. Several hundred yards from the camp, on the north bank of the Kabul River, a large concentration of tribesmen kept up a steady drizzle of sniping fire. Even with armed escorts, the British and Indians found it almost impossible to wash their dust-quilted bodies in the river; so artfully did the sharpshooters conceal themselves that firing back was a waste of ammunition. Not only to circulate the overheated air but as protection against bullets, all tents had to be pitched above giant foxholes.

Every day, however, there would be a cease-fire, when a few Mohmands crossed the river and set up stalls where they sold fresh vegetables, fruit and eggs to supplement the putrefying British rations. As soon as they returned to the north bank, the rifles began popping away once more.

It got so bad that an amphibious assault team was finally formed to chase off the Mohmands. Five Royal Navy launches were brought up-river for the crossing, and for several days troops practiced rowing in a partly sheltered cove while others egged them on with shouts of "Go it Oxford!" and "Go it Cambridge!" Wrote Molesworth: "The Mohmands must have thought we had gone mad." But the operation was duly carried out; thenceforth, sniping became less of a nuisance.

And on May 24, the troops could even stand in the open and cheer as a venerable Handley-Page bomber lurched a few hundred feet over-head on its way to attack no less an objective than Kabul. The aircraft's pair of 100-pound bombs killed no one and caused little property damage, although the explosions did empty Amanullah's harem and caused the Amir to soothe his hysterical wives with the music of a military band. But the strike was important nonetheless, because it signalled the next stage of the British advance. On May 28, the Dakka force was ordered to resume its westward march and occupy Jalalabad.

No one much cared, not even the men of the Somersets, who wore "Jalalabad" on their badges—the regiment having once been the 13th Foot that had held out with Sir Robert Sale's "Illustrious Garrison" in 1842.* The whole force, to be sure, could hardly wait to put the dust and flies and stink of Dakka behind it, but Jalalabad did not seem worth a thirty-mile hike in 100-degree heat across a desolation of baking earth and rock that concealed snipers and knifemen at every turn. By then, in fact, open disaffection had broken out again in the British ranks. Protests over the delay in demobilization grew more audible almost by the hour. The advance on Jalalabad was called off.

The troops' discontent, however, played only a small part in the can-cellation of the offensive. The real reason could be found nearly 100 miles to the south, where the British had been caught flat-footed and were facing a full-scale invasion of Indian soil.

In the Afghan forces of 1919, there was only one field commander with anything like a grasp of twentieth-century military strategy and tactics, and the initiative to put that knowledge to use. He was General Nadir Khan, Amanullah's third cousin once removed, and in 1919 he stood on the threshold of a long and distinguished career of service to Afghanistan. Only a few months earlier, Nadir had been Commander-in-Chief of the Afghan Army, but suspicion of his possible complicity in Habibullah's murder had forced Amanullah to demote him. This may have been fortunate for the British: had Nadir led the Afghan troops in the all-important Khyber offensive, he might have carried the pass and even reached Peshawar. Instead, he had been placed in charge of the forces in the Khost District, which lay just across the Durand Line from the British Kurram Valley and Waziristan regions. As it proved, however,

* It also became the last British regiment to leave India, in 1947.

this position gave him the opportunity to do the British at least as much direct damage, and indirectly, a great deal more.

Early in May, Nadir had tried unsuccessfully to stir up a jihad among the tribes in the British territory adjoining Khost. That he failed may have been due to Afghan reverses under Saleh in the Khyber area, but this did not discourage him. As the Indian Army concentrated its effort in the north and stepped up the drive on Kabul via Jalalabad, Nadir soon perceived that his own troops in Khost faced what may have become the most lightly defended sector on the Frontier. The main strongpoint, Thal, about twenty miles to the east at the bottom of the Kurram Valley, was the railhead of a narrow-gauge line from Kohat, but its fort was held by barely 800 militiamen with a pair of ten-pound mountain guns. Against this garrison Nadir could hurl at least 3,000 Afghan infantry regulars and two cavalry regiments, supporting his advance with ten 100-mm. Krupp guns and seven 75-mm. Krupp howitzers. Thal offered easy pickings.

Further to Nadir's advantage, the line of his advance on Thal ran only a few miles north of a short east-west dogleg of the border; for all the British knew, he might execute a sudden right wheel and drive down on the northern Waziristan post of Miram Shah. A move in that direction could bring the Afghans right up to the administrative boundary and actually threaten the settled district of Bannu. When the British learned of Nadir's presence, they had made haste to reinforce both Thal and Miram Shah, but they had made haste slowly, and until the very last moment they had no idea of which objective Nadir would select.

On May 25, they found out. To a great rumbling of drums, braying of bugles and trumpeting of supply camels and artillery elephants, Nadir's Afghan forces marched unopposed across the border and headed northeast toward Thal. The huge green battle flags of the unwieldy columns were almost invisible beneath a thunderhead of dust thrown up by the even more ragged formations of several Pathan lashkars, 12,000 strong. Previously, the tribes had hung back. Now, they saw the chance that had been denied them in the Khyber.

The news of Nadir's tribal reinforcements spread across the Frontier like a lighted train of gunpowder. Although Thal was the immediate Afghan objective, Nadir's advance had its most lasting repercussions in Waziristan. To Roos-Keppel's fury, the Upper Tochi posts of Northern Waziristan were evacuated in near-panic. In Southern Waziristan, the militia garrison at Wana mutinied and seized the fort. The garrison commander, Major Russell, managed to shoot his way free with a handful of officers and loyal sepoys; their sixty-mile fighting retreat to Fort Sandeman in Baluchistan may have been the most gallant exploit of the campaign, but it was no less a retreat. Other Waziristan posts fell like ninepins. Scattered militia and Indian Army units could barely hold their own against some 20,000 Wazir and Mahsud tribesmen, many of whom had fought with the British on the Western Front and in East Africa. More than two years would go by before order could be restored in Waziristan.

Meanwhile, Nadir was having it all his own way at Thal. Although his troops were separated from the British by the Kurram River, he placed the fort under siege on May 27, when his elephants dragged the Krupps up to the south bank, 2,200 yards from the walls. Even low-level bombing-strafing runs by a pair of Royal Flying Corps BE2Cs failed to silence Nadir's artillery. Within twenty-four hours, an Afghan infantry column had forded the river, shot and bayoneted its way into the village adjoining the fort, and cut off the defenders' water supply. Militiamen and British troops inside the fort dug pits and lined them with tarpaulins for water catchment, in the wistful hope that rain would fall on their bone-dry precincts.

Hope for a lifting of the siege faded swiftly. Thanks to a shortage of locomotives on the Toonerville line from Kohat, a relief column had become stalled somewhere over the eastern horizon. Its troops had been forced to advance on foot; it was altogether possible that they would not arrive before Nadir's Krupps finished their own work. By May 31, the Krupps had knocked out one of the mountain guns and were beginning to kick open a breach in the southern wall of the fort. In the surrounding hills to the north and east, thousands of Pathans waited to pour into the hole as soon as it became large enough. With the fort in Afghan possession, Nadir would have both a stronghold against the relief column and a springboard for further penetration into British territory.

But shortly after sunrise on June 1, Nadir's troops saw a fogbank of dust rising in the northeast. The relief force was approaching—perhaps belatedly, but better late than never. The 3,000-man British-Indian column, backed up by a dozen large-caliber field guns, was commanded by General Dyer, who had not yet been brought to book for Amritsar. Whatever his views on riot control, Dyer was a good soldier. Although most of his troops were without combat experience, he deployed them intelligently, striking first at the Pathan concentrations before closing with Nadir's Afghan regulars. As usual, the tribesmen could withstand shellfire only so long; well before the day was out, they had fled from the hills in confusion and Dyer's main force had taken up attack positions just two miles north of the fort itself. The relief of Thal now seemed likely within three days.

In fact, it came the next day, when an Afghan officer approached the British lines under a flag of truce and handed Dyer a note. Nadir and the other Afghan field commanders had just been ordered by Amanullah to "suspend hostilities until the door of discussion and communication is opened" with the British. Dyer told the officer that he would forward Nadir's note to his own divisional commander. Then he fixed the man with an immediate reply. By nightfall, after Dyer's artillery had put at least six of the Afghan Krupps out of action, Nadir's columns were commencing a disorderly withdrawal toward the border as British armored cars and RFC Handley-Pages hastened them on their way with Lewis guns and bombs. On the following morning, Dyer ordered the pursuit halted when he received a telegram announcing an armistice.

The twenty-nine-day war was over.

Both sides claimed to have won. The British sent planes over the Frontier, dropping leaflets that proclaimed in Pushtu that Amanullah had been the first to sue for peace; the bombardment almost caused several tribes to go back on the warpath. Amanullah for his part disregarded Indian government proposals that a peace conference be held, thus creating the impression that he no longer considered formalities necessary to affirm Afghan independence. It was not until the British threatened a renewal of hostilities that he finally agreed to send a delegation to the Punjab city of Rawalpindi in July.

During the interval, the two victors continued to flex their respective muscles. Late in May, the Soviet Union had recognized Afghanistan, and both countries now exchanged ambassadors while British-paid Tajik and Turkmen agents in Central Asia simultaneously toiled to sabotage Afghan-Soviet friendship. General Sir Wilfrid Malleson, who ran the undercover project, had made a grand botch-up of things as a brigade commander in East Africa in the early days of the war, but seemed better suited to cloaks and daggers. His operatives came within an ace of creating another Panjdeh incident by circulating rumors and half-truths that presently had Afghan and Russian armies massing against each other near the scene of the 1885 crisis. The panic atmosphere helped to delay the arrivals of both ambassadors at their posts.

Britain and Afghanistan also weighed the possibilities of pursuing high-handed lines at the peace talks. Curzon, now Foreign Secretary, insisted that Afghanistan's foreign affairs remain a Whitehall affair, although he ran into opposition from realists who perceived a growing worldwide sympathy for nationalist aspirations in Asia. In Kabul, Amanullah busily instructed his cousin Ali Ahmed, whom he had chosen to head up Afghanistan's four-man delegation at Rawalpindi. Subject to only one condition, Ali Ahmed was given a completely free hand in the negotiations. Amanullah's single stipulation was plain enough: under no circumstances was Ali Ahmed to return to Kabul without Afghanistan's total independence.

Early on July 24, the delegation left Kabul. On the twenty-seventh, it reached Rawalpindi, where Ali Ahmed was welcomed by India's Foreign Secretary, Sir A. Hamilton Grant, who had been chosen to head the British panel at the talks. The Afghans might have arrived half a day sooner but for a delay at Dakka, where a search had to be made for one delegate's missing Savile Row top hat. (It was not found, having been stolen by a private of the Somersets.) And in fact the mission might as well have spent a week in Dakka for all that was accomplished at Rawalpindi during the same length of time. Nearly the entire opening session was given over to a meandering dispute between Ali Ahmed and Grant on the exchange of Peshawar's Afghan postmaster and the British agent in Kabul, both of whom had been detained. Grant insisted on the agent's immediate return to India. Bristling, Ali Ahmed replied that Grant was never to give him orders but only make requests. After the meeting had been adjourned, another member of the British delegation got off a note to Chelmsford, describing Ali Ahmed as "a vain, full-blooded coxcomb."

At the next session, Grant told Ali Ahmed that the Indian Government would close down the Frontier passes if Afghanistan did not cease what he called "coquetting" with the Soviet Union. Ali Ahmed said that the Soviets had been doing the coquetting. This touched off interminable fusillades of nit-picking by both sides. The talks almost broke down completely during the third session, when Grant read the draft of a treaty in which Afghanistan accepted responsibility for starting the war and apologized for having done so. Ali Ahmed threatened to pull out his delegation. Grant took a softer tone, and Ali Ahmed presently smiled. "If you treat me kindly as a friend," he said, "you can make me do anything you like."

This proved to be less than accurate at the fourth session. Ali Ahmed asked for a personal interview with Chelmsford, and Grant told him, with almost eighteenth-century courtesy, that this would not be possible. In that case, peace too is impossible, declared Ali Ahmed, again preparing to leave. Grant asked for time to make the delegation's train ready. Ali Ahmed told him the delegation would walk. Somehow, the delegation stayed on.

On the following day, August 6, the conferees finally got around to the only item on the agenda that really mattered: the question of whether Afghanistan should control her own foreign relations. Grant now showed himself to be anything but an obstructionist. Along with a growing number of Indian Government officials and policy-makers in Britain, he was sensibly alive to winds of change and had come to see Afghan independence as a fait accompli. Several days earlier, in fact, he had sought and received Chelmsford's permission to yield on the foreign policy issue—subject only to London's approval. That endorsement arrived by cable just before the August 6 meeting began, and Grant was able, therefore, to hand Ali Ahmed a letter he had already written, acknowledging the removal of Afghan foreign affairs from British custody.

Ali Ahmed now balked briefly over the wording of a proposed treaty, which did not refer to Amanullah as "His Majesty" but as "His Highness"; surely, so small an alteration would be simple enough, protested Ali Ahmed. "You do not know King George," replied Grant. Ali Ahmed did not press the matter, and on August 8, the heads of both delegations signed a "Treaty of Peace Between the Illustrious British Government and the Independent Government of Afghanistan." Ali Ahmed had done his master's bidding.

Amanullah was properly appreciative, although Ali Ahmed may not have thought so on returning to Kabul, where he was immediately placed under house arrest. Barely a week later, however, he was released, and on the same day married one of Amanullah's sisters. In fact, his detention had been little more than a sop to Mahmud Tarzi and some of the ultra-diehards, who felt that in return for independence, Ali Ahmed had made too many concessions to the British.

To more than one Briton it seemed the other way round. "What has impressed me most unfavorably," grumbled one member of the House of Lords, "is the attitude of victors which seems throughout to have been assumed by the Afghans." But that attitude was hardly out of place. The Afghans had won it all.

At the same time, however, most British and Indian Government officials did not view Afghan independence as signifying the collapse of the British Empire. Some even predicted that Britain would continue to pull the strings in Kabul. "Liberty is a new toy to the Afghan Government," said Grant. "Later on, if we handle them well, they will come to us to mend their toy when it gets chipped or broken."

Grant was an intelligent politician but without expertise in consulting crystal balls. He would have done well to have heeded Roos-Keppel's prediction that "Amanullah has lit a fire that will take us a great deal of trouble to put out." That glum warning, to be sure, had been voiced at the outbreak of hostilities in the spring, but it still held. And would hold for many years.

PART EIGHT

Last Post

30

The Memsahib Gets Hijacked

Apart from its rare capacity for nourishing intrigue and violence, the North West Frontier was unique in being the only key trouble spot of the British Empire to which the British could never send the Royal Navy. And the fleet would never have come in handy on the Frontier than during the last twenty-eight years of British rule in India.

This became evident almost immediately after the signing of the Treaty of Rawalpindi in August 1919. For that document did more than just affirm Afghanistan's independence. It also gave meaning to the old Pathan saying that Frontier wars never really begin until peace has been proclaimed.

Amanullah apparently subscribed to this theory. Drunk on the wine of his liberation from British bondage, he and other Afghan leaders lost no time in encouraging a continued struggle for freedom on the Indian side of the Durand Line. In December 1919, Nadir Khan, who had nearly chased the British out of the Kurram Valley six months earlier, had another try at the enemy. Inviting representatives of every Frontier clan to a great jirga at Jalalabad, he handed out black war flags and called for a redoubling of the tribal effort against the Feringhi. At least a partial result of this incitement to riot became visible during the next twelve months, with a rash of no fewer than 611 armed forays into the settled districts—or nearly two raids every day. The toll among British subjects during this mini-offensive ran to well over 1,100 in killed, wounded and kidnapped. It was peace with a vengeance.

Waziristan was the hottest spot. There the tribes had only begun to fight. During their stampede on the heels of Nadir's invasion in the summer of 1919, the Mahsuds and Wazirs had all but reconquered their own country from the British and had begun to think of themselves, not altogether incorrectly, as the victors. This notion fed and thrived on rumors, circulated by one of Amanullah's generals, that the Indian Government was planning to evacuate Waziristan as a condition of the Rawalpindi treaty. When the rumors proved false, the tribesmen undertook to rewrite the treaty in stepped-up shooting-looting sprees across the administrative border. By November, the British had struck back hard with two Indian Army columns. They fought twenty actions in thirty days, with nothing to show for the effort but casualties. And casualties continued to mount as the days became weeks and the weeks became months.

A military operation in Waziristan always seemed to exceed its predecessor in carnage, and the "police action" of 1919-20 was no exception. In one fight for possession of a narrow cleft through some rocks, 5,000 Indian Army regulars and 10,000 Mahsuds went at each other in five consecutive days of hand-to-hand combat that resulted in more than 2,000 British and Indian dead and wounded. It was the highest butcher bill ever paid by Empire troops in the history of Frontier warfare.

But 4,000 Mahsuds also fell in the same brawl, and, over the long haul, such attrition was too great a drain on tribal manpower to continue indefinitely; if nothing else, the British had reserves. By early 1921, Waziristan had become a miniature Verdun, Somme and Passchendaele rolled into one. Mahsud and Wazir jirgas began coming in to make their submissions, and it was not long before another so-called peace had returned to Waziristan.

This time, however, the British intended to make it stick. Early in 1922, an Indian Government committee of inquiry descended on the Frontier to find out why officialdom had so consistently tripped over its own feet in the place that the chairman, Sir Denys Bray, called "a devil's kitchen of mischief." Bray recognized Waziristan as the focal point of unrest beyond the administrative border, and further noted that "the crux in Waziristan is not the Wazir but the Mahsuds." Most to the point, he saw why this was: the Mahsuds were located in the very center of Waziristan and thus beyond the effective reach of authority. "In their very inaccessibility lies their strength," said Bray.

Bray's committee therefore went on to outline a peacetime strategy aimed at bringing the Mahsuds under control. It would not be carried out by military occupation but by what amounted to exactly the same thing. In theory, Mahsud territorial integrity was to be scrupulously respected: as in the past, tribal police and a Mahsud militia were entrusted with keeping the peace. The difference, however, was that the British presence now made itself felt with the complete scrapping of the Curzon policy that had held regular army forces on a leash behind the administrative border. Almost within rifle range of the northern and southern Mahsud boundaries, the forts of Razmak and Wana underwent massive troop buildups, as did the post at Miram Shah, slightly farther north; Razmak alone accommodated no fewer than six brigades. The idea was that the Mahsuds would think twice about running wild with the Indian Army breathing down their necks.

That was not all. New roads were also built, not only to connect Razmak and Wana with the settled districts but to accelerate lateral communications between the two forts themselves. Thus both posts came to offer swift access to every trouble spot in the Mahsuds' 2,500-square-mile wasteland. The garrison of each fort was to stand on twenty-four-hour alert for twelve months of every year. Previously, the Indian Army had had to carry out long and often fruitless forced marches in pursuit of elusive Mahsud raiding bands or lashkars. Under the new system, instant retaliation lay almost within what Pathans called "one shout's distance." At least so it was hoped.

Originally applied to the Mahsuds alone—and indirectly to all Waziristan—this scheme presently became operative with various modifications across the whole tribal area of the Frontier. Known alternately and semiofficially as "peaceful penetration" and the "Modified Forward Policy," its idea was to allow the widest possible tribal autonomy while standing ready to stamp swiftly and decisively on mass antisocial behavior. If the formula appeared to be little more than a rehash of old recipes that had failed, that was because it was. But there seemed little harm in giving it a try. The chance always existed that some combination of ideology and action might one day begin to absorb the Empire's tetchiest community into the imperial family.

The British did not delude themselves with the notion that the Modified Forward Policy would be welcomed; if nothing else, the tribes could ask what was so modified about it. They also had room to wonder what was in it for them. Government could make huge outlays for military roads and simultaneously play the pauper when it came to improving the hillman's lot. True, the British had initiated land development programs, but they were nowhere nearly enough. Tribes, clans, individual growers and herders were all badly in need of low-interest loans for farm implements, seeds, fodder. The anemic streams of the hills cried out for the dams that would bring hydroelectric power, which in turn would irrigate the bone-dry soil; water storage tanks on the Frontier were a rich man's indulgence. Virtually nothing was being done to open up livestock and produce markets. In Afghanistan, dried fruit had become a thriving industry; in the Frontier tribal belt, most of the fruit simply withered. Every incentive to disorder remained.

And so, during the 1920s, legitimate grievances joined with plain orneriness to bring the Frontier to new heights of anarchy. In 1902, provincial courts had tried 709 cases of violent crime; by 1929, the annual figure was up to 2,045, including 900 murders—most of the victims being British Indian subjects in the administered districts. "With its population of two and a quarter millions only," wrote the Indian Government's Sir William Barton in an informal study of British-Pathan relations, "this tale of crime stamps the Frontier Province as the most lawless country on the face of the earth." The visiting journalist Robert Bernays put it more tersely: "This is not British India, but enemy territory."

Neither man overstated it. Although a railway through the Khyber Pass was completed in 1925, the pass itself remained not much less the funnel of danger that Mountstuart Elphinstone had once known. At sunset, all pickets were withdrawn from posts along the permanent way and the motor road, all wheeled traffic was halted for the night. Travelers could proceed through the pass on foot, but Government would not answer for their safety. At times, Government could not even answer for its own. Late in the afternoon on a day in April 1923, two officers of the Seaforth Highlanders went for a stroll outside the fort at Landi Kotal. Hardly had they taken their first breath of the early evening air than bullets smashed through each man's skull while a pair of tribal snipers high above them vanished into a maze of boulders.

Other Frontier military posts, previously guarded only by sentries at night, were now ringed with heavy barbed wire entanglements and illuminated by floodlights to keep off tribal wire-cutters. At Fort Lockhart, only fifty yards from the administrative border on Tirah's Samana range, cordons of armed sepoys stood watch over tennis matches and biweekly band concerts. The gardens around the houses of army officers were cut down and swept away—their foliage offered too much concealment to marauders.

Even Peshawar's fast-growing European population lived in a state of partial siege. Tap water in private homes sometimes had to be tested for poison even before it was boiled. Spectators at the racecourse never knew when a bomb might go off on the track or in the grandstand. Sentries were a fixture at cocktail parties, dinner dances and theatricals. The wives and daughters of British officers, administrators and businessmen were forbidden, by Government order, to ride their own horses outside the city limits without armed escorts.

At least, however, the British took it all with their celebrated stiff upper lip. During a particularly violent riot in Peshawar, all of the city's Englishwomen were herded into the billiard room of the Peshawar Club for their safety. This caused an army officer some consternation. According to Barton, he went to the club secretary and complained: "Isn't it a bit thick to jam a colonel's wife among all these other women? Couldn't you give her the bridge room to herself?"

Escalating concern for British wives and daughters could at first have been thought of as touched with paranoia if one considered the Pathan attitude toward women. They were chattels, to be sure. All the menial labor in a tribal family was woman's work alone. Girls were bought and sold as brides like so many perfumed sheep and goats. Yet, as a Frontier army officer once wrote, tribesmen "sell women only to those who will honourably wed them. . . . The honour of his wife, and his women-folk generally, is of first importance to a Pathan." And, except when he sliced off a wife's nose or ears as punishment for adultery, the hillman abided by a rigid Mafia-like code which proscribed violence toward the opposite sex. The abovementioned officer also wrote that some clans "mutilate in a very peculiar way" the bodies of men known to have molested women. Of even greater importance, as long as the Frontier had been part of the Raj, even the boldest hill warrior had always had the intelligence to recoil from the unthinkable act of tampering in any way with the sacrosanct British memsahib.

After the First World War, however, chivalry and common sense began yielding to a new outlook. In 1920, an officer of the Indian Army Medical Services, one Colonel Foulkes, and his wife were knifed to death while asleep inside the Cantonment at Kohat. "The cold-blooded outrage, involving, as it did, the murder of an English lady," wrote another officer, "was of a nature quite different from anything which [has] occurred before in the long history of the frontier."

It was also just a rehearsal. In April 1923, a gang of Afridis broke into the Kohat home of Major Archibald Ellis, an officer in the Kurram militia. After gunning him down and gutting his wife, the bandits then seized the couple's seventeen-year-old daughter Mollie and carried her off into the hills of Tirah, where she was held for ransom. The Mutiny itself had not given white supremacy in India quite so rude a jolt as did the Mollie Ellis kidnapping.

On recovering from their initial sputterings of outrage, authorities took a careful look at their extremely ticklish situation. Although it was clearly not the moment for a punitive expedition, the Chief Commissioner, Sir John Maffey, also realized that dealing with the perpetrators through their own tribe could easily backfire with tragic consequences. Most of the Tirah Afridis, to be sure, expressed sincere dismay, even open fury, over the act; the kidnappers had long criminal records and were looked on as near-outlaws even by kith and kin. Nonetheless, their crime in no way invalidated the Pakhtunwali code of asylum; certainly it did not soften Afridi feelings toward the British—who under no circumstances could negotiate personally. As Maffey well knew, Mollie Ellis' life would probably not be worth two annas if he sent in even a single white man to negotiate for her release.

So he sent in a white woman.

Whether or not this was sound thinking, it at least symbolized peaceful intentions. The go-between, Mrs. Lillian Starr, was a mission hospital nurse who had won a great deal of respect among the Afridis. She was also the first and last European woman ever to enter the forbidden land of Tirah voluntarily, and her journey through the rifle-bristling hills did not encourage further tourism. To avoid drawing fire automatically from every rock and bush within range, she had to discard her pith helmet and wear the Pathan *chadar*, or veil. When she reached the house of one of the region's chief mullahs, even her Afridi guide—who was also a high-ranking member of Maffey's staff—seemed an inadequate shield as hundreds of armed tribesmen formed a muttering circle around her. In fact the mission almost came to an abrupt and violent end at this point, with receipt of a letter from the mullah himself. It stated: "Absolutely, lady-doctor and her company are prohibited. This is very urgent order. In default of this there will occur very long fighting." Mrs. Starr and her party could only withdraw in some haste to a less hostile quarter of the hills.

At last, however, Mrs. Starr managed to make contact with Mollie Ellis and, after bringing to bear a mix of cajolery and bluff that would have won a salute from Kipling, she took the girl unharmed back across the administrative border. The RAF then buzzed Tirah, a heavy fine was imposed on the clans that had been implicated, and several villages were razed by Government order, for whatever effect the punishment had on the kidnappers, who had long since escaped.

Seven months later, the same band struck again, this time at the remote border outpost of Parachinar, where the Kurram Militia's Captain Watts had not too wisely taken his wife. For some reason, no one paid immediate attention to a sudden eruption of rifle fire and screams. Nearly an hour went by before a servant noticed the pair of bullet-riddled and knife-scored cadavers lying alongside a bloody trail of sandal prints that led into Afghanistan.

And all the while, the barbed wire continued to go up and the floodlights went on while the gardens went down and bridle paths remained off limits to unescorted Englishwomen. It was, said Barton, "a gloomy commentary on British border administration."

If so glum a view of things had been elicited by the hill Pathans alone, the situation on the Frontier might have been just barely tolerable. But the tribesmen, as usual, had the backing of their fellow Afghans to the west—and Afghanistan herself was cultivating the friendship of a new neighbor. That friendship threatened a geopolitical earthquake on the Frontier, an upheaval whose shock waves might even roll across India.

31

Queen Souraya Removes Her Veil

Since the October Revolution of 1917, the Soviet Union had made no secret of its intention to sabotage and destroy British influence—and British rule, wherever it existed—in Asia. The thrust of the Russian effort centered on Afghanistan, for the same reasons that had impelled the Czars toward that country. In 1927, a British diplomat lamented: "If Afghanistan were bounded on the northwest by an Arctic Ocean, she would be merely a petty border state which could give no concern to H.M.G." But that of course was not the case. During the 1920s, Afghanistan seemed well on the way to becoming the arena of another Great Game.

Unwittingly or deliberately—probably both—Amanullah gave the Russians a leg up. He may not have heard Grant's comment that the British expected as a matter of course to be called on to fix the broken "toy" of Afghan independence, but he knew quite well that the Indian Government thought it still held a privileged position in his country. To help dispel that notion, he discarded the title of Amir and proclaimed himself King in 1926. But much more significantly, he had already begun playing Russia and Britain against each other, much to the disadvantage and great discomfiture of the latter.

On the surface, Amanullah was properly neutral. In 1921, he signed a new treaty with Britain and shortly afterward received Sir Francis Humphrys as the first accredited British Minister to Afghanistan since

Cavagnari.* But in the same year, Amanullah also ratified a treaty with the Soviets, who had already enjoyed a diplomatic edge because their own Legation in Kabul had been open since 1919. The head start, apparently, had not been neglected; according to Fraser-Tytler, the British Military Attache in Kabul, "friendly caresses by the Russian Bear owed a great deal to the personality of the Ambassador, M. Leonide Stark, who rather resembled a bear himself." Fraser-Tytler could have added that Stark also behaved like a fox.

Stark was a man of unbounded affability. He liked to mingle freely and engagingly with all classes of Afghan society, while the strikingly handsome Humphrys tended to emulate Cavagnari by remaining within the walled confines of the British Legation. Although Humphrys at least showed the good sense to disregard Curzon's instruction that he never appear in the streets without six Bengal Lancers riding before him and six after, his relative seclusion almost certainly left a fairly clear field open for Stark. The Soviet envoy was even able to organize a vest-pocket KGB in Kabul; for a while, the Afghan chief of police himself was on Stark's payroll, after promising to jail any Briton the Russians might label a spy.

By no means all of Stark's gains were covert, although none pleased the British. In 1921, Moscow presented Amanullah with two fighter planes (originally a gift to Russia from England); by 1928, the Soviet Union had control of the Afghan Air Force. All of its dozen-odd craft were manned by Russian pilots, part of whose salaries, the British believed, were "regularly set aside for propaganda purposes." Russia also offered the services of its nationals in a variety of commercial and cultural areas. The British voiced concern over proposals to open an Afghan branch of Vneshtorg, the Soviet trading organization. Consternation broke out in India when rumors surfaced that a Russian bank would be established in Kabul, and possibly used as a front for undercover agents. Nothing Russian was too insignificant to be suspect. Humphrys once received a worried query from the Indian Government as to "whether the report is true that some of the Russian women [in Afghanistan] are young, well educated in languages, and desirous of giving lessons to the wives and daughters of Kabul sardars."

Stark also continued to play his cloak-and-dagger game. Like Alexander Burnes, he was a ravenous womanizer, with the difference that there was method in his philandering. Further, nearly all of his many wives and mistresses were not Afghan but Russian (the British described one as "a lady of some physical attractions who does not believe in masking her batteries"), and each happened to have a frail constitution requiring

* The Legation staff held a party to celebrate Humphrys' presence in Afghanistan for six weeks without being murdered.

340

Last Post

frequent rest in the warm climate of Jalalabad. The coincidence was interesting. Because of its proximity to the Frontier, Jalalabad had long been a hotbed of Afghan intrigue, and the British had somehow prevailed on Amanullah to place it out of bounds to Russian officials. But the ban did not apply to convalescing women, who no doubt had many things to tell Stark when they returned to Kabul. The Afghans for their part closed at least one eye to this less-than-subtle device.

This is not to say that Russian-Afghan relations always proceeded smoothly. In 1926, there was an ugly border incident when Soviet troops occupied an island on the Oxus, but Moscow deftly exploited the crisis to the benefit of its image in Kabul by withdrawing after Amanullah's strong protest. Amanullah, however, was more often disinclined to challenge the Russians. In fact, he seemed to shrink from offending them even in the smallest way. In Kabul's movie theater, when a film about the Russo-Japanese War began to take an apparently pro-Japanese line, Amanullah leaped from the royal box and ordered the projector turned off. As much as anything, this and other seemingly insignificant gestures caused Humphrys to write that "there is every reason to believe that the Russian menace will increase."

But Humphrys could also inform the British Foreign Office: "It is a matter of first importance to keep Amanullah on his throne. Unsatisfactory as he is, there is no one better in prospect; and revolution is what the Bolsheviks are playing for." In using the word "revolution," Humphrys had the northwest frontier very much in mind. Although Amanullah's intrigues among the tribes on the heels of the Rawalpindi Treaty reflected less than mature statesmanship, the British hoped that such excesses would subside and that boundary differences would be ironed out once Amanullah grew into his job and recognized his new responsibilities as an independent monarch. It seemed to stand to reason that as the Soviets gained strength in Kabul, Frontier turmoil might well prove as dangerous to Amanullah's position as to the security of India.

Indeed, Amanullah once told Humphrys: "I am aware that Soviet agents are trying to spread revolutionary doctrines among my people and I am not so blind as to suppose that a Communist Government could be anything but hostile to myself and my throne."

And in many respects, Amanullah also behaved responsibly toward the British. While challenging the legality of the Durand Line, his dissent was often expressed through proper channels—including Humphrys, the Viceroy of India, the Afghan Minister in London and his own country's official newspaper, *Aman-i-Afghan*. In 1928, when he became the first Afghan ruler to visit England, he personally laid his case before Sir Austen Chamberlain, the Foreign Secretary. But Britain for her part refused to yield an inch on any of these representations, and although her position would have stood up in a court of international law, just the slightest bit more flexibility might have helped allay Amanullah's understandable anxiety that the Modified Forward Policy might be aimed at Afghanistan. Fraser-Tytler himself acknowledges that "it was a frightening thing, this slow, relentless advance into areas which no Afghan had ever looked on as forming part of India."

For which reason Amanullah also showed a less diplomatic side. He continued to disseminate Anglophobic propaganda in the tribal belt. He kept the Afghan side of the Durand Line open to Pathan fugitives from British territory. Tribesmen went on receiving Afghan subsidies and even Afghan arms. In Waziristan, Amanullah had what Fraser-Tytler said "almost amounted to a militia." Abdur Rahman himself could not have played the role of Frontier obstructionist with more zeal.

The first real showdown took place early in 1923, when Amanullah went to Jalalabad and personally presided over a large jirga attended by many Pathan leaders from the Indian side of the Durand Line. The gathering was less an orderly assemblage than a call to arms. Lavish distributions of money and inflammatory talk about jihad brought on a rash of Frontier outrages—so obviously inspired by Afghanistan that they finally exhausted British patience. Bluntly, Humphrys told Amanullah that unless he mended his ways at once, diplomatic relations would be no less swiftly severed. For all his truculence toward his former masters, loss of diplomatic recognition by Britain was something Amanullah could ill afford to risk, particularly at so early a stage of Afghan independence. Humphrys' warning had its effect in a visible diminution, although not a cessation, of Afghan Frontier intrigues.

Concurrently, another episode showed that the British were not above playing their own brand of dirty pool. The tribesmen who killed the two Seaforth officers in the Khyber were Afghan subjects and had escaped to their own country. When Humphrys demanded that they be arrested and tried in Afghan courts, he was insisting (despite personal reservations) on a procedure that violated Britain's own extradition laws. A similar ultimatum was laid down with respect to the Mollie Ellis kidnappers, who were also more or less at large in Afghanistan. When Amanullah seemed to hedge on the demands, Humphrys applied the strong arm of extortion. A shipment of arms was then on its way to Afghanistan via India; until and unless the criminals were brought to justice, said Humphrys, the cargo would remain on the Bombay docks.

Both the Seaforth and Mollie Ellis cases hinged on touchy legalistic points, which were complicated by the Afghan instinct for offering asylum, and were also thrown into total confusion by the fugitives' relative freedom to move about the country. Eventually, however, Amanullah gave in to the point of deporting the kidnap ringleader to Afghan Turkestan, and one of the murderers was accidentally shot by Afghan troops as he tried to give himself up. These things seemed to satisfy Humphrys, and the arms shipment was duly released. To Amanullah, however, Britain's behavior in the affair smacked altogether too much of British high-handedness during the Roberts dictatorship four decades earlier.

It also came close to losing him the Afghan throne. "No Amir," he said bitterly, "has previously made reparations of any kind to the British Government. My submission has enormously weakened my position on the frontier." That was putting it mildly. By caving in, not only on the Frontier criminals but under the threat of British nonrecognition, Amanullah touched off a major tribal uprising against him. In March 1924, the Ghilzai Pathans of Khost went into open revolt and their lashkars began an advance on Kabul. It was not long before the tribal armies were only thirty-five miles from the capital.

The British now became alarmed at what they had set in motion. Just as Amanullah had not dared risk an open diplomatic breach with Britain, so too did Britain fear losing the only Afghan ruler who seemed even remotely accommodating. The interests of the Modified Forward Policy would hardly be served if the unstable Amanullah were replaced by a less predictable and far less manageable rabble of Frontier Pathans. Besides which, the Foreign Office had no wish to be indicted in the eyes of the world for complicity in the overthrow of a legally constituted monarch.

Accordingly, two aging RAF pursuit planes were sold to Amanullah, who promptly hired a pair of German mercenary pilots to strafe the rebel tribesmen with leaflets. The plot thickened—or curdled—when the Soviet Union got into the act. Evidently and perhaps surprisingly no less averse than Britain to losing the pliable or seemingly pliable Amanullah, Moscow now came up with another gift of planes, whose Russian pilots dropped some real bombs on the insurgent formations. No one was killed, but the explosions scattered the lashkars and broke up the revolution.

Amanullah's position, however, had become shaky. By taking steps against fellow Afghans who had done no more than vent their rage over his capitulation to the Feringhi, he had lost not only a great deal of popular support, but the counsel of his ablest advisor. This man was Nadir Khan, who, after refusing to lead troops against the Ghilzais, had been removed as War Minister and kicked upstairs to head the Afghan Legation in Paris. Nadir was virtually worshipped by the Frontier tribesmen; they took his demotion and exile as an affront to themselves. In the country where the Pathan voice was loudest and the Pathan fist strongest, the Pathan Amanullah had committed a serious blunder.

For all this, however, Amanullah could probably have restored himself to favor had he not also, by the mid-1920s, made plain his intention to sabotage the entire Afghan way of life.

Even at the outset of his reign, the young ruler's modernist views had been suspect among a people crippled since time immemorial by fanatical bigotry and stone-age superstition. As a disciple of the journalist Mahmud Tarzi, who had seen with his own eyes the beginning of Turkey's rapid transformation from decaying medieval empire to twentieth-century constitutional police state, Amanullah seldom lost an opportunity to bemoan in public Afghanistan's own stagnation in the mire of ancient custom. To say the least, this sort of thing did not go down well with the Afghan people—much less with the incalculably powerful Afghan religious leadership. And so it was that national uneasiness grew during the first six months of 1928, when Amanullah made an extended state visit to European and Middle Eastern capitals. Afghans were scandalized to learn that their ruler had worn a top hat to prayers in a Cairo mosque, even more shocked by photographs of an unveiled Queen Souraya in a Western evening gown. But this was only a taste of what Amanullah had in store for his hidebound fellow countrymen.

The first real inkling came after his return to Kabul in July 1928, when he issued proclamations that urged if they did not quite demand the wearing of European clothes, light veils for women and short haircuts for men; at least one tribesman was actually arrested because his hair was too long. In August, when Amanullah summoned the Loe Jirga—a sort of Afghan national assembly—to announce a new legislative program, the delegates played it safe by humoring their monarch's sartorial whims. Fraser-Tytler called the gathering "an unhappy and pathetic sight. Clad in black morning coats and trousers, with white shirts, black ties, and soft hats, [the members] looked very much more like caricatures of Nonconformist clergy than Ghilzai, Mangal and other tribesmen."

But the clown suits were only the beginning. Amanullah next proceeded to outline Afghanistan's New Deal. Among other things, it offered an elected legislature, separation of church and state, compulsory education for both sexes and the total emancipation of women. On the heels of this catalogue of affronts, Amanullah delivered a series of public lectures describing the reforms in detail; the high point came when Queen Souraya dramatized Afghan women's liberation by mounting the dais and ripping off her veil. By the autumn of 1928, not just the Ghilzais of Khost had become aroused. The whole country was up.

This time there was no stopping the rebels. Led by a charismatic brigand named Habibullah Khan—better known as Baccha-i-Saqao, the "son of the water carrier"—a berserk tribal phalanx brushed aside token Afghan Army resistance and swelled its ranks with disaffected regulars in a swift drive on Kabul. On January 3, 1929, Amanullah cancelled all his reforms, with the same effect of a cup of warm water thrown on a forest fire. Nine days later, as insurgent riflemen entered the outskirts of Kabul, he abdicated, managing somehow to escape from the city and eventually to achieve the sumptuous degradation of royal exile in Italy. The son of the water carrier then proclaimed himself the Amir Habibullah Khan.

But his crown fitted badly, for the simple reason that he was not a Pathan but a Tajik, and in Afghanistan, no one but a Pathan could expect to reign long, let alone rule. Within two months of Baccha-i-Saqao's accession, Nadir Khan had returned from France and was mobilizing a counterrevolutionary Pathan army in Khost. By October 1929, the tribal forces were in possession of Kabul, Baccha-i-Saqao had fled (to be gunned down by tribesmen three years later), and Nadir Khan had become King Nadir Shah. The 182-year rule of the Durrani House had been interrupted for barely nine months.

In terms of Frontier security, the news of Nadir's accession was less than cheering to the British. Amanullah, though troublesome enough, had been manageable to a point, while Baccha-i-Saqao's interregnum had been so abbreviated as not to matter much. Nadir was an entirely different proposition.

Outwardly, perhaps not; Nadir's well-trimmed beard, steel-rimmed spectacles and bland expression brought to mind a Viennese psychiatrist rather than a Central Asian warlord. According to Fraser-Tytler, he and the members of his family were "outstanding in Court circles in Kabul for courtesy, good breeding and a certain indefinable air of authority.... [They] were also men of the world who did not allow their political outlook to interfere with their personal relationships." But that was as far as Nadir was prepared to go when it came to dealing with the British.

Ever since his attack on Thal in 1919, Nadir had never made any bones about his resolve to remove the British presence from the Frontier or, at the very least, to make that presence as miserable as he possibly could. In raising the army that overthrew Baccha-i-Saqao, he had defied the Raj by enlisting thousands of Mahsuds and Wazirs from the British side of the Durand Line. In lieu of payment to these tribal irregulars (the Afghan treasury was then empty), he even encouraged their lawlessness by allowing them to loot Kabul, which they did with a will. The royal palace itself was not overlooked; for many years afterwards, Chippendale chairs and handsome Persian carpets, together with medals, jewelry and silverware bearing the royal Afghan star, turned up in the bazaars of cities as far distant as Peshawar and even Lahore. But when the smoke cleared, there was no one who doubted for a moment that Nadir Shah was now in full charge of Afghanistan.

To be sure, one result of the trashing of Kabul's palace was that the Mahsuds and Wazirs came to look on themselves as kingmakers. Nadir himself would later discover this. In the meanwhile, however, the tribesmen remained Nadir's anything but secret weapon. Frontier authorities had valid reason for concern that the Pathans would have the new King's blessing and aid—and Russia's, too—as they renewed their efforts to deep-six the Modified Forward Policy.

And if Nadir had mischief in mind when he came to the Afghan throne in 1929, he could not have chosen a more opportune moment to work it. For the British at this juncture were facing another red alert on the Frontier. It was a crisis different from any they had ever known before.

32

Red Shirts and Cafard

ONE OF THE BIGGEST SURPRISES ever sprung on the Raj by the Frontier Pathan was his relatively sudden, and head-first, entry into politics at the end of the First World War. Previously, officialdom had known of tribal political stirrings, but there does not seem to have been a thorough awareness of how eloquent and passionate a spokesman for his own causes the hillman was capable of becoming. And certainly the last thing Government could have expected was the Pathan's emergence not just as a pugnaciously activist Frontier politico, but as an extremely dangerous militant in the Indian nationalist movement.

In any case, when the lid finally blew off at the end of the 1920s, the British were caught flat-footed.

While the hill tribesman had always been a political animal—albeit a wild one—he had begun, since the turn of the century, to express his legitimate aspirations and legitimate grievances with instruments other than the rifle and curved sword. Thanks to British encouragement of Western education, Peshawar's Edwardes and Islamia colleges were turning out not only a cadre of highly capable Pathan civil servants but an influential intelligentsia of tribal ideologues. Although the dream of ultimate Pathan independence was always there, the original goal of these leaders was more realistic: to bring the Frontier to political equality with the rest of India. Initially, that objective hardly seemed subversive. In many quarters it was considered both reasonable and desirable. While Curzon's reforms had been far from enough, While helping elevate the Pathan's national self-esteem, the reforms themselves were to a great extent administrative and kept the tribes in a political backwater. In the wake of the First World War, Gandhi's powerful Indian National Congress had wrung important concessions from the British. By the Montagu-Chelmsford reforms of 1919, India's central legislature had been given an elected majority, while the Viceroy handed over many of his functions to provincial governors. It was a small yet significant step toward responsible self-rule, but it had not touched the Pathan homeland. The Frontier's young and inexperienced political leaders had therefore sought to achieve the same gains that had been granted elsewhere on the subcontinent, and to achieve them without bloodshed. But Allah and the Raj decreed otherwise, and as the 1920s drew to a close, constitutional procedure swiftly began giving way to armed insurrection.

One reason why the Frontier had been excluded from the Montagu-Chelmsford reforms had been its status as a Chief Commissioner's rather than a Governor's province. This was, however, a technicality that probably would not have mattered much but for the incumbent Chief Commissioner himself. Sir George Roos-Keppel was a typical paradox of the British Empire: the loving father who held his children on a short leash. "More than any other Englishman," writes Caroe, Roos-Keppel was thought of by the tribes "as a sort of malik *in excelsis*, a Pathan among Pathans." He also looked and acted the part (and maybe even dreamed it in Pushtu, having compiled the first standard dictionary of that language). Burly, glowering, hot-tempered, sharp-witted, he could cow the most belligerent warrior with an icy glance or charm the most fractious jirga with a few well-chosen verses from Khushhal Khan. If for no other reason than his role in the founding of Islamia College, Roos-Keppel probably did more to advance the interests of the tribes than any Pathan since Ahmad Shah Durrani.

But if Roos-Keppel was a super-Pathan, he was also a super-paternalist who did not believe that his "children" were ready for Western democracy; it mattered not that almost alone among the subject peoples of British India, the Pathans had had their own representative institutions for centuries. Roos-Keppel liked to say that extending the secret ballot to the Frontier would be akin to lighting matches in a powder magazine. With the introduction of the Montagu-Chelmsford proposals, he brought all of his not inconsiderable influence to bear with the British Government to deny these advances to the Frontier. When he left office, in the same year that the reforms were conferred everywhere else in India, he had made certain that his own fief would be left out in the cold.

The Frontier's response was swift and enraged. It was also nonviolent, at first. One protest took the form of the so-called *Hijrat* movement, a mass Pathan exodus from British territory into Afghanistan, in emulation of the Prophet's *hijra* from Mecca to Medina. Betrayed, as they believed, by their infidel rulers, thousands upon thousands of tribesmen and their families poured through the Khyber Pass to make new homes in a country where the Koran was the law of the land. Most were promptly ordered back across the border by the Afghan Government, and many women and children perished in the scorching summer heat on the return journey. Although Amanullah would probably have preferred to let everyone stay, he could not afford the political and diplomatic risks involved. But neither could the British shrug off so dramatic an extravaganza of dissent.

Far more disturbing was the almost simultaneous emergence of the activist *Khilafat* organization, which took its name from the Turkish Caliphate—the Sultan of Turkey, before his overthrow, having been generally regarded as the spiritual leader of all Islam. The piston rod of this machine was a six-foot, four-inch firebrand named Abdul Ghaffar Khan, for whom Frontier prison gates were almost a revolving door. No other Pathan spoke more eloquently and forcibly—if not always ac-curately—for his people's cause. A well-educated member of an aristo-cratic Yusufzai family, he had once considered entering the Indian Army, but changed his mind and his way of life when he saw a British subaltern abusing a very senior Muslim officer. From that time on, Abdul Ghaffar made it a point never to speak English or wear European clothes, and he became known as *"Fakhre-Afghan"*—"Pride of the Pathans."

Abdul Ghaffar's other sobriquet, "the Frontier Gandhi," was more fitting, since he placed the Khilafat movement into what may have been history's weirdest political bedfellowship: the alliance of Muslim Pathans and the overwhelmingly Hindu Indian National Congress.

In no other part of British India could so unlikely a union have been formed. It came about, and worked, mainly because the Frontier was ninety-four percent Muslim. The Pathans had no need to fear a Hindu takeover, while they simultaneously welcomed Congress money and political know-how. Congress leaders also had something to gain; however fragile, amalgamation was their party's only chance of securing a foothold on the Frontier; without some sort of Pathan endorsement, a Hindu politico would have courted instant gelding if he had so much as set foot in tribal territory. So the uneasy associates held meetings and distributed propaganda and awaited an opportunity to strike a blow at their common British enemy.

The chance came in 1929, when Britain's Simon Commission recom-mended that certain constitutional advances be granted to the Frontier. Rather than being hailed as a political victory by the Pathans, the pro-posed reforms were seen—correctly—as too little and too late, and the Frontier's Hindu-Muslim engine went into high gear. With the blessing of Congress, Abdul Ghaffar had already set about mobilizing an ostensibly nonbelligerent army of Pathan youths. Calling themselves the *Khudai Khidmatgars*, or "Servants of God," they were better known as the Red

Shirts because they could not afford uniforms and coated their clothes with brick dust. Very much an expression of Gandhi's civil disobedience philosophy, the Servants of God did not quite reflect Gandhian views on passive resistance. The Red Shirts were, in fact, more like the Green Berets. With military titles and rank insignia, using drill instructions written by Abdul Ghaffar, they trained in the manner of regimental combat teams.

And after the nonreforms of 1929, training swiftly became the real thing. In Peshawar alone, the Red Shirt chapter had gained so much strength that it was virtually in a position to seize the city by force. By April 1930, that nearly happened when Abdul Ghaffar orchestrated a Red Shirt rally in a school building. Among its features was what authorities called "the performance of a seditious play, calculated to bring the Government into hatred and contempt." Two days after the curtain went down, the British arrested Abdul Ghaffar and several Red Shirt leaders and thus played directly into the hands of the movement as a full-scale insurrection swept the city.

For well over a month, Peshawar was a landlocked Belfast. Regular infantry and cavalry regiments sometimes came close to being scattered and routed in volleys of bricks that were supported by charges of Red Shirts carrying clubs and knives. Police vehicles had their tires slashed. Armored cars were inundated by the mob; Red Shirts poured gasoline over some of the cars and set them alight. At least one motorcycle dispatch rider got the same treatment; many others were luckier, simply being stoned from their pillions. It took nearly six weeks of hand-to-hand fighting, punctuated continually by machine gun bursts, before army and police could bring the outbreak under control.

Actually, it had only begun, for the flames by then had spread into tribal territory. Two RAF bomber squadrons had to fly missions over Waziristan to discourage a mobilization of Mahsuds and to disperse a Wazir lashkar that was laying siege to a militia garrison. The cauldron seethed even more fiercely to the north, where Red Shirt agitators were stirring up a hornets' nest in Tirah—some 7,000 Afridi hornets. By early June, this lashkar had marched to within a mile of Peshawar; only the teamwork of Indian cavalry and RAF fighter planes kept the Afridis from breaking into the city. In August, however, the tribesmen returned. Again they failed to take Peshawar, but they did flank the walls to the north, penetrate the city's outskirts and seize an army supply depot. Although armored car attacks and pinpoint RAF bombing-strafing runs presently dislodged them, insurgency had made its point. On August 16, 1930, the British placed the entire Peshawar district under martial law.

As usual, the action came a little too late. "For the first time in nearly a century of British rule," wrote Barton, ". . . the Frontier capital [had] been attacked and threatened, not by a foreign enemy but by tribesmen in theory subjects of the British Crown. Never in history has sedition been allowed such complete freedom to paralyse authority."

That exaggerated, of course, but Barton was not off base in observing that the Red Shirts now had "what was almost a parallel government" in Peshawar. Certainly they wielded enough clout to make demands that had to be heeded. Abdul Ghaffar was presently released from prison to resume his incendiary organizing, and Congress rewarded him with the title of "Generalissimo of Volunteers." He earned the honor; by the end of 1931, Peshawar had reached the brink of another insurrection.

The authorities now took swift measures to nip it in the bud, declaring the Red Shirts an illegal organization, arresting nearly 100 of their leaders and deporting Abdul Ghaffar from the province. In so doing, they may have kept Peshawar, and the whole Frontier, from going up in smoke.

But again Government proved tardy—Abdul Ghaffar had done his work too well. In 1932, thanks largely to earlier Congress-Red Shirt pressure, the 1919 reforms were finally conferred on the Frontier, which now became a full-fledged Governor's province with an appointed in-digenous minister at the head of local government. The latter office was what really counted; at long last, the Pathans had achieved political parity with the rest of British India.

To be sure, the man chosen by the Indian Government as the Frontier's chief minister was a relative moderate. Sahibzada Sir Abdul Qayyum, Roos-Keppel's old friend, had an outstanding record as a political officer, and his work within the system had won him a knighthood. But the British could never forget that Abdul Qayyum was no less a Pathan than Abdul Ghaffar. He had continually nagged viceroys, governors and commissioners for responsible government on the Frontier, and when he had been told—invariably—that the Frontier was too small, he had always replied that fleas were small, too, but a nuisance in one's trousers. Although the tribes would probably have preferred a fire-eating nationalist to Abdul Qayyum, they at least knew that they now had a fellow tribesman to speak for them in the highest councils of Frontier administration.

There was more to come. In 1935, the Government of India Act not only extended the franchise, but made the provincial chief minister an elected rather than an appointed official. Frontier politics became a much more serious matter than ever before. In the 1937 elections, the tribes swept Abdul Qayyum out of office and returned Abdul Ghaffar's brother, Dr. Khan Sahib, in a landslide. Khan Sahib's English wife and Edinburgh University medical degree belied an ideology at least as militant as Abdul Ghaffar's, and no less strong an identification with Gandhi and Nehru. The British could only scratch their heads and begin to ask themselves whether the unnatural Hindu-Muslim alliance, which they had previously thought of as impermanent at best, might not become a lasting force on the Frontier.

In 1930, at the height of the Red Shirt riots in Peshawar and the concurrent outbreaks in Waziristan and Tirah, numerous Pathan delegations had visited Kabul to seek money, arms and other assistance from Nadir Shah. The Anglophobic Afghan monarch was the quintessence of Oriental hospitality, receiving his guests warmly in the royal palace, where they were served vast amounts of mutton kebabs and spiced saffron pilaf, vermicelli with almonds, raisins and pistachios, sliced fried bread in essence of rose, sherbet in at least two dozen flavors and all the opium-laced coffee they could drink. Nadir also offered the Pathans a great deal of advice. And he gave them nothing.

If this unexpected coolness surprised and chagrined the tribesmen, it surprised and delighted the British, who had fully expected—with very good reason—that their old *bête noire* would certainly not have spurned so juicy an opportunity to torpedo the Modified Forward Policy. But for the first time in Britain's nine-decade occupation of the trans-Indus hills, an Afghan ruler appeared to have voluntarily waived his own claim to the Frontier Pathans as Afghan subjects. Nadir's refusal to exploit the 1930 crisis suggested strongly that his years in Paris might have softened his belligerence, that he might have taken a long new look at his responsibilities as a chief of state, that he may have felt it in his country's best interests to honor treaty obligations and respect international boundaries—in short, a good neighbor rather than a thorn in the flesh. It was the only ray of light for the British in one of their darker hours on the Frontier.

This was not to say that Nadir had suddenly come to love his old enemies. No British nationals were permitted employment anywhere in Afghanistan—not even as English teachers in schools, with the result that many Afghans became fluent in French and German and spoke halting English in the "Babu" accents of their Indian instructors. But they knew even less Russian, for Nadir was determined to maintain an iron neutrality toward the two giants on his borders. Considering Soviet inroads under Amanullah, Nadir's nonalignment, for all its iciness, could only gratify the British Foreign Office.

Nadir's domestic policy also encouraged the British because it too reflected statesmanship. Without trying to reintroduce Amanullah's more impetuous reforms, Nadir did not hesitate to move his country forward in less immoderate, but definitely progressive, ways. He created a new Cabinet, National Council and Upper House. A genuinely modern army—with something like a real air force—came into being. Communications made a quantum leap with the construction of the "Great North Road" over the Hindu Kush. Nadir's regime also witnessed the growth of secular education, the building of hospitals, the development of irrigation projects, mineral exploitation and foreign trade. Afghanistan was at last beginning to establish bona fide credentials as a more or less stable twentieth-century sovereign nation. And stability in Afghanistan was directly related to stability on the northwest frontier of British India.

Forbearance on the Frontier, however, proved Nadir's Achilles' heel. When Amanullah had caved in under British border demands, a tribal revolt had been mounted against him. Now, the exiled Amanullah's supporters in Afghanistan seized on the same hot potato as the means of ousting the man who had supplanted Amanullah. Rumors soon began circulating that Nadir had made a secret pact with the British. Although totally without foundation, these tales were more than enough to start the Frontier volcano rumbling. On the British side of the Durand Line, great lashkars of Mahsuds and Wazirs began massing. Having put Nadir on the throne, these tribes were now prepared to remove him. With no opposition, they crossed the border into Khost. It was only by good fortune and Nadir's own foresight that a powerful Afghan Army column finally intercepted the lashkars and sent them sprawling. But Nadir's troubles had only begun.

For frontier hysteria had taken hold in Kabul. By 1932, the leader of the pro-Amanullah faction, one Ghulam Nabi, was conspiring so openly for Nadir's overthrow that Nadir ordered his summary execution. The consequence of this act was the unedifying spectacle of a Pathan blood feud that centered on Afghanistan's royal house. It came to an abrupt end in 1933, while Nadir was handing out prizes to pupils in a school ceremony. One of the winners was a natural son of Ghulam Nabi. As Nadir approached him, he drew a pistol and pumped three bullets into the King's chest. In the panic and rioting that ensued, it looked for a few moments as if the assassination would plunge Afghanistan back into her former state of Cro-Magnon anarchy.

But Nadir had done his job too thoroughly. Before the day was out, his younger brother, Shah Mahmud, had stepped into the breach and used his near-absolute powers as War Minister to nip any insurrection in the bud and assure the succession of Nadir's nineteen-year-old son Zahir. Under the guidance of another of Nadir's brothers, Prime Minister Hashim Khan, Zahir reigned, and eventually ruled, in Afghanistan for forty years. The orderly continuation of the royal line may have been the most accurate measure of the degree to which Nadir had united Afghanistan in spite of herself.

The smooth transfer of power in Kabul was just as important to the British, who saw diminishing reason to anticipate any disruptive changes in the Frontier policy that Nadir had established—nothing, at least, that would interfere seriously with the slow but not altogether discouraging progress of their own Modified Forward Policy. In 1933, with the worst of the Red Shirt troubles apparently behind them, Frontier authorities could begin to hope that "peaceful penetration" might at last be gaining something vaguely like acceptance among the tribes.

This did not mean that the hills had become a pacifist commune. In 1933, with Red Shirt help, the Mohmands to the north of Peshawar kicked over the traces and went on a two-year rampage of intermittent but jarring collisions with the best troops the Indian Army could put into the field. The future Field Marshal Sir Claude Auchinleck won his spurs in this campaign. One action in 1935 saw a Sikh rifle company and a Gurkha machine gun platoon hold back a raging sea of Mohmands that rolled in on them for an entire night. Tribesmen continually breached the British defenses, seized machine guns by their overheated muzzles and clubbed sepoys to the ground with the butts of their own rifles—only to be evicted violently each time by bayonets and kukri blades. Not since Ambela in 1863 had the Frontier witnessed so wild a melee. But for all its ferocity, the Mohmand uprising was an isolated affair that never won Frontier-wide support, even among its own clans. And Barton could write of this period that "the policy of peaceful penetration [had] not been entirely unsuccessful where conditions [were] not unfavourable."

That assessment was not invalid. Visible if not spectacular improvements had been wrought by Government to improve the tribesman's economic lot. As early as 1929, a detailed report on Frontier resources had even sounded a note of unprecedented optimism: "Historically speaking, [the region] is decidedly more tranquil today than it was a decade or two ago and there has slowly come into existence a new spirit of economic striving. . . . There is a growing realisation . . . that the pursuits of peace are not unproductive in themselves." Considering that the Red Shirt outbreaks were about to occur, the report was overly sanguine, but it did indicate at least the stirrings of a trend.

Nowhere did this appear more true than in the old Armageddon of Waziristan, where the abbreviated dustup of 1930 had been the only really explosive moment in an otherwise uninterrupted decade of relative quiet. Of course, no Wazir or Mahsud could be expected to abstain totally from taking occasional potshots at fellow tribesmen, from the sporadic theft of a neighbor's goats or wives or from the waylaying of a stray army lorry. But in general, the Mahsuds and the Wazirs behaved themselves, content to accept their Government allowances and Government wages for labor on roads and other public works. Some tribesmen even exploited the British road network by starting private bus services to compete with the camel trade. Sir Evelyn Howell, who had once had his plate full with the Mullah Powinda and had since become India's Foreign Secretary, could write that the Mahsuds "have abandoned their sullenness and talk openly, although perhaps not altogether sincerely, of the day when they will submit to disarmament and become full-fledged British subjects."

Waziristan was one of the showcases of the Modified Foreign Policy, and its newly acquired decorum was enforced at arm's length by the great British strongholds of Wana, Razmak and Miram Shah—but most directly by the tribe's own constabulary and militia forces. The *Khassadars*, or tribal police, wore no uniforms except armbands with the letter "K," which may have given them a partial anonymity in their task of guarding roads against brigands. From midget forts, strategically located throughout tribal territory, they carried out an unending fine-tooth-comb patrol of all Waziristan. Neither they nor the Khassadars ever stamped out feuding, looting and shooting entirely—nor was it expected that they would—but their presence, as often as not, was enough to discourage delinquency on the grand scale.

The novelist John Masters, whose service as a junior officer with a Gurkha regiment in Waziristan during the 1930s enabled him to write many lively personal reminiscences of Frontier war and peace, has a nice assessment of the two tribal forces. He thought of the Khassadars as "probably a necessary step in the development of local responsibility for law and order," and because "tribesmen were reluctant to shoot at *khassadars* for fear of becoming engaged in a blood feud." Masters added that "unfortunately, the *khassadars* were equally reluctant to fire on their naughty fellows for precisely the same reason. Furthermore, all *khassadars* seemed to be permanently in a temper about pay or promotion, and a high proportion of the stray shots fired at the army in Waziristan was fired by peevish *khassadars*."

Masters had kinder words for the militia. "Scouts on the march were a magnificent sight. The British officers were indistinguishable from the men—all brown as berries, all wearing khaki turbans, grey shirts flapping loose outside khaki shorts, stockings, and nailed sandals. . . . [They] covered enormous distances at high speed. Each man carried thirty or fifty rounds of ammunition, a water bottle, a bag of raisins, a few disks of unleavened bread, and a lump or two of coarse sugar. The whole party, numbering perhaps one hundred and eighty, shared the burden of the heavy baggage—four stretchers and a basket of carrier pigeons." In a punitive action, said Masters, the Scouts "pounced before dawn on some fortress village . . . arrested the startled headman, and whisked him lightfoot to headquarters, there to explain just what hand the young men of his village had taken in last week's mail robbery. . . . In ordinary times they would keep the peace because they were light-armed and fast, and because they were themselves Pathans."

"In ordinary times"—that was the operative phrase. If and when the situation in Waziristan should ever get out of hand, Government could call on the big battalions in the three big forts. And the forts were big indeed, accommodating a total of more than 30,000 Indian Army troops, together with a more or less formidable assortment of artillery, armor and aircraft. At the slightest sign of a real tribal rampage, the gates of the fortresses would swing open and three immense iron dragons would thunder forth, spewing out a deadly vomit of bombs and bullets and blades.

But it said something about Waziristan's peace that the British forts were breeding grounds of cafard: a two-year tour of garrison duty was not unlike a jail sentence. "The Razmak barracks," wrote Masters, "were low and made of stone and stood in straight lines inside a low stone wall three or four miles long that surrounded the whole fortress. . . . Beyond the wall stood a row of electric lights on tall posts, and, just beyond the lights, three double aprons of barbed wire. Beyond the wire the tilted plateau sloped away to jagged mountains, and across the plateau tribesmen strode slowly with the full, free lilt of their kind, leading their camels behind them. We watched them enviously from the safe imprisonment of the wall and the wire."

The army tried to keep officers and men contented by providing such amenities as movies, shopping centers and fields for race meetings, football, hockey, squash and tennis. In the officers' mess, said Masters, "lived an echo from silver trumpets of the past. . . . At dinner the Colours, cased and capped and crossed, stood . . . against the wall. . . . On guest nights they were unfurled and lit the room with the embroidered battle honours of two hundred years." But these reminders of tradition—and of home—only served to intensify a very real feeling of exile to a dead asteroid in outer space.

The most important comfort of all, moreover, was strictly forbidden; Razmak, the biggest of the three forts, was also called, with joking frustration, the world's largest monastery. There were sporadic efforts at unauthorized relief. Several subalterns riding a lorry in a Razmak-bound convoy were found to be young Englishwomen from Peshawar in disguise. A venturesome peeress on a round-the-world journey donned the robes and veil of a Mahsud woman, with a view to entering Razmak, but was stopped nearly twenty miles from her goal; no one had told her that the fort was off limits even to Pathan women—or, perhaps, especially to Pathan women. If nothing else, however, such episodes at least made topics of sex-starved conversation.

To keep officers and men from going stir-crazy, periodic cross-country hikes had to be arranged. Lasting a week or ten days, they were carried out on the pretext of showing the flag and flexing the muscles for the benefit of some headman or clan suspected of evil designs against the peace of the neighborhood. In some ways, these maneuvers had the flavor of a picnic. "At evening," wrote Masters, "the day's march done and the stone wall built, we sat, sweat-stained, around the cookers and smoked and drank strong tea. At night as we made our rounds of duty the stars gleamed on the bayonets of the silent sentries along the wall. At dawn we awoke to the shrill sweet call of the mountain artillery trumpets blowing a long reveille. The call seemed to last a golden age while I huddled deeper into my blanket and embraced my returning senses." Then, fully awake and once more on the march, "we rampaged up and down the mountains, playing at being scouts and soldiers. . . . It was a game—but we never pulled the trigger on one another, as we would have done in similar mock battles in England, because here every weapon was loaded with ball."

Nor were triggers often squeezed in anger; the tribes seldom gave that much offense. Enough, yes, so that the North West Frontier Province of the post–World War I decade was the only remaining part of the British Empire—except for Kenya's Northern Frontier District—where young men could still find the stuff of high adventure in the Kipling tradition. But the hills generally tended to offer something that could almost have passed for peace. T. E. Lawrence called Miram Shah "the station of a dream" when he served there during the late 1920s as an RAF enlisted man under the alias of T. E. Shaw. "As though one had fallen right over the world," he wrote a friend, "and had lost one's memory of its troubles. And the quietness is so intense that I rub my ears, wondering if I am growing deaf."

For the legendary Lawrence of Arabia, of course, this idyllic existence had to be short-lived. Hardly had he settled down to his clerk-typist duties at Miram Shah than reports began circulating of his involvement as a secret agent for the rebels in the uprising that unseated Amanullah from the Afghan throne. Despite an official Afghan denial ("We do not believe in Colonel Lawrence's power and skill. He is only an Englishman."), the British had to quash the rumors by transferring Lawrence back to England. Nor was Lawrence the only Briton to be deprived suddenly of peace in Waziristan. In that place, so unnatural a stillness could not continue indefinitely. In the 1930s it would come to a swift and shattering end.

33

The Caves of the Fakir of Ipi

ONE SUMMER DAY in 1936, a Wazir tribesman entered the town of Bannu in the settled district of that name. By dint of personal charm or the blade of his knife or both, he prevailed on one Chand Bibi, the wife of a Hindu merchant, to accompany him back across the administrative border and marry him in a Muslim ceremony. Chand Bibi's original husband then sought to win her back by going to court with a charge of kidnapping.

The trial became India's Patty Hearst case. Government looked on uneasily as the tribesmen began to smolder over what they considered an affront to their own version of Muslim law. Shortly after the verdict came down in the Hindu's favor, several thousand Wazirs ambushed the Indian Army's Bannu Brigade, killing and mutilating 130 officers and men and making off with a bumper crop of rifles and ammunition. The "Islam Bibi" case had become a casus belli; as one Frontier official put it: "here a pretty face moved, not a thousand ships like Helen of Troy, but at least two British divisions."

Perhaps the whole thing would have simmered down but for a Wazir holy man known as the Fakir of Ipi. Small in stature by Pathan standards, he had been going about his priestly duties for years without attracting notice, but beneath his unassuming exterior bubbled a hatred for the unbeliever that was certifiable in its intensity. The Fakir of Ipi also possessed the skills of a field marshal and enough rabble-rousing charisma to mobilize a tribal army. The "Islam Bibi" case was his long-awaited opportunity to

[357]

demonstrate these attributes. Not since the Mullah Powinda would a Waziristan Pathan pose so grave a threat to British Frontier authority.

The Fakir got off to a good start. By early 1937, his lashkars had carried out nearly three dozen major raids into administered territory, leaving in their wake a smoking trail of gutted houses and shops and disemboweled Hindu cadavers. They also caught the British flat-footed. Patrols and pickets came under continual sniper fire. One war party ambushed an army convoy of fifty lorries, shooting and slicing up seventy-two officers and men. Tribal columns threatened Razmak's supply lines. Under the Fakir of Ipi's blows, the military arm of the Modified Forward Policy seemed at first to be strangely lacking in sinew.

Then the British struck back. Two Indian Army brigades, composed mainly of Sikh and Gurkha regiments, spearheaded the counteroffensive. In May 1937, they trapped the Fakir of Ipi, who had been found holed up in some caves near Wana. A strong Gurkha force converged on the position, and its forward rifle companies deployed outside the caves as sappers tossed in several bushels of hand grenades. Then the Gurkhas went in with bayonets fixed. They found the Fakir's cook-fires still burning, but they did not find the Fakir, who had slipped out through a fissure in the rocks only moments before the grenades went off.

Yet the near-miss was not without its effect; one of the larger and more belligerent Wazir clans accepted British surrender terms and an armistice was proclaimed.

It meant nothing whatever while the Fakir of Ipi remained at large. Within six months of the armistice, nearly 50,000 British and Indian troops were in the field, festooned with automatic weapons, girdled with field guns and howitzers, chaperoned by flotillas of tanks and armored cars, shaded by the umbrella of the Royal Air Force. An oversize punitive expedition had escalated into a full-scale war.

Arrayed against the Government forces were probably fewer than 10,000 Wazirs and Mahsuds, but numerical superiority and twentieth-century combat hardware did not tip the scales in favor of the Indian Army. Tanks and armored cars proved as much liability as asset in country that mangled treads and shredded tires. Aircraft had to overcome special obstacles, which will be described. Despite their well-earned reputations as in-fighters, the Gurkhas and Sikhs were tangling with a savvy guerrilla soldiery that enjoyed the incalculable advantage of defending its own ground. There was no fixed front. "The core of our problem," said John Masters, who fought through the whole campaign, "was to force battle on an elusive and mobile enemy."

For the tribesmen made it a point to avoid the head-on clashes that they could never win, favoring instead the same kind of evasive broken-field tactics that were to humiliate the cream of American generalship in Vietnam three decades later. On the rare occasions when the British maneuvered smartly enough to close with a lashkar, the tribal forces needed only to scatter and re-form as soon as they were beyond reach of the ungainly steel juggernaut. As often as not, they slipped off across the Durand Line into Afghanistan, where the British could not even scout them. "We felt," wrote Masters, "as if we were using a crowbar to swat wasps."

The wasps also had sharp stings. They sniped. They laid ambushes. They poisoned wells. They improvised booby traps from stolen hand grenades. They tore up isolated encampments and outposts in quick-silver night attacks, melting off into the blackness before the defenders could get off an answering volley or even form up. They were masters of deceit: the tribesman would surrender and then pull a knife; he would evade notice by dressing as a woman or a trader. Often, he simply played possum; an entire Sikh or Gurkha regiment might march past several dozen dead Wazirs or Mahsuds who would then come to life and blast away at the rear guard. A British company commander once ordered his men to open fire on a tribal funeral procession. Some instinct had told him—correctly, as it proved—that the "female" mourners carried rifles under their robes and that the coffin itself contained a pair of especially notorious guerrilla leaders who had been packed inside with several thousand rounds of ammunition.

Lines of communication were a favorite Pathan target. Even railway supply lines behind the administrative border might go sky-high above tribal land mines made from unexploded British shells. Most vulnerable of all were the army's slow, lurching motor convoys—bushwhacked so regu-larly that as many as 10,000 troops sometimes had to be used simply to keep the roads clear, or try to. Masters called guarding convoys against ambush "the hardest task the Frontier offered, because every day we covered the same stretch of road, and every day it become more difficult to obey the cardinal Frontier principle of never doing the same thing in the same way twice running." To disregard that rule even for a part of a second was to court a bullet between the eyes.

Or worse, to invite capture. The tribes were not signatories to the Geneva Convention. A prisoner could feel grateful if he was simply decapitated; even live castration showed forbearance. Just as often, the captive might have his tongue torn out at the roots and twigs pushed into his urethra while he was being flayed alive. Another popular execution was the so-called "death of a thousand cuts," highlighted by thorns being thrust into each wound as it was sliced open. Or the prisoner would be pegged to the ground and his jaws wedged apart with a stick, so that each woman of a clan could squat over him and urinate down his throat until he drowned. There were other variations on these themes.

It was the sort of thing that sometimes put a strain on the British to remember their own rules of fair play, although they were continually reminded of them—to their great exasperation—by the political officers who accompanied most units. Masters acknowledged that "Political Agents would have been useless if they had not identified themselves thoroughly with the tribesmen's thoughts and feelings," but added that "we felt they often carried it too far." An echo of Winston Churchill's old complaint about Harold Deane, the conflict between military and civil officers in Waziristan turned on the difference between what Masters called "the soldier's downright description of the Pathan as an 'enemy,' and the political's opinion of him as a 'misguided fellow citizen.'" The campaign abounded with episodes in which a political agent would remark to an army officer: "I thought our chaps did rather well today"—the chaps being some lashkar that had just inflicted heavy casualties on a British, Gurkha or Sikh unit.

The army had its own reply. "We took very few prisoners at any time," wrote Masters, "and very few indeed if there was no Political Agent about."

It went a bit farther than that. A well-worn anecdote of the Waziristan campaign concerned the Sikh detachment that came across the body of one of its officers; his private parts had been stuffed into his mouth and his skin was drying in the sun a few yards away. When the British commanding officer was sure that the sepoys had had a good look, he then ordered that no further prisoners be taken under any circumstances. Several days later, the order was disobeyed when one of the men brought in a Mahsud whose thighs had been shattered by a grenade burst. This so irked the officer that he had the prisoner spreadeagled to a rock for the rest of the day, beneath a sun whose ferocity toppled even Pathans. He further ordered that every sepoy passing the prisoner kick him in the testicles. It is not known whether the Mahsud succumbed to his wounds, the kicks or the 130-degree heat.

The British fought dirty in other ways. A youthful tribesman taken into custody on strong suspicion of brigandage that could not be proved had his rifle temporarily confiscated. "Under pretext of examining it," wrote Masters, the battalion armorers "took the weapon in a vice and secretly bent the barrel a fraction of an inch, not enough to notice but enough to cause an explosion and perhaps blow the young man's hand off next time he fired." The most widespread practice was to have ordnance men remove the propellant charges from rifle cartridges, substitute high explosives and then strew the doctored bullets across the countryside. Masters notes with satisfaction that "the tribesman, always short of ammunition, picked them up, with bad results for his hand or face when he fired his treasure trove."

It was enough that the troops had to deal with political officers. They were also up against British war aims. It had been laid down by the

Indian Government that the objective in Waziristan was not to win, but to restore order; authorities maintained, not without reason, that if a resounding humiliation were inflicted on the tribes it would only sow the seeds of further unrest and violence. With this in mind, a set of combat regulations was drawn up. Its effect, said Masters, was that "we fought with one hand behind our backs."

The rules were clear and strict. Offensive action was forbidden outside so-called "proscribed areas," which were more or less arbitrarily delimited as legitimate combat zones. Even inside a proscribed area, however, troops could not open fire on bands of fewer than ten tribesmen, and the Pathans could still be immune to attack if they carried no visible weapons and stayed on the road. "These were dangerous conditions," Masters observed drily, "in a country where arms can be concealed close to flowing clothes, and where paths are tracks invisible from a hundred yards." Masters did not have to add that such conditions favored the Pathans even more because the rules did not apply to them.

Aircraft were also bound by the rules. RAF fighter-bombers proved useful in strafing runs that generally scattered tribal formations discovered creeping up on British convoys or troops on the march, but only if the creeping was being done in a proscribed area. Bombing missions could not be carried out unless approved by the local political officer and endorsed along a chain of authority extending from the Waziristan Resident to the Governor of the Province and sometimes to the Viceroy. Even then, however, aircraft had to fly over the target clan a week in advance and release a snowstorm of white leaflets announcing the upcoming attack. The warning would also specify a safety zone where tribesmen could take their families and livestock. Six days later came a red alert: red leaflets with twenty-four-hour notice of the bombing. After that it was all systems more or less "go."

Obviously, few Wazirs or Mahsuds were ever killed in air raids. But the tribesmen did at least find their confinement more than a minor nuisance, since the "safe" area was generally a barren postage stamp in which hundreds and sometimes thousands of men, women, children, sheep and goats had to cram together for days and occasionally weeks at a time, with virtually no food, water or grazing. Occasionally the result would even be a mass surrender, which was a good thing: an entire month might go by before the clan's able-bodied males were back in action.

Air warfare may have created more problems than it solved. A great furor was raised in the League of Nations over the wanton bombing of helpless women and children. It seemed to escape the critics' notice that children were always safe, and that the only women ever killed by the RAF were those occasional old crones whom the tribesmen tied up outside secure areas with a view to collecting blood money from Government. Nor did anyone in the League get around to observing that Wazir and Mahsud women sometimes joined their menfolk in action, or that women usually showed more inventiveness when it came to disfiguring prisoners.

Above all, there appeared to be no awareness of the Pathan's remarkable skill in bringing down low-flying planes with rifle fire. RAF crews always carried special papers—against the possibility of forced landings—which promised safe conduct and large cash rewards to any tribesmen who delivered them intact to the British lines. Armed with these documents, captured airmen were an infinitely better insurance risk than captured ground troops, although immunity from live dismemberment could never be absolutely certain.

What may have exasperated the army even more than the restrictions on its fighting potential was the high-level policy of negotiating with the belligerents. Instead of making it plain that Government terms had to be accepted on a tribal-wide basis, the British dealt piecemeal with individual sections or clans. The result of this was that even if two or three or four groups submitted, other large Pathan forces would still remain in the field, and thus assure shelter for the Fakir of Ipi—the cause of the whole thing—while they continued to hound and harass and mutilate and simply drag the war on.

And so it went for nearly three years without so much as a glimmer of light at the end of the tunnel, while the British tried vainly to cope with a pitiless and diabolical foe on a blasted desolation of his own choosing—a land that fried the brains in the hot months and split the marrow when the arctic winter clamped down. In July 1938, the army trapped the Fakir of Ipi for the second time. Again he had burrowed into a cave, and again a powerful force converged on his hideout, this time sealing off all avenues of escape. But all avenues of entry were also blocked; the terrain of the broken-tooth range where the Fakir had concealed himself proved so rugged that even the mountain-wise Gurkhas could not come within miles of the cave. Once more, the capture of the Fakir of Ipi had to be written off.

By way of thumbing their noses, the tribes now went on a vest-pocket offensive as a 200-man commando force crossed the administrative border and leveled Bannu. Artillery and light machine guns soon pried the attackers out of the town, but neither soon enough nor far enough to suit Bannu's Hindu population. As one man, the Hindus packed their belongings in fear-stricken haste and fled east across the Indus. British prestige on the Frontier never altogether recovered from that particular humiliation.

In the end, though, the British "won." As 1938 drew to a close, the sheer force of Indian Army numbers and the sheer weight of its metal had begun to make themselves felt on the tribes. The Wazirs and Mahsuds had led the army a merry chase and had usually made fools of its commanders, but they could not afford a slow but seemingly endless siphoning-off of their own manpower. Clan after clan began accepting the British terms, and by early 1939 the war had all but petered out. The most serious problem, the British now discovered, lay in dealing with the hordes of previously hostile tribesmen who were making formal application for Waziristan campaign medals. "I think their request was reasonable," said Masters.

As for the Fakir of Ipi, he remained at large. His career as troublemaker, in fact, had hardly begun.

From the British standpoint, the Waziristan campaign, apart from casualties, had cost more than £50 million—with nothing to show for the outlay but the fragility, if not the worthlessness, of the Modified Forward Policy.

Yet this was not quite so; if nothing else, Waziristan had proved immensely useful as what Sir William Barton called "a school for soldiering." Masters certainly agreed. "The campaign had taught me much," he wrote, "that was to be of value in the coming world war.* Many Aldershot-type officers maintained that we learned only bad habits in this tribal warfare against what they called 'ragged-arsed barnshoots.' It was not true. From the Frontier itself we learned unwinking, unsleeping alertness. From the Pathans we learned more about the tactical value of ground than any of our . . . future enemies knew. (In 1944 after a heavy Japanese night attack on my brigade had failed . . . Subadar Manjang shook his head and said to me with a slightly disapproving cheerfulness, 'If these *Japani-baru* were Pathans we'd have a very bad time.')"

Masters added: "I also learned to respect the enemy—any enemy. Whoever he was, he was only a man doing something that he believed right."

The training came none too soon. Even as the Waziristan campaign wound down, Adolf Hitler was masterminding an exotic Frontier conspiracy aimed at throwing sand in the gears of British global strategy. His field manager was the former Grand Mufti of Jerusalem and his chief agent a Syrian holy man known as the Shami Pir, who had once lived in Afghanistan and was related by marriage to the exiled Amanullah. Late in 1938, the Shami Pir went to Waziristan, made some stem-winding speeches to the tribes, and raised a lashkar to march on Kabul. At the eleventh hour, the Indian Government scotched the whole thing with a £25,000 bribe to the Shami Pir and a plane that carried him back to the Middle East. It was fortunate that the plot backfired. Hitler knew that Amanullah was believed to have strong pro-German sympathies, and

* From which Masters himself emerged as a general.

that his reinstatement might well throw the whole Frontier into an anti-British eruption perhaps even more violent than the 1897 revolt. Restoring order might require not just two divisions but quite possibly nearly all of the Indian Army.

That of course was Hitler's idea; should the Empire find itself locked in conflict with Germany again—and perhaps also with Japan—it would be in serious trouble if at least half a million British and Indian soldiers were shackled to a northwest frontier in an uproar. The handwriting was on the wall.

Indeed, when hostilities finally broke out in 1939, the Pathans did rise. The duration of the war witnessed acts of mass tribal violence and atrocity on a previously unimagined scale—all of them perpetrated in British uniform in Europe, North Africa and Burma. As in the First World War, the British were gratified to know that Pathans could respond to threats from infidels other than those who ruled India. Concurrently, the hills themselves went into hibernation, enjoying six consecutive years of unprecedented peace. It later became a standing joke among Indian Army officers to ask one another: "Were you in the war or on the frontier?"

Then the tribes came home from the wars and the peace came to an end.

34

The Last Viceroy

On February 20, 1946, in fulfillment of a Labour Party campaign promise, Prime Minister Clement Attlee announced to the world that Britain would quit India within two years. Rather than being greeted with elation on the Frontier, the news touched off a wave of alarm and consternation. To the hillmen, Indian freedom seemed to promise only a leap from frying pan into fire. The subcontinent's population consisted of 300 million Hindus and 100 million Muslims, which meant that the Hindus' Congress Party would inevitably shape the course of Frontier affairs. The Raj was intolerable enough, but at least one could find room to respect the British; now, the hills were to be ruled by the despicable Hindu, and the tribesmen would not have it.

At this time, Congress was still the majority party on the Frontier. During the 1920s and 1930s, tribal political leaders had found it expedient and safe enough to accept Hindu funds and exploit Hindu organizational talents against the common British oppressor. In 1945, Dr. Khan Sahib had been returned to office as the Frontier's Chief Minister on a Congress ticket that swamped the candidate of Muhammad Ali Jinnah's Muslim League in the provincial elections. But with the impending departure of the British, the political face of the Frontier began to change in a sudden erosion of Congress influence and a corresponding rise of tribal support for the Muslim League.

Previously, Jinnah's backing had come almost exclusively from Muslim communities in the Punjab and other parts of India, while the Pathans, who might have been expected to raise the loudest clamor for a separate

[365]

Muslim state, had simply not taken the two-nation concept seriously. Now, however, Pakistan became a very real thing almost overnight. Muslim League enrollment on the Frontier swelled to the point where no less a Congress figure than Jawaharlal Nehru decided that something had to be done. In the summer of 1946, Nehru personally stumped the province to shore up his party's collapsing edifice.

It was the act of a very brave man. When Nehru stepped off his plane at Peshawar's airport, a strong police cordon just managed to hold back an angry sea of tribesmen brandishing black war flags and screaming epithets at the loathsome Brahmin who had the effrontery to think he and his cow-worshipping ilk were going to sway true sons of the Prophet. The abuse became louder and more enraged as Nehru proceeded into the hills. Brickbats continually bounced off his car; one drew blood from his forehead. In the Khyber Pass, a gang of Afridi toughs rushed the car and would have overturned it if police batons had not clubbed them senseless. It was a small wonder that Nehru managed to return to Delhi intact. But the message was clear enough: to all practical purposes, Congress was through on the Frontier.

Nehru would not accept that verdict; he pumped more funds into Khan Sahib's machine. The investment failed to bring a return. By early 1947, anti-Congress riots were sweeping the Frontier. In the capital of the Dera Ismail Khan District, Indian Army tanks had to be brought up to disperse brigade-size mobs that had been looting and burning Hindu shops by the score. The town of Tank near the Waziristan border was the scene of savage street fighting between heavily armed Muslim League demonstrators and strong units of the South Waziristan Scouts. As the battle raged, terrified Hindu merchants and moneylenders offered astronomical sums to Mahsud tribesmen to guard their homes, shops, families and persons. Payment was on a per diem basis, and the gleeful mercenaries, stationing themselves behind windows and doors and on rooftops, prolonged the action for several days with random but continual potshots at anything and everything that moved.

Khan Sahib's position had grown precarious. He ordered the arrest of the Muslim League's Peshawar chairman, together with hundreds of his followers. This only intensified the tribes' fury. Women climbed the walls of the Peshawar prison to wave the green flag of Islam in defiance. Effigies of Khan Sahib were dragged through the streets by donkeys and burned in the bazaars. Railway service was disrupted when the tracks of the Peshawar Mail were pulled up and several trains derailed. The situation promised to grow a great deal worse before it got better.

A contributing factor in the escalating violence was the April visit to the Frontier of India's last Viceroy. The dashing, politically astute Admiral Lord Louis Mountbatten had been appointed by Attlee for the specific task of liquidating the Raj. As King George VI's cousin and Queen Victoria's great-grandson, Mountbatten had understandably sought to duck the assignment, but once it had been forced on him he resolved to carry out Britain's evacuation with dignity, honor and fairness—and, if possible, in an orderly fashion. Along with Gandhi, Nehru and the entire Congress leadership, Mountbatten was implacably opposed to India's partition into separate Hindu and Muslim states, but two things changed his mind. One was the even more unbudgeable Jinnah, who all but guaranteed to drown the subcontinent in its own blood if denied Pakistan. The other was the Frontier.

Before he went to the province, Mountbatten's acquaintance with Muslim nationalist fervor had probably been less practical than theoretical. On his arrival in Peshawar, however, theory became jolting fact as 100,000 rifle- and knife-toting Pathans converged on his party and shredded the air with their strident demands for independence. The Viceroy and Lady Mountbatten left their car and approached the mob. Demands became curses and animal howls. The noise could almost be cut with a knife. Tribesmen began picking up stones. For a few ugly moments it looked as if the two most awesome living symbols of the Raj would meet a squalid end at the hands of hoodlums.

But Mountbatten had better luck running for him than had Alexander Burnes 106 years earlier. Among other things, he had shown the good sense not to deck himself out in the resplendent gold lace, the red sash, the glittering stars and medals, the imperious cocked hat or any other adornments of the infidel rule so fiercely hated by the tribesmen. Instead, he simply had on the same wartime jungle green uniform that he had worn as Supreme Allied Commander in Southeast Asia. Thousands of Pathans had also worn that uniform in Burma. And green, of course, was the color of Islam. It did not take the tribesmen long to notice these things. Now, shouts of "Jihad!", "Violator of camels!" and "Pig dung!" were quickly drowned out by louder voices crying "Salaam alaikum!", "Shabash, Sahib!" and "Mountbatten *zindabad!*"—Long live Mountbatten! If Mountbatten breathed a sigh of relief he concealed it.

But the lesson had not been lost on him: the concept of Pakistan was anything but an idle intellectual exercise or academic hypothesis. It was very much alive, a fierce, pulsating thing. Right or wrong, these tribesmen were determined to have their own country. Mountbatten thought them wrong, but he could not deny the simple honesty of their passion— much less the threat they posed to Indian stability. Under the strongest pressure from Jinnah, he had already come to suspect that only by partition might India be saved from herself. His confrontation with the tribesmen in Peshawar, reinforced by talks with Sir Olaf Caroe, the Frontier's highly knowledgeable and intensely pro-Pathan Governor, firmed Mountbatten's thoughts into a conviction.

Not without great difficulty, Mountbatten prevailed on Nehru to accept the inevitable. Although Gandhi for his part refused to be swayed, Mountbatten at least talked him into refraining from exerting the full force of his opposition; that alone may have been his most important achievement as Viceroy. Certainly it helped enable him to announce to the people of the Frontier that on July 20, they would be allowed to choose between India and Pakistan in a provincial referendum.

Not that the outcome of that vote had ever been in doubt. When the ballots were counted, it was 2,874 for India; 289,224 for Pakistan.

Exactly twenty-five days later, on August 14, 1947, Mountbatten, in Karachi, administered the oath of office to Jinnah, making him the first Governor General of a newborn Pakistan. The outgoing Viceroy then boarded a plane for Delhi to take part in an identical ceremony with Nehru at midnight—except that Nehru became India's first Prime Minister.* The Raj was now history.

Several hours earlier, at sunset, the Union Jack had been lowered for the last time from every flagstaff on which it flew across the subcontinent. Since the North West Frontier and Baluchistan happened to be the westernmost bastions of the old British India, the flag flew just a few moments longer in those regions. But the few moments were very short. As the sun dropped behind the peak of Sikaram at the far end of the Safed Koh range and the shadows of night crept through the Khyber Pass with the stealth of Afridi bandits, the gathering darkness seemed to swallow the naked staff atop the battlements of Landi Kotal fort in one swift gulp. The last notes of "Last Post" echoed faintly in the overhanging hills. Then a great silence came down like a blanket, enveloping the Khyber Rifles bugler and color guard as they returned to their barracks.

Britain's imperial trials had not yet ended; she still had to face bloodbaths in Malaya, Kenya, Cyprus, Aden and Northern Ireland. After the Frontier, they would seem to be town meetings.

*Jinnah could have had the same office in Pakistan, but preferred being Governor General.

EPILOGUE

"Blow the Hell Out of Everybody"

IT COULD HARDLY have been otherwise: the partition of India and the departure of the British in 1947 did little, if anything at all, to end strife on the North West Frontier. In many ways the past three decades in the hills have been just one long demonstration of the old Pathan saying that war begins with peace.

What might be called a rehearsal took place less than three months after the ballots of the Frontier referendum had been counted. In October 1947, several motorized Pathan lashkars rolled out of Peshawar and headed east for the fabled Vale of Kashmir. With its predominantly Muslim population, the Kashmir province had been slated to join Pakistan, but its Brahmin maharaja had wheeled and dealed delays until the Frontier tribesmen simply decided to seize the place. Nothing stood between them and Kashmir's capital, Srinagar, except for some Hindu bazaars which of course had to be looted and burned, and a Catholic mission filled with nuns ripe for the raping. These diversions lasted only a day or so, but that was just long enough for the Indian Army to fly a Sikh rifle company to Srinagar's airstrip—the key to the occupation of Kashmir. The Sikhs managed to hold the position until the arrival of strong infantry and armored units that presently hammered the lashkars to a safe distance from the capital. This was followed by two years of alternate negotiating and fighting, which came to an end in 1949 when a cease-fire agreement gave most of Kashmir to India. The whole province would belong to Pakistan today had not the Pathans stopped for their picnic.

It did not matter that the tribal invasion of Kashmir had had the secret backing of the Pakistan Government. Even while the frontiersmen's trucks were barrelling toward Srinagar, Pakistan itself had already become what was to be a full-time Pathan target as the redoubtable Abdul Ghaffar Khan took center stage once more at the head of a movement to drive the tribes' new rulers from the hills forever. His objective was nothing less than full sovereign status for the Frontier, which would become an independent nation called Pakhtunistan.*

Abdul Ghaffar had not even waited for partition before starting his campaign, but had ordered his still substantial Red Shirt following to boycott the referendum after a third question—that of Frontier independence —had been refused a place on the ballot. And hardly had the vote been counted than he began littering the province with revolutionary pamphlets while bombarding every city, town and village with public jeremiads inciting to riot and worse. His tirades were not without effect; in 1948, a Pakistan court sentenced him to six years in prison.

But the ball had started rolling, and a host of dedicated followers was ready to carry on the good fight. Among the most active was another of Britain's old biting fleas, the Fakir of Ipi, who became interim 'President" of Pakhtunistan. From his Waziristan caves, the Fakir and his "cabinet" masterminded an endless series of razzias against Frontier villages, together with frequent ambushes of Pakistan border forces. During these actions, the raiders also circulated copies of a monthly propaganda newsletter which the Fakir's people turned out on a Pushtu printing press. In 1960, the Fakir died, and received a long obituary in *The Times*, which described him as "a man of principle and saintliness" who would be remembered by his former British adversaries as "a doughty and honourable opponent." British reaction was probably expressed more accurately by a Pakistan official who called the Fakir "a vicious old man, twisted with hate and selfishness."

Meanwhile, the mantle of leadership had passed back to Abdul Ghaffar Khan, not in the least discouraged by his incarceration or advancing years. In 1956, at the age of 66, he had stumped the Frontier once more and delivered no fewer than 84 raging harangues against Pakistan in barely three months. He had also been jailed again, but in passing a lenient sentence, the judge explained that "the accused is an old man . . . and at times has had to remain in the hospital." On his release, the sick old man set about streamlining the Red Shirts, who now became the National Awami (People's) Party—better known as NAP. The party's president was Abdul Ghaffar's own son, Abdul Wali Khan,** who quickly

---

* Also spelled Pushtoonistan, Pashtoonistan, Pathanistan, etc.
** Dr. Khan Sahib was killed by a tribal dissident in 1958.

proved himself a chip off the old block as NAP meetings and public demonstrations took on an increasingly seditious tone.

Actually, NAP might have been no more troublesome to Pakistan than any oversize gang of armed bandits but for the support it received from Afghanistan. From the outset, King Zahir and the Kabul power structure had seen the Pakhtunistan movement as the ideal instrument with which to win back Afghanistan Irridenta, and no effort was spared to help the Frontier nationalists advance the cause of self-determination in the hills. Besides firing off regular fusillades of anti-Pakistan propaganda through its own press and radio channels, the Afghan Government also poured money and arms into the NAP slot. At the Khushhal Khan School in Kabul, Pakistani Pathan youths not only received first-rate tuition-free educations but were indoctrinated as Pakhtunistan activists and trained in the techniques of terrorism. Alumni quickly began carrying out night raids, ambushing patrols, blowing up bridges and railway tracks and generally touching off a cyclone of sabotage across the whole Frontier. The result, in 1961, was a two-year suspension of diplomatic relations between Pakistan and Afghanistan. Not since Abdur Rahman had the dispute over the trans-Indus lands come so close to reaching flash point.

NAP's leadership did not seem to realize or care that Frontier independence with Afghan backing would inevitably make Pakhtunistan a client state of Kabul if not an outright Afghan province. In 1965, Abdul Ghaffar Khan went to Kabul and announced his intention to carry on the struggle from Afghanistan, declaring that until and unless Pathan freedom was achieved, he would never return to the land of his birth. The Old Bolshevik became a close confidante of General Muhammad Daud Khan, a sort of mustachioed Telly Savalas who was King Zahir's cousin, brother-in-law and Prime Minister rolled into one—and what counted most, the real mastermind of Afghan Frontier strategy.

In the summer of 1973, Daud proved himself no less able an intriguer in another field. At that time, Zahir had gone to Italy for mud and mineral baths, leaving his country in Daud's hands. Abdur Rahman would never have committed such a blunder. After an almost bloodless overnight coup, Daud proclaimed himself President of the spanking-new Republic of Afghanistan, and announced that the nation was to become a "genuine democracy," whatever that meant. NAP leaders probably hoped it meant a full-scale escalation of Afghanistan's Frontier offensive against Pakistan.

The time could not have been more ripe. In 1971, the state of Bangla Desh had emerged from the revolution in East Pakistan, and Abdul Ghaffar Khan had subsequently reneged on his pledge of perpetual self-exile, returning to the Frontier to be midwife at the violent birth of a second Bangla Desh. Early in 1973, Abdul Wali Khan had announced the imminent labor pains, telling a British journalist: "My people are not going to be bullied . . . . They will pick up their arms and blow the hell out of everybody. We all have guns here. East Pakistan did not have so much as a penknife." Not without reason, the government of Pakistan's Prime Minister Zulfikar Ali Bhutto braced itself for new and unprecedented shock waves from the NAP shock troops.

They were not long in coming. On the heels of Abdul Wali Khan's threat, a disorganized but heavily armed Pathan phalanx marched into the Punjab, in what NAP called a "caravan of democracy," to conduct a protest demonstration at Rawalpindi. The rally quickly degenerated into a city-wide fire fight, with insurgent and Government forces taking heavy casualties. Shortly afterwards, Abdul Wali Khan all but promised a program of assassinations that would reach straight to the top. "The bullet that can hit us or the head of a dog," he shouted in a speech, "can also enter the head of Bhutto." This was not just impassioned talk. During an address by Bhutto at Quetta, a youth in the crowd was observed behaving suspiciously; as police closed in on him he became nervous and an armed hand grenade dropped from his pocket, atomizing him instantly while Bhutto finished his speech. Bombs continued to explode through 1973 and 1974, while raids, looting, kidnapping and sabotage increased. By early 1975, the brushfire seemed to be running out of control as its flames spread south into Baluchistan.

Push now came to shove. In January 1975, Abdul Wali Khan confronted a high-ranking Frontier official, one Muhammad Khan Sherpao, and warned him: "You have no wife, but I will see that your old mother is thrown out on the road." This did not happen, but on February 9, as Sherpao addressed a large student gathering in the auditorium of Peshawar University, a bomb went off and blew him through the ceiling. That tore it for the Pakistan Government. With a speed exceeded only by its constitutional scruple, NAP was formally dissolved and outlawed, while Abdul Ghaffar Khan and Abdul Wali Khan were arrested, tried and sentenced to long prison terms. All that remained of the Pakhtunistan movement, at least for the time being, was a question. Why had it failed?

It was a $64,000 question. Abdul Wali Khan had not been far off the mark in saying that East Pakistan "did not have so much as a penknife." Frontier Pathans, on the other hand, went about armed to the teeth, while Pakistan's army, though well equipped and highly disciplined, had nothing approaching the strength of numbers the British had been able to bring to bear in their century of failure to tame the tribes. How was it, then, that NAP had failed to blast out its own Bangla Desh? How much of the Frontier's revolutionary ardor was no more than the usual Pathan high spirits and traditional love affair with mayhem for mayhem's sake?

And was it just possible that most tribesmen had found themselves relatively content with being Pakistanis?

In all probability, yes. One of Pakistan's earliest formal acts had been the evacuation of the forts at Razmak and Wana, in pursuance of a Frontier policy that could never have worked under the British. Essentially, this policy turned on a nonmilitary approach to relations with the tribes. It was and is possible simply because Pakistan is a Muslim nation, governed by Muslims who deal with fellow-Muslims on the Frontier. Abdul Ghaffar Khan to the contrary notwithstanding, the cement of Islam has seemed, in the hills, to have contained the ingredients of peace—or, at the very least, of armed truce.

But it might have become an armed camp had Pakistan confined its Frontier program to troop withdrawals alone. Instead, the past three decades have witnessed an all-out agricultural development campaign in the hills. Government has initiated massive irrigation schemes and settlement projects in new fertile regions. Modern fertilizers and superior seeds have become available at cheap subsidized prices. Market outlets have been opened up for farm and ranch produce. All these things, together with agricultural fairs and livestock shows, have stimulated a previously unfamiliar kind of rivalry among the hill clans—and have given the Pathan a pride in skills other than marksmanship and knife artistry. If Pakistan has not quite equaled the Israeli achievement in making the desert bloom, she has still accomplished far more than the British ever attempted (and, it must be admitted, more than the tribes might have allowed the British to try). Where muscle failed, persuasion has seemed to work.

Arnold Toynbee summed it up after a visit to the Frontier, when he wrote that "instead of becoming saboteurs of civilization . . . [the Pathans] are becoming converts to it."

Not that the fist of authority or the threat of trouble have vanished. Pakistan maintains a small but highly mobile and very tough Frontier force that has the support of jet fighter-bombers. And although the Pakhtunistan movement seemed at least quiescent as late as 1977,* with real gestures toward detente by Afghanistan and Pakistan, there remained room to wonder whether Kabul would—indeed, could—ever truly relinquish its historic claim to the trans-Indus region. Above all, recent years have seen the world's two great Communist giants cast increasingly long shadows across the disputed land. Although the general pattern of alignment has placed Russia behind Afghanistan and China in Pakistan's corner, any kind of shift is possible in so volatile a part of Asia. If nothing else, the simple proximity of the Soviets and Red Chinese serves as an unpleasant reminder of what a nuclear-age "Great Game" is capable of touching off. In all likelihood, the game will never be played, but even so, perhaps the only reason why the Frontier has not become another Middle East as these words are written is because no one has yet got around to discovering oil in Bannu or Waziristan.

In any case, during the late 1970s, visitors were unlikely to have noticed signs of tension, even less apt to have found more serious trouble than a flat tire. To get oneself shot or knifed, it was necessary to be an Afghan or a Pakistani Pathan, and even with those credentials the odds were small. For tourists, Kabul and Peshawar seemed no more than oversize casbahs with decent hotel accommodations. The scheduled bus trip from Peshawar to Quetta, through the very heart of Waziristan, offered a much better insurance risk than a stroll into Central Park at night. At the Fort Jamrud checkpoint near the eastern entrance to the Khyber Pass, the most forbidding threat that faced a driver was a large sign reading: DEAD SLOW—WE LOVE OUR CHILDREN.

This does not mean that the Frontier has finally been disarmed, or that it ever will be. If nothing else, guns remain the Pathan's advertisement to the rest of the world that he is still very much his own man. By no means inaccurately, the rifle slung across any tribesman's back can be thought of as his way of telling outsiders (definitely including the non-Pathan authorities of the Pakistan Government) that they are his welcome and honored guests, that they are completely at liberty to drink in the tonic of his beloved hills—so long as they behave.

Shortly before this book was completed, a veteran British journalist went out to the Frontier and took a good long look. He recognized what he saw. He called it "the last free place on earth."

Bibliography

Abdul Qaiyum. *Gold and Guns on the Pathan Frontier.* Bombay: Hind Kitabs, 1945.

Abdur Rahman. "Instructions to My Son on His Visiting England." *Monthly Review* 4 (1901).

——. *The Life of Abdur Rahman.* 2 vols. London: John Murray, 1900.

Balfour, Lady Betty. *The History of Lord Lytton's Indian Administration, 1876 to 1880.* London: Longmans, Green, 1899.

Barnes, Maj. R. Money. *A History of the Regiments and Uniforms of the British Army.* London: Seeley Service & Co., 1950.

Barton, Sir William. *India's North-West Frontier.* London: John Murray, 1939.

Bellew, H. W. *Journal of a Mission to Afghanistan in 1857.* London: Smith, Elder & Co., 1862.

Beloff, Max. *Imperial Sunset. Britain's Liberal Empire, 1897–1921,* vol. 1. New York: Knopf, 1970.

Bernays, Robert. *Naked Fakir.* London: Victor Gollancz, 1931.

Beveridge, Annette S. "The Khaibar Pass as the Invaders' Road for India," *Journal of the Central Asian Society* 3, 4 (1926).

Beynon, Lt. W. G. L. *With Kelly to Chitral.* London: Edward Arnold, 1896.

Blood, Gen. Sir Bindon. *Four Score Years and Ten.* London: G. Bell & Sons, Ltd., 1933.

Broadfoot, Maj. W. *The Career of Major George Broadfoot, C.B.* London: John Murray, 1888.

Bruce, Richard I. *The Forward Policy and Its Results.* London: Longmans, Green, 1900.

Burnes, Alexander. *Cabool: A Personal Narrative of a Journey to, and Residence in That City in the Years 1836, 7, and 8.* Philadelphia: Carey & Hart, 1843.

——. *Travels into Bokhara.* 3 vols. London: John Murray, 1835.

Caroe, Olaf. *The Pathans, 550 B.C.–A.D. 1957.* New York: St. Martin's Press, 1958.

——. *Soviet Empire: The Turks of Central Asia and Stalinism.* London: Macmillan, 1953.

Churchill, Winston S. *My Early Life.* New York: Scribner, 1930; Avon Books, 1972.

——. *The Story of the Malakand Field Force.* London: Longmans, Green, 1898.

Coatman, J. "The North-West Frontier Province and Trans-Border Country Under the New Constitution." *Journal of the Royal Central Asian Society* 18 (1931).

Collen, Maj. Gen. Edwin, and Yate, A. C. "Our Position on the North-West Frontier of India." *The Empire Review* 2 (1901).

Collins, Larry, and Lapierre, Dominique. *Freedom at Midnight*. New York: Simon & Schuster, 1975.

Cotton, Lt. Gen. Sir Sydney. *Nine Years on the North-West Frontier of India*. London: Richard Bentley, 1868.

Crocker, Lt. Col. H. E. "The Khyber Pass." *Journal of the Royal Central Asian Society* (1931).

Cross, Colin. *The Fall of the British Empire*. London: Hodder & Stoughton, 1968.

Curzon, George N. *Russia in Central Asia*. London: Longmans, Green, 1889.

———. *Tales of Travel*. London: Hodder & Stoughton, 1923.

Davies, C. Collin. "British Relations with the Afridis of the Khyber and Tirah." *The Army Quarterly* 22 (1932).

———. "Lord Curzon's Frontier Policy and the Formation of the North West Frontier Province, 1901." *The Army Quarterly* 13 (1927).

———. *The Problem of the North-West Frontier, 1890-1908*. Cambridge: At the University Press, 1932.

Dilks, David. *Curzon in India*. Vol. 1. New York: Taplinger, 1970.

Diver, Maud. *Kabul to Kandahar*. London: Peter Davies, 1935.

Dupuy, R. Ernest, and Dupuy, Trevor N. *The Encyclopedia of Military History*. New York: Harper & Row, 1970.

Eden, Hon. Emily. *Up the Country*. 2 vols. London: Richard Bentley, 1866.

Edwardes, Emma. *Memorials of the Life and Letters of Major-General Sir Herbert B. Edwardes*. London: Kegan Paul, Trench & Co., 1886.

Edwardes, Maj. Herbert B. *A Year on the Punjab Frontier*. 2 vols. London: Richard Bentley, 1851.

Elphinstone, Hon. Mountstuart. *An Account of the Kingdom of Caubul, and Its Dependencies in Persia, Tartary and India; Comprising a View of the Afghaun Nation, and a History of the Dooraunee Monarchy*. 2 vols. London: Richard Bentley, 1839.

Enriquez, C. M. *The Pathan Borderland*. Calcutta and Simla: Thacker, Spink & Co., 1921.

Ewart, J. M. *Story of the North West Frontier Province*. Peshawar: Government Printing & Stationery Office, 1930.

Eyre, Lt. Vincent. *The Military Operations at Cabul, with a Journal of Imprisonment in Afghanistan*. Philadelphia: Carey & Hart, 1843.

Ferrier, J. P. *Caravan Journeys and Wanderings in Persia, Afghanistan, Turkistan and Beloochistan*. London: John Murray, 1856.

Forrest, G. W. *Life of Field-Marshal Sir Neville Chamberlain*. London: Blackwood, 1909.

———. *The Life of Lord Roberts*. London: Cassell, 1914.

Fraser, George MacDonald. *Flashman*. New York: World Publishing, 1969.

———. *Flashman at the Charge*. New York: Knopf, 1973.

———. *Flashman in the Great Game*. New York: Knopf, 1975.

Fraser-Tytler, W. K. *Afghanistan*. London: Oxford University Press, 1950.

Gardner, Brian. *The East India Company*. New York: McCall Publishing Co., 1971.

Gonzales de Clavijo, Ruy. *Clavijo: Embassy to Tamerlane*. London: George Routledge & Sons, 1928.

Gray, John Alfred. *At the Court of the Amir.* London: Richard Bentley, 1895.

Griffiths, John C. *Afghanistan.* New York: Praeger, 1967.

Habberton, William. *Anglo-Russian Relations Concerning Afghanistan, 1837–1907.* Urbana: University of Illinois Press, 1934.

Haward, E. "India's Defence as an Imperial Problem." *Journal of the Central Asian Society* (1926).

Holdich, Sir Thomas. "England's Strength in Asia." *Proceedings of the Central Asian Society* (1905).

———. *The Gates of India.* London: Macmillan, 1910.

———. *Political Frontiers and Boundary Making.* London: Macmillan, 1916.

Holmes, T. Rice. *Sir Charles Napier.* Cambridge: At the University Press, 1925.

Hutchinson, Col. H. D. *The Campaign in Tirah, 1897–1898.* London: Macmillan, 1898.

Ibn Battúta. *Travels in Asia and Africa.* London: George Routledge & Sons, 1929.

Jackson, Maj. Donovan. *India's Army.* London: Sampson Low, Marston & Co., n.d.

Jacob, Maj. Gen. A. LeG. "Waziristan." *Journal of the Central Asian Society* (1927).

Kally Prosono Dey. *The Life and Career of Major Sir Louis Cavagnari.* Calcutta: J. N. Ghose & Co., 1881.

Kaye, Sir John W. *History of the War in Afghanistan.* 3 vols. London: Wm. H. Allen & Co., 1874.

Keppel, Arnold. *Gun-Running and the Indian North-West Frontier.* London: John Murray, 1911.

Kessler, Melvin M. *Ivan Viktorovich Vitkevich 1806–39: A Tsarist Agent in Central Asia.* Washington: Central Asian Collectanea, 1960.

Kipling, Rudyard. *Barrack-Room Ballads.*

Konishi, Masatoshi. *Afghanistan.* Palo Alto, Calif.: Kodansha International, Inc., 1969.

Lumsden, Gen. Sir Peter S., and Elsmie, George R. *Lumsden of the Guides.* London: John Murray, 1899.

Mackenzie, Lt. Gen. Colin. *Storms and Sunshines of a Soldier's Life.* 2 vols. Edinburgh: David Douglas, 1884.

MacMunn, Maj. Gen. Sir G. F. "The North-Western Frontier of India To-Day." *The Journal of the Royal Artillery* 51 (1924–25).

Macrory, Patrick, ed. *Lady Sale.* Hamden, Conn.: Archon Books, 1969.

———. *Signal Catastrophe.* London: The History Book Club, 1967.

Marshman, J. C. *Memoirs of Major-General Sir Henry Havelock, K.C.B.* London: Longman, Green, Longman & Roberts, 1860.

Martin, Frank A. *Under the Absolute Amir.* London and New York: Harper & Bros, 1907.

Marvin, Charles. *The Russian Advance towards India.* London: Sampson Low, Marston, Searle & Rivington, 1882.

Masson, Charles. *Narrative of Various Journeys in Balochistan, Afghanistan, the Panjab, and Kalat, during a Residence in Those Countries.* 4 vols. London: Richard Bentley, 1844.

Masters, John. *Bugles and a Tiger.* London: Michael Joseph, 1956.

Mayne, Peter. *The Narrow Smile.* London: John Murray, 1955.

Mohan Lal. *Travels in the Panjab, Afghanistan & Turkistan, to Balk, Bokhara, and Herat; and a Visit to Great Britain and Germany.* London: W. H. Allen & Co., 1846.

Molesworth, Lt. Gen. G. N. *Afghanistan 1919.* New York: Asia Publishing House, 1962.

Morris, James. *Heaven's Command.* New York: Harcourt Brace Jovanovich, 1974.

Moynahan, Brian. "The Free Frontier." *Sunday Times Supplement,* 21 March 1976.

Nevill, Capt. H. L. *Campaigns on the North-West Frontier.* London: John Murray, 1912.

Payne, Robert. *Lawrence of Arabia.* New York: Pyramid Books, 1962.

Pearson, Hesketh. *The Hero of Delhi: A Life of John Nicholson.* London: Collins, 1939.

Pennell, T. L. *Among the Wild Tribes of the Afghan Frontier.* London: Seeley & Co., 1909.

Polo, Marco. *The Book of Ser Marco Polo.* 2 vols. London: John Murray, 1871.

"The Problem of Afghanistan." *Journal of the Central Asian Society* 13 (1926).

Rafee, M. A. *The Industries and Economic Resources of the North West Frontier Province.* Calcutta: Government of India, Central Publications Branch, 1929.

Rawlinson, Maj. Gen. Sir Henry. *England and Russia in the East.* London: John Murray, 1875.

Ridley, Jasper. *Lord Palmerston.* London: Constable, 1970.

Roberts, Field Marshal, Earl of Kandahar. *Forty-One Years in India.* New York: Longmans, Green, 1908.

Rose, Kenneth. *Superior Person: A Portrait of Curzon and His Circle in Late Victorian England.* New York: Weybright & Talley, 1969.

Sale, Lady. *A Journal of the Disasters in Afghanistan.* London: John Murray, 1843.

Shand, A. I. *General John Jacob.* London: Seeley & Co., 1900.

Smith, H. Bosworth. *Life of Lord Lawrence.* London: Thomas Nelson & Sons, n.d.

Spain, James W. *The People of the Khyber.* New York: Praeger, 1963.

Stewart, Rhea Talley. *Fire in Afghanistan, 1914-1929.* New York: Doubleday, 1973.

Stocqueler, J. H. *Memoirs and Correspondence of Major-General Sir William Nott.* 2 vols. London: Hurst & Blackett, 1854.

Swinson, Arthur. *North-West Frontier.* London: Hutchinson, 1967.

Sykes, Sir Percy. *The Right Honourable Sir Mortimer Durand.* London: Cassell, 1926.

Thomas, Lowell. *Beyond Khyber Pass.* New York: Century, 1925.

———. *A History of Afghanistan.* Vol. 2. London: Macmillan, 1940.

Thornton, T. H. *Colonel Sir Robert Sandeman.* London: John Murray, 1895.

Toynbee, Arnold. *Between Oxus and Jumna.* London: Readers Union, Oxford University Press, 1963.

Vambéry, Arminius. *Arminius Vambéry, His Life and Adventures.* London: T. Fisher Unwin, 1884.

———. *Central Asia and the Anglo-Russian Frontier Question.* London: Smith, Elder, 1874.

———. *Travels in Central Asia.* New York: Harper & Bros., 1865.

Vigne, G. T. *A Personal Narrative of a Visit to Ghuzni, Kabul, and Afghanistan, and of a Residence at the Court of Dost Mohamed: With Notices of Ranjit Singh, Khiva, and the Russian Expedition.* London: Whittaker & Co., 1840.

Warburton, Col. Sir Robert. *Eighteen Years in the Khyber.* London: John Murray, 1900.

Younghusband, G. J. *The Story of the Guides.* London: Macmillan, 1908.

Younghusband, G. J. and Frank E. *The Relief of Chitral.* London: Macmillan, 1895.

Index

Index

NOTE: *Unless otherwise indicated, the title "amir" refers to a ruler of Afghanistan. Governors-general (until 1858) and viceroys were the British heads of government in India.*